Seeing Us in Them

What causes some people to stand in solidarity with those from other races, religions, or nationalities, even when that solidarity does not seem to benefit the individual or their group? *Seeing Us in Them* examines outgroup empathy as a powerful predisposition in politics that pushes individuals to see past social divisions and work together in complex, multicultural societies. It also reveals racial/ethnic intergroup differences in this predisposition, rooted in early patterns of socialization and collective memory. Outgroup empathy explains why African Americans vehemently oppose the border wall and profiling of Arabs, why Latinos are welcoming of Syrian refugees and support humanitarian assistance, why some white Americans march in support of Black Lives Matter through a pandemic, and even why many British citizens oppose Brexit. Outgroup empathy is not naive; rather it is a rational and necessary force that helps build trust and maintain stable democratic norms of compromise and reciprocity.

Cigdem V. Sirin is Associate Professor of Political Science at the University of Texas at El Paso. Her research interests center on examining the microfoundations of interstate and intrastate conflict processes and outcomes.

Nicholas A. Valentino is Professor of Political Science and Research Professor in the Center for Political Studies at the University of Michigan. He studies political campaigns, racial attitudes, emotions, and social group cues in political communication.

José D. Villalobos is Associate Professor of Political Science at the University of Texas at El Paso. His research examines public opinion and policy making dynamics in the areas of the US presidency, race and ethnicity, and immigration.

Cambridge Studies in Public Opinion and Political Psychology

Series Editors
Dennis Chong, *University of Southern California and Northwestern University*
James H. Kuklinski, *University of Illinois at Urbana–Champaign*

Cambridge Studies in Public Opinion and Political Psychology publishes innovative research from a variety of theoretical and methodological perspectives on the mass public foundations of politics and society. Research in the series focuses on the origins and influence of mass opinion, the dynamics of information and deliberation, and the emotional, normative, and instrumental bases of political choice. In addition to examining psychological processes, the series explores the organization of groups, the association between individual and collective preferences, and the impact of institutions on beliefs and behavior.

Cambridge Studies in Public Opinion and Political Psychology is dedicated to furthering theoretical and empirical research on the relationship between the political system and the attitudes and actions of citizens.

Books in the series are listed on the page following the Index.

Seeing Us in Them

Social Divisions and the Politics of Group Empathy

CIGDEM V. SIRIN
University of Texas at El Paso

NICHOLAS A. VALENTINO
University of Michigan

JOSÉ D. VILLALOBOS
University of Texas at El Paso

CAMBRIDGE
UNIVERSITY PRESS

CAMBRIDGE
UNIVERSITY PRESS

University Printing House, Cambridge CB2 8BS, United Kingdom

One Liberty Plaza, 20th Floor, New York, NY 10006, USA

477 Williamstown Road, Port Melbourne, VIC 3207, Australia

314–321, 3rd Floor, Plot 3, Splendor Forum, Jasola District Centre,
New Delhi – 110025, India

79 Anson Road, #06–04/06, Singapore 079906

Cambridge University Press is part of the University of Cambridge.

It furthers the University's mission by disseminating knowledge in the pursuit of
education, learning, and research at the highest international levels of excellence.

www.cambridge.org
Information on this title: www.cambridge.org/9781108495844
DOI: 10.1017/9781108863254

First published 2021

A catalogue record for this publication is available from the British Library.

ISBN 978-1-108-49584-4 Hardback
ISBN 978-1-108-79784-9 Paperback

For Sean and Dylan –
may you stay forever young and empathic.
For Dom, Toby, and Stella –
your kindness, curiosity, and love are your greatest gifts.

Contents

Figures

Tables

Prologue

It all started with a news story. We were scrolling through the news in 2011 when we came across the story of Irum Abbasi, a headscarf-clad US citizen of Pakistani descent, being escorted off a plane by a Transportation Security Administration (TSA) agent because a flight attendant allegedly heard her say "It's a go" on her cell phone just before takeoff. Abbasi explained that she had actually said "I've got to go" when the flight was ready to depart. Despite the fact that TSA agents cleared her to fly after searching her bag and patting down her headscarf, the pilot and crew would not let her back on board, claiming that she made them feel uncomfortable. Abbasi reported feeling humiliated and overwhelmed by this treatment. She missed her flight from San Diego to San Jose, where she was working on a graduate degree in psychology at San Jose State University. The mother of three later stated: "This time they said 'we weren't comfortable with the headscarf.' Next time, they won't be comfortable with my accent or they won't be comfortable with my South Asian heritage."[1]

Accounts of racial profiling, intergroup conflict, and ethnic tensions seem all too common in the current political moment. Decisions by law enforcement officials to target specific groups for extra scrutiny are often justified out of an abundance of caution, not an attempt to racially profile or discriminate. Still, this particular story jumped out at us: even the simple choice to wear a hijab can transform banal words and phrases into deadly threats. "I've got to go" becomes "It's a go," presumably a green light for launching a terrorist attack of the type burned into the American psyche since September 11, 2001. It seems as though terrifying plots bloom in people's imaginations, triggered by the tiniest and most inconsequential behaviors of those around them, especially when someone is perceived differently and reminds them of perpetrators of past tragedies. We

---

[1] The Associated Press (2011), "Muslim Passenger Pulled from Plane Seeks Apology: US Citizen Wants Southwest Crew Disciplined for Refusing to Let Her Fly," NBC News, www.nbcnews.com /id/42117799/ns/travel-news/t/muslim-passenger-pulled-plane-seeks-apology/#.XUy2aeNKiUl.

suspect the incident described would have been less likely if the passenger were not wearing a headscarf, had no accent, displayed a lighter complexion, and were named Jones rather than Abbasi. In that alternate reality, the flight attendant may not have even heard a suspicious phrase uttered, since one's selective attention to information and perceptions of threatening behavior are consistent with commonly held outgroup stereotypes.

Stories of racial profiling are common. What surprised us even more than the news story itself was the variety of reader comments that followed.[2] As we might have feared, many were vitriolic and hostile, criticizing the woman for speaking out against her treatment that day and delineating the many reasons non-Muslim passengers had to be anxious about flying with people dressed as she was. On the other hand, numerous other commenters across multiple news websites running that story took her side. "Charlotte" wrote she was "disgusted with the amount of comments agreeing with the airline on here, not only the humiliation that poor woman suffered, but the fact she missed a critical experiment in her studies for this. I genuinely feel for her." "Moe" felt it was a "disgusting example of discrimination. Of course, had it been a white person who had said something worse, we all know that the situation would be different." "Jan" said: "The fact that most on this site is [sic] saying that what happened is OK is just apauling [sic]. If this EVER happens to you, I hope you get what you deserve … strip search! Let's see who's [sic] side you take then. This [sic] actions are deplorable, racist, and a total violation of our rights."

The balance between critical versus supportive comments was negatively lopsided in our informal search. Nevertheless, there was quite a lot of variation, with many commenters defending Abbasi and expressing concern about her ordeal. What would drive someone to speak up and show support for an unfairly targeted person in such cases? One guess would be that only those with a close group attachment or kinship with the victim would react this way. People come to the aid of their family and close friends in order to protect them from harm. This is an ancient human instinct for social animals living in small groups surrounded by myriad threats. Anticipating and promptly reacting to threats toward close kin would increase the chance that our offspring would survive to reproductive age. Empathy at this intimate level – the skills and motivation to put oneself in the shoes of another and to care about their plight – could trigger a helping response even when the risks of self-harm and sacrifice are high. But most theories of empathy find that its reach is quite restricted, extending only to those we know well enough to believe that they might someday return the favor or pass on our genes to the next generation. Empathy is seen as a critical building block for bonds of reciprocation and ingroup protection. In situations like the one Abbasi found herself in, where she was stereotypically perceived by many as a member of a potentially threatening

---

[2] The comments are compiled from www.dailymail.co.uk/news/article-2047733/Muslim-woman-removed-flight-security-heard-say-Its-phone.html.

outgroup, we would expect most people to act just as they did – siding with the flight crew rather than Abbasi. Even those with high levels of interpersonal empathy could react with anxiety and aversion, hoping to reduce potential threats to their families, close friends, and local communities. But some chose to side with her.

These diverse reactions to what seemed, even among non-Muslims, like a case of anti-Muslim profiling struck us as fundamentally similar to another puzzle that had emerged in some of our data on immigration opinion in the United States. When we looked at racial/ethnic group differences in policy views about immigration from a national survey collected in 2010, we found that African Americans were significantly more likely than whites to prefer more open immigration policies. Black respondents in our surveys were significantly more likely than whites to oppose English as the sole official language of the United States; to support giving undocumented immigrants a path to citizenship; and to oppose armed citizen militias patrolling the US border with Mexico.

We were therefore not surprised to read another news story, titled "The One Group That Opposes Trump's Border Wall More Than Latinos."[3] A Quinnipiac poll discovered 87 percent of African Americans opposed the wall in April 2018, compared with 71 percent of Latinos and only 51 percent of whites. Why would African Americans, who are more likely to compete with Latinx immigrants for jobs and wages, seem so willing to extend a hand nonetheless? While differences in partisan attachments seem a plausible explanation, we find in our own data that partisanship is not enough. The theory we propose suggests that prosocial reactions in these situations are highly conditional on a particular set of skills and motivations that varies significantly from person to person: the ability to take another group's perspective, understand and share their emotions, and care about their welfare. We call that set of skills and motivations "group empathy." The title of our book is meant to convey this phenomenon – the political consequences of bridging social divisions of all types by seeing us in them.

In our own lives we have often witnessed the power of group empathy. One of our students served three tours in Iraq and happens to be African American. When we told him about the story of Abbasi, he was immediately reminded of a personal experience he wanted to share. On one of his plane trips, there was a Middle Eastern–looking couple in Islamic clothing boarding the aircraft. He said most passengers looked uncomfortable and uninviting while the couple was looking for a place to sit (it was one of those airlines where you can sit anywhere available). He said he pointed to the empty seats next to him and told them, "Come, my brother and sister, you can sit here." Many passengers looked at him in disbelief; he said he was wearing his "dog tag," so people would know

---

[3] Eugene Scott (2018), "The One Group That Opposes Trump's Border Wall More Than Latinos," *Washington Post*, https://wapo.st/2HiopP2?tid=ss_mail.

he was a soldier, and perhaps they somehow considered his action as contradictory. But for him it was unpatriotic to deny them a seat because of how they looked – he said he knew how it felt when people generalize negative, stereotypical notions about a whole group, stigmatizing every member as violent or threatening.

Going back to that airplane where Abbasi was singled out – and among those who read the news story about her mistreatment – some people empathized more strongly than others, and some felt the same frustration, sadness, and disappointment that she felt. Our theory proposes that those who have had similar life experiences with discrimination and unfair treatment – either personal, witnessed, or learned from others – will be the most empathic toward other groups. And this empathy for other groups should be strongest among members of stigmatized groups, as they are already familiar with the range of emotions and thoughts that such unjust treatment brings. Events and issues like the airplane incident and Trump's wall are natural stimuli we can use to observe the power of group empathy. In fact, we decided to turn the plot of that airplane story into a series of controlled experiments and to elaborate it into different political contexts, including national security, immigration, and foreign policy. In other words, stories like these and the wide variety of reactions we saw were a springboard for what we call Group Empathy Theory.

On our journey, we have had the great good fortune to speak with many colleagues and friends who gladly provided vital guidance, criticism, and help. We would like to give special thanks to a host of scholars who gave us fantastic feedback, including Paul Allison, Charles Boehmer, Amber Boydstun, Ted Brader, Lawrence Cohn, George Edwards, Ryan Enos, Emily Falk, Stanley Feldman, Nehemia Geva, Daniel Gillion, Joe Heyman, Ben Highton, Leonie Huddy, Kosuke Imai, David Jones, Kerem Ozan Kalkan, Don Kinder, Rick Lau, Valerie Martinez-Ebers, Lily Mason, Monika McDermott, Tali Mendelberg, Marc Meredith, Jennifer Merolla, Fabian Neuner, Marzia Oceno, Markus Prior, David Sears, Gary Segura, Jim Sidanius, Lynn Vavreck, Claes de Vreese, and Carly Wayne. We are deeply grateful for the encouragement and expert insights of Sara Doskow, our editor at Cambridge University Press, in tackling the big questions related to group empathy. Our gratitude further extends to the reviewers for their thoughtful, detailed, and constructive feedback.

Our national survey experiments on airport security and immigrant detention were funded in part by grants from the University of Michigan and the University of Texas at El Paso. We thank Bill Weaver and UTEP's Center for Law for supporting a portion of our survey costs. We also thank Jamie Druckman and Jeremy Freese, principal investigators of the Time-sharing Experiments for the Social Sciences (TESS) funded by the National Science Foundation (SES-1628057), for fielding our national survey experiment on group empathy in the domain of foreign policy. We are greatly indebted to Jane Green and the rest of the leadership team at the British Election Study (BES) for allowing us space in their survey for our Group Empathy Index (GEI).

Samantha Luks from YouGov and Stefan Subias from GfK also deserve our special thanks for all their help with fielding our national surveys and collecting reliable data.

Finally, we thank our dearest for reminding us daily about the importance of empathy. To Bebe Zuniga-Valentino, we are grateful for the unwavering love and support that produced the space for this book to grow. To our children, our debt is equally large. When one becomes a parent, the happiness, sadness, pain, anger, fear, and hope of your children become your own. Trying to look at the world (and at ourselves) through the eyes of our wonderful children gives us a new perspective every day. We are proudest of their kindness, caring, and empathy for others – even when it is as simple as sharing their last M&M.

The Puzzle

Empathy for Outgroups amid Existential Threats and Ingroup Interests

> No one is born hating another person because of the color of his skin, or his background, or his religion. People must learn to hate, and if they can learn to hate, they can be taught to love, for love comes more naturally to the human heart than its opposite.
>
> Nelson Mandela, *Long Walk to Freedom* (1994)[1]

Sugar, ketchup, and mustard – common condiments became tools of racial harassment during the "sit-in movement" that started in 1960, as four black college students in Greensboro, North Carolina, protested segregation in public spaces by sitting at a whites-only lunch counter of a local store. Denied service, they quietly remained in their seats until the store closed that day. Soon the movement spread across the South, with thousands of students and activists joining this nonviolent act of defiance. The rules of the sit-in movement were simple: no matter what they do, no matter what they say, remain calm and peaceful. Whenever protestors were hauled away by police, or injured so badly they could not continue, others would take their place. An iconic photo from a sit-in on May 28, 1963, in Jackson, Mississippi, shows three demonstrators – two women and one man – stone-faced and determined at a lunch counter. Their hair and clothes were covered in sugar, ketchup, and mustard (and blood, seeping from the man's head), surrounded by a sneering white mob. The photo is a powerful image of civil rights activism in the face of racism and hatred. But there is more to the story. Two of the three demonstrators were *not* African American.[2]

---

[1] From *Long Walk to Freedom* by Nelson Mandela, copyright © 1995. Reprinted by permission of Little, Brown and Company, an imprint of Hachette Book Group, Inc.

[2] John Hunter Gray (2005), "That's Me in the Picture: Hunter Gray Is Attacked at a Civil Rights Protest in Jackson, Mississippi, 28 May 1963," *The Guardian*, www.theguardian.com/artanddesign/2015/mar/27/hunter-gray-1963-jackson-mississippi-sit-in.

During the civil rights movement, racial animus had a substantial impact on the policy attitudes and political behavior of many white Americans, both Southerners and non-Southerners, who strongly resisted efforts to integrate schools and public spaces. Many of them saw the struggle for equality as a threat to their culture and values, as well as to their political and economic interests. And, of course, some of that was surely true: the prevailing racial hierarchy benefited them, their families, and their co-ethnics. So the behavior of the angry mob surrounding the demonstrators in the picture – as appalling and disgusting as it was – is not surprising or unusual within the broader history of race relations in the United States. One might be puzzled, however, about what motivated the two nonblack demonstrators to support their African American compatriot – and the entire movement? What would compel members of one group to stand (and, in this case, *sit*) in solidarity with an outgroup in their fight for justice and equality, even when that act carries great personal risk and material sacrifice?

In this book, we will explore the roots of political solidarity with marginalized outgroups. We suspect that political support for outgroups who are suffering cannot be reduced to the absence of racial animus, disregard for existential threat, a naive willingness to sacrifice ingroup interests, or an overriding moral, liberal, or egalitarian worldview. Many "nonracists" are passive bystanders to racism. Many progressives are not motivated even to vote, let alone to protest discriminatory policies that target marginalized outgroups. On the other side, many who care deeply about their own safety and security are nonetheless compelled to defend the political interests of vulnerable outgroups. A central piece of the puzzle is what we call group empathy: the ability and motivation to take another group's perspective, feel emotionally connected to their struggles, and care about their welfare even when doing so puts the individual's interests, or those of their group, at risk.

Many scholars have puzzled over similar questions for decades (Monroe 1996; Scuzzarello et al. 2009), focusing on individual acts of altruism, benevolence, and compassion toward others under extraordinary circumstances. Why did some non-Jewish Germans – and other Europeans – routinely risk their lives to save strangers of Jewish descent during the Holocaust? We hope to add our own perspective to that discussion by documenting, carefully and empirically, how empathy for outgroups shapes public opinion and political behavior not just under extreme circumstances but also in more mundane times.

We have collected a great deal of evidence demonstrating that outgroup empathy is a major force in shaping political attitudes and behavior across groups and national boundaries and in a wide variety of policy domains. In the next section, we continue our discussion of the puzzle in two key policy domains – terrorism and immigration. Considering reactions to outgroups affected by policies and actions taken in these contexts, we highlight some surprising differences *across* social divisions and *within* groups that commonly invoked explanations based on existential threats, ingroup material interests, and symbolic identities cannot explain. That is where Group Empathy Theory comes in.

GROUP EMPATHY IN THREATENING CONTEXTS: TERRORISM AND IMMIGRATION

Following the tragic events of September 11, 2001, Americans of Arab and Middle Eastern descent became the subject of scrutiny and suspicion in their own country (Cainkar 2002; Panagopoulos 2006). The public's anti-Arab reaction after 9/11 may seem simple at first blush: existential threats posed by terrorist groups from the Middle East led many Americans to fear and then stigmatize fellow citizens who had nothing to do with the perpetrators and who were themselves just as likely to be victims. Indeed, persistently negative and threatening portrayals of Arabs as terrorists (Merskin 2004) might well have made national identity more salient for many (Transue 2007), prompting non-Arab Americans to support punitive anti-terrorism policies even at the expense of civil liberties. This "existential threat" hypothesis would further predict that those facing the greatest risk from terrorism would be the most antagonistic toward anyone ethnically similar to the group that brought death and destruction to their homeland on that terrible day. Surprisingly, perceptions about the risk of future terrorist threats turned out to have only limited power to predict public reactions to security policies and the treatment of Arab Americans.

One puzzle emerged in the form of large differences in opinion across racial/ethnic groups in the United States concerning the appropriate policy response to 9/11. African Americans generally perceived *greater* risk from terrorism than did whites after the attacks (e.g., Eisenman et al. 2009; Huddy et al. 2005). In a national study on behavioral and life changes in the aftermath of the 9/11 attacks, Torabi and Seo (2004) found that African Americans were more likely than whites to improve home security, limit outside activities, and change their mode of transportation in fear of terrorism. Given the logic of the existential threat hypothesis, one would then expect blacks to express more support for strict homeland security policies in order to prevent another attack. However, in national survey data collected in the immediate aftermath of 9/11, African Americans were much less willing to trade civil liberties for security than whites and Latinos even when they were quite concerned about another terrorist attack (Davis & Silver 2004; Davis 2006).

These large racial gaps in opinion about national security policies after 9/11 were not fleeting. A CBS News/*New York Times* survey conducted in 2011 with New York City residents for the tenth anniversary of the attacks found that 44 percent of African Americans thought it was "extremely likely" that Arab Americans were being singled out unfairly in the post-9/11 era, compared with just 34 percent of whites who felt that way.[3] More surprising, perhaps, was that this gap existed above and beyond racial group differences in party

---

[3] CBS News and the *New York Times* (2011), "CBS News/*New York Times* New York City Poll, August #2, 2011," http://doi.org/10.3886/ICPSR34468.v1.

identification and other socio-demographic factors like education and income.[4] In other words, these differences in opinion did not spring from partisan politics or personal material stakes.

Blacks' resistance to draconian security policies and higher sensitivity to Arab racial profiling did not spring from feelings of relative security either. Among the same 2011 CBS News/*New York Times* survey participants, African American and white residents of New York did not differ significantly in their perceived risk of another terrorist attack targeting their city, with about one-third of each group saying an attack in the near future was "somewhat likely." Meanwhile, more than twice as many African Americans (25 percent) compared to whites (12 percent) felt that New Yorkers had "not at all recovered" emotionally from the attacks. Therefore, even ten years after the attacks, African Americans were significantly more cognizant of the unfair treatment of Arab Americans, despite perceiving the same risk and experiencing more emotional distress about terrorist attacks compared with whites.

Of course, this circumstantial evidence cannot disprove the existential threat hypothesis. Indeed, people who lived in Manhattan during the attacks were more likely to move from the Democratic Party toward the Republican Party (Hersch 2013) and became somewhat more supportive of anti-terrorism spending (Hopkins 2014). It is not surprising that such a powerful event would impact those who witnessed such immense political violence first-hand. As other studies have shown, personal and group interest play a role in policy opinions when the stakes are high and salient (Chong et al. 2001). So why didn't African Americans, who were more likely on average to live in urban areas that might become targets of terrorist groups, move toward policies and candidates promising greater security?

Another survey conducted in 2011 for the tenth anniversary of the 9/11 attacks inquired whether respondents thought there were more violent extremists among Arabs than among other ethnic groups.[5] In that study, 54 percent of African Americans and 47 percent of Latinos thought there were fewer or about the same number of violent extremists among Arabs compared to other groups. Only 32 percent of whites felt this way. A follow-up survey conducted in 2012 revealed other notable racial/ethnic differences: 66 percent of African Americans and 54 percent of Latinos said they felt "mostly" or "very" favorable toward Arabs, compared to 47 percent of whites.[6] Going back to the surveys conducted shortly after 9/11, feeling

---

[4] The analytical results of the survey data discussed in this chapter are provided in the online appendix.

[5] PIPA/Anwar Sadat Chair Poll (2011), "The American Public and the Arab Awakening [dataset]. USUMARY2011-04," Ithaca, NY: Roper Center for Public Opinion Research.

[6] PIPA/Anwar Sadat Chair Poll (2012), "Americans on the Middle East [dataset]. USUMARY2012-09," Ithaca, NY: Roper Center for Public Opinion Research.

thermometers had indicated that African Americans and whites displayed similar levels of negative affect for Arabs while Latino ratings of Arabs were somewhat lower than the other two respondent groups (Davis 2006, 206). However, ten years later, African Americans and Latinos expressed much more favorable sentiments about Arabs than whites did. What was the driving force behind this opinion shift over the decade that moved African Americans and Latinos away from whites and toward more positive evaluations of Arabs as an outgroup?

Fast-forward to 2017, when Donald Trump issued his so-called Muslim ban. This policy barred immigrants, refugees, and visitors from several Muslim-majority nations that Trump's administration branded as "terror-prone." Consequently, Arabs and other predominantly Muslim Middle Eastern communities were once again stigmatized as threats to homeland security. Perhaps not coincidentally, hate crimes against these communities rose, but so did positive affect toward these groups. A 2017 Arab American Institute (AAI) poll shows that 52 percent of those surveyed expressed a favorable opinion of Arab Americans compared to 40 percent in 2015.[7] In the same poll, 51 percent rated American Muslims favorably compared to 33 percent two years prior. This was the first time in AAI polling that a majority of Americans favorably rated both groups. A majority of respondents displayed strong opposition to the profiling of Arab and Muslim Americans and expressed awareness of a rise in hate crimes. In addition to these overall public opinion trends, a 2019 study by the Institute for Social Policy and Understanding (ISPU) revealed large intergroup differences concerning opinions of Muslims.[8] African Americans were seven times more likely to hold positive than negative opinions of Muslims while Latinos were five times as likely to do so. In comparison, whites were almost as likely to hold favorable as unfavorable opinions. What explains these positive shifts in US public attitudes toward Arab and Muslim Americans, and large racial/ethnic group differences in opinion, in the face of Trump's policies and rhetoric criminalizing these communities?

Again, we think it is unlikely that these public opinion dynamics in reaction to terrorism and groups negatively affected by harsh security policies are fully explained by threats or material interests. Another common explanation for these puzzles is symbolic politics (Sears 1993), which denotes the psychological attachments to party and race that structure the way people think about politics above and beyond their personal economic circumstances. Nonwhites are indeed more likely to be Democrats and to hold more liberal views on civil rights, immigration, and a host of other issues related to race/ethnicity and redistribution. But we also think the most-often-cited alternative explanations,

---

[7] See www.aaiusa.org/aai_american_attitudes_poll_in_the_press.

[8] Dalia Mogahed and Azka Mahmood (2019), "American Muslim Poll 2019: Predicting and Preventing Islamophobia," *Institute for Social Policy and Understanding*, www.ispu.org/wp-content/uploads/2019/04/AMP-2019_Predicting-and-Preventing-Islamophobia.pdf.

including partisanship and "symbolic" predispositions related to group identification (Sears 1993), are not sufficient. While we will discuss our reasons for this skepticism more in the chapters to come, for now we would simply point out that large and statistically significant differences in policy opinions remain even after controlling for these alternative political dimensions. Furthermore, racial/ethnic differences in opinion are largest and most consistent concerning domestic, redistributive policies (Kinder & Winter 2001). Why, then, are these patterns emerging on policy issues like national security, so removed from standard racial political debates?

Immigration constitutes another central issue of our time. Immigrants have become a highly stigmatized group, characterized by some politicians and natives as a threat to the homeland's economy, culture, and security (Branton et al. 2011; Chavez 2008; Hainmueller & Hiscox 2010; Lahav & Courtemanche 2012). Amid these negative perceptions, public animosity toward immigrants can run high (Alvarez & Butterfield 2000; Branton et al. 2011; Chavez 2008; Perea 1997), though the causes of this often substantial variation in support for more or less immigration is still debated (e.g., Valentino et al. 2019). Hostile public attitudes may have profound policy implications: harsh treatment of immigrant children, opposition to the Dream Act, and even troubling instances of human rights violations documented in immigrant detention centers across the country (Villalobos 2011). However, similar to the case of terror threats, opinions over such issues are not necessarily uniform across different segments of society. To date, most research has focused on whites' opinions on immigration, while much less is known about the dynamics of opinion among minority groups.

If public opposition to immigration is driven mostly by concerns about economic or existential security threats, we would expect the most vulnerable domestic groups to register the greatest opposition. African Americans experience greater downward wage pressure and employment competition compared to whites due to the influx of working-class immigrants (Borjas 2001; Borjas et al. 2010; Gay 2006). On these grounds alone, one might expect African Americans to react more negatively than whites to immigration.

So how do perceptions of immigrants vary across racial/ethnic lines? The evidence is mixed at best. On the one hand, several studies point to interminority conflict between African Americans and other nonwhite groups over political rights and resources (Cummings & Lambert 1997; Gimpel & Edwards 1999; but see Morris 2000). Still, African Americans are also found to be significantly *more* supportive than whites of policies favorable to immigrants in general (Kinder & Sanders 1996; Schuman et al. 1997). Further, unlike whites, blacks tend to reject news that stigmatizes Latinx immigrants (Brader et al. 2010), and their immigration attitudes tend to be unmoved by threatening political appeals (Albertson & Gadarian 2013). For instance, polls consistently show that African Americans' opposition to Trump's border wall surpasses that of all other groups in the United States, even Latinos.[9] This presents an intriguing puzzle: Why might African Americans be more supportive of immigrants than whites are, even when they face larger and more direct material threats and no obvious short-term benefits from immigration?

The puzzle may also extend to the Latinx community, though in a different way. Scholars find Latinos are more supportive than whites of policies – such as amnesty – that assist undocumented immigrants and their families (Binder et al. 1997). At first blush, ethnic ties with immigrants from Latin America might seem a plausible explanation for this (de la Garza et al. 1993). The US news media have depicted immigration as an almost exclusively Latinx phenomenon (despite the actual diversity of newcomers) for some time, leading many citizens to view the issue through a narrow ethnic lens (Valentino et al. 2013). However, little is known about how Latinos view *non-Latino* immigrants. Ingroup attachment is a less convincing explanation if Latinos are more favorable toward undocumented immigrants of *non-Latino origin*. We find they are. What explains such views?

Beyond such large racial/ethnic gaps in opinions in these policy domains, there is significant within-group variation as well. For instance, college-educated whites compared to whites without college degrees, and white women compared to white men, are much more likely to oppose Trump's family separation policy.[10] Even partisan groups are sometimes heterogeneous, as in the case of substantial support for the Dreamers (undocumented immigrants who were brought to the United States as children) among Republican identifiers.[11] So there is a great deal of heterogeneity in opinion dynamics surrounding certain policy issues that cannot be explained simply in terms of symbolic politics, threat perceptions, ingroup interest, or even personal stakes. The fact is many people – within both white and minority communities – live in areas targeted by terrorists but nevertheless oppose lopsided trade-offs of civil liberties for security. Among these, substantial fractions refuse to trade humanitarian principles for border security, as seemed clear when polls overwhelmingly revealed opposition to the family separation policy of the Trump administration.

To explain heterogeneity in reactions to a broad range of threats to the nation, we develop Group Empathy Theory (Sirin et al. 2016a, 2016b, 2017). The theory posits empathy felt by members of one group toward another can alter reactions to existential threats and even counteract ingroup interest, thereby reducing intergroup conflict, boosting opposition to punitive policies, and elevating

---

[9] See https://poll.qu.edu/images/polling/us/us04112018_ugnt28.pdf/. See also www.pewresearch .org/fact-tank/2017/02/24/most-americans-continue-to-oppose-u-s-border-wall-doubt-mexico- would-pay-for-it/ and https://poll.qu.edu/images/polling/us/us12182018_ubwn20.pdf/.

[10] See www.vox.com/policy-and-politics/2018/6/18/17475740/family-separation-poll-polling-border- trump-children-immigrant-families-parents.

[11] See https://news.gallup.com/poll/235775/americans-oppose-border-walls-favor-dealing-daca .aspx.

support for civil rights protections. Of course, we expect empathy for potentially threatening outgroups to be less common than empathy for close intimates and for members of one's ingroup. We further expect outgroup empathy to develop under a variety of circumstances, particularly when one group's experiences map onto historical patterns of unfair treatment experienced by another. The theory explains why African Americans and Latinos are more likely than whites to support policies that protect stigmatized groups *other than their own*. However, group empathy is politically consequential among all groups: whites who demonstrate high levels of group empathy (albeit via different socialization processes and experiences) are also more supportive of policies that reduce inequality and protect disadvantaged groups.

In study after study, we find that the ability to put oneself in the shoes of a member of an outgroup experiencing distress fundamentally structures political opinion and action across all racial/ethnic groups, above and beyond the forces that have been known for some time to influence these decisions. We find that group empathy is as strong as or stronger than alternative explanations such as party identification, ideology, racial resentment (Sears 1988), authoritarianism (Altemeyer 1981, 1996; Feldman & Stenner 1997), and social dominance orientation (SDO; Sidanius & Pratto 2001) for opinions about terrorism, immigration, foreign aid, humanitarian crises, military interventions, contemporary social movements (such as Black Lives Matter), and a variety of other policies and issues affecting group rights and resources. Group empathy is not simply a substitute for ingroup identity or outgroup animus, and it powerfully influences mass policy opinions in the United States and Britain.

What we offer in the end is a broad and original theory about how whites and nonwhites think not just about their own groups but about others, as well as how variation within and across these groups helps explain broader public opinion dynamics regarding threats to the nation from without and within. The theory and empirics transcend the typical focus on the black–white dynamic in the United States, which remains an essential area of research but must also be broadened as societies around the world become more diverse and multicultural. The book ends with contemplation about how individuals and ultimately entire nations might foster group empathy in order to improve comity in their increasingly multicultural societies amid the revival of far-right, populist, and exclusionary politics.

EMPIRICAL TESTS OF GROUP EMPATHY THEORY

The tests we bring to bear come from seven nationally representative studies, plus several smaller studies on convenience samples, conducted between 2012 and 2020.[12] Six of the nationally representative studies are based on the US

---

[12] The Appendix at the end of the book provides information on sampling methodology, descriptive statistics, response rates, and the full items for several measures not detailed within the text.

public and one on respondents from Great Britain. The US samples in these studies contain large representative subsamples of black and Latinx citizens, so we can learn about the dynamics of opinion within at least two prominent minority groups, not just among the majority. The data were collected across the two markedly different presidential eras of Barack Obama and Donald Trump, giving us confidence that the influence of outgroup empathy is not fleeting. The number of independent tests using a variety of measurement approaches and issue domains suggests the impact of group empathy is robust.

We measure empathy for outgroups alongside other group-related and political predispositions, such as SDO, ethnocentrism, partisanship, ideology, and the like. When we run experiments, it is to vary racial/ethnic cues in vignettes within key threat contexts, including terrorism, immigration, and humanitarian crises abroad, in order to see if different racial and ethnic groups indeed respond differently to the same threatening events. They very often do. We then explore whether this variation is explained by differences in outgroup empathy. It very often is. The general measure of group empathy we created – the Group Empathy Index (GEI) – is more abstract than many of the other standard measures of group-oriented predispositions and evaluations such as racial resentment or feeling thermometers. The GEI, as we will discuss further in Chapter 3, does not ask about how strongly each respondent empathizes with particular groups in society. This makes for a more conservative test of the theory while minimizing endogeneity concerns, since outgroup empathy as a general predisposition should be less specifically linked to political conflicts between particular groups in a given country.

Our two major tests come from a two-wave national survey with two embedded experiments fielded by GfK (formerly known as Knowledge Networks) in December 2013–January 2014. We refer to this as the "2013/14 US Group Empathy Two-Wave Study." GfK provides a probability-based platform known as "KnowledgePanel." A total of 1,799 respondents participated in the survey, with a randomized sample of 633 whites and randomly selected stratified oversamples of 614 African Americans and 552 Latinos.[13] Of 1,799 first-wave respondents, a second wave reinterviewed 1,344 respondents. Roughly half of these (244 whites, 217 African Americans, and 212 Latinos) took part in an airport security ("Flying While Arab") experiment while the other half (244 whites, 217 African Americans, and 210 Latinos) participated in an immigrant detention experiment.

We also provide an online appendix with additional information for all the data used in this book (including the survey and experimental materials) along with various manipulation checks and sensitivity analyses.

[13] When we use the label "whites" in this book, we are referring to self-identified non-Latino whites. This is to distinguish the group from Latinos, who also may identify as white. Many of our studies are performed on samples comprised solely of respondents who identify as (1) non-Latino white, (2) African American, or (3) nonwhite Latino because our hypotheses specifically concern intergroup attitudes and behavior involving these groups.

Measures of group empathy (the fourteen-item version of the GEI) appeared in the first wave of this study. The first wave also contained measures of SDO, ethnocentrism, authoritarianism, threat perceptions about terrorism and immigration, trust in government, and a spate of additional items tapping policy opinions and behavioral tendencies. We administered experimental treatments and policy questions in the second wave. The experiments compare white versus African American and Latino reactions to vignettes (in the form of news stories) depicting ambiguous but potentially threatening incidents (either in the context of airport security or immigrant detention) in which racial/ethnic cues were nonverbally manipulated. The news story was accompanied by a photo of the targeted passenger or immigrant detainee. We randomly assigned a photo of a white, Arab, black, or Latino male without any explicit racial/ethnic identifiers.

We conducted a pilot of the "Flying While Arab" experiment (also fielded online by GfK in August/September 2012) with a separate pool of 621 participants (a randomized sample of 221 whites and randomly selected stratified oversamples of 193 African Americans and 207 Latinos). We refer to this as the "2012 US Group Empathy Pilot Study." This first experiment helped us improve our instrumentation and serves as a robustness check of the airport security experiment fielded in December 2013–January 2014. It also included measures of linked fate, which allowed us to rule out the possibility that empathy for outgroups is simply standing in for linked fate with those groups. We also performed a couple of surveys with smaller, nonrepresentative samples using Mechanical Turk (MTurk) – an online crowdsourcing platform – in order to improve our measurement and provide additional robustness and manipulation checks in various chapters. We refer to this set of MTurk surveys as the "2015 US Group Empathy Study."

We tested Group Empathy Theory with another national survey experiment, this time in the context of foreign policy, fielded online by GfK in late September and early October 2016. This study was supported by Time-sharing Experiments in the Social Sciences (TESS), so we refer to this as the "2016 US Group Empathy TESS Study." A total of 508 respondents participated in the study, which consisted of a random sample of 173 whites and randomly selected stratified oversamples of 172 African Americans and 163 Latinos. The pretest questionnaire included a range of items designed to measure preexisting foreign policy attitudes, including foreign aid and humanitarian interventions, along with the fourteen-item GEI. Participants were then exposed to the experimental treatment in the form of a hypothetical news report about the violent actions of an oppressive government in an island nation – either in the Balkans or in the Arabian Peninsula – accompanied by a photograph of a young victim. The individual appeared to be either European or Arab. We measured respondents' reactions to these vignettes in terms of both their support for a variety of policy actions that the United States may take in response to the humanitarian crisis (such as providing asylum to refugees escaping conflict) and their own behavioral intentions (such as donating money to help victims).

To test the premises of Group Empathy Theory during Trump's presidency, we conducted yet another national survey, fielded online by YouGov in October 2018, with a total number of 1,050 respondents. We refer to this as the "2018 US Group Empathy Study." The dataset is composed of a random sample of 350 whites and stratified, random oversamples of 350 African Americans and 350 Latinos. The survey included a shorter, four-item version of the GEI in question format and covered major ground by including a series of key questions about various salient policy issues in the Trump era such as the Muslim ban and Deferred Action for Childhood Arrivals (DACA), among others.

We continued our investigation of the role group empathy plays in public reactions to the Trump administration's political agenda by looking into two key controversial immigration policies – the border wall and family separation – using data from the American National Election Studies (ANES) pilot study fielded by YouGov in December 2018. We thus refer to this as the "2018 ANES Pilot Study." The survey was conducted with a total of 2,500 respondents and included the short, four-item GEI in question format along with measures of some other key socio-political predispositions including racial resentment.

We also performed a comparative test of the theory by exploring the impact of group empathy on political attitudes and behavior in the United Kingdom. The British Election Study (BES) included the short, four-item GEI in statement format in a wave fielded online by YouGov in May 2018. We thus refer to this as the "2018 British Election Study." A representative general population sample of 31,063 respondents was interviewed. The BES is one of the longest-running election studies in the world, collecting data on British public opinion for nearly sixty years. This study gave us the chance to examine the reliability of the shorter scale and the generalizability of the theory in a second important national context in which immigration policy is hotly debated and populist politics are on the rise.

Our latest national survey was conducted in mid-March of 2020, around the time the novel coronavirus (COVID-19) outbreak was declared a global pandemic. It was fielded by YouGov with a total of 850 respondents. We refer to this as the "2020 US Group Empathy Study." The survey included the four-item, question-format version of the GEI we piloted in 2018. With the data collected, we were able to empirically test the effects of group empathy on self- and other-oriented responses to the threat of COVID-19.

OUTLINE OF THE BOOK

In Chapter 2 we introduce Group Empathy Theory. We define group empathy as a multidimensional construct composed of cognitive, affective, and motivational elements. We discuss why we expect group-level empathy to differ from individual-level empathy, especially in terms of its higher potential for explaining and predicting political attitudes and behavior. The theory predicts racial/ethnic differences in group empathy due to variation in socialization patterns and life experiences. Chapter 2 further discusses how Group Empathy Theory challenges one of the key tenets of Social Identity Theory (SIT). According to SIT, one's motivation to establish a positively distinct social identity leads to ingroup favoritism and outgroup discrimination. Accordingly, one would predict that the *higher* one's ingroup identification, the *lower* one's level of outgroup empathy due to stronger intergroup empathy bias. By comparison, Group Empathy Theory predicts that this relationship will appear only among the dominant group – whites in the American case. In contrast, compared to low ingroup identifiers, minorities who *identify more strongly* with their ingroup will actually display *higher empathy* for outgroups – a prediction counterintuitive to SIT. In short, Chapter 2 lays the groundwork for unique theoretical expectations and hypotheses that we then test in the subsequent chapters.

Chapter 3 introduces an original, multi-item measure of group empathy: the Group Empathy Index (GEI). The GEI modifies the Interpersonal Reactivity Index (IRI), which was developed by Davis (1983) to measure individual-level empathy. The latter primarily taps the bond of family and friendship. The GEI taps empathy for members of socially distinct groups. The two measures are similar on their face, but they are in fact conceptually and functionally distinct. The chapter also explores the measurement properties of a long and short version of the GEI, employing data from our multiple surveys. Both versions of the GEI are reliable and valid indicators of the underlying construct. We also find that the GEI is not reducible to personality dimensions such as authoritarianism or other group-oriented predispositions such as SDO, racial resentment, ethnocentrism, ideology, and partisanship.

Chapter 4 explores the origins of group empathy using data from the first wave of our 2013/14 US Group Empathy Two-Wave Study. We investigate the association of group empathy with key socio-demographic factors and life experiences related to intergroup contact, discrimination, and competition. The chapter also tests predictions about the link between ingroup identification and outgroup empathy among whites, blacks, and Latinos, using data from our 2018 US Group Empathy Study. We find strong support for our theoretical expectation that higher ingroup identification is linked with outgroup empathy rather than outgroup animosity among nonwhite respondents. As mentioned, this challenges one of the basic assumptions of SIT.

Chapters 5 and 6 present the results from two national survey experiments in which we manipulated racial/ethnic cues in ambiguous news vignettes depicting a potentially threatening situation either at an airport or at an immigrant detention center. Compared to whites, African Americans and Latinos exhibited substantially higher levels of group empathy and policy support for minority groups other than their own. In both experiments, white respondents were less likely to side with nonwhite targets compared to a white target. African Americans and Latinos, on the other hand, were more likely to side with minority targets, support civil rights policies, and commit to political action on behalf of stigmatized groups as compared to white respondents. These reactions occurred even though African Americans and Latinos reported greater perceived personal risk from terrorism and similar levels of perceived personal threat of immigration compared to whites. Group empathy helps explain the different reactions we observed here.

Chapter 7 presents the results of our 2016 US Group Empathy TESS Study on the link between group empathy and foreign policy opinion. Consistent with our previous findings, African Americans and Latinos expressed significantly higher empathy toward refugees, Arabs, and Muslims than did whites. Such differences again helped explain racial/ethnic gaps in policy preferences as well as distinct reactions to experimental vignettes about humanitarian crises in other countries. On average, those high in group empathy attributed higher responsibility to the United States to protect other nations in need and were much more supportive of foreign aid. Group empathy was also associated with increased support for the United States providing humanitarian assistance and asylum for Syrian civilians, as well as for humanitarian military intervention. We also find that group empathy was the primary determinant of opposition to then-presidential candidate Donald Trump's Muslim ban proposal, with the magnitude of its effect exceeding that of all other factors in the model including partisanship and ideology.

Chapter 8 investigates the effects of group empathy on attitudes regarding a variety of policy changes that took place after Trump's election using data from our 2018 US Group Empathy Study and from the 2018 ANES Pilot Study. We examine how group empathy affects support for the Trump administration's border wall plan and family separation policy, as well as its attempts to end the Obama-era DACA program. We also revisit the issue of Trump's travel and immigration ban on several Muslim countries after he turned his controversial campaign promise into government policy through an executive order. We further explore how group empathy influences opinions about some additional group-related political issues such as hurricane relief for Puerto Rico; misappropriation of Native American names, symbols, and imagery in sports; and the removal of Confederate statues and monuments. Though most of the book is focused on mass opinion about immigration and national security, in Chapter 8 we also examine the relationship between group empathy and support for contemporary social movements, namely Black Lives Matter, #MeToo, and LGBTQ rights, which came to the forefront of public discussion with Trump's election. In all these tests, we find that group empathy is a powerful determinant of public reactions to the Trump administration's policies above and beyond partisanship, ideology, and many other socio-political predispositions.

Chapter 9 extends our examination of Group Empathy Theory outside the United States. As mentioned, the four-item version of our GEI was included in Wave 14 of the British Election Study (BES) in May 2018. The BES data also allowed us to compare the predictive power of intergroup empathy versus interpersonal empathy as it included a ten-item individual-level empathy scale. Group empathy significantly predicts the British public's opinion across a myriad of policy issues, including opposition to Brexit, favorable perceptions of immigration, and support for equal opportunity policies, social welfare, and foreign aid. By comparison, individual empathy has very little effect on opinions about these topics. In line with our theory and consistent with the findings from the United States, nonwhite minorities in the United Kingdom score higher on the GEI than whites do while no significant intergroup differences are observed when it comes to individual-level empathy. The data indicated large gaps in policy opinions between whites and nonwhites, and group empathy once again proved to help explain this variation.

Chapter 10 provides an overview of all our findings and offers additional avenues of research. We also discuss the many policy implications and political ramifications of group empathy, including what happens when it is lacking in specific contexts. The eight-year span of our data collection covers a stark transformation of the American policy landscape as the United States transitioned from Barack Obama's presidency to Donald Trump's ascension into the White House. This allows us to contemplate whether and how levels of group empathy might have shifted over time within and across racial/ethnic groups in the United States. We further consider how to cultivate group empathy in order to improve intergroup relations and social justice. The conclusion chapter is followed by an Epilogue, where we discuss and present empirical evidence on the role group empathy plays in reactions to the COVID-19 pandemic that upended the world, causing massive loss of life and socio-economic devastation, as we were finishing our book.

2

Group Empathy Theory

And I will tell you, Class of 2013, whatever success I have achieved, whatever positions of leadership I have held have depended less on Ivy League degrees or SAT scores or GPAs, and have instead been due to that sense of connection and empathy – the special obligation I felt, as a black man like you, to help those who need it most, people who didn't have the opportunities that I had – because there but for the grace of God, go I – I might have been in their shoes. I might have been in prison. I might have been unemployed. I might not have been able to support a family. And that motivates me. So it's up to you to widen your circle of concern – to care about justice for everybody, white, black, and brown. Everybody. Not just in your own community, but also across this country and around the world. To make sure everyone has a voice and everybody gets a seat at the table; that everybody, no matter what you look like or where you come from, what your last name is – it doesn't matter, everybody gets a chance to walk through those doors of opportunity if they are willing to work hard enough.

Barack Obama, commencement address at Morehouse College (May 19, 2013)[1]

Empathy is frequently invoked in popular culture to describe a wide variety of human experiences. The exhortation to "put yourself in someone else's shoes" is a common nod to the benefits of empathy, especially in a multicultural society. Yet there is a lot of confusion about what empathy really is and what it causes. Some people use the word synonymously with reactions like sympathy, compassion, kindness, caring, or pity for those in distress. Others think of it as generosity or charity. Still others think it means interpersonal affinity, like-mindedness, or fellowship. Dictionary definitions also carry a range of meanings, but most center on the notion that empathy is the ability to recognize, understand, and share the emotions, thoughts, and experiences of

---

[1] See https://obamawhitehouse.archives.gov/the-press-office/2013/05/19/remarks-president-morehouse-college-commencement-ceremony.

another person. It is the ability to imagine what it feels like to be in that person's situation, even without having been told.[2]

Such imprecise definitions in everyday conversation are common, but vague concepts make for blunt analytic tools that rarely solve scientific puzzles. If empathy means all those things we mentioned, invoking it may not really help explain much (Coplan 2011). Why do some people with so much to lose still sometimes protect others who are perceived as a threat? Maybe some people are just soft-hearted and kind? Or weak and unable to advocate for themselves? Or perhaps they just identify with the other as a member of some superordinate group the analyst had not considered. If all of those things are empathy, we have not narrowed down our explanation enough.

In this chapter, we first review existing psychological definitions of individual-level empathy and then introduce our own related construct. Our central argument is that a less common form – outgroup empathy – is conceptually related to but empirically distinct from the dominant forms studied by social psychologists. We further argue that group empathy, like empathy for one's closest intimates, is more a trait than a state – learned early and largely stable over the life span. We then discuss where we think outgroup empathy comes from. Is it nature or nurture? If the latter, how do we acquire the ability to empathize with those who are very different than us, as well as the motivation to use that ability in politics? Finally, we discuss the theoretical relationship between social identity and group empathy. The two forces are distinct yet probably linked. Group Empathy Theory suggests they will be related differently among majority versus minority group members.

WHAT IS EMPATHY?

The scholarly literature on empathy has displayed some conceptual ambiguity, though surely not as much as is present in lay understandings of the word (see Breyer 2020 for a discussion). Some conceive of empathy primarily as an *affective* response (see Mehrabian & Epstein 1972): the reflexive tendency to experience the emotions of another. A mother's automatic physiological reaction to her infant's cries is an example. These reactions are quite unavoidable. Seeing a loved one laugh or cry often triggers strong feelings even before we understand why.

Other conceptual definitions focus on the *cognitive* ability to put oneself in the place of another, so we might see the world through their eyes (e.g., Dymond 1949; Kerr & Speroff 1954). Baron-Cohen and colleagues (1997, 2001) developed a test called "Reading the Mind in the Eyes" to measure just this dimension. The test involves pictures cropped to show only a person's eyes, and each respondent is given a set of four emotion words to match to the expression displayed in the

---

[2] See, for example, https://dictionary.cambridge.org/us/dictionary/english/empathy, www.lexico.com /en/definition/empathy, and www.merriam-webster.com/dictionary/empathy.

picture. The test was originally developed to diagnose milder forms of Autism Spectrum Disorder (ASD) based on the premise that such individuals were impaired, to various degrees, in their ability to correctly attribute mental states to another person. Baron-Cohen et al. (2001, 241) refer to this ability as "Theory of Mind," asserting that it "overlaps with the term 'empathy.'" Indeed, this more narrow definition has received some attention in political psychology, with one study demonstrating that scores on the Mind in the Eyes test are associated with support for social welfare spending and moderated by preexisting beliefs about how effective government is at solving problems (Feldman et al. 2020).

We believe the affective and cognitive dimensions of empathy are both important, but they omit a key piece of the puzzle: motivation. Without the *motivation to care* about another person's well-being, simply having the ability to experience their emotional state and take their perspective would not necessarily lead to an empathic attitudinal and behavioral response (Batson & Coke 1981; Batson et al. 2002; Lamm et al. 2007). To put it most dramatically, sociopaths are known for their keen ability to detect emotions in others but tend to use that knowledge to manipulate and deceive rather than help (e.g., Book et al. 2007).

The motivation to empathize is often assumed when we are thinking about close kin and friends. Of course, we are motivated to care about people we share so much of our intimate lives with, on whom we depend for company and affection, and without whom we might feel unsafe. However, scholars have begun to recognize that there is wide variation in the motivation to empathize with others, especially those who are outside our family and friendship circles (Weisz & Zaki 2018). We believe motivation is especially key to predicting who will extend political rights and resources across social divisions, even to groups that are perceived to be threatening and in competition.

In line with a wide swath of research in this area, therefore, we consider empathy to be a multidimensional construct, encompassing affective, cognitive, and motivational components (Davis 1980, 1983, 1994; Decety & Jackson 2004; Duan & Hill 1996; Hoffman 1990). The affective dimension involves an automatic emotional response to others, especially those encountering struggle, discrimination, or need. The cognitive dimension captures an individual's capacity for putting themselves in someone else's shoes. The motivational dimension represents one's concern about and desire to alleviate the pain and distress felt by another. We define empathy as *the ability to take the perspective of others and experience their emotions with the motivation to care about their welfare.* Outgroup empathy arises when such ability and motivation is directed toward social collectives with whom one has little in common.

FROM INDIVIDUAL TO GROUP EMPATHY

Work in evolutionary psychology suggests that empathy is most adaptive in family units and small social groups. In such settings, each individual's chance of survival is improved when everyone is attuned to the emotions of others, since emotions serve as early warning signals for threats and opportunities in the immediate environment (Preston & De Waal 2002). Empathy enables individuals to quickly identify problems, resolve conflicts, and coordinate within the collective to defend against external threats.

Empathy is such a powerful survival tool that it has been found throughout the natural world, even among nonprimate mammals. To investigate empathically motivated prosocial behavior in rodents, Ben-Ami Bartal et al. (2011) conducted an experiment in which a free rat was placed with a former cagemate who was trapped in a restraining device. Over several sessions, the free rat figured out how to open the restrainer and free the trapped cagemate while not making the same effort to open empty or object-containing restrainers. Rats rescued their former cagemates even in the absence of a reward. Most surprisingly, the rats helped each other even when they were in competition for highly palatable food. When placed in an area with a second restrainer containing chocolate, rats typically chose to open both restrainers and shared the chocolate with the cagemate they liberated. Ben-Ami Bartal et al. (2011, 1430) concluded: "The ability to understand and actively respond to the affective state of a conspecific is crucial for an animal's successful navigation in the social arena and ultimately benefits group survival."

Not surprisingly, then, empathy in humans also seems widespread and individually rewarding. The experience of interpersonal empathy is associated with a number of positive psychological conditions such as life satisfaction, enriched social networks, self-esteem, and decreased aggressiveness (e.g., Eisenberg et al. 2006; Richardson et al. 1994). There is also a strong link between empathy and prosocial behavior. People high in empathy are more likely to volunteer in their communities (Unger & Thumuluri 1997), donate to charities (Cialdini et al. 1997), and cooperate to achieve shared goals (Rumble et al. 2010).

From an evolutionary perspective, empathy is adaptive for ingroup protection (Decety et al. 2012). It helps to connect emotionally with those upon whom one depends for safety, security, and reproductive success. Under many circumstances, we might therefore expect those high in empathy for close kin and friends to be the least likely to extend empathy to strangers, especially members of outgroups. This would presumably help individuals avoid risks by distancing themselves from those who might threaten their kin and close friends. Of course, this implies that empathy and moral values are not synonymous (Batson et al. 1995), since protecting a close ingroup member could significantly conflict with the collective good (Batson & Ahmad 2009a).

The bottom line is that empathy is no simple, unidimensional phenomenon with obvious social and political consequences, either for good or for evil. The impact of empathy depends on the context, especially perhaps the scope and range of the person's ability to experience and care about the plight of others. As that scope broadens, and the individual can see and vicariously experience others' perspectives and emotions across greater lines of difference, political preferences should also change. In this book, we focus on a form of empathy that most existing theories suggest will be quite rare: empathy for strangers from different social groups, backgrounds, and cultures. We suspect that, as people broaden their scope of empathy beyond their intimate family and friendship circles, this form of empathy becomes more common and important political consequences arise.

We think outgroup empathy emerges when one's own group experiences act as a lens through which the circumstances of other groups are evaluated. We envision group empathy as *a predisposition that motivates members of one group to vicariously experience and care about the perspectives and emotions of members of other groups.* Our conceptualization of "group empathy" thus centers on intergroup empathy (i.e., empathy toward members of outgroups) rather than intragroup empathy (i.e., empathy toward one's ingroup members).

While empathy for outgroups should be much less common than for close intimates, we suspect it is adaptive in increasingly pluralistic, multicultural communities. As our societies become more and more diverse, the ability to empathize with people of distinct racial/ethnic, cultural, religious, and various other backgrounds can produce great personal and even ingroup benefits. It could mean the difference between recognizing a beneficial compromise and walking away from one. Outgroup empathy should therefore have significant social, political, and economic consequences. Suggestive evidence comes from studies finding links between empathy and helping behavior directed at members of stigmatized groups such as AIDS patients (e.g., Batson et al. 1997). Empathy can also be experienced for racial/ethnic outgroups, effectively reducing prejudice, stereotyping, and ingroup favoritism (Finlay & Stephan 2000; Galinsky & Moskowitz 2000). We know less, however, about the role of outgroup empathy in mass political preference formation and behavior.

While empathy for close intimates has important social consequences and highly positive effects on interpersonal relations, outgroup empathy is more *politically* potent because it can influence opinions and actions that affect entire social groups. We find that the effects of group empathy go beyond ordinary altruistic views and behaviors often associated with individual-level empathy, such as donating to charity or helping the needy in one's local community. For instance, Chapter 3 demonstrates that our measure of group empathy is the single best predictor of attending a rally to defend another group's rights, above and beyond partisanship, ideology, authoritarianism, and other predispositions. Generalized empathy for outgroups, but not individual-level empathy, also drives opposition to punitive immigration policies. Chapter 9 shows that group empathy powerfully influences the opinions of British citizens about Brexit, immigration, and welfare. Standard measures of individual-level empathy carry no significance for these policy views. So while empathy for one's close family and friends is surely common and adaptive, it often does not have large political consequences in the way outgroup empathy does.

GROUP EMPATHY: TRAIT OR STATE?

We conceive group empathy as a trait that develops in early childhood, is cultivated over time through life experiences, and remains mostly stable in adulthood. As Duan and Hill (1996) point out, empathy has been conceptualized both as a long-term trait (e.g., Buie 1981; Sawyier 1975) and a short-lived, event-specific experience (Rogers 1959; Stotland 1969; Truax & Carkhuff 1967). Trait empathy captures individual differences stemming from some combination of genetics and socialization (Davis 1980; Hoffman 1984). Some grow into more empathic individuals than others (Cao 2010). Situational triggers may invoke affective reactions across all individuals and groups independent of one's baseline trait empathy (e.g., Batson & Coke 1981; Batson et al. 2002; Cao 2010; Zillmann 2006). However, while certain situations may invoke affective reactions such as sympathy or pity even among those low in trait empathy, we think those who are predispositionally high in group empathy react much more powerfully and prosocially to situations involving members of outgroups in distress.[3]

Trait empathy should guide political attitudes and behavior consistently across situations and might override more immediate emotional reactions to threats and opportunities. By comparison, short-term emotional triggers may lead one to temporarily discard political habits and values, focusing instead on the immediate environment. Think about the haunting picture of the three-year-old Syrian boy who was lying face down on a Turkish beach, drowned while his family was trying to escape the violence in their country on an overloaded boat not safe to cross the Mediterranean.[4] The troubling image turned the world's spotlight, if only for a brief moment, on the horrors of the civil war in Syria. Tens of thousands of people donated to help Syrians after seeing the photo. We suspect many of those who responded to the picture were driven by situational sympathy, not high levels of trait empathy. This would help explain why there has been such strong public opposition to Syrian refugee resettlements across many developed countries, including the United States and most of Europe, even though many were saddened by the photo.[5]

Martin Luther King Jr. once criticized such short-term charity, driven solely by paternalistic, impersonal pity rather than a genuine concern for the well-being of an oppressed group. The irony, he pointed out, was that "millions of missionary dollars have gone to Africa from the hands of church people who

---

[3] We find empirical support for this expectation in Chapter 3.

[4] See http://100photos.time.com/photos/nilufer-demir-alan-kurdi.

[5] See, for example, https://news.gallup.com/poll/209828/syrian-refugees-not-welcome-eastern-europe.aspx.

would die a million deaths before they would permit a single African the privilege of worshipping in their congregation" (King 2012, 28). In keeping with King's point, we suspect some of those who were moved by that heart-wrenching photo would nonetheless oppose admitting even a single Syrian refugee into their country. But those high in group empathy would not only react in the moment to the death of a small child but also be more likely to support a variety of policies and actions to help Syrian civilians fleeing violence.[6]

Group empathy may also play a persistent, even lifelong, role in shaping political attitudes and behavior. If so, those high in this trait should evaluate political conflict very differently across contexts. This would not be the case for short-term emotional reactions to an outgroup's suffering, triggered by specific events. Think back to the picture of the drowned Syrian toddler. The initial uproar provoked by the unsettling image faded after only a few short weeks. As Slovic et al. (2017) show, throughout the week following the release of the photo, the number of daily donations to a Red Cross campaign designated to aid Syrian refugees grew 100-fold. Yet, after just four weeks, those numbers plummeted back to baseline. Unlike such fleeting effects of situational affective reactions, group empathy as a trait characteristic should have enduring effects on political attitudes and behavior, since it is the product of socialization and recurrent life experiences rather than a single sensational incident.

Besides its long-lasting effects on favorable attitudes and prosocial behavior toward outgroups in distress, group empathy should be rather stable and independent of specific events. However, we would not rule out changes in outgroup empathy as a result of very significant social trends. Even over the course of our own research on this topic from 2012 through 2020, we witnessed some significant changes in the proportion of Americans who report that they put themselves in the shoes of groups very different than their own. The contemporary political moment may be increasing the opportunity to witness group conflict and discrimination in close quarters. Trait empathy may thus very well shift as the environment changes, leading especially young people to be socialized differently than previous cohorts.

There are plenty of examples of the impact of distinct socializing experiences on adult political habits. Peffley and Hurwitz (2010) discuss how blacks and whites perceive different realities when it comes to justice in America. Many whites may sincerely believe that the criminal justice system is fair and color-blind. However, as more and more vivid and frequently deadly incidents of police brutality and other systemic injustices appear on television screens or social media circles, it becomes more apparent that the reality for minorities is indeed different. This might lead some whites

---

[6] We provide evidence in support of this prediction in Chapter 7, in the context of foreign policy threats.

to develop greater empathy for marginalized outgroups – and even begin to support civil rights movements like Black Lives Matter as well as policies that would protect those most vulnerable. While a single image may trigger sympathy for a person in distress, repeated exposure to an outgroup's suffering might enhance the ability to empathize and the motivation to apply that ability in a variety of circumstances.

With these considerations in mind, we suspect that populist, exclusionary politics may be met with a countervailing force: group empathy. Even those whose lives are far removed from the realities of persecuted groups may begin to see the systemic discrimination and violence fanned by demagogues. For instance, as mentioned in Chapter 1, the results of a 2017 Arab American Institute (AAI) poll show that a majority of Americans had begun to express more favorable views of Arabs and Muslims – for the first time in AAI polling. This coincides with a significant spike in hate crimes targeting the Muslim American community and with increased Islamophobic discourse in the Trump era. In fact, we observe an uptick in group empathy among whites in the years after Trump took office.

Of course, repeated exposure to incidents involving members of an outgroup in distress will not guarantee the development of empathy toward those people. There are multiple obstacles to consider. First, empathy for large, amorphous groups is much more difficult to generate than empathy for an individual, even a stranger. Empathic reactions do not grow linearly with the ranks of the suffering. On the contrary, Västfjäll et al. (2014) find a substantive *decrease* in donations to help children in distress as the number of those in need increases. They refer to this effect as "compassion fade" that occurs when an incident featuring a single person expands to a group of even as few as two people. Slovic (2007, 79) argues that people experience "psychic numbing" in reaction to genocide, noting: "Most people are caring and will exert great effort to rescue individual victims whose needy plight comes to their attention. These same good people, however, often become numbly indifferent to the plight of individuals who are 'one of many' in a much greater problem." Repeated exposure to situations where large groups are suffering can lead to habituation and emotional fatigue, dulling our ability to experience empathy. People may feel overwhelmed about the number of those suffering, so, to avoid stress and other negative emotions caused by an empathic state of mind, they may psychologically detach themselves as a defense mechanism (Shaw et al. 1994; Stephan & Finlay 1999; see also Bloom 2017).

Second, rather than an empathic reaction, outgroups in distress may actually cause antipathy for some, especially when framed as taking advantage of the kindness and generosity of one's ingroup and exploiting their resources. This is perhaps how Trump's negative framing of undocumented immigrants and asylum seekers heading to the US border as an "invasion" inoculates his base from experiencing empathy and extending policy support to these outgroups, instead rallying support for punitive measures.[7]

Further, not everyone who is exposed to situational triggers will internalize them. One historical example comes from the 1960s civil rights era. A key strategy of Martin Luther King Jr. and several other civil rights leaders was visually documenting nonviolent protests of African Americans amid violent backlash in order to increase white sympathy. Such graphic documentation of African Americans published by the news media showing their peaceful resistance to Jim Crow racism despite all the beatings, bullying, and unfounded arrests indeed mounted up to gather white sympathy (at least in regions of the United States where racial attitudes were less solidified) and the sympathy of the international community. This, in turn, intensified the pressure on the US government for extending civil rights and protections to African Americans (see Ward & Badger 1996). And this was accomplished at a time when there were no smartphones to live stream police interactions, multiple news channels running HD footage of the protests, or social media circulating and evaluating such events. However, even if "white sympathy" aroused by the images and footage of violence might have contributed to key legislative changes, only a portion of those who sympathized would also develop trait empathy for outgroups. We would expect a smaller share to stand in solidarity with their black compatriots in their struggle for genuine societal and political change. In fact, according to Berger (2011), the very pictures credited with eliciting white sympathy might have simultaneously conditioned many to perceive blacks as powerless, thus limiting policy reforms.

For all these reasons, empathy should be more common for ingroup members rather than strangers, individuals rather than groups, and those whom elites do not have an incentive to vilify. Still, there are a variety of reasons to expect politically consequential outgroup empathy to occur in a range of circumstances common in modern multicultural societies. Those who empathize across lines of cultural, religious, racial/ethnic, and other differences might be better able to compromise and collaborate in ways that maximize collective harmony and productivity. Indeed, we suspect the benefits of diversity (Page 2007) – touted by educators, economists, and leaders – can be achieved only after individuals begin to extend empathy toward groups from the wider world. While the incentives to look inward and guard against outgroups perceived as threats are still great, so are the potential gains to be captured by connecting with others who have different experiences, skills, and energy. In politics, outgroup empathy has the potential not just to reduce conflict and hatred but also to maximize security and economic growth.

---

[7] Anthony Rivas (2019), "Trump's Language about Mexican Immigrants under Scrutiny in Wake of El Paso Shooting," ABC News, https://abcnews.go.com/US/trumps-language-mexican-immigrants-scrutiny-wake-el-paso/story?id=64768566.

DEVELOPING EMPATHY FOR OUTGROUPS: NATURE VERSUS NURTURE?

The social range of empathic reactions remains a subject of intense study in cognitive and evolutionary psychology. How broadly does empathy apply to the social world before it becomes maladaptive for individuals, opening them up to risks from outgroup members who may take advantage? One critical question that springs from this concern is whether empathy is innate, and therefore essentially fixed at birth, or whether it is mostly learned, as a result of interacting with others in social settings. If the latter, this would make it more likely that we would find empathy for outgroups as society becomes more diverse. It turns out there is some evidence for this possibility in the animal kingdom as well.

Recall Ben-Ami Bartal et al.'s (2011) work on empathy in rats discussed earlier. In another experiment, Ben-Ami Bartal et al. (2014) found that rats helped strangers of their own strain but not strangers of a different strain they were unfamiliar with. However, if they were previously housed with a rat from a different strain, they would help strangers phenotypically similar to their cagemate. Most remarkably, rats fostered from birth with another strain and with no exposure to their own strain would only help strangers of the fostering strain, not their own. The results suggest that prosocial behavior in rats is greatly moderated by social experience, not simply by genetic similarity.

So what about humans? It is almost impossible to conduct perfectly controlled laboratory experiments, like the ones Ben-Ami Bartal and her colleagues did with rats, to untangle the socialization processes that lead to variation in empathy in humans. Still, considering the experimental set-up of Ben-Ami Bartal et al., one particular question comes to mind: Why would some people be indifferent to seeing immigrants and asylum seekers, among them even children, held in cages in detention facilities, while others would strongly oppose such conditions and even take political action to help release them?

Chapter 4 discusses in detail the origins of outgroup empathy. The focus is on how individuals in a large multicultural society may have distinct experiences that lead to greater or lesser empathic ability and motivation. We predict differences across race/ethnicity, gender, education, and age, all as a result of the ways membership in these groups shapes one's life experiences. We include a discussion here regarding the impact of race/ethnicity, since gaps in public opinion across racial/ethnic groups are often large and not fully explained by differences in threat perceptions, material interests, partisanship, or other standard predictors. We think outgroup empathy can help us solve those puzzles particularly well.

To date, studies in social psychology have almost exclusively examined empathy for nonracial/nonethnic stigmatized groups such as the homeless, drug addicts, convicted murderers, and AIDS patients (e.g., Batson et al. 1997, 2002). Work that does examine ethnocultural empathy tends to focus on the conditions under which majority group members empathize with minorities (e.g., Finlay & Stephan 2000; Galinsky & Moskowitz 2000; Wang et al. 2003). Moreover, little attention has been paid to whether common social experiences between different racial/ethnic groups trigger empathic processes and, if so, with what political consequences (Johnson et al. 2009). Our theory, however, focuses on empathy for outgroups exhibited not only by the majority but also by minorities, and predicts cross-group variation in empathy to explain distinct reactions to very similar political threats.

While empathy for victimized groups can develop among members of the majority, we expect that historically disadvantaged minorities are particularly likely to be empathic toward members of other groups. As Masuoka and Junn (2013, 5) put it, "race is not simply a demographic characteristic or a product of personal preference but a structural attribute imposed on an individual with important consequences for individual life chances and political experiences." These experiences impact the social lens through which a person sees the world as one grows from a young child into adulthood. The internalized cultural narratives of marginalized groups should trigger empathy toward other groups with similar experiences.

Group Empathy Theory posits that minority group members will find it easier, cognitively speaking, to imagine themselves in the position of those from another group being unfairly treated. According to Segal et al. (2011, 439), minorities have "the dual task of understanding and negotiating their own culture and the culture of the dominant class." Similarly, Swigonski (1994, 390) argues that, in order to thrive, less powerful groups "have the potential for 'double vision' or double consciousness – a knowledge of, awareness of, and sensitivity to both the dominant worldview of society and their own perspective." Accordingly, we expect historically oppressed groups to be better able to "put themselves in the shoes" of others experiencing discrimination, especially when it mirrors their own histories. An individual's direct experience with discrimination should thus serve as a primary causal antecedent of empathy toward others (Eklund et al. 2009; Hoffman 2000). After all, in order to take the perspective of another person, it helps to hold a repertoire of similar experiences (Cao 2010).

Batson and Ahmad (2009b) suggest individuals can develop both self- and other-oriented perspective-taking abilities. Self-oriented perspective taking (also known as the "imagine-self" perspective) involves imagining what one might think in another's situation or "shoes." Self-oriented perspective taking seems to reduce stereotyping and boost positive evaluations of individuals and even entire outgroups. By comparison, other-oriented perspective taking (aka the "imagine-other" perspective) entails one's ability to imagine what another person thinks given their situation. Batson and Ahmad (2009b) find that other-oriented perspective taking leads not only to increased situational attribution and concern for the plight of a targeted individual but also more positive attitudes toward the individual's outgroup as a whole. Given their own experiences of unfair treatment, Group Empathy Theory asserts that minority groups should possess, on average, higher levels of both self- and other-oriented perspective taking.

In addition to cognitive perspective taking, stigmatized minorities may also develop a keener sense of *affective* empathy. Previous work suggests affective empathy can be *reactive* – responding to the emotional experiences of another – and *parallel* – experiencing emotions similar to those of another (see Davis 1994; Stephan & Finlay 1999). For instance, witnessing racial profiling may trigger sympathetic concern and compassion for the targeted person's well-being – a form of reactive empathy. But, if the observers also experience anger and disgust in response to such unfair treatment, they are paralleling the emotions of the other. Parallel empathy requires a very fine-tuned emotional system that develops over time from personal experience. Since minorities are more likely to have had such personal experiences, or to have been exposed to the cultural narratives of their group, Group Empathy Theory would predict that affective empathic processes – in both reactive and parallel forms – likely occur more often among minority group members than the majority.

African Americans and Latinos have historically struggled with discrimination, lower income, and higher unemployment (McClain & Stewart 2002). Such shared experiences of exclusion and constraint can increase perceptions of commonality (e.g., Craig & Richeson 2012; Masuoka & Junn 2013; Sanchez 2008), and coalition-building can occur between these groups (Barreto et al. 2013; Tedin & Murray 1994; but see Kaufmann 2003). Having superordinate goals may facilitate intergroup cooperation and diminish social divisions (Gaertner & Dovidio 2000), which in turn helps foster outreach between groups (Stürmer et al. 2006). On the other hand, perhaps due to resource scarcity, African Americans and Latinos can perceive one another as economic competitors (Bobo & Hutchings 1996), and some research suggests such intergroup competition could strongly countervail the development of empathy for outgroups (Cikara et al. 2011). This latter line of research implies minority groups are unlikely to view each other as members of a larger collective.

Despite intergroup competition, which could undermine any sense of co-identification or linked fate between oppressed groups, we think empathy may still powerfully condition reactions to external threats. The reason is that empathy for outgroups may be triggered quite automatically by instances of racial/ethnic-based discrimination, and can therefore be impactful even when groups are in competition with each other and do not strongly co-identify. In short, our theory predicts that group-based empathy can override one's existential, economic, and cultural concerns about an outgroup.

As mentioned, we perceive group empathy as a trait that develops through early life socialization experiences where one's membership in a disadvantaged group is salient. Compared to the members of a racial/ethnic majority in a given society, group-based trait empathy should be stronger among disadvantaged minorities due to their life experiences and collective memories of oppression and discrimination. If so, minorities will be more reactive to ambiguous situations that could be interpreted as discriminatory against a member of a different minority group. Therefore, while anyone high in trait empathy should react similarly, we expect significant differences across racial/ethnic groups at the aggregate level.

Minority groups do not necessarily experience identical forms of discrimination. For instance, Latinos are often branded as foreigners even if they are native-born, English-speaking citizens (Branton et al. 2011; Masuoka & Junn 2013). Arab Americans have their own distinct experiences with marginalization as outsiders, often stereotypically connected to fears about terrorism (Sides & Gross 2013). Both of these groups' experiences are notably different from the African American experience – born of slavery and tied to a continuous history of oppression and discrimination. And, of course, whites may also hail from ethnic backgrounds with a history of being the targets of discrimination and oppression (such as Italian or Irish Americans). Such diverse experiences and cultural specificities should not, however, inhibit the development of outgroup empathy. There is common ground for different groups to perceive societal discrimination as a shared experience, even as the details differ.

Those who see other members of their group experiencing similar challenges are certainly quick to show support and unify under a common banner. Beyond such ingroup empathy, a cornerstone of Group Empathy Theory rests on the notion that groups have the potential to see past social divisions and conflicting interests (e.g., job competition between blacks and Latinos) and to extend empathy to one another, with powerful implications for their political views and behavior. Individuals familiar with discrimination should be among the first to come to another marginalized group's defense, even when the circumstances of injustice differ from those of their ingroup. If so, personal experience of discrimination – regardless of its specific forms – should still amplify one's sensitivity to the unfair treatment of others.

Group Empathy Theory further predicts minorities will extend empathy not only to other marginalized groups but also to whites in times of distress. For instance, in a survey experiment (presented in Chapter 7) set in the context of an international humanitarian crisis scenario involving a European nation versus an Arab nation, minority respondents were as empathic toward European victims as they were toward Arabs. Specifically, African Americans and Latinos displayed higher support than whites for a US humanitarian military intervention against an oppressive regime depicted in the experimental vignette in both European and Arab nation conditions. Moreover, for both the European and Arab nation conditions, African Americans and particularly Latinos were much more likely to sign a petition supporting humanitarian aid for the victims of the violent conflict.

Albeit via different socialization processes, we expect whites who score highly on group empathy to display similarly high levels of policy support and helping behavior toward stigmatized outgroups as minorities would do. A major historical example is the march from Selma to Montgomery in 1965 (see Pratt 2017). On what became known as "Bloody Sunday" on March 7, 1965, television coverage of the tear gas attacks and brutal beatings of peaceful protestors at the hands of state troopers led to national outrage and helped mobilize hundreds of whites to respond to King's call on short notice to join the ranks of the black demonstrators to reattempt the march. This is one of the iconic moments illustrating how empathy for an outgroup can overcome existential threats and even lead people to risk their own lives to assist others in their fight for justice and equality. James Reeb, a white Unitarian minister from Massachusetts, and Viola Liuzzo, a white woman from Michigan, were both killed by white supremacists during the protests, demonstrating just how real and imminent the threat was. Upon reaching the steps of the capitol in Montgomery, Alabama after a five-day march with thousands of people in tow, King stated: "There never was a moment in American history more honorable and more inspiring than the pilgrimage of clergymen and laymen of every race and faith pouring into Selma to face danger at the side of its embattled Negroes" (Otfinoski 2018, 80).

There have indeed been major instances where some whites have stood in solidarity with oppressed groups, risking their lives. Take, for example, the protest against white nationalism that occurred in Charlottesville, Virginia, during the "Unite the Right" rally in August 2017, as well as the Black Lives Matter protests that spread across the nation (and the globe) following the murder of an unarmed black man, George Floyd, at the hands of police in May 2020. In Chapter 8, we discuss these incidents in detail and also show that the effect of group empathy on reactions to exclusionary policies and issues in the Trump era is significant across all three racial/ethnic respondent groups in our sample.

In short, the explanatory power of our theory captures the political attitudes and behavior of both minority groups and the dominant majority. In other words, it is not confined to minorities, with empathy only being extended from one marginalized group to another. While whites are overall less likely than minorities to extend empathy toward marginalized outgroups, we still expect group empathy to be a key driver of white political opinion and behavior. We also do not consider group empathy as a prosocial reaction exclusively reserved for historically disadvantaged outgroups; rather, minorities should demonstrate similar levels of support and helping behavior in cases where the members of the majority find themselves in dire situations, such as natural disasters or school shootings.

INGROUP IDENTIFICATION AND OUTGROUP EMPATHY

While we believe race/ethnicity, in and of itself, is an important demographic factor in shaping one's life experiences that help cultivate group empathy, *identification* with one's racial/ethnic ingroup is a vital social mechanism that affects the internalization of such life experiences as part of a collective and guides one's interactions with other groups. A number of scholars find that shared group membership strongly facilitates empathy and that such "ingroup empathy bias" has neurological, physiological, and psychological bases (Brown et al. 2006; Cheon et al. 2011; Mathur et al. 2010; Suleiman et al. 2018). As mentioned, just like individual empathy is directed primarily toward one's family and friends, the general assumption is that empathy is more easily exhibited for members of one's ingroup. This does make intuitive sense from an evolutionary as well as a social perspective. One is more likely to perceive similarity in interests and life challenges with fellow members of one's ingroup than outgroups. So people may thus find it much easier to put themselves in the shoes of ingroup members. Other scholars suggest that feeling empathy for outgroups is not only harder but is negatively associated with empathy for one's ingroup, especially when groups are in competition, so much so that the struggles that an outgroup faces may even lead to *schadenfreude* – malicious pleasure at an outgroup's misfortune – rather than an attempt to alleviate suffering (Leech et al. 2003; Cikara et al. 2011).

Our theory departs from these assumptions in that we suspect outgroup empathy may be triggered (1) even when individuals are strongly empathic toward their ingroup and (2) even for outgroups perceived to be threatening. Since empathy is a trait learned early on and applied somewhat automatically, we predict it will shape policy reactions whenever an outgroup is subjected to treatment the observer believes to be unfair, especially if the injustice resonates with the life experiences of one's own group. It should then matter which group one belongs to and identifies with, because that identification helps internalize the experiences that lead to outgroup empathy in the first place. Let us elaborate.

According to Social Identity Theory (SIT; Tajfel & Turner 1979), people who identify more strongly with their ingroup will favor their ingroup more and discriminate against outgroups (see also Perreault & Bourhis 1999). SIT's close relative, self-categorization theory (Turner et al. 1987, 42) further points to a basic need for individuals "to differentiate their own groups positively from others to achieve a positive social identity." If so, one might predict that those who identify more strongly with their ingroup will also display higher levels of ingroup empathy, as a reflection of ingroup favoritism, and lower levels of outgroup empathy, owing to outgroup discrimination.

Furthermore, SIT makes similar predictions for groups of both high and low social status with regard to outgroup attitudes, though the pathways are somewhat different. Individuals in high-status groups have it easy: they benefit from their membership and therefore focus positive attitudes on the ingroup and negative attitudes on outgroups who might threaten their higher status. When group status is low, on the other hand, members have several choices. First, they might "exit" the group if such a move is possible, since identifying with a low-status group might hurt their self-esteem. If a member of a low-status group can "pass" as a higher-status group member, they might attempt it. Second, they could attempt to redefine the group's status more positively even without making any real substantive changes to the group's position. Finally, they could challenge their group's low status directly, attempting to bring about real social change by reducing inequality (Tajfel & Turner 1979; Turner et al. 1987).

From our perspective, what is most important about these theoretical claims for both high- and low-status group members is that they all make the same prediction about the relationship between ingroup and outgroup attitudes. Strong group identifiers are most often going to embrace their ingroup membership rather than try to join a different group (Ethier & Deaux 1994; Tajfel 1981). The more people think of themselves as members of a group, be it the majority or the minority, the more likely they are to express positive attitudes toward their group and the less likely they are to empathize with members of another. Group Empathy Theory makes a very different prediction.

Group Empathy Theory would expect that the direction of the relationship between ingroup identification and outgroup empathy changes, depending on the relative social status and collective experiences of the groups in question. As SIT would predict, highly identified majority group members should be expected to empathize strongly with other members of their group in order to derive the maximum benefits of membership. They should also be less likely to extend empathy to other groups who are seeking to topple them from their position in the social hierarchy.

The relationship should, however, be different for minority group members. If, as we have argued, marginalized groups face more systematic discrimination throughout their lives, they may become much more sensitive to situations where other groups are experiencing unfair treatment. Chong and Kim (2006) find that even economically upwardly mobile minority group members remain conscious of their group status and do not forgo support for policies that address racial/ethnic inequality. These authors suggest that continued encounters with prejudice and discrimination remind minorities that their identity matters. We suspect that the more strongly such individuals identify with their group, the more often they will be reminded of their unfair status in the social hierarchy, and, in turn, the more empathy they will extend to other marginalized groups that face similar challenges. This effect might hold even when minority groups are in competition with each other for limited resources at the bottom rungs of the social system, because the application of empathy is learned early on and automatically triggered.

In the US case, we therefore predict that outgroup empathy will be linked to ingroup identification much differently for whites versus minorities. Among whites, ingroup identification should inhibit empathy for members of most other racial/ethnic groups – just as SIT would predict. Higher ingroup identification among whites may even lead to outgroup antipathy if driven by racial bias, ethnocentrism, and social dominance (see Forgiarini et al. 2011; Perreault & Bourhis 1999). Note that outgroup discrimination is not necessarily synonymous with outgroup animus, and low levels of outgroup empathy will not always be accompanied by high levels of outgroup antipathy (see Brown et al. 2006). For example, Jardina (2019) finds that not all whites who identify with their ingroup are driven by racial resentment or animosity toward minorities. At least some are expressing a preference for their ingroup, particularly when they feel their ingroup interests are threatened, without strongly disliking others. Nevertheless, as Brewer (1999, 438) points out, "Ultimately, many forms of discrimination and bias may develop not because outgroups are hated, but because positive emotions such as admiration, sympathy, and trust are reserved for the ingroup and withheld from outgroups" (see also Brewer 1979; Greenwald & Pettigrew 2014). So, with or without strong malice toward others, whites who identify strongly with their ingroup likely possess less *empathic motivation to care* about the struggles of those who have to navigate a system that favors whites. Given whites' dominant position in society, coupled with the fact that they face less discrimination and systemic injustice on average, strong white identification should be *negatively* correlated with empathy for outgroups.

By comparison, we expect a strong *positive* correlation between ingroup identification and outgroup empathy among African Americans, since that group has experienced a great deal of discrimination over many generations. Blacks' long history of slavery carries deep "cultural trauma" that grounded their identity formation (Eyerman 2001). This collective memory led not only to heightened ingroup identification but also to political solidarity over time, especially since their struggle for civil rights continues. Further, it is often not a viable option for a black person to "exit" one's identity (Yancey 2003). Even African Americans who have achieved a high socio-economic status experience negative stereotypes and discrimination (Chong & Kim 2006; Hughes & Thomas 1998). Therefore, when African Americans witness racism and discrimination, even if the targets are other minorities with which they share little in common, they should be more likely than those in the majority to react with politically consequential empathy.

The same general pattern should emerge among Latinos, though the mechanism concerning the relationship between Latino identification and outgroup empathy might be more complex than for blacks. This is due to important differences between the political histories and demographic make-up of these two minority groups in America. Compared to African Americans, Latinos are a more heterogeneous community in terms of nation of origin, immigrant status and generation, and culture. Some Latino citizens identify with their national origin while others embrace a panethnic "Hispanic" or "Latino" (or "Latinx") umbrella categorization or take on a race-based social identity as members of a marginalized, nonwhite minority group (see Masuoka 2008). And for some Latinos, the process of assimilation and acculturation may weaken their traditional cultural ties to their community and lessen the strength of ingroup identification (see de la Garza et al. 1993, 1996). In addition, it may be easier for some Latinos compared to blacks to "exit" their minority identity and identify as white (Tafoya 2007). In that instance, we would expect Latino attitudes and behavior to be closer to that of whites than that of blacks (Yancey 2003). Nevertheless, many Latinos – particularly those with darker complexions, those who speak Spanish, or those speak English with an accent – may find assimilation and acculturation more difficult (see Padilla & Perez 2003). In that instance, African American and Latino ingroup identification dynamics should be more similar. Among such individuals, the association between ingroup identification and outgroup empathy should be in the *positive* direction, and the political consequences of group empathy should be more pronounced.

We therefore assert that ingroup identification serves as one of the causal antecedents of outgroup empathy. We must be clear, however: if our theory is true, empathy for an outgroup is not simply derivative of co-identification. In Chapter 3, we show that blacks and Latinos generally feel no stronger linked fate toward other minority groups than they do toward whites. Members of racial/ethnic groups more often identify with distinct social categories, rather than superordinate collectives whose socio-political and economic fates are linked. While there may be circumstances where such linkages between minority groups are salient, empathy across lines of difference does not depend upon prior identification with another group.

CONCLUSION

Group Empathy Theory builds on a line of scholarship that recognizes the power of social identities to shape political preferences and behavior. Previous work has focused on the ways symbolic group identities often outweigh individual material interests in decision processes. Scarcer, however, are insights about why, how, and when members of one group would subordinate their personal or group interests to those of another, even when the two groups are in material or existential conflict. We think the answer lies in group empathy – the ability and motivation to cognitively and emotionally walk in the shoes of someone very different than oneself.

This vital predisposition is likely to be more common among minorities, due to life experiences that give them more practice at empathizing with those experiencing discrimination. However, outgroup empathy can be found in all groups. In modern, socially diverse societies, the ability to empathize across lines of difference is not a liability. In fact, those who hold this skill and the motivation to use it might be much more likely to succeed by building diverse and successful coalitions both socially and occupationally.

Given its scope of concern that transcends social divisions, group empathy is much more politically consequential than individual empathy. As an enduring trait, group empathy is also more potent than state empathy in shaping political attitudes and behavior, since it leads to general concern about social equity and institutional bias affecting entire groups rather than addressing harm in specific episodes that highlight single individuals. As we demonstrate empirically in the coming chapters, group empathy is consequential across many different policy domains concerning the well-being of marginalized outgroups, above and beyond standard explanations based on partisanship, ideology, or other key predictors of such opinions.

Group Empathy Theory is parsimonious yet carries a strong central claim: empathy for outgroups, independent of other predispositions, drives support for policies that extend help to those in distress. If true, the theory could expand our understanding of public opinion in both the domestic and foreign policy realms, where puzzles abound. Why would blacks oppose a wall on the US southern border even more than Latinos, on average, if they may perceive immigrants to be competing for their jobs and wages? Why would Latinos defend the civil liberties of Arab Americans stereotypically associated with terrorism, even though they consider themselves to be at high risk of future terror attacks? And why would some whites feel so differently than the rest of their ingroup about Trump's signature policies that harm marginalized groups, even after controlling for party identification, ideology, and racial resentment? We think the answer lies in the large differences in outgroup empathy that exist across social divisions.

We believe group empathy is a set of skills and motivations learned prior to other more complex and abstract political attachments, such as partisanship, political ideology, authoritarianism, and the like. The dimension might be both ubiquitous and powerful in its effects in societies around the globe. Group Empathy Theory therefore holds extensive interdisciplinary implications for sociology, psychology, communications studies, social work, and other related fields. The theory further holds normative and practical implications that are potentially very profound as multicultural societies attempt to navigate the contemporary challenges that come with living so close to people who are so different from one another. Discerning how different social groups react distinctly to threats – both foreign and domestic – as well as more deeply understanding the mechanisms underlying intergroup conflict and cooperation are among the most important challenges of our time.

We think Group Empathy Theory is more broadly applicable than existing theories (and their empirical instruments) about racial opinion dynamics in the

United States. For example, the concept of racial resentment (Kinder & Sanders 1996), a close relative of symbolic racism (Henry & Sears 2002; Kinder & Sears 1981), focuses specifically on the long historical conflict between blacks and whites in the United States, and its measurement primarily invokes opinions about those groups. The explanatory power of racial resentment is well established, but the scale itself is hard to justify as a measure of general outgroup animus in the United States, and it is very difficult to transport to other national contexts with different group cleavages and histories. The items we use to operationalize group empathy do not mention specific groups, and thus the resulting measure can be used to test predictions across groups and national settings.

Throughout the rest of the book, we will test our theory with a host of surveys and experiments covering a wide range of policy domains, including national security, immigration, and humanitarian crises. We will take the theory on the road to see if it helps understand politics in other countries, namely in the case of the Brexit crisis in the United Kingdom. We will deploy the theory to help explain large gaps in opinion across racial/ethnic groups both in the United States and in Britain. But before we get to all of that, we must first explain how we capture group empathy empirically.

3

Measuring Group Empathy
The Group Empathy Index

> The measure of a country's greatness is its ability to retain compassion in times of crisis.
>
> Thurgood Marshall (1972)[1]

In the previous chapter, we defined group empathy as the ability and motivation to take the perspective of members of another group, experience their emotional state, and care about their welfare. A precise definition of the concept is crucial because that will allow us to make clear and testable claims about where group empathy comes from and what group empathy should lead to in the political sphere. In this chapter we review our strategy for producing a measure of group empathy that captures each key dimension of the concept.

Prior work on empathy reveals the importance of employing a multidimensional measurement approach. As Davis (1983, 113) points out, "Our understanding of empathy can improve only with the explicit recognition that there are both affective and cognitive components to the empathic response." Cikara et al. (2011, 149) also discuss empathy as a "suite of cognitive and affective capacities," including perspective taking, emotional contagion, and the motivation to alleviate the suffering of others. Studies that use functional magnetic resonance imaging (fMRI) find strong neural evidence for the concomitant role of cognitive and affective abilities, bolstered by motivational tendencies in generating empathic responses (e.g., Lamm et al. 2007).

THE GROUP EMPATHY INDEX (GEI)

To measure outgroup empathy, we draw heavily on Davis's (1980, 1983) "Interpersonal Reactivity Index" (IRI), which is the most widely used

---

[1] See www.nytimes.com/1972/06/30/archives/excerpts-from-opinions-on-death-penalty.html.

measure of individual-level empathy in social psychology. The IRI consistently demonstrates high test–retest reliability across various samples and cross-national contexts (Davis 1994; Pulos & Lennon 2004). Building on this measure, we first generated a fourteen-item "Group Empathy Index" (GEI) by adapting the perspective taking and empathic concern subscales of the IRI. We modified the items to tap respondents' experiences with outgroups rather than their interpersonal experiences mainly with close intimates.

Table 3.1 lists the group-specific versions of the IRI items in these subscales. For example, we altered the perspective taking item "I try to look at everybody's side of a disagreement before I make a decision" to focus on outgroups: "I try to look at everybody's side of a disagreement, including those of other racial or ethnic groups, before I make a decision." The empathic concern item "I often have tender, concerned feelings for people who are less fortunate than me" was likewise changed: "I often have tender, concerned feelings for people from another racial or ethnic group who are less fortunate than me." As with the original IRI, response options for the fourteen-item GEI were placed on a 5-point scale ranging from "does not describe me well at all" to "describes me extremely well."[2]

Davis's original IRI includes two additional subscales besides perspective taking and empathic concern. One is "fantasy," which taps respondents' tendencies to "transpose themselves imaginatively into the feelings and actions of fictitious characters in books, movies, and plays," and the other is "personal distress," which taps "'self-oriented' feelings of personal anxiety and unease in tense interpersonal settings" (Davis 1983, 114). We suspect that the fantasy and personal distress dimensions are not as politically relevant, so we did not include them in our adaptation. This decision is in line with a majority of recent studies that focus on the perspective taking and/or empathic concern subscales of the IRI (e.g., McFarland 2010; Miklikowska 2018).

Concerns about social desirability biases in self-reported measures of empathy like the IRI have recently been raised. In particular, some worry that items in the original measure – such as the one asking respondents about "tender, concerned feelings for people less fortunate" – are highly gendered in nature (Feldman et al. 2020). If men and women differ in the degree to which they view empathy as a societally valued trait, they may differentially misrepresent their true level of empathy. The rationale for this argument arises mostly from the smaller gender gap some observe in an alternative

---

[2] The IRI does not contain a specific "motivation" subscale, but each item – in both the cognitive and affective subscales – does tap motivation. For instance, the phrase "I try" that appears in many of these items captures one's motivation to take on another group's perspective or experience their emotional state. Expressions such as feeling "protective" toward outgroups that are treated unfairly tap one's motivation to care about their welfare. In fact, the affective subscale is named "empathic concern" as it captures not only the skills to experience others' emotional states but also one's motivational concern about their well-being.

TABLE 3.1 *The Group Empathy Index (GEI)*

Perspective taking items (Cognitive subcomponent of group empathy)

- I believe that there are two sides to every question and try to look at them both, including for issues involving other racial or ethnic groups.
- I sometimes find it difficult to see things from the "other person's" point of view, particularly someone from another race or ethnicity. (R)
- When I'm upset at someone from another racial or ethnic group, I usually try to "put myself in their shoes" for a while.
- I try to look at everybody's side of a disagreement (including those of other racial or ethnic groups) before I make a decision.
- I sometimes try to better understand people of other racial or ethnic groups by imagining how things look from their perspective.
- If I'm sure I'm right about something, I don't waste much time listening to the arguments of people, particularly those of other racial or ethnic groups. (R)
- Before criticizing somebody from another racial or ethnic group, I try to imagine how I would feel if I were in their place.

Empathic concern items (Affective subcomponent of group empathy)

- I often have tender, concerned feelings for people from another racial or ethnic group who are less fortunate than me.
- The misfortunes of other racial or ethnic groups do not usually disturb me a great deal. (R)
- I would describe myself as a pretty soft-hearted person toward people of another racial or ethnic group.
- When I see someone being treated unfairly due to their race or ethnicity, I sometimes don't feel very much pity for them. (R)
- Sometimes I don't feel very sorry for people of other racial or ethnic groups when they are having problems. (R)
- When I see someone being taken advantage of due to their race or ethnicity, I feel kind of protective toward them.
- I am often quite touched by things that I see happen to people due to their race or ethnicity.

Note: R = Reversed items. Response options are: (1) Does not describe me well at all; (2) Describes me slightly well; (3) Describes me moderately well; (4) Describes me very well; (5) Describes me extremely well.

measure of empathic ability we discussed in Chapter 2, called the "Reading the Mind in the Eyes" test (RMET; Baron-Cohen et al. 1997). We accept the possibility of some gender bias in our measure. However, even if gender differences in self-reported empathy are partly due to social desirability, that bias could not explain the differences between entire racial/ethnic groups that we consistently find in this book. While we are intrigued by the possibility of incorporating alternative measures of group-level empathy, we believe the GEI is distinctly useful for several reasons.

As we discuss later in this chapter in more detail, the 2018 ANES Pilot Study included a four-item, shortened measure of the GEI. ANES administered randomized versions of the empathic concern items with variation in question wording to check if the responses were sensitive to social desirability pressures that might be gendered. More specifically, half the respondents were asked "When you see someone being *taken advantage of* due to their race or ethnicity, how often do you feel protective toward them?" whereas the other half were given the alternate version: "When you see someone being *treated poorly* due to their race or ethnicity, how often do you feel protective toward them?" Similarly, half the respondents were asked "How often would you say that you *feel concerned about* people from another racial or ethnic group who are less fortunate than you?" instead of "How often would you say that you *have tender, concerned feelings for* people from another racial or ethnic group who are less fortunate than you?"

It is plausible that the phrase "tender, concerned feelings" might inflate differences between men and women as a result of the gendered social norms surrounding the expression of tenderness. Nevertheless, while the overall mean for "tender, concerned" version is somewhat higher (.59) than the "feel concerned" one (.49), the difference in means between males versus females is nearly identical – about .10 on a 0–1 scale – in both versions of the item. As for the other randomized item, the means for the "taken advantage of" versus "treated poorly" versions are identical (.65). The gender difference in means observed in the original "taken advantage of" version is actually slightly smaller (less than .05) compared to the "treated poorly" one (over .07). Furthermore, analyzing the effect of the GEI on several outcome variables that appear in the 2018 ANES Pilot Study – including support for immigration, as presented in Table 3.2 – yields similar results for both versions of these questions.[3] Since the analyses are robust to these changes in question wording, we decided to keep the original wording for our version of the short GEI.

Even more importantly, the GEI captures something the RMET does not: motivation. As Gleichgerrcht and Decety (2014, 244) point out, "Recently, work from developmental and affective and social neuroscience converge to consider empathy as a multidimensional construct comprising dissociable components that interact and operate in parallel fashion, including *affective, motivational* and *cognitive* components [emphasis ours]." As we have argued, the skill to identify an emotional state experienced by another is a necessary condition for empathic responses but may not be sufficient. Empathizing also

---

[3] We measured support for immigration on a 7-point scale based on the following ANES question: "Do you think the number of immigrants from foreign countries who are permitted to come to the United States to live should be increased, decreased, or kept the same as it is now?"

TABLE 3.2 *The relationship between group empathy and support for immigration – sensitivity analyses with alternate question wordings of the Group Empathy Index (GEI)*

	Version 1 w/ original wording		Version 2 w/ alternate wording		Both versions pooled	
	β	S.E.	β	S.E.	β	S.E.
Group empathy	.20***	.05	.19***	.05	.19***	.04
Racial resentment	−.37***	.05	−.32***	.05	−.34***	.03
Party ID	−.08*	.04	−.10**	.03	−.09***	.03
Ideology	−.12*	.05	−.09†	.05	−.11**	.04
Black	−.01	.04	−.06*	.03	−.04†	.02
Latino	−.01	.03	−.03	.03	−.02	.02
Other minority	.05	.05	.05	.04	.05	.04
Female	−.01	.02	−.03†	.02	−.02	.01
Education	.01	.04	.05	.03	.03	.03
Age	−.15***	.05	−.13***	.04	−.14***	.03
Income	.05	.04	.01	.05	.03	.03
Married	−.01	.02	.03	.02	.01	.01
Employed	.0004	.02	−.04*	.02	−.02	.02
Catholic	.02	.02	.0003	.02	.01	.02
Constant	.69***	.06	.67***	.05	.68***	.04
N	951		940		1,891	

Note: Coefficients estimated using OLS regression. Data are weighted. All variables are rescaled to run from 0 to 1. †$p \leq .10$, *$p \leq .05$, **$p \leq .01$, and ***$p \leq .001$, two-tailed.
Source: 2018 ANES Pilot Study (YouGov)

requires one to be motivated to take the perspective of others, to vicariously experience their emotional states, and to develop concern for their well-being. Its multidimensional structure thus makes the GEI a better measurement choice for tapping empathy for outgroups. Our evidence further demonstrates that the GEI is a valid, reliable, and functionally distinct indicator of group-level empathy.

RELIABILITY AND VALIDITY OF THE GEI

We first administered the full fourteen-item GEI in our 2013/14 US Group Empathy Two-Wave Study, fielded by GfK with a total of 1,799 participants, employing a randomized sample of whites and randomized, stratified oversamples of African Americans and Latinos. We ran several analyses to examine the internal reliability and dimensionality of the GEI. The internal consistency of the measure is high (Cronbach's alpha = .84). In addition, the measure is reliable for all three racial/ethnic subgroups in the sample (a_{Whites} = .86; a_{Blacks} = .83; $a_{Latinos}$ = .79). An exploratory factor analysis further justifies the formation of a single GEI.[4] The fit indices suggest a unidimensional underlying structure. The first factor predicts 62 percent of the variance, with an eigenvalue of 3.08 and factor loadings ranging from .75 to .81. No other eigenvalue is greater than .6. Moreover, the χ^2 difference test confirms a significantly superior fit for the one-factor model over higher factor structures. The perspective taking and empathic concern dimensions are highly correlated (r = .75).

The fact that the GEI does not return a two-factor solution with perspective taking and empathic concern as separate dimensions might seem contradictory to prior conceptualizations of empathy. However, this finding is consistent with recent studies that demonstrate the two subscales are part of a global unidimensional structure (e.g., Alterman et al. 2003; Cliffordson 2001; Litvack-Miller et al. 1997). We therefore consider perspective taking and empathic concern to be two key subdimensions of group empathy that together tap the general trait.

We also ran a predictive validity test to check whether the GEI captures the motivational aspect of group empathy. Our survey included a question tapping respondents' motivation to intervene in a socially awkward situation, where someone from a *different* racial/ethnic group might feel insulted by a third party's jokes. More specifically, we asked respondents how likely they would be to tell a person making a racist joke to stop, even if the joke was not about the respondent's own racial/ethnic group. Response options ranged, on a 5-point scale, from "not at all likely" to "very likely." We expected a particularly strong correlation between group empathy and responses to this item. By comparison, we would not expect other group-relevant predispositions such as social dominance orientation (SDO), authoritarianism, and ethnocentrism to predict this sort of social intervention, because those scales do not specifically tap the ability and motivation to take an outgroup's perspective.

SDO taps the degree to which an individual feels groups in society are organized hierarchically, with some on top and others on the bottom. For this test, we used a shortened version of the SDO battery consisting of agreement with four statements: (1) "It's probably a good thing that certain groups are at the top and other groups are at the bottom"; (2) "Inferior groups should stay in their place"; (3) "We should do what we can to equalize conditions for different groups" (reverse-coded); and (4) "We should increase social equality" (reverse-coded).[5]

---

[4] We checked for the direction-of-wording effects by employing the strategy of item parcels with each parcel containing one pro-trait and one con-trait item.

[5] This shortened SDO scale is used by Sidanius and colleagues in multiple studies (e.g., Kteily et al. 2011; Matthews et al. 2009).

To measure authoritarianism, we employed the ANES's four-item authoritarianism scale tapping child-rearing attitudes. Respondents choose between pairs of desirable qualities in children that they deem more important: (1) independence versus respect for elders; (2) obedience versus self-reliance; (3) curiosity versus good manners; and (4) being considerate versus being well-behaved. Those who choose "respect for elders," "obedience," "good manners," and "being well-behaved" receive the maximum score on authoritarianism, and those who choose "independence," "self-reliance," "curiosity," and "being considerate" score at the minimum. The child-rearing scale has been shown to be a valid and reliable measure of authoritarianism as a predisposition (Feldman & Stenner 1997; Stenner 2005).[6] It is also more exogenous to the policy attitudes and political actions it seeks to predict compared to Altemeyer's (1981, 1996) Right-Wing Authoritarianism scale yet still correlates well with it (Feldman 2003; Hetherington & Weiler 2009).

To measure ethnocentrism, we adopted Bizumic et al.'s (2009) ethnocentrism scale. It consists of four *intergroup* dimensions (i.e., ingroup preference, superiority, purity, and exploitativeness) and two *intragroup* dimensions (i.e., group cohesion and devotion). For example, to tap intergroup exploitativeness, we asked how strongly respondents agreed or disagreed with the statement "In dealing with other ethnic and cultural groups, our first priority should be that we make sure we are the ones who end up gaining and not the ones who end up losing." We chose one item from each dimension and generated a six-item index.

As expected, the GEI correlates well with one's motivation to intervene to discourage a racist joke ($r = .38$). By comparison, zero-order correlations between SDO, authoritarianism, and ethnocentrism and responses to the racist joke question are much lower ($r = .13$, $r = .02$, and $r = .08$, respectively). In addition, the GEI is not redundant with these other predispositions. It is moderately correlated with SDO ($r = .37$), but weakly associated with authoritarianism ($r = .02$), ethnocentrism ($r = .18$), party identification ($r = .19$), and ideology ($r = .13$). Group empathy also powerfully outperforms these other predictors in an ordered logistic regression analysis. The GEI delivers a statistically significant positive effect on one's propensity to discourage racist jokes targeting outgroups, whereas other group-relevant predispositions have no

---

[6] Pérez and Hetherington (2014) question the cross-racial validity of the child-rearing scale by suggesting that it relies heavily on a metaphor about hierarchy (dominance at home parallels dominance in society) that is valid for majority group members but not for minorities. If the child-rearing scale is an invalid measure of authoritarianism among minority respondents, then we might be underestimating the effect of authoritarianism in the sample as a whole. To address this possibility, we conducted robustness checks with subsamples consisting of only whites by replicating the analyses presented in Tables 3.3, 3.4, and 3.5. The results are nearly identical to those obtained from the full sample and are available in the online appendix. The GEI retains its statistical significance and magnitude while the coefficient size of authoritarianism is not much larger in these subgroup analyses.

significant effect (see Model 1 in Table 3.3). The probability of doing nothing to stop a racist joke about another group drops from 64 percent to only 7 percent as one moves from the lowest to highest score on the GEI.

We also verify the content validity of the GEI. If the GEI taps only compassion or sympathy rather than empathy, then the empathic concern subdimension rather than the perspective taking items should be driving most of our results. We replicated all of our results using each subscale rather than the general GEI measure. The findings show that the perspective taking items are always significant in their own right and never distinguishable from the empathic concern dimension. For example, when we replicate the validity check broken down by each subdimension, we find that perspective taking and empathic concern are equally powerful predictors of intervening to discourage a racist joke (see Models 2 and 3 in Table 3.3). This evidence suggests that the GEI is not simply tapping compassion or sympathy but instead captures a broader form of empathy consisting of both cognitive and affective subdimensions.

We next test the predictive validity of the GEI vis-à-vis several policy attitudes and political behaviors. Group empathy should uniquely and powerfully predict policy opinion and political action in domains such as immigration and national security, independent of other political predispositions. We explore two policy opinion domains: (1) attitudes toward undocumented immigrants and (2) the trade-off between civil liberties and national security with regard to terrorism. For political action, we look into (1) volunteerism to help outgroups and (2) rallying behavior to defend outgroup rights. The goal is to provide a strict test of the GEI's predictive power in these domains, so we control for a host of group-relevant and general political predispositions including SDO, authoritarianism, ethnocentrism, party identification, and ideology. The GEI should predict political attitudes and behavior even after controlling for key life experiences such as personal experiences with discrimination and socio-demographic variables.

To measure views about undocumented immigrants, we adopted a scale developed by Hetherington and Weiler (2009) that presents respondents with a pair of statements about undocumented immigrants and asks them which statement comes closer to their own point of view. Statement A asserts: "Undocumented immigrants are lawbreakers, plain and simple, and Congress needs to pass laws that make them pay for breaking the law." Statement B asserts: "Undocumented immigrants often come to the United States to make a better life for their families. Even if they technically violate the law, we need to give them some way of making it here." Respondents chose which statement was closer to their view and indicated how strongly they felt that way. We then built an ordinal measure on a 6-point scale where higher values indicate favorable attitudes toward undocumented immigrants. To measure opinions about the civil liberties/national security trade-off, we asked the following: "When it comes to the issue of national security, how concerned

TABLE 3.3 *Group empathy as a predictor of motivation to stop derogatory jokes about another racial/ethnic group*

	Model 1: Full GEI		Model 2: Empathic concern subscale		Model 3: Perspective taking subscale	
	β	S.E.	β	S.E.	β	S.E.
Group empathy	3.22***	.40	2.90***	.42	2.75***	.36
SDO	−.20	.38	−.23	.38	−.41	.38
Authoritarianism	.03	.24	−.04	.25	.14	.24
Ethnocentrism	−.22	.57	−.37	.56	−.32	.56
Party ID	−.09	.29	−.14	.29	−.11	.28
Ideology	−.06	.40	−.02	.40	−.06	.39
Black	.28	.18	.21	.19	.32†	.18
Latino	.33†	.18	.30†	.18	.37*	.18
Female	.49***	.14	.47***	.14	.52***	.14
Education	.21	.60	.22	.59	.17	.60
Age	.17	.36	.20	.36	.20	.35
Income	−.27	.34	−.32	.34	−.29	.34
Married	.10	.15	.08	.16	.10	.15
Employed	.03	.16	.03	.16	−.01	.15
Metropolitan residence	−.24	.20	−.26	.20	−.23	.20
Catholic	−.04	.16	−.05	.16	−.05	.15
Household size	.37	.48	.40	.48	.38	.47
N	1,724		1,724		1,724	

Note: Coefficients estimated using ordered logistic regression. Data are weighted. All variables are rescaled to run from 0 to 1. †$p \leq .10$, *$p \leq .05$, **$p \leq .01$, and ***$p \leq .001$, two-tailed.
Source: 2013/14 US Group Empathy Two-Wave Study (GfK)

are you about the possibility of a violation of civil rights and liberties?" Response options ranged from "not at all concerned" to "very concerned" on a 5-point scale.

Table 3.4 displays the results of ordered logistic regression analyses. To gauge the magnitude of group empathy's effects, we simulate changes in predicted probabilities for various outcomes of our dependent variable at different levels of group empathy while keeping the other variables in our model at their observed values. The probability of very strongly supporting undocumented immigrants is 8 percent if we set the GEI at its minimum. It almost triples to 23 percent when the GEI is at its maximum. Group empathy is the largest predictor of concern about violations of civil rights and liberties in order to protect national security. Moving from the lowest to highest level of the

TABLE 3.4 *The relationship between group empathy and opinions about immigration and national security*

	Favorable attitudes about undocumented immigrants		Concern about civil liberties/ national security trade-off	
	β	S.E.	β	S.E.
Predispositions				
Group empathy	1.37***	.42	1.57***	.45
SDO	−2.24***	.47	−.67	.47
Authoritarianism	−.08	.25	−.52*	.25
Ethnocentrism	−.88†	.53	1.22*	.58
Party ID	−1.15***	.29	.02	.24
Ideology	−.78*	.36	.58†	.33
Life experiences				
Discrimination	.12	.28	.59*	.30
Contact quality	−.20	.41	.35	.48
Contact quantity	−.45	.28	.87**	.29
Economic competition	−.29	.28	.19	.27
Socio-demographics				
Black	.21	.19	.05	.18
Latino	.97***	.20	.04	.18
Female	.01	.14	.31*	.14
Education	1.03†	.62	−.79	.57
Age	−.01	.40	−.43	.39
Income	.02	.35	−.37	.35
Married	−.07	.16	.26†	.15
Employed	−.25	.17	.08	.16
Metropolitan residence	.39*	.19	−.22	.20
Catholic	.20	.17	−.14	.17
Household size	.08	.49	−.16	.46
N	1,682		1,693	

Note: Coefficients estimated using ordered logistic regression. Data are weighted. All variables are rescaled to run from 0 to 1. †$p \leq .10$, *$p \leq .05$, **$p \leq .01$, and ***$p \leq .001$, two-tailed.
Source: 2013/14 US Group Empathy Two-Wave Study (GfK)

GEI triples the probability of being highly concerned about civil liberties (from 14 to 42 percent). These results hold with controls for other key social and political predispositions, life experiences, and socio-demographics. This is reassuring, because it further suggests that group empathy's downstream consequences are not simply a function of politics or other group attitudes.

Group empathy is a very powerful and consistent predictor of how people view undocumented immigrants, as well as how they balance civil liberties and national security concerns.

As for other predispositions, SDO has a highly significant and negative effect on attitudes toward immigrants. Expectedly, the stronger one identifies as a Democrat or a liberal, the more positive one's views are toward undocumented immigrants. Authoritarianism and ethnocentrism, on the other hand, are not significantly related to attitudes about immigrants in the model. With respect to the trade-off between civil liberties and national security, the effects of SDO, authoritarianism, party identification, and ideology are either insignificant or much smaller than group empathy. Also interestingly, ethnocentrism seems to drive up civil liberties concerns. This may be because people who are ethnocentric are also concerned about the violation of their *own* group's civil rights and liberties.

We further explored the predictive validity of the GEI by examining its effects on civic volunteerism and political activism to benefit outgroups. The survey instructed respondents: "Imagine someone asked you to volunteer to clean up a neighborhood in a dangerous part of town where most of the residents were from a racial or ethnic group different than yours. How likely would you be to agree to do that?" We also asked respondents: "Imagine you knew a rally to protest discrimination against a racial or ethnic group different than yours was taking place in your town. How likely would you be to attend?" The response options for both items ranged from "not likely at all" to "extremely likely" on a 5-point scale.

The results presented in Table 3.5 demonstrate that group empathy is the strongest predictor of civic and political action measures. Less than 1 percent of those scoring lowest on the GEI would likely volunteer to help clean up another group's neighborhood, but this rate climbs to 20 percent when the GEI is at its maximum. Similarly, the predicted probability for being "not likely at all" to attend an anti-racism rally in defense of an outgroup's rights is 79 percent when the GEI is set to its minimum but drops to 29 percent for those scoring highest on the GEI. Among other social and political predispositions, only ideology has a significant effect on volunteerism; liberals report a higher likelihood of volunteering to help outgroups. When it comes to attending an anti-racism rally, SDO has a significant and negative effect, while the effects of authoritarianism, ethnocentrism, and party identification are insignificant. Liberals are somewhat more likely to attend such a rally. The results again hold despite controls for key life experiences and socio-demographics. Overall, these findings reassure us about the validity of the GEI.

SHORT GROUP EMPATHY INDEX

The fourteen-item GEI comprises all of the empathic concern and perspective taking items that constituted the original IRI, adapted to reference outgroups. While the full GEI measure appears valid and reliable given the evidence

TABLE 3.5 *The relationship between group empathy and civic/political action*

	Volunteerism to help other groups		Rallying to defend the rights of other groups	
	β	S.E.	β	S.E.
Predispositions				
Group empathy	3.85***	.47	2.43***	.49
SDO	−.40	.46	−1.24**	.43
Authoritarianism	.30	.25	−.26	.25
Ethnocentrism	−.19	.58	−.66	.53
Party ID	.30	.26	−.27	.27
Ideology	−.89*	.35	−.83*	.38
Life experiences				
Discrimination	.33	.29	.78**	.27
Contact quality	.87*	.42	.57	.42
Contact quantity	.46†	.27	.14	.25
Economic competition	−.36	.26	.13	.27
Socio-demographics				
Black	−.11	.19	.49*	.19
Latino	.06	.19	.13	.19
Female	−.28*	.14	−.14	.15
Education	−.48	.52	−1.08†	.62
Age	−.07	.34	−.80*	.37
Income	.12	.29	−.14	.32
Married	−.13	.15	.12	.17
Employed	.32*	.15	−.13	.16
Metropolitan residence	.19	.18	−.22	.21
Catholic	−.22	.17	.10	.18
Household size	.20	.45	.18	.44
N	1,700		1,687	

Note: Coefficients estimated using ordered logistic regression. Data are weighted. All variables are rescaled to run from 0 to 1. †$p \leq .10$, *$p \leq .05$, **$p \leq .01$, and ***$p \leq .001$, two-tailed.
Source: 2013/14 US Group Empathy Two-Wave Study (GfK)

presented so far, it is important to have a shortened version that is parsimonious yet proves as valid and reliable, and performs as powerfully in predicting group-based political attitudes and behavior. Such a shortened scale is not only useful to prevent respondent fatigue and maintain attention but also necessary when conducting national surveys with limited space. Offering a shorter scale also facilitates the broader adoption of the measure and, in turn, replication of our findings by other scholars.

To develop the shortened GEI, we selected two perspective taking items and two empathic concern items with the highest factor loadings from our 2013/14 US Group Empathy Two-Wave Study. The reliability remained very high (Cronbach's alpha = .86). The results of a confirmatory factor analysis further justified the formation of a single-dimensional group empathy scale (eigenvalue = 2.83). Replicating all of the reliability and validity tests reported earlier with the short GEI yielded nearly identical results. For both the full fourteen-item GEI and the short, four-item GEI, we also generated simple summative index versions of the measure in addition to the factor-based measurement. The summative index versus the factor-based scale revealed no substantive differences in any of the results. We employ factor-based measures in the analyses to better account for variation in the loadings of each item.

The four-item version of the GEI (still using the same Likert-type statement format as in the original full scale) was included in Wave 14 of the 2018 British Election Study (BES). In the final design for the shortened version, we converted the original Likert statement format of the index into a construct-specific question format to reduce concerns about acquiescence or positivity biases that may arise from using positive traits (see Table 3.6).[7] This latest version of the shortened scale appeared in the 2018 ANES Pilot Study. The Cronbach's

TABLE 3.6 *Four-item Group Empathy Index (GEI) in construct-specific question format*

Perspective taking items

- How often would you say you try to better understand people of other racial or ethnic groups by imagining how things look from their perspective?
- Before criticizing somebody from another racial or ethnic group, how often do you try to imagine how you would feel if you were in their place?

Empathic concern items

- How often would you say that you have tender, concerned feelings for people from another racial or ethnic group who are less fortunate than you?
- When you see someone being taken advantage of due to their race or ethnicity, how often do you feel protective toward them?

Note: Response options are: (1) Not often at all; (2) Not too often; (3) Somewhat often; (4) Very often; (5) Extremely often.

---

[7] Employing two waves of the 2012 ANES data, Lelkes and Weiss (2015) demonstrate that both construct-specific and agree/disagree formats were equally reliable and valid, even among respondents most likely to show acquiescence bias.

alpha for the four-item scale was .90 for BES and .88 for ANES. A principal-component factor analysis using oblique rotation yielded an eigenvalue of 3.08 (all other factors were below .4) with factor loadings .86 and above for the four GEI items in the BES dataset. Factor analysis of the four GEI items in the ANES data also yielded a single-factor model with an eigenvalue of 2.97 (with other factors .44 and lower) and factor loadings ranging from .82 to .90. Our findings are consistent and robust across different datasets using these alternative formats. We thus consider both the statement and question formats of the GEI to be reliable and valid.

Employing the short GEI, we conducted a discriminant validity test by identifying an outcome variable that should theoretically be unrelated to group empathy. The 2018 ANES dataset included the following question: "During the past 12 months, do you think US policy has been too tough, about right, or not tough enough with these countries?" Canada and Mexico were among the countries inquired about. This allowed us to compare respondents' policy reactions to Canada, the USA's neighbor at the northern border with a predominantly white population, versus their policy reactions to Mexico, the USA's neighbor at the southern border with a predominantly nonwhite demographic. Our theory suggests that group empathy will be a primary driver of policy opinions, particularly in response to the unfair treatment of a historically disadvantaged outgroup. We therefore expect those who score high in the GEI to be significantly more likely to perceive US policy toward Mexico – a developing nation with hard living conditions – as "too tough," whereas we do not expect the GEI to be a significant predictor of opinions about Canada – a developed, wealthy country with high living standards. The results of ordered logistic regression analyses show that the GEI successfully passes this discriminant validity test (see Table 3.7). In line with our expectations, the coefficient for the GEI is statistically insignificant for the Canada model (p > .10) whereas the GEI has a significant and positive coefficient when the target is Mexico (p ≤ .05). As the GEI moves from its minimum to maximum value, the predicted probability of perceiving US policy with Mexico as "too tough" increases by about 15 percentage points even after controlling for racial resentment, party identification, ideology, political interest, and key socio-demographic factors.

THE GEI VERSUS THE IRI

Some might wonder if the GEI, designed to measure intergroup empathy, is really distinct from and superior to the original IRI, a measure of interpersonal empathy. We assert that, as a group-centric measure, the GEI should be a much better predictor of political opinions and behavior than the IRI because many policy issues – particularly those such as immigration, affirmative action, and social welfare – are geared toward allocating rights

TABLE 3.7 *Discriminant validity test – the Group Empathy Index (GEI) as a predictor of policy opinions about Canada versus Mexico*

	US policy with Canada being "too tough"		US policy with Mexico being "too tough"	
	β	S.E.	β	S.E.
Group empathy	.28	.48	.93*	.46
Racial resentment	−1.45**	.47	−2.83***	.45
Party ID	−1.09**	.35	−1.28***	.30
Ideology	−.98*	.47	−.39	.43
Political news exposure	−1.05**	.37	.23	.29
Black	−.04	.37	−.53[†]	.29
Latino	−.63*	.32	.61*	.31
Other minority	−.52	.47	.39	.40
Female	.15	.18	−.13	.17
Education	1.29***	.40	.08	.34
Age	−.70	.51	−1.11*	.45
Income	−.05	.66	.44	.47
Married	−.01	.21	.07	.18
Employed	−.05	.20	−.13	.19
Catholic	.51*	.24	.07	.21
N	940		942	

Note: Coefficients estimated using ordered logistic regression. Data are weighted. All variables are rescaled to run from 0 to 1. [†]$p \leq .10$, *$p \leq .05$, **$p \leq .01$, and ***$p \leq .001$, two-tailed.
Source: 2018 ANES Pilot Study (YouGov)

and resources between social groups rather than between individuals. This expectation aligns well with a long line of scholarship that demonstrates group ties as a primary way citizens make sense of the political world (e.g., Brady & Sniderman 1985; Dawson 1994; Sanchez 2006; see also Transue 2007).

To compare the predictive power of the GEI versus the IRI, we conducted online interviews with 300 participants recruited from the Mechanical Turk (MTurk) interface. Half of these participants were randomly assigned the items that made up the GEI, and the other half the IRI. All participants also answered questions about policies aimed at capturing and deporting undocumented immigrants as well as attending a rally to protest discrimination levied against another racial/ethnic group. If the GEI taps a distinct, group-level construct, then it should be a more powerful predictor of these outcome variables than the IRI.

TABLE 3.8 *Comparing the Group Empathy Index (GEI) and the Interpersonal Reactivity Index (IRI) as predictors of civil rights–related policy attitudes and political action*

	Opposition to punitive immigration policies				Rallying to defend the rights of other groups			
	Model 1a		Model 1b		Model 2a		Model 2b	
	β	S.E.	β	S.E.	β	S.E.	β	S.E.
GEI	3.01***	.85			4.61***	1.15		
IRI			.54	.68			1.71*	.75
Party ID	−.45	.96	−.66	.97	2.16†	1.19	−.99	1.00
Ideology	−4.39***	1.06	−3.89***	1.17	−5.34***	1.41	−.70	1.22
Minority	−.20	.36	.57†	.33	.49	.47	−.04	.42
Female	.49	.34	.31	.33	.69†	.42	.07	.34
Education	.83	.86	.55	.74	−.29	.87	−.22	.76
Age	−2.47**	.87	−1.68*	.76	−3.32**	1.23	−1.12	.77
Income	−1.19†	.71	−.02	.58	−.53	.77	−.45	.67
Catholic	.14	.37	−.58	.55	.06	.46	.47	.50
N	150		150		150		150	

Note: Coefficients estimated using ordered logistic regression. All variables are rescaled to run from 0 to 1. †$p \leq .10$, *$p \leq .05$, **$p \leq .01$, and ***$p \leq .001$, two-tailed.
Source: 2015 US Group Empathy Study (MTurk)

The results of ordered logistic regression analyses, displayed in Table 3.8, indicate that the GEI, but not the IRI, is a significant predictor of attitudes about undocumented immigrants, even after controlling for partisanship, ideology, and key socio-demographic factors. This association is substantively important as well; moving from the minimum to maximum level of the GEI leads to a 44 percentage point decrease in the likelihood of very strongly supporting punitive immigration policies. The GEI is also a stronger predictor of one's likelihood to engage in political action to help outgroups. While both the GEI and IRI have statistically significant effects on one's intention to attend a rally in defense of another racial/ethnic group's rights, the association with the GEI is far larger. The average change in the predicted probabilities of attending such a rally is 31 percentage points as one moves from the minimum to maximum score of the GEI – almost double the size of the IRI's effect (16 percentage points). The GEI is therefore not simply tapping individual empathy; it outperforms the IRI in predicting political attitudes and behavior. It also performs similar to ideology and better than partisanship, at least in this sample and on these dependent variables.[8]

The same pattern emerges in the British context, where we tested the explanatory power of the GEI with a nationally representative sample. The 2018 British Election Study (BES) Wave 14 includes not only the four-item version of the GEI but also a ten-item individual empathy scale. As we will show in Chapter 9, the GEI predicts British political attitudes and behavior much more strongly than the individual-level empathy measure. In most analyses, when both group empathy and individual empathy are included together, the effect of individual empathy is not significant while group empathy is a powerful predictor. The power of the GEI over individual-level empathy is demonstrated in domains as varied as Brexit, immigration, welfare, foreign aid, perceptions of discrimination against marginalized groups, and equal opportunity policies.

OR IS IT SIMPLY LINKED FATE?

Perhaps African Americans and Latinos simply feel a sense of linked fate with other minority groups, and this, rather than group empathy, is what drives the findings related to the intergroup differences we present throughout the book. To test this alternative, we analyzed data from the 2012 US Group Empathy Study – a national survey experiment fielded online by GfK with a pool of 621 randomly selected participants (with oversamples of African Americans and Latinos) that included a measure of linked fate. Specifically, we asked respondents: "When you hear that something good or bad happens to each of the following groups, to what extent do you feel that your life is similarly affected by the fate of each group?" The results, illustrated in Figure 3.1, demonstrate that African Americans and Latinos, on average, feel *no stronger linked fate* toward other minority groups than they do toward whites.

GROUP EMPATHY AND RACIAL RESENTMENT

We have shown that the GEI is empirically distinct from a variety of political predispositions including authoritarianism, party identification, and ideology. We have also found that group empathy is different from individual empathy. It also taps into a force distinct from several other major group-based predispositions such as ethnocentrism, SDO, and linked fate. In fact, the GEI predicts many important group-related policy attitudes and political behaviors *at least as powerfully* as these other factors.

Nevertheless, one might still wonder if the GEI is simply standing in for racial animus toward particular groups in society. Racial resentment (Kinder &

---

[8] These analyses were conducted with the full fourteen-item GEI and IRI. We replicated these analyses using the four-item GEI and the results are nearly identical.

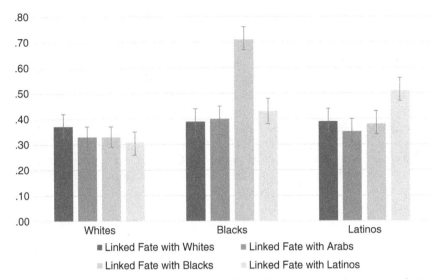

FIGURE 3.1 Levels of ingroup and outgroup linked fate, by respondents' race/ethnicity
Note: The bars represent estimated group means calculated using MANCOVA. The lines represent 95 percent confidence intervals. Models also control for party identification, ideology, gender, education, age, income, marital status, household size, employment status, metropolitan residence, and religion (Catholic). Data are weighted. All variables are rescaled to run from 0 to 1. Estimates from full model available in the online appendix.
Source: 2012 US Group Empathy Pilot Study (GfK)

Sanders 1996), also referred to as symbolic racism (Sears 1988), is a widely deployed measure of white American attitudes about African Americans in the post–civil rights era (Kinder & Sanders 1996; Sears & Kinder 1981). The concept is defined as a blend of negative affect about blacks as a group, combined with the view that many members of the group regularly violate traditional norms of individualism and a commitment to hard work. It is typically measured with four questions that ask respondents how strongly they agree with statements such as "Irish, Italians, Jewish and many other minorities overcame prejudice and worked their way up. Blacks should do the same without any special favors."[9]

The racial resentment scale has been criticized on a number of grounds. One of the early concerns that surfaced involved the similarity between some of the items used to measure the construct and the policy opinions that racism

---

[9] Other agree/disagree items include: "Generations of slavery and discrimination have created conditions that make it difficult for blacks to work their way out of the lower class" (reverse-coded); "Over the past few years, blacks have gotten less than they deserve" (reverse-coded); and "It's really a matter of some people not trying hard enough; if blacks would only try harder they could be just as well off as whites."

purportedly explained (Schuman 2000; Sniderman & Tetlock 1986). For example, asking how strongly someone agrees with the statement "It is wrong to set up quotas to admit black students to college who don't meet the usual standards" – one of the items in a version of the original scale (Sears & Kinder 1981) – is quite similar to asking about support for affirmative action in general. Subsequent revisions of the measure (Kinder & Sanders 1996) largely eliminated these concerns, but the item that suggests blacks should work their way up without "special favors" might still invoke support for or opposition to affirmative action policy rather than attitudes about blacks per se. That said, validity checks by Henry and Sears (2002) find that even when the phrase "special favors" is stripped from this item, the scale works as powerfully as before.

Another persistent concern has been that the items in the scale do not measure racial attitudes at all but instead reveal the respondent's acceptance of universal norms like individualism or conservative values like preference for a limited role of government in determining life opportunities for all citizens regardless of race (Sniderman & Piazza 1993; Sniderman et al. 2000). The standard response to these concerns is to include controls for ideology and other nonracial values in models where racial resentment is being used to explain various policy outcomes (Kinder & Mendelberg 2000). Indeed, the measure powerfully and consistently predicts public opinion on racialized policies like affirmative action, welfare, crime, immigration, and a host of others. Race reemerged as a dominant fault line in electoral politics even before Barack Obama's election in 2008 (Tesler & Sears 2010; Valentino & Sears 2005). Since then, the measure has robustly predicted an even wider array of policies that were once completely independent of race (Tesler 2016). Nevertheless, concerns remain that the measure is irrevocably "tinged" with ideology (Feldman & Huddy 2005, 170) and performs differently for liberals than it does for conservatives.

The GEI is less likely to suffer from these challenges. First, the items do not invoke thoughts of public policies at all, focusing the respondent's attention on whether and how often they find themselves looking at the world through the perspective of an outgroup member, as well as how that perspective makes them feel. We think this abstract approach is a strength, much like the approach to measuring authoritarianism using questions about child-rearing (Feldman & Stenner 1997). The GEI is therefore likely to be more independent of ideology or specific issue opinions than is racial resentment, though we include statistical controls for many of these dimensions in our analyses throughout the book. In Chapter 8, we also compare the predictive power of the GEI and racial resentment using data from the 2018 ANES Pilot Study and find the former to maintain a substantively significant effect on a host of contemporary policy positions even with the latter included in the model.

Finally, advocates of racial resentment prize the cultural specificity of the measure, arguing that it is designed uniquely to understand white attitudes about blacks in the post–civil rights America. In other words, racial resentment was intended to measure only white Americans' attitudes about African Americans – it was not designed to measure the racial attitudes of nonwhites. And it was designed to address a puzzle tied to a specific, though obviously important, period in American history. The puzzle, of course, was why so many white Americans strongly endorsed egalitarian norms while rejecting policies designed to achieve racial equality.

The GEI captures a more general dimension of intergroup attitudes than racial resentment or other group-specific measures. By operationalizing the construct of group empathy in such a general way, we of course run the risk of confusing respondents, with the result that our explanations of policy opinions and political behavior that depend on group empathy would fail. On the other hand, the prize in such an attempt is large, both theoretically and analytically. If we have succeeded in validly and reliably measuring this general dimension of outgroup empathy, then we have a tool for examining policy opinion dynamics across racial/ethnic respondent groups in the US and even abroad, and one that should operate more or less stably across time. This is an advantage of the GEI, given the increasing importance of understanding a diverse array of groups and social divisions around the world. Note that we do not believe group empathy conceptually supersedes or replaces racial resentment – the two should be correlated empirically. We simply propose that group empathy can explain policy opinions and political choices above and beyond attitudes about specific groups.

The 2018 ANES Pilot Study indicates that, while the GEI is a powerful determinant of immigration attitudes, racial resentment remains influential not only for whites but for minorities as well. However, racial resentment may be capturing a different construct among nonwhites. For blacks who score high on the racial resentment measure – in other words, those who display resentment against their own ingroup – the measure is no longer about negative sentiments toward an outgroup but may instead be capturing SDO. For Latinos, high scores may also be a product of SDO and assimilation into a white-dominant system. On the other hand, as a general measure of empathy toward *all* outgroups, the GEI can capture that same underlying construct across all racial/ethnic respondent groups and thereby possesses higher internal validity and reliability.

To be sure, the GEI and racial resentment are moderately correlated (−.44) in the 2018 ANES data. This is not surprising, since both capture reactions to outgroups. However, we suspect outgroup empathy and racial resentment are not simply the opposite sides of the same coin. When we include both measures in the same models, as we do here and also in Chapter 8, both powerfully predict a variety of policy opinions. While not entirely orthogonal to racial resentment, group empathy then helps explain policy views above and beyond animus toward blacks. The GEI also turns out to be much less tightly linked to party identification (r = .33) and ideology (r = .36) than is racial resentment (r = .63 and r = .67, respectively) in the 2018 ANES data. This further reduces concerns about conceptual redundancy that have been raised in debates about the latter construct.

Moreover, the GEI taps a positive emotional state (empathy) whereas racial resentment is geared toward measuring negative affect (resentment). Research on discrete emotions suggests that these distinct emotional states may lead to differential processes and outcomes along with significant differences in the magnitude of their effects (Sirin & Villalobos 2019). For instance, regarding the roles that the GEI and racial resentment play in political participation, the effect of the GEI is much larger than that of racial resentment and moves in the opposite direction. Figure 3.2 illustrates the predictive margins for the outcome we call "political apathy" by setting the political participation index from the 2018 ANES data to 0. Group empathy substantively decreases the probability of political apathy from 60 to 24 percent as one moves from the minimum to maximum values of the GEI. Such marginal effect is much larger than that of racial resentment, which increases the probability of political apathy from 31 to 44 percent – the magnitude of the GEI's effect on mobilization is thus almost triple that of racial resentment.

All of this, as mentioned, is not to argue racial resentment should be discarded in favor of the GEI. Racial resentment has performed consistently as one of the best predictors of racial policy opinions in the United States over the last forty years. Group empathy, however, is a distinct construct and a powerful predictor of political attitudes and behavior above and beyond white racial prejudice. On a practical level, even simple feeling thermometers and stereotype measures cannot be asked in places that forbid applying racial labels to groups in the public domain. The GEI, on the other hand, can easily be applied across groups, cultural contexts, and national borders without such concerns.

MEASURING GROUP-SPECIFIC EMPATHY

In addition to the GEI, which is general in nature, we also measured empathic concern and perspective taking toward specific groups in society. We did this to further help determine whether empathy is expressed exclusively for members of one's own group or is also extended to members of outgroups. We expect minorities to display higher empathy for all outgroups, but particularly those who are disadvantaged. The results we discuss in the upcoming chapters (in particular, Chapters 4 and 7) show that this is indeed the case.

To measure group-specific empathic concern, we asked respondents: "For each of the following specific groups, how concerned do you feel about the challenges they face in our society these days?" Response options ranged on a 5-point scale from "not at all concerned" to "very concerned." To measure group-specific perspective taking abilities, we asked respondents: "Regardless

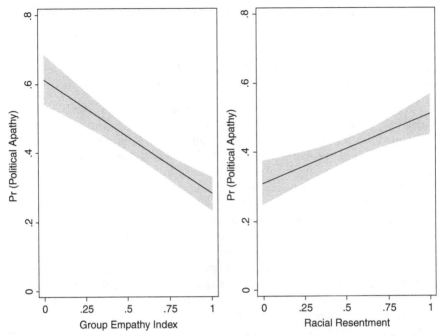

FIGURE 3.2 Comparing group empathy and racial resentment as predictors of political apathy
Note: The lines represent the marginal effects of group empathy and racial resentment on political apathy estimated using ordered logistic regression. The shaded areas represent 95 percent confidence intervals. Models also control for party identification, ideology, race/ethnicity, gender, education, age, income, marital status, employment status, and religion (Catholic). Predicted values generated by holding all other variables in the model at their observed values in the sample. Data are weighted. All variables are rescaled to run from 0 to 1. Estimates from full model available in the online appendix.
Source: 2018 ANES Pilot Study (YouGov)

of the challenges another group faces, sometimes it is easier and other times more difficult to understand what members of a given group are going through. How easy is it for you to 'put yourself in the shoes' of individuals from each of the following groups in our society?" Response options ranged on a 5-point scale from "not easy at all" to "very easy." Respondents evaluated several specific groups along these dimensions, including whites, African Americans, Arabs, Latinos, Native Americans, Catholics, Jews, Muslims, and undocumented immigrants.[10] We additively combined scores for the empathic

---

[10] The list of particular groups we included in our group-specific empathy measures varied across different datasets based on the purpose and focus of each study we conducted.

concern and perspective taking submeasures to generate our group-specific empathy measures.

MEASURING GROUP EMPATHY–BASED REACTIONS
TO SITUATIONAL TRIGGERS

As we discussed in Chapter 2, we theorized that those high in group empathy – particularly minorities – will react much more strongly to incidents that involve people suffering and/or experiencing discrimination even if they are members of an outgroup, and these stronger empathic reactions will then lead to more powerful attitudinal and behavioral responses. We put this assumption to empirical test with the 2013/14 US Group Empathy Two-Wave Study, which included two national survey experiments conducted with white, black, and Latino respondents. The experiments featured vignettes depicting ambiguous situations where either an airline passenger or an undocumented immigrant detainee might be unfairly targeted by law enforcement officers. In these vignettes, we visually manipulated the race/ethnicity of the passenger/detainee who appeared to be either white, Arab, black, or Latino. While we will discuss these experiments extensively in Chapters 5 and 6, here we provide evidence from the experimental data on the significant association between the GEI and group empathy–based reactions to such incidents.

Batson and Ahmad (2009b, 143–4) discuss four distinct but related psychological states in empathic reactions to situations at the group level. Two of these four refer to nuanced forms of affective response: "feeling *for* an out-group member" and "feeling *as* an out-group member feels." The former affective state is akin to what Stephan and Finlay (1999) would call *reactive* empathy, and the latter is a reflection of *parallel* empathy, as we discussed in Chapter 2. The other two psychological states encompass the cognitive elements of group-level empathy with nuanced forms of perspective taking: "imagining how *an out-group member* thinks and feels" ("imagine-other") and "imagining how *one* would think and feel in an out-group member's situation" ("imagine-self"), also mentioned in the previous chapter. In designing measures of group-empathic reactions to situational triggers, we aimed to capture all of these psychological states. Upon exposure to the experimental vignettes, we measured affective empathic reactions of the respondents by asking them to indicate on a 5-point scale to what extent they experienced (1) feelings of sympathy and compassion (to capture reactive empathy) for the person featured in the news story and (2) feelings of anger and disgust (to capture parallel empathy) regarding the person's treatment by law enforcement. We next measured cognitive-based empathic reactions to the vignettes by asking respondents to indicate on a 5-point scale how well the following statements described them: (1) "I could easily imagine how the passenger/detainee felt in this situation" (to capture "imagine-other"–oriented perspective taking); and (2) "Apart from imagining how the passenger/ detainee felt, I could also easily imagine how I personally would feel if I were in that person's situation" (to capture "imagine-self"–oriented perspective taking). We then combined all these items (Cronbach's alpha = .85) to compare overall group-empathic reactions of three racial/ethnic respondent groups to the experimental vignettes along with their mediational effects on the outcomes of interest.[11]

We examined the relationship between trait-level general group empathy, tapped by the GEI in the first-wave pretest survey, and empathic reactions to the targeted groups featured in our experimental vignettes in the second wave. This analysis is important for internal validity purposes. If general group empathy is not linked to respondents' empathic reactions to the experimental vignettes, our proposed causal mechanism cannot explain our findings. The results of an OLS regression analysis (presented in Table 3.9) reveal that the GEI is indeed the primary predictor of empathic reactions evoked in response to the experimental vignettes, even after controlling for perceived terrorism threat, perceived immigration threat, party identification, ideology, and a host of socio-demographic factors (p ≤ .001).[12]

CONCLUSION

In this chapter, we analyzed the measurement properties of the GEI we designed to operationalize the concept of group empathy. We crafted the GEI based on Davis's (1980, 1983) widely used Interpersonal Reactivity Index (IRI) by transforming its items originally designed to measure empathy at the individual level into the group level. This transformation led to a measure of intergroup empathy that is conceptually and empirically distinct from interpersonal empathy as well as much more consequential in shaping political attitudes and behavior.

The GEI consists of both cognitive and affective elements, catalyzed by one's motivation to care. This sets it apart from some other alternative measures of empathy such as the RMET (Baron-Cohen et al. 1997). We think empathy goes beyond the ability to recognize the affective state of another person or to take

---

[11] We adapted the affective (i.e., reactive and parallel) measures of empathy from Stephan and Finlay (1999) and the cognitive (i.e., imagine-self and imagine-other) measures from Batson and Ahmad (2009b).

[12] As we discussed in Chapter 2, trait empathy and situational empathy are not identical constructs. Some situations may trigger empathy even among those low in trait empathy (see Batson & Coke 1981; Zillmann 2006). Indeed, the correlation between general group empathy as a trait (measured in the first wave using the GEI) and group-based empathic reactions to the experimental vignettes (measured in the posttest of the second wave) is only .26. As such, our analysis of the link between general group empathy and empathic reactions to group-related situational triggers is not tautological.

TABLE 3.9 *Internal validity test – the Group Empathy Index (GEI) as a predictor of empathic reactions to experimental vignettes*

	β	S.E.
Group empathy	.16**	.05
Experimental context	.02	.02
Terrorism threat	.02	.04
Immigration threat	−.04	.04
Party ID	−.05	.04
Ideology	−.16**	.06
Black	−.01	.02
Latino	.04	.02
Female	.01	.02
Education	.19*	.08
Age	.05	.05
Income	−.08*	.04
Married	−.001	.02
Employed	.0002	.02
Metropolitan residence	−.01	.03
Catholic	.005	.02
Household size	.16*	.06
Constant	.12†	.07
N	1,296	

Note: Coefficients estimated using OLS regression. Data are weighted. All variables are rescaled to run from 0 to 1. †p ≤ .10, *p ≤ .05, **p ≤ .01, and ***p ≤ .001, two-tailed.
Source: 2013/14 US Group Empathy Two-Wave Study (GfK)

their perspective. It also involves a motivational concern about that person's well-being – which is especially important when such concerns are tied to the welfare of an entire social group. By capturing not only cognitive and affective empathic abilities but also the motivation to care about members of other groups, the GEI demonstrates high predictive power in explaining policy preferences and political action tendencies.

Through multiple robustness checks and analyses, we find that group empathy – as we have measured it – is not a byproduct or simply a reverse form of other group-based predispositions such as SDO, ethnocentrism, and racial resentment. In study after study, the statistical and substantive impact of the GEI persists even after controlling for these and other political predispositions such as authoritarianism, party identification, and ideology.

An even stronger claim, one that we theorize but cannot empirically test at the moment, is that group empathy causally precedes these other predispositions in early childhood development. It therefore represents a quite fundamental force on adult political attitudes and behavior. Could outgroup empathy develop even before a person learns much about politics in their particular society, before they even know what party they belong to or where they stand in the social hierarchy? We suspect this is quite possible.

First, we know that infants automatically mirror the emotions of close others and may even be consciously aware of this effect that others have on them (Hoffman 2000). This awareness boosts concern and helping behavior toward others as early as the second year of life (Zahn-Waxler et al. 1992). Whether and when in the developmental process this prosocial behavior toward close intimates gets applied to complete strangers from very different backgrounds is, of course, an open question. Hoffman (2000) speculated that this level, what he referred to as "empathy for another's life condition," develops during later childhood.

There is scant evidence about when other racial/ethnic group attitudes and identities are crystallized, though some have speculated this might occur before adulthood (Allport 1954; Sears & Levy 2003). Sears's theory of symbolic racism suggested that the rather complex blending of anti-black affect and racially specific individualist norms probably required some experience with the political world and therefore could take until perhaps late adolescence or early adulthood to become stabilized. Some empirical evidence supports this claim, though change can occur throughout adulthood (Henry & Sears 2009). We know even less about the developmental trajectory of predispositions like authoritarianism, racial identity, or SDO, though defenders of each of these concepts argue for a crystallization process similar to that of racial resentment. Partisan identification becomes anchored during mid- to late adolescence as a result of highly salient political events (Sears & Valentino 1997; Valentino & Sears 1998).

At the moment, we do not have evidence that could untangle definitively whether outgroup empathy or other group attitudes and identities come first in structuring political thoughts and action. Given that ingroup empathy develops at a very young age, outgroup empathy might also be acquired early, as a result of socialization experiences within the family. At various points, we will discuss the kinds of evidence future studies might collect to explore this important question.

While we cannot be sure whether outgroup empathy arrives first on the scene, we still can determine how important a player it is compared to other predispositions. In addition, the GEI is a general measure and does not contain references to specific groups or specific cultural contexts. It is therefore a useful tool for studying respondents from a wide variety of racial/ethnic backgrounds, across national boundaries, and over time. We will provide a strong example of this analytic advantage in Chapter 9, where we examine British public opinion toward Brexit and a host of other policy domains. Respondents in various countries, or even in various regions of the United States, may well imagine different specific outgroups when answering the questions in the GEI. That variation is a strength, not a weakness, in our approach. If we are wrong, more specific measures of outgroup animus should be sufficient for explaining policy views. But, if our theory is correct, it is empathy toward salient outgroups that drive policy views, regardless of which groups those are.

4

An Origin Story

Socializing Group Empathy

> The sense of being an outsider – of being one of the people who had suffered oppression for no sensible reason – it's the sense of being part of a minority. It makes you more empathetic to other people who are not insiders, who are outsiders.
>
> Ruth Bader Ginsburg (2018)[1]

On August 23, 2014, in Forney, Texas, police pulled over an African American mother with four young children in tow and held them at gunpoint in response to a 911 caller claiming a black man was waiving a gun while driving recklessly in a tan Toyota. The woman drove a red Nissan. Despite this fact, the mother was ordered to get out of the car with her hands up and walk backward toward the police, where she would be handcuffed while her children were screaming in fear. The police soon realized they had pulled over the wrong car and lowered their guns when her six-year-old boy emerged from the car, terrified, with his hands in the air. The scene was eerily reminiscent of the "Hands up, don't shoot" refrain that became a widespread symbol of police brutality against African Americans following the fatal police shooting in Ferguson, Missouri, earlier that same month. Though the police later admitted they made a mistake, they still insisted the response was appropriate, given the original caller's depiction of a dangerous situation involving a firearm.[2] Afterward, the mom said in a Facebook post that she had a "heart to heart" talk with her children "about how your life can change in a matter of seconds." She added that she was so proud of her children and advised them "not to be bitter or angry" and instead "try to stay calm in a situation like this."[3]

---

[1] In conversation with Jane Eisner, available online at The Forward, https://forward.com/culture/391971/ruth-bader-ginsburg-and-jane-eisner-in-conversation-everything-you-need-to/.

[2] See https://abc30.com/news/police-pull-mother-and-children-over-at-gunpoint-by-mistake/278215/.

[3] See https://dfw.cbslocal.com/2014/08/25/forney-police-apologize-after-mom-kids-pulled-over-at-gunpoint/.

There is a phenomenon well known in the black community called "The Talk," which the *New York Times*[4] and Vox[5] have profiled. The Talk is a discussion that many African American parents feel they must have with their young children in order to prepare them for dealing safely with law enforcement. They feel their kids are at much higher risk than other members of the community and fear that even benign interactions with the police can turn deadly as a result of misunderstandings, misstatements, or even the slightest unintentional move. Unfortunately, these concerns are well warranted.

Police perceive black youth to be older, more dangerous, and physically larger than whites who are identical in age and size (e.g., Goff et al. 2014).[6] As a result, black parents feel the need to explain to their kids how to keep their hands visible at all times, move slowly, and listen carefully to police commands. They engage in role-playing exercises to help their kids stay calm and avoid getting frustrated even when they feel police have unfairly targeted them because of their race. In many of these news stories, black parents note that they value the police, and know officers are doing a difficult and risky job, but they also perceive systemic biases in the way their families and communities are treated. In the *New York Times* story, one man says, "It doesn't mean that every police officer is inherently a bad person, but what it does mean is that the police force – that institution – does not look out for your best interest."

Examples of what many consider racial profiling and unfair treatment at the hands of police appear regularly in the news, especially when they turn violent. Less intense incidents of everyday bias – for example, minorities feeling unfairly scrutinized by police, by store security, or in public places as they go about their daily lives – are less likely to make the news. However, they are probably much more common. Twitter contains a record of such incidents under several hashtags such as "#alivewhileblack," "#livingwhileblack," "#livingwhilebrown," and "#privilege." One can read about thousands of mundane eyewitness accounts of encounters with racism.[7] The experience of discrimination, day by day, helps one understand how discouraging and demoralizing it can be. Subsequently, we think that an individual who personally experiences discrimination might also be more sensitive and opposed to similar mistreatment of others (Eklund et al. 2009;

---

[4] Geeta Gandbhir and Blair Foster (2015), "Op-Doc: A Conversation with My Black Son," *New York Times*, www.nytimes.com/video/opinion/100000003575589/a-conversation-with-my-black-son.html?action=click&gtype=vhs&version=vhs-heading&module=vhs&region=title-area.

[5] German Lopez (2016), "Black Parents Describe 'The Talk' They Give to Their Children about Police," *Vox*, www.vox.com/2016/8/8/12401792/police-black-parents-the-talk.

[6] For instance, in the fatal shooting of twelve-year-old Tamir Rice, who was playing with a toy gun in a Cleveland park, the police severely overestimated the child's age: the recording of the incident reveals the officer saying: "Shots fired. Male down. Black male, maybe twenty." See www.theguardian.com/us-news/2014/nov/26/tamir-rice-video-shows-boy-shot-police-cleveland.

[7] Of course, there is no way to verify every one of these accounts or to prove that the actions of any officer were motivated by racial bias. But those challenges are beside the point for the current discussion.

Hoffman 2000). This sensitivity is one of the key foundations of outgroup empathy, a predisposition that can powerfully structure policy opinions and political behavior.

We suspect empathy for outgroup members emerges in childhood as a result of various socialization processes. One's experiences with discrimination over time should constitute a vital part of these socialization processes that activate group empathy. We therefore would predict that on average, minorities will score at least modestly higher on measures of intergroup empathy compared to whites. On the other hand, interpersonal empathy (reserved mainly for one's family and friends) should be more or less evenly distributed across racial/ethnic groups, since all humans hold a similar capacity for perspective taking and concern for their closest kin.

In addition to race/ethnicity, group empathy is likely to vary by gender. Gender differences in self-reported empathy at the individual level are well established (Davis 1980; De Corte et al. 2007). These differences may emerge from the gender imbalance in the duration and quality of child-rearing experiences between men and women in most societies. Eagly's (1987) Social Role Theory, for example, suggests that the historical division of labor in heterosexual relationships – which has set women as primary caregivers – might explain the gender differences we currently observe in attitudes and behavior (see also Eagly et al. 2009). Besides cultural stereotypes about gender roles that lead to different socialization experiences for women and men, some studies also reveal neuroscientific evidence consistent with the gender gap in interpersonal empathy. For instance, using functional magnetic resonance imaging (fMRI), Schulte-Rüther et al. (2008) find that female brains recruit areas containing human mirror neurons to a higher degree compared to male brains during both self- and other-related processing in empathic interactions (see also Christov-Moore et al. 2014).

If individual empathy is mainly directed toward one's offspring and family, and since women often score higher in this form of empathy, one might expect women to actually score *lower* on empathy toward outgroups that are perceived as a threat to their kin. Such perceptions of outgroup threat may be more significant for women, not only because they are often primary caregivers but also because they experience relatively higher physical and economic vulnerability in the social sphere. Therefore, when an outgroup is framed as an existential threat (such as in the case of Trump's depiction of Mexican immigrants as "rapists"), one might expect women to view that outgroup much more negatively.[8] Even if the perceived threat of an outgroup is mainly on economic rather than security-based grounds, women might exhibit lower outgroup empathy as they already suffer from a substantial pay gap in the

---

[8] Aaron Blake (2018), "Trump Conjures a New Immigrant Rape Crisis," *Washington Post*, https://wapo.st/2q7BmBz?tid=ss_mail.

workplace that may be further exacerbated by an influx of low-skilled workers willing to accept lower wages.

Despite all this, there are also several reasons that lead us to expect that women will instead display *higher* – not lower – empathy for vulnerable outgroups even when they feel threatened. Just as with racial/ethnic minorities, women are likely to experience discrimination and prejudice as they reach adulthood. Many women feel that they are being treated as second-class citizens, often branded unqualified, unintelligent, weak, irrational, and emotionally fragile. They are underrepresented, underpaid, and overworked in many public- and private-sector occupations. Women also lack equality in political representation in the United States and in many other nations. Indeed, as of May 2020, the United States ranked 83 out of 193 in the percentage of female legislators at the federal level, lagging grossly behind many developing nations such as Mexico (which ranked fifth).[9] Women's reproductive rights are under constant threat, severely limited, or entirely violated in many countries around the world. Women also experience unfair treatment in the criminal justice system. They face victim blaming and shaming in cases of sexual harassment and assault, while most sexual perpetrators walk free or serve minimal prison time. As a result of exposure to gender discrimination and disadvantage, we expect that women on average might find it easier than men to imagine themselves in the position of an outgroup member being unfairly treated.

While we expect direct personal experiences with discrimination are strong catalysts for empathy toward disadvantaged outgroups, time spent in places where the struggles of other groups can be witnessed, and where personal connections can be built across lines of difference, might also boost outgroup empathy among whites and nonwhites alike. This prediction is directly parallel to the contact hypothesis (Allport 1954), which posited that the benefits of interethnic contact could, under specific conditions, substantially reduce racial prejudice and discrimination. The specific conditions that Allport posited, and which have been explored since by Pettigrew (1998) and others, were equal status, common goals, the absence of direct competition for rights and resources, and support for interethnic comity from trusted authorities, societal elites, and governmental institutions.

While these conditions for positive intergroup contact are rarely met, especially simultaneously, school might be one place where they are most likely to occur (Cooper 2011). The quality and quantity of contact with other groups is likely to be higher in school than in other contexts. School is often the place where young people first encounter challenging intergroup dynamics. Young people may become more aware of other groups' historical struggles and current challenges via educational activities such as events organized for "Black

---

[9] Inter-Parliamentary Union (IPU) (2020), "Percentage of Women in National Parliaments," https://data.ipu.org/women-ranking?month=5&year=2020.

History Month" or service learning opportunities. In short, we expect education to facilitate life experiences conducive to developing empathy for outgroups.

Individual empathy also seems to increase with age (Erikson et al. 1989), though its growth may not be linear across the lifespan (O'Brien et al. 2012). As people move from adolescence to adulthood, they build increasingly sophisticated cognitive representations of other people's emotional experiences (e.g., Collins 2003). Friendships, child-rearing, and workplace relationships may enhance the development of empathy. According to Sze et al. (2012, 1138), increased empathy and prosocial behavior observed in older cohorts may reflect a number of other changes that are associated with age: (a) increased emotional reactivity to situations that signal the need for help and reparation; (b) motivational transformations from self- and future-oriented goals into socially oriented ones; and (c) shifts toward social contribution.

We expect age differences in individual-level empathy might extend to group-level empathy, as people gain more experience with social group dynamics and recognize the consequences of group conflict. If group empathy is a product of socialization via certain life experiences, such as contact with outgroups or personal exposure to discrimination, those effects might be expected to accumulate with age. Even members of dominant social groups, though less likely to experience unfair treatment, may develop higher levels of group empathy over time as they witness different forms of discrimination and struggle that minority groups endure in various settings.

To illustrate, younger generations whose teenage years mostly coincided with the Obama presidency (January 2009–January 2017) may take for granted that an African American can be elected to the highest office in the country. Seeing an African American in the White House may also inadvertently convey a sense of a color-blind society to these younger generations. Older cohorts, by comparison, are likely struck by the historical uniqueness of Obama's presidency. As First Lady Michelle Obama put it at the Democratic National Convention in 2016: "I wake up every morning in a house that was built by slaves, and I watch my daughters, two beautiful, intelligent, black young women, playing with their dogs on the White House lawn."[10] Those who lived through the civil rights movement in the 1960s may more fully recognize the significance of this statement. Indeed, across both sides of the aisle, many people appeared deeply moved by Michelle Obama's remarks. Some were more critical, such as then–Fox News conservative host Bill O'Reilly, who retorted that, while the First Lady was "essentially correct" that slaves took part in the construction of the White House, they were nonetheless "well fed."[11] Although age is surely bound up

---

[10] Olivia B. Waxman (2016), "Michelle Obama Reminded Us That Slaves Built the White House. Here's What to Know," *Time*, https://time.com/4423691/michelle-obama-dnc-speech-history/.

[11] Melissa Chan (2016), "Bill O'Reilly Says Slaves Who Built White House Were 'Well-Fed,'" *Time*, https://time.com/4426003/bill-oreilly-slaves-white-house-michelle-obama/.

with many other forces that might push outgroup empathy up or down, we expect that, ceteris paribus, older generations will display higher levels of group empathy.

HYPOTHESES AND DATA

We hypothesize that socio-demographics influence levels of outgroup empathy as a result of the variation they produce in exposure to discrimination, diversity, and competition. Therefore, race/ethnicity, gender, education, and age should all be associated with group empathy by structuring the socio-economic contexts in which people live (H1). More specifically, we expect minorities, females, the educated, and older generations to show higher levels of group empathy. The life experiences that spring from these socio-demographic contexts – mainly, exposure to discrimination, the quality and quantity of contact with other groups, and perceptions of intergroup economic competition – should also predict group empathy (H2). These life experiences should mediate the effect of socio-demographic factors on group empathy (H3).

To test these hypotheses, we employ data from the first wave of our 2013/14 US Group Empathy Two-Wave Study, fielded by GfK. The sample is composed of 633 randomly selected whites and stratified oversamples of 614 African Americans and 552 Latinos, making a total of 1,799 participants. The analyses that follow use poststratification sampling weights provided by GfK on racial/ethnic group strata to bring the oversampled groups to their population proportions.

RESULTS

We first evaluate whether group-based empathy is conditioned by the socio-demographic contexts and subsequent life experiences of the respondents. Table 4.1 presents OLS regression results for socio-demographic factors and life experiences (Models 1 and 2) along with an omnibus model (Model 3). The results of Model 1 confirm the significant impact of socio-demographic factors on general group empathy, measured by the GEI. As predicted, African Americans and Latinos both display higher levels of empathy for outgroups than whites. In addition, females, those with higher educational degrees, and older respondents display more group empathy. These results are supportive of H1.

We also explored the impact of income, marital status, employment status, metropolitan residence, Catholic religious identification, and household size on group empathy. Respondents who are married display lower levels of outgroup empathy. Catholic respondents in our sample also exhibit somewhat *less* group empathy compared to non-Catholics, but this is after we control for Latino identity, a heavily Catholic group. Anglo Catholics, in other words, show less outgroup empathy than other whites in this sample. By comparison, those living in larger households display higher outgroup empathy. That said, the statistical

TABLE 4.1 *Antecedents of group empathy*

	Model 1: Socio-demographics		Model 2: Life experiences		Model 3: Full model	
	β	S.E.	β	S.E.	β	S.E.
Black	.04**	.02			.03*	.01
Latino	.04*	.02			.03†	.02
Female	.04**	.01			.02*	.01
Education	.15**	.05			.06	.05
Age	.13***	.03			.13***	.03
Income	−.01	.03			−.02	.03
Married	−.03†	.02			−.03**	.01
Employed	−.02	.01			−.04**	.01
Metropolitan residence	−.01	.02			−.02	.02
Catholic	−.03†	.02			−.03†	.01
Household size	.08†	.05			.10**	.04
Discrimination			.03*	.01	.03*	.01
Contact quality			.38***	.03	.38***	.03
Contact quantity			.08***	.02	.08***	.02
Economic competition			−.05**	.02	−.06**	.02
Constant	.39***	.04	.30***	.02	.23***	.04
N	1,781		1,760		1,742	

Note: Coefficients estimated using OLS regression. Data are weighted. All variables are rescaled to run from 0 to 1. †$p \leq .10$, *$p \leq .05$, **$p \leq .01$, and ***$p \leq .001$, two-tailed.
Source: 2013/14 US Group Empathy Two-Wave Study (GfK)

significance of these effects are marginal ($p \leq .10$). Income, employment status, and metropolitan residence appear to be unrelated to group empathy in this model.

Table 4.1, Model 2, analyzes the link between key life experiences and group empathy. Specifically, this model includes personal experience of discrimination, the quality and quantity of intergroup contact, and perceived economic competition with other groups. To measure personal experience of discrimination, we asked respondents how fairly – ranging from "very fairly" to "very unfairly" – on a 4-point scale they felt they have been treated by law enforcement. To measure the quality of intergroup contact, we asked respondents to evaluate the nature of their interactions with members of other groups across five dimensions: superficial, voluntary, cooperative, pleasant, and equal in status (adopted from Islam & Hewstone 1993). With these five items, we generated a summative scale for contact quality. To measure the quantity (i. e., frequency) of intergroup contact, we asked respondents: "In general, how often do you have contact with people of other racial or ethnic groups in your daily life?" Response options ranged, on a 5-point scale, from "almost never" to "very often." We also included a measure (adopted from Oliver & Wong 2003) that taps into perceptions of economic competition based on respondents' level of agreement with the following statement: "More good jobs for other racial or ethnic groups mean fewer good jobs for my own group." Response options ranged from "strongly disagree" to "strongly agree" on a 5-point scale.

The results indicate that those who report they have experienced unfair treatment by law enforcement exhibit significantly higher levels of group empathy. This is in line with the theoretical expectation that personal experience with discrimination sensitizes respondents to the unfair treatment of individuals from other groups. To further check if this is indeed the case, the survey not only asked respondents how fairly they felt they have been personally treated by law enforcement officials but also how fairly they think law enforcement treats two key marginalized outgroups of interest – Arabs and undocumented immigrants. Response options again ranged on a 4-point scale from "very fairly" to "very unfairly." Pairwise comparisons of group means indicate that African Americans and Latinos have significantly higher perceptions of discrimination against the outgroups we inquired about. Figure 4.1 displays a profile plot of the relationship between respondents' personal experience with discrimination and perceived discrimination against Arabs and undocumented immigrants, broken down by the race/ethnicity of the respondents. While higher personal experience with discrimination correlates with heightened perceptions of discrimination against these two marginalized outgroups across all racial/ethnic respondent groups, the relationship is far stronger for both African Americans and Latinos. This pattern is in line with our theoretical expectations. The power of exposure to discrimination as a catalyst for outgroup empathy is expected to be strongest among nonwhites precisely because nonwhites are more likely to experience discrimination more directly, intimately, and intensely.

Going back to the results presented in Table 4.1, Model 2, the quality of contact with other groups has an even larger association with group empathy – in fact the *largest* of any variable in the model. The frequency of contact with other groups also boosts group empathy, though more modestly. Perceived economic competition, on the other hand, is negatively associated with group empathy, as we predicted. Overall, the results corroborate theoretical expectations about the link between life experiences and group empathy (H2).

We next combine the socio-demographic factors and life experiences to generate an omnibus model (see Table 4.1, Model 3). Personal experience with discrimination, the quality and quantity of intergroup contact, and perceived economic competition all remain highly significant in the fully specified model. These results signal that such life experiences may be more

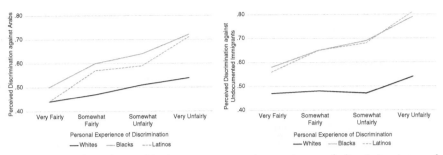

FIGURE 4.1 The relationship between personal experience of discrimination and perceived discrimination against Arabs and undocumented immigrants, by respondents' race/ethnicity

Note: The lines represent estimated marginal means calculated using multivariate analysis of covariance (MANCOVA). Other covariates are gender, education, age, income, marital status, household size, employment status, metropolitan residence, and religion (Catholic). All variables are rescaled to run from 0 to 1. Estimates from full model available in the online appendix.

Source: 2013/14 US Group Empathy Two-Wave Study (GfK)

proximal predictors of group empathy and that some of the effects of the key socio-demographic factors may function indirectly through them, as theorized. The coefficients for race/ethnicity, gender, and particularly, education – except for age – all appear to be diminished in this model. As for the other socio-demographic covariates, the coefficient for employment status achieves statistical significance in this model, while income and metropolitan residence continue to be insignificant. Respondents who are married, employed, and Catholic display lower empathy for outgroups, whereas those who live in larger households score higher on the GEI.

EXPLORING SOCIALIZATION PROCESSES

We next explore whether life experiences mediate the effects of the primary socio-demographic factors that we find to be powerful predictors of outgroup empathy in Table 4.1, Model 1.[12] We employ generalized structural equation modeling (GSEM) to examine path models leading from socio-demographic factors through life experiences to group empathy. To do so, we first estimate the effects of race/ethnicity, gender, education, and age on (1) personal

---

[12] Since these data come from a cross-sectional observational design, we cannot conclusively rule out other theoretically plausible causal models. For example, it could be the case that those who score high on group empathy differ from those who score low on some other dimension that was not controlled for. Still, if the GSEM results are in line with our theoretical predictions, we can modestly claim that there is empirical support for the proposed causal pathways.

experience of discrimination, (2) contact quality, (3) contact quantity, and (4) economic competition. We then estimate the effects of these life experiences on group empathy. These structural models control for all of the other socio-demographic factors included in the omnibus model presented in Table 4.1. After obtaining path coefficients, we test the significance of indirect effects using a bootstrap procedure that yields bias-corrected confidence intervals.

Figure 4.2 displays the role that life experiences play in explaining racial/ethnic differences in group empathy. We find that both African Americans and Latinos report significantly more experience with discrimination than whites and that experience significantly boosts group empathy. The bootstrap tests indicate that the indirect effect of personal experience with discrimination is statistically significant. The quantity of contact also seems to drive some of the empathy differences between African Americans and whites, but the same is not true for Latinos. Surprisingly, perhaps, neither the quality of intergroup contact nor perceived economic competition influence the size of racial/ethnic differences in group empathy.

Figure 4.3 displays the results for gender as the distal predictor. Women report much lower levels of perceived economic competition with other groups, which in turn further boosts their group empathy. So even though women suffer from a substantial gender wage gap, it appears they do not necessarily blame other groups for such inequalities in the workplace, nor do they see themselves in economic competition with outgroups that could potentially undermine their financial well-being. As for the other mediational paths, gender is marginally associated with contact quality and not significantly linked to contact quantity. Most surprisingly, women report less, not more, frequent experiences with discrimination. However, this may be due to the question wording that focuses on unfair treatment by law enforcement. We suspect if we also inquired about people's experiences with sex-based discrimination, such as in one's daily interactions or in the workplace, we would have a more direct measure of gender-specific life experiences that likely elicit higher group empathy among females. Overall, gender differences are still significant even after taking these particular mediating paths into consideration. The explanation for gender differences in group empathy therefore requires further attention.

Figure 4.4 displays the results of path analyses as before but with education as the distal predictor. As expected, education significantly decreases the likelihood of experiencing discrimination. That said, the empathy-boosting effects of education appear to be occurring through other socialization processes. Education is strongly and positively associated with both contact quality and quantity. These life experiences for the highly educated in turn powerfully increase outgroup empathy. The analyses also reveal that education significantly reduces the sense that groups are in economic competition, as predicted. Because education often brings people into diverse environments, it may help individuals develop the complex cognitive and

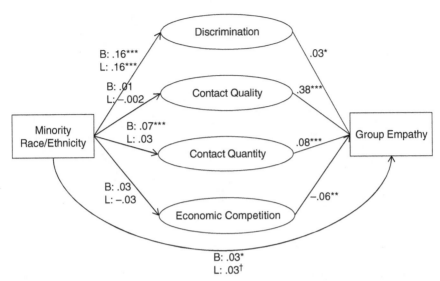

FIGURE 4.2 The role of race/ethnicity in structuring life experiences and group empathy
Note: Path coefficients estimated using generalized structural equation modeling based on the full models. "B" denotes blacks and "L" denotes Latinos. White respondents constitute the baseline category. Data are weighted. All variables are rescaled to run from o to 1. †p ≤ .10, *p ≤ .05, **p ≤ .01, and ***p ≤ .001, two-tailed.
Source: 2013/14 US Group Empathy Two-Wave Study (GfK)

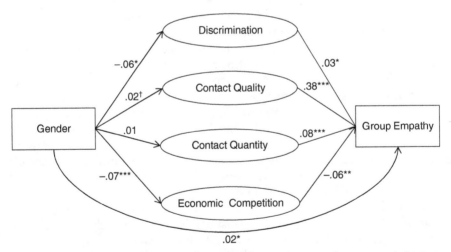

FIGURE 4.3 The role of gender in structuring life experiences and group empathy
Note: Path coefficients estimated using generalized structural equation modeling based on the full models. Data are weighted. All variables are rescaled to run from o to 1. †p ≤ .10, *p ≤ .05, **p ≤ .01, and ***p ≤ .001, two-tailed.
Source: 2013/14 US Group Empathy Two-Wave Study (GfK)

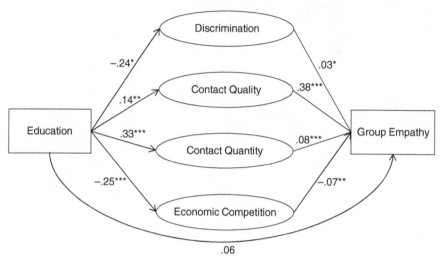

FIGURE 4.4 The role of education in structuring life experiences and group empathy
Note: Path coefficients estimated using generalized structural equation modeling based on the full models. Data are weighted. All variables are rescaled to run from 0 to 1. †p ≤ .10, *p ≤ .05, **p ≤ .01, and ***p ≤ .001, two-tailed.
Source: 2013/14 US Group Empathy Two-Wave Study (GfK)

affective representations necessary to empathize with others while also diminishing perceived economic conflict.

We also explore the indirect paths between age and group empathy. Those who are older report lower levels of personal experience with discrimination. This finding is somewhat counterintuitive but consistent with prior research that shows younger generations tend to be more conscious of discrimination and ready to report unfair treatment (e.g., Zainiddinov 2016). Surprisingly, age does not appear to be significantly linked to contact quality or quantity or to perceived economic competition in our sample. Further, the direct path between age and group empathy remains highly significant after controlling for these life experiences. Therefore, other forces must be at work to explain the generational differences in group empathy we find.

Overall, these results confirm our expectation that differences in group empathy spring at least in part from distinct life experiences that emerge from key socio-demographic factors (H3). Since African Americans and Latinos are more likely to grow up experiencing discrimination, they are more likely to be cognizant when it is happening to someone from another group. Lower perceptions of economic competition proves to be another significant mediator for the more highly educated as well as for women. As the quality and diversity of contact increases with years of education, so does group empathy. The life forces that significantly affect the age-group empathy path require further inquiry. Of course, while other causal relationships could result in the correlations observed here, these results provide a foundation for future work to explore the socialization processes that may lead to variation in levels of group empathy.

MINORITY DIFFERENCES: HIGHER EMPATHY FOR OUTGROUPS OR ANTIPATHY TOWARD THE MAJORITY?

We further explore the link between race/ethnicity and group empathy by calculating the predictive marginal means after conducting OLS regression analyses, while controlling for all other socio-demographic factors included in our previous models. The results are illustrated in Figure 4.5. African Americans and Latinos report higher levels of not only general outgroup empathy but also empathy directed specifically toward a wide variety of minority groups.

Importantly, African Americans (.41) and Latinos (.39) express as much empathy toward whites as whites do for their own group (.41). This suggests that group empathy is not simply a measure of ingroup preference among whites, much less a measure of outgroup antipathy among African Americans and Latinos toward whites. Of course, one would expect each group's empathy score for their own group to be higher than that for other groups. This is especially true for African Americans, who score .78 in empathy toward their ingroup. But African Americans also express nearly the same level of empathy toward Latinos (.60) as Latinos do for their own group (.62). These results fall in line with Mathur et al.'s (2010) findings based on the functional magnetic resonance imaging (fMRI) of neural activity, which indicate that, while African Americans tend to respond with empathy to the pain of ingroup members, this does not dampen their empathy toward outgroup targets.

If the GEI simply taps ingroup identification or outgroup animosity, we would expect a *negative* correlation between ingroup and outgroup empathy. This would be especially true for empathy displayed for whites among African Americans and Latinos, who might see whites as the major source of discrimination against their group. However, our theory suggests that group empathy is acquired early in life and then applied generally to outgroups. Therefore, we expected that African Americans and Latinos who empathize with their own group would also be more – not less – likely to empathize with whites and other groups. This is exactly what we find. African Americans who empathize with their own group are also significantly more likely to empathize with whites (r = .23) and Latinos (r = 41). There are in fact no negative correlations between ingroup and outgroup empathy for any of the groups under study.

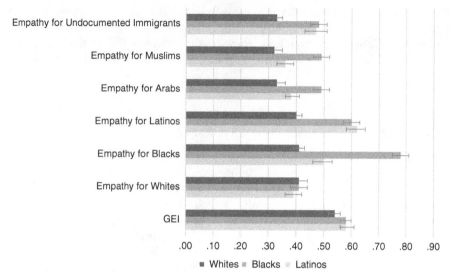

FIGURE 4.5 Racial/ethnic differences in group empathy
Note: The bars represent predictive margins calculated after OLS regression. The lines represent 95 percent confidence intervals. Models also control for gender, education, age, income, marital status, household size, employment status, metropolitan residence, and religion (Catholic). Data are weighted. All variables are rescaled to run from 0 to 1. Estimates from full model available in the online appendix.
Source: 2013/14 US Group Empathy Two-Wave Study (GfK)

MINORITY–MAJORITY DIFFERENCES IN GROUP EMPATHY VERSUS INDIVIDUAL EMPATHY

Group Empathy Theory predicts higher intergroup empathy among minorities due to their personal and collective ingroup experiences with discrimination. Meanwhile, interpersonal empathy should be similar across different groups in society. One would expect that human beings generally display a similar tendency for empathic concern and perspective taking toward their family and friends regardless of their race/ethnicity. We asserted that socialization processes that lead to minority–majority differences in group empathy are distinct from those that engender individual empathy.

We tested this suggestion using the 2015 US Group Empathy Study via MTurk, in which we administered the GEI to half of the participants and the Interpersonal Reactivity Index (IRI) to the other half. As predicted, the results of OLS regression analyses indicate that minorities are significantly higher in group empathy (β = .10, S.E. = .04, p ≤ .05) but do not differ from the majority when it comes to individual empathy (β = -.04, S.E. = .05, p > .10) even after controlling for other key socio-demographic correlates of group empathy.[13] These findings corroborate the expectation that minority–majority differences in group empathy are not simply mimicking existing differences in individual empathy. We replicate these findings in the United Kingdom with a nationally representative sample using data from Wave 14 of the 2018 British Election Study (BES). We discuss those results in detail in Chapter 9; simply put, British nonwhites display significantly higher levels of group empathy than British whites, yet we observe no significant differences in individual empathy between the minority and majority groups. It thus appears that these two different forms of empathy may have distinct causes, with race/ethnicity as one of the key antecedents for intergroup empathy but not for the interpersonal form.

INGROUP IDENTIFICATION AND OUTGROUP EMPATHY

In Chapter 2 we made a provocative assertion that, while ingroup identification should be negatively correlated with outgroup empathy among whites, we expect a *positive* association between ingroup identification–outgroup empathy among minorities. In other words, counter to one of the central claims of Social Identity Theory (SIT) about ingroup–outgroup bias, we predict that minorities who identify more strongly with their ingroup should show *higher* – not lower – levels of empathy for outgroups. This is because minorities with strong ingroup identification are more likely to embrace their group's collective consciousness and memory, which should boost their sensitivity to the unfair treatment of fellow group members and, in turn, trigger sensitivity to the struggles of other groups that are similarly marginalized. Accordingly, socialization processes (especially experiences with discrimination) that cultivate empathy for disadvantaged outgroups should be more salient among minorities with strong ingroup identification. In contrast, whites who strongly identify with their ingroup are more likely to embrace their group's dominance in society, which would make it more difficult to take the perspective of stigmatized outgroups. From a psychological standpoint, whites who are strong ingroup identifiers are likely to be less sensitive to discriminatory practices targeting minority outgroups to avoid cognitive and emotional dissonance that such an awareness would elicit given their ingroup's role as the majority in power in an unjust system. Some members of the majority with strong ingroup identification may even seek to justify such discriminatory treatment – such as racial profiling – by associating minority

---

[13] We also control for gender, education, age, income, and Catholic religious identification in the model. The MTurk sample did not include measures of household size, marital status, employment status, and metropolitan residence; however, these additional controls did not display significant effects on group empathy in the previous model (see Table 4.1), so this model is parsimonious. Full results are available in the online appendix.

groups with negative dispositional attributes – such as higher proclivity to commit crime.

To empirically test this assertion, we included measures of ingroup identification in the 2018 US Group Empathy Study fielded nationally online by YouGov. Adapting Huddy and colleagues' (2015) partisan identity scale to racial/ethnic ingroup identification, we asked our participants the following: (1) "How important is being [black/Latino/white] to you?" (2) "How well does the term [black/Latino/white] describe you?" (3) "When talking about [blacks/Latinos/whites], how often do you say 'we' instead of 'they'?" (4) "To what extent do you think of yourself as [black/Latino/white]?" Huddy et al.'s partisan identity scale covers several key components of social identity such as salience of identity and connectedness. Yet it does not include an affective component, which is likely an important part of one's racial/ethnic ingroup identity. To compensate for this, we added a fifth item to the measure: "How often do you feel proud that you are [black/Latino/white]?" All items were on a 5-point ordinal scale. Since the objective was to measure ingroup identification, the question wording [black/Latino/white] was programmed to correspond to the race/ethnicity of the respondent. The Cronbach's alpha for the five items measuring the concept of racial/ethnic ingroup identification yielded a score of .84, indicating high internal consistency. The principal-component factor analysis with oblique rotation further suggested a single-factor model underlying these five items, with an eigenvalue of 3.06 and factor loadings ranging from .71 to .83.[14]

Consistent with our theoretical expectations, ingroup identification and outgroup empathy are negatively correlated among whites ($r = -.21$; $p \leq .001$) but positively associated for both African Americans and Latinos ($r = .40$ and $r = .43$, respectively; $p \leq .001$). As a more stringent test, we also conducted OLS regression analyses. The coefficient of ingroup identification among whites – with group empathy modeled as the outcome variable – is negative and statistically significant ($p \leq .05$). By comparison, ingroup identification significantly increases outgroup empathy among African Americans as well as Latinos ($p \leq .001$). Figure 4.6 graphs the marginal effects of ingroup identification on group empathy by race/ethnicity. As the graph illustrates, blacks and Latinos behave very similarly to one another and in the opposite direction to whites. Whites who identify *least* with their ingroup display the *highest* levels of group empathy. In contrast, blacks and Latinos who identify *least* with their ingroup are also the *least* empathic toward outgroups. As ingroup identification increases, outgroup empathy decreases for whites but substantively increases among both minority groups – leading to a large group

---

[14] As a more direct measure regarding the strength of one's ingroup identification, respondents were also asked: "How strongly do you identify with [black/Latino/white] people?" The results are robust to the use of this alternative measure in sensitivity analyses and are available in the online appendix.

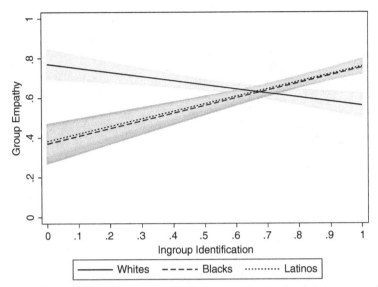

FIGURE 4.6 The relationship between ingroup identification and group empathy, by respondents' race/ethnicity
Note: The lines represent the marginal effects of ingroup identification on group empathy estimated using OLS regression. The shaded areas represent 95 percent confidence intervals.
Source: 2018 US Group Empathy Study (YouGov)

empathy gap between the majority and minorities at the highest levels of ingroup identification.

These trends make sense if denouncing one's minority identity stems from a desire to "exit" a low-status group and move up in the social strata, instead of choosing to positively redefine one's identity or challenge the status quo (Tajfel & Turner 1979). Weak ingroup identification among minority members would then likely elicit (a) higher levels of empathy for members of the dominant group and (b) lower levels of empathy for marginalized groups. This is what we find in analyzing the marginal effects of ingroup identification on empathy for specific groups, as illustrated in Figure 4.7. Among low ingroup identifiers, minorities are as empathic toward whites as whites themselves are toward their own ingroup; yet they are much less empathic than whites toward stigmatized groups such as undocumented immigrants and Arabs. However, the pattern dramatically reverses if one's ingroup identification is strong. In other words, minorities' identification with their ingroup does not reduce empathy toward whites and powerfully increases empathy for other minority outgroups. By comparison, ingroup identification for whites significantly reduces empathy for all minority groups while boosting empathy for their own group. In short,

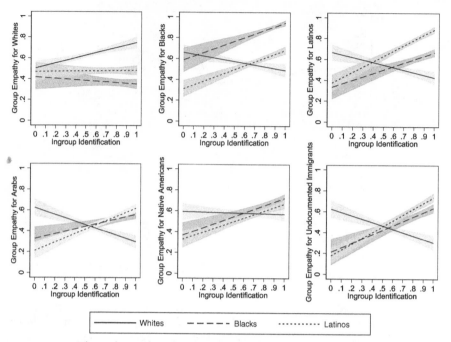

FIGURE 4.7 The relationship between ingroup identification and group-specific empathy, by respondents' race/ethnicity
Note: The lines represent the marginal effects of ingroup identification on group-specific empathy estimated using OLS regression. The shaded areas represent 95 percent confidence intervals.
Source: 2018 US Group Empathy Study (YouGov)

ingroup identification may serve as a significant precursor to group empathy, and the underlying mechanism is entirely different for minorities versus whites.

CONCLUSION

In this chapter we tested our theory's central claim about the origins of group empathy. We argued that socio-demographic dimensions – primarily race/ethnicity, gender, education, and age – are likely to shape key life experiences such as encounters with discrimination, the quality and quantity of intergroup contact, and perceived economic competition between groups. These socialization processes, in turn, trigger one's sensitivity to the struggles of outgroup members and lead to group empathy. Such experiences are likely to vary significantly across groups, and they shape the lens through which people see the world. Minority children, for example, might develop empathy for stigmatized outgroups as a result of their own experiences with discrimination, as well as through the stories they hear about the struggles of their family and friends. The resulting variation in empathy toward social groups other than one's own may have powerful political consequences, which we further demonstrate in subsequent chapters.

It has long been noted that elite discourse and media depictions of various minorities may prime and reinforce negative stereotypes about such groups. Criminalizing depictions of undocumented immigrants is one example (e.g., Chavez 2008). The construction of Arabs as hostile and violent after the attacks of September 11, 2001, is another (e.g., Merskin 2004). African Americans have also long suffered from persistent, biased racial cues that circulate via media and elite messaging that stereotypically associate them with unlawfulness, drugs, and welfare dependency (e.g., Valentino et al. 2002). Very little work has been done, however, to see how such portrayals are received by minority versus majority groups in society. Based on our findings, we would expect much different reactions conditioned by the distinct life experiences of minority groups, particularly vis-à-vis discrimination.

Our results show that African Americans and Latinos display significantly higher levels of empathy for marginalized groups yet also have as much empathy for whites as whites themselves do.[15] This is consistent with the notion that empathy is learned at an early age and is applied generally and rather automatically based on one's social context and life experiences. Empathic reactions to others in distress constitute the default response for such people.

We thus expect group empathy to be relatively weak only when relevant socialization processes do not occur. Majority group members, for instance, may not grow up experiencing discrimination on the basis of their race. On average, though certainly not for every member of the dominant group, these individuals might not be as sensitive to the plight of groups experiencing unfair treatment in society. Still, life experiences such as contact with other groups, learning about the struggles of historically disadvantaged communities via education, and personally witnessing injustices targeting minorities over the years may trigger group empathy even if a person lacks direct experience with discrimination.

Additional research is needed, of course, to further determine how and when group empathy is acquired during the lifespan. Our research design is not suited for longitudinally tracking socialization processes, since it is a one-shot

---

[15] We conceive group empathy to be primarily directed at those who are in distress. It is thus not surprising that blacks and Latinos show much higher levels of empathy for nonwhite groups than they do for whites. Still, the fact that their outgroup empathy toward whites is on par with the level of empathy whites show for their own ingroup indicates these minority communities do not harbor antipathy for whites.

observational design and our sample does not include children or adolescents. Of course, studying socialization processes directly among young people is challenging, especially since no existing panel studies explicitly tap group empathy. Even a short panel design among adolescents with variation in their experiences with group-based discrimination, contact, and competition, however, could help trace the development of this dimension in a more direct way.

5

Group Empathy and Homeland Security

The Case of "Flying While Arab"

> Meanwhile, far away in another part of town / Rubin Carter and a couple of friends are drivin' around / Number one contender for the middleweight crown / Had no idea what kinda shit was about to go down / When a cop pulled him over to the side of the road / Just like the time before and the time before that / In Paterson that's just the way things go / If you're black you might as well not show up on the street / 'Less you wanna draw the heat
>
> Bob Dylan and Jacques Levy, "Hurricane," from the album *Desire* (1976)[1]

In the post–9/11 world, it seems that terrorist threats abound and frequently fill the news waves. Consider, for example, the so-called Shoe Bomber's attempt in 2001 on a flight to Miami; the Christmas Day Bomber's attempt on a flight to Detroit in 2009; the Boston marathon bombings of 2013; the terror attacks in Paris and San Bernardino in 2015, Orlando in 2016, and London in 2017; not to mention the countless other atrocities committed by terrorist groups such as ISIS and Boko Haram, and the list goes on. Sporadic terrorist incidents rekindle animosity and collective blame toward the Arab community, even when the perpetrators are not of Arab descent. In the case of the 2013 Boston bombings, for instance, anti-Arab sentiments were promulgated by law enforcement officials and a variety of mainstream news sources presuming, among other things, the appearance (dark-skinned), race/ethnicity (Arab, Middle Eastern), and nationality (Saudi, Moroccan) of the bombing suspects before their actual identities – two Caucasian males of Chechen descent – were confirmed days later.[2]

---

[1] "Hurricane," written by Bob Dylan and Jacques Levy. Copyright © 1975 by Ram's Horn Music; renewed 2003 by Ram's Horn Music.

[2] Larry Celona (2013), "FBI Grills Saudi Man in Boston Bombings," *New York Post*, http://nypost .com/2013/04/16/fbi-grills-saudi-man-in-boston-bombings/. See also Gene Demby (2013), "Ethnicity, Religion and the Tsarnaev Brothers," NPR, www.npr.org/sections/codeswitch/ 2013/04/22/178461447/ethnicity-religion-and-the-tsarnaev-brothers.

In this chapter we examine the role of group empathy in shaping public attitudes, policy preferences, and political behavior in the aftermath of these terror attacks. Given that the US public has stereotypically perceived Arabs as the world's primary source of violent extremism since September 11, 2001 (Cainkar 2009; Huddy et al. 2005; Panagopoulos 2006), one might expect simple perceptions of threat to drive public opinion about Arabs. We predict, instead, group empathy powerfully drives political views and actions concerning the civil rights and treatment of Arabs. The domain of terrorism and national security, therefore, is a key test bed for Group Empathy Theory.

THE EVOLVING IMAGE OF ARABS IN THE UNITED STATES

The Arab population in the United States has been growing steadily for over a century. In the 1880s, modest numbers of Arab immigrants started assimilating into a mainstream American culture that prized "Anglo-conformity" (Kulczycki & Lobo 2001). The Arab population began to grow more rapidly following the 1965 Immigration and Nationality Act, which lifted national origin quotas and encouraged family reunification (Keely 1971). Conservative estimates suggest that Arabs living in the United States grew from about 712,000 in 1980 to well over a million by 1990, with nearly three out of five Arab Americans recorded as US native-born by that time (Zogby 1990). According to the 2018 American Community Survey conducted by the US Census Bureau, more than 2.1 million US residents are of Arab descent.[3] The Arab American Institute, a nonprofit private organization, suggests that the adjusted Arab-American population might actually be closer to 3.7 million, with about one-third residing in California, New York, and Michigan.[4]

Arab Americans are officially classified by the US census as white, and their average incomes and homeownership rates are comparable to whites (Gaddis & Ghoshal 2015). Nevertheless, the image of the Arab in mainstream American culture has been mostly negative and *othered*, with very little attention paid to the group's struggles for acceptance. As Jamal (2008, 116) puts it, "This racialization process essentially sees Muslims and Arabs as different from and inferior to whites, potentially violent and threatening, and therefore deserving of policies that target them as a distinct group of people and criminalize them without evidence of criminal activity."

Long before the 9/11 attacks, the US media portrayed the Arab community negatively, highlighted by events such as the 1956 Suez crisis, the Israeli-Palestinian conflict, Islamic revivalism, and the 1993 World Trade Center bombing (e.g., Ghareeb 1983; Hamada 2001; Jackson 1996). In other words, regardless of their citizenship status, Arabs have been represented as an *external*

---

[3] United States Census Bureau (2018), "People Reporting Ancestry," American Community Survey, https://data.census.gov/cedsci/table?q=C04006&tid=ACSDT1Y2018.C04006.

[4] See www.aaiusa.org/demographics.

threat to American society in mass media for some time (Slade 1981). Lind and Danowski's (1998) study of ABC, CNN, and PBS television content from 1993 to 1996 found that most media coverage of Arabs linked the group to war, violence, and threat.

News reporting often presumes Arab involvement in terrorist attacks that are later revealed to be home-grown. For instance, almost immediately after the 1995 Oklahoma City bombing, news outlets began speculating about the possibility that Arab terrorists were behind the attack before confirming that Timothy McVeigh – an American of Irish descent – had actually carried out the bombing (Hamm 1997). Shaheen's (2003, 172) examination of 900 American films found that Arabs have often been portrayed as "Public Enemy #1 – brutal, heartless, uncivilized religious fanatics and money-mad cultural 'others' bent on terrorizing civilized Westerners, especially Christians and Jews." Similarly negative depictions of Arabs in America have been documented in songs, cartoons, comics, advertisements, editorials, movies, television dramas, and even educational textbooks (e.g., Semmerling 2006; Terry 1985).

In light of such studies, scholars point to the development of a collective memory in American media and popular culture that fuses the terms "Arabs, Muslim, and Middle East into one highly negative image of violence and danger" (Jackson 1996, 65), a stereotypical schema often referred to as the "monolithic evil Arab" (Merskin 2004; Said 1997). According to Merskin (2004, 161), this schema "facilitates the binding of people together as an *us* and sends those who are not *us* into 'symbolic exile' as *them*" (see also Hall 1997; Kalkan et al. 2009). Consequently, perceptions of negative events connected to certain detested Arab figures (e.g., Osama bin Laden, Saddam Hussein, and Muammar Gaddafi) may be erroneously applied en masse to anyone resembling a person of Arab descent (Merskin 2004; see also Ghareeb 1983; Hamada 2001; Suleiman 1988, 1999).

This caustic stigmatization of the Arab community spiked following the September 11, 2001, terrorist attacks. Arab Americans were subjected to acts of violence, discrimination, defamation, and intolerance at a "level unparalleled in their 100-year history in the US" (Cainkar 2002, 22). Within one week of the 9/11 attacks, approximately 645 incidents of bias and hate crimes were reported by Arab and South Asian Americans (CAIR 2002; SAALT 2001). By late September 2001, a majority of Americans supported the profiling of Arabs at security checkpoints before boarding airplanes (Cainkar 2002, 23; see also Huddy et al. 2005). Again, in the immediate aftermath of the attacks, 83 percent of Americans favored restricting immigration from Arab and Muslim countries, and almost one-third of the US public believed that the government should place Arab Americans under special surveillance (Panagopoulos 2006). Almost one-third of Americans even supported extreme policies such as interning Arab Americans in camps until their innocence could be determined (Schildkraut 2002, 2009).

This sharp surge in hostility toward Arab and Muslim Americans stabilized several years after the 9/11 attacks, but the balance of opinion about the group remained largely negative (Merolla & Zechmeister 2009; Panagopoulos 2006). Since the election cycle of 2016, hate crimes against Arabs and Muslims have once again been on the rise. According to a Pew Research Center analysis of hate crimes statistics from the FBI, the number of hate-driven assaults in 2016 against Muslims in the United States surpassed even the number of incidents observed in 2001 – the year of the 9/11 attacks.[5] Some scholars attribute this spike to the highly incendiary anti-Muslim and anti-Arab rhetoric Donald Trump employed during his presidential bid, which continued after taking office. Modi (2018) found that one in five perpetrators of hate violence targeting Muslims in the United States referenced Trump, a Trump policy, or a Trump campaign slogan in the year after his election.[6]

A number of studies have systematically documented the links between perceptions of terrorist threat and hostility toward Arabs in the post-9/11 era. For instance, Huddy and colleagues (2005, 2007) find that Americans who anticipate future terrorist attacks are more likely to hold negative stereotypes of Arabs, approve restrictive immigration policies, and support invasive surveillance and security measures directed at the Arab community. In a nationally representative survey experiment, Conrad et al. (2018) find that Americans overall are far more likely to approve of the government's use of torture when a detainee is of Arabic descent and the alleged crime is terrorism. These patterns are consistent with prior psychological research that demonstrates the prominent role existential threats play in triggering the vilification of outgroup members who are perceived to be responsible (e.g., Skitka et al. 2004; Staub 1989). Public reactions to terror threats thus have

---

[5] Katayoun Kishi (2017), "Assaults against Muslims in US Surpass 2001 Level," Pew Research Center, www.pewresearch.org/fact-tank/2017/11/15/assaults-against-muslims-in-u-s-surpass-2001-level/. Note that the actual number of hate crime incidents is likely higher than the reported numbers. The FBI itself acknowledges that its statistics vastly undercount anti-Arab hate crimes partly because they are based on voluntary reporting by local law enforcement agencies. Indeed, the category "Anti-Arab" hate crime in the FBI reports was eliminated in 2001 (interestingly, in the year of the 9/11 attacks, when Arab Americans became the primary target of hate crimes), only to be reintroduced in 2015. See Omar Baddar (2018), "Hate Crimes Continue to Surge in America: Underreporting Remains Significant Problem in FBI's Annual Statistics," The Arab American Institute, www.aaiusa.org/hate_crimes_continue_to_surge_in_america. See also Masood Farivar (2018), "Report: FBI Vastly Undercounts Anti-Arab Hate Crimes," Voice of America, www.voanews.com/a/report-fbi-vastly-undercounts-anti-arab-hate-crimes/4491928.html.

[6] Radha Modi (2018), "Communities on Fire: Confronting Hate Violence and Xenophobic Political Rhetoric," South Asian Americans Leading Together (SAALT), http://saalt.org/wp-content/uploads/2018/01/Communities-on-Fire.pdf. See also Chris Fuchs (2018), "Reported Anti-Muslim Hate Incidents, Rhetoric Rose in Year after Election, Report Finds," NBC News, www.nbcnews.com/news/asian-america/reported-anti-muslim-hate-incidents-rhetoric-rose-year-after-election-n843671.

dangerous consequences, not just for the Arab community but also for democratic institutions (see Merolla & Zechmeister 2009).

If negative attitudes toward Arabs are fueled by the view that the group poses a serious existential threat to the nation, then we might expect *all* non–Arab American groups to react similarly to them. On the other hand, if other marginalized groups such as African Americans and Latinos empathize with Arabs after witnessing the stigmatization they have endured since the 9/11 attacks, such groups should display more tolerant views about Arabs and resist punitive policies that target them. If Group Empathy Theory is correct, these attitudinal differences should persist even among African Americans and Latinos who perceive themselves and the nation to be at greater risk from future attacks. If so, group empathy is indeed a powerful antidote for perceived threats and reduces one's willingness to trade off civil rights and liberties for promises of security at the expense of stigmatized groups stereotypically associated with such threats.

HYPOTHESES

In Chapter 3 we found group empathy to be a strong predictor of attitudes about the trade-off between civil liberties and national security in combating terrorism and to potentially drive political action in order to protect the rights of targeted groups. Here, we explore the impact of group empathy on policy preferences and behavioral intentions concerning Arabs in times of high terror threat.

Group empathy should increase one's awareness of the "Arab-as-terrorist" stereotype in the US (H1a). Further, we expect group empathy drives opposition to discriminatory national security policies targeting Arabs (H1b). It should also boost opposition to deporting undocumented immigrants of Arab descent (H1c). Of course, we expect these associations to hold above and beyond the forces that have been widely studied in the previous literature on this topic, including partisanship, ideology, threat perceptions, and other key political predispositions.

In Chapter 4 we found significant racial/ethnic differences in levels of group empathy. If significant intergroup differences emerge on the outcomes of interest, we expect that differences in group empathy should help explain those gaps. African Americans and Latinos should display more favorable attitudes toward Arabs. Outgroup empathy helps explain why these minority groups would protect Arabs from unfair treatment, independent of other predispositions, threat perceptions, and socio-demographics (H2).

Group Empathy Theory further predicts that African Americans and Latinos will react differently than whites to ambiguous but potentially threatening scenarios involving the racial profiling of Arabs. We perform an experiment to test this hypothesis. We expect that minorities will exhibit far more support for Arabs in these situations than will whites. African Americans and Latinos should be more likely than whites to side with an Arab passenger who has been singled out for additional search and questioning at an airport due to an alleged terror threat, especially compared to the same situation involving a white passenger (H3a). This pattern of reactions should also emerge in evaluations of probable cause for law enforcement decisions (H3b). We also predict that African Americans and Latinos will show higher support for civil rights policies (H4a) and a stronger commitment to political action for addressing the plight of profiled groups (H4b). Last, group-based differences in empathic reactions to these vignettes should significantly mediate intergroup variation in policy opinions and behavioral intentions, even more so than threat perceptions (H5).

GROUP EMPATHY AND ATTITUDES TOWARD ARABS

We first examine the data from the Wave 1 portion of the national survey experiment we fielded online in December 2013–January 2014 via GfK's probability-based sampling panel that included 633 whites, 614 African Americans, and 552 Latinos (a total of 1,799 respondents). African Americans and Latinos were oversampled and stratified for the purpose of the experiment in Wave 2. Survey weights are applied to the Wave 1 analyses to bring the sample into line with nationally representative population proportions. For ease of interpretation, we rescaled all measures to run from 0 to 1. We employ the fourteen-item Group Empathy Index (GEI) to measure general group empathy. The models control for social dominance orientation (SDO), ethnocentrism, authoritarianism, trust in political authorities, key threat perceptions (mainly, perceived threat of Arabs, terrorism, and immigration), party identification, ideology, and a host of socio-demographic factors. We also control for personal experience of discrimination to demonstrate that group empathy – while enhanced by this specific life experience – is not identical to it. Therefore, these models offer highly conservative tests of our hypotheses.[7] The results of ordered probit analyses are presented in Table 5.1.

We expected group empathy to increase awareness of the "Arab-as-terrorist" stereotype (H1a). To test this hypothesis, we asked respondents: "In your opinion, to what extent does the US public perceive that Arabs are responsible for most terrorist attacks around the world?" Response options ranged from "not at all responsible" to "very responsible" on a 5-point scale. As shown in the first set of columns in Table 5.1, the GEI's effect on one's awareness of the "Arab-as-terrorist" stereotype is the third largest in the model following

---

[7] Predicted probabilities and marginal effects were calculated using the observed-value approach (see Hanmer & Kalkan 2013).

TABLE 5.1 *The relationship between group empathy and attitudes about Arabs*

	Awareness of "Arab-as -terrorist" stereotypes		Opposition to profiling Arabs		Opposition to deporting undocumented Arab Immigrants	
	β	S.E.	β	S.E.	β	S.E.
Group empathy	.70***	.21	.33†	.20	.61**	.22
Experience of discrimination	−.53***	.14	.54***	.14	.23	.15
SDO	−1.43***	.23	−.86***	.22	−.22	.23
Ethnocentrism	−.46	.30	−.67**	.27	.14	.33
Authoritarianism	−.37**	.14	−.26†	.14	−.16	.13
Political trust	−.67***	.16	−.07	.16	.19	.17
Perceived Arab threat	1.70***	.16	−1.37***	.15	−1.30***	.15
Terrorism threat	.26	.18	−.28†	.16	−.10	.16
Immigration threat	.19	.17	−.72***	.15	−.91***	.17
Party ID	.14	.13	−.44**	.14	−.51***	.14
Ideology	−.28	.19	.14	.17	.11	.18
Black	−.10	.10	.18†	.10	.09	.10
Latino	−.11	.10	.20*	.10	.15	.11
Female	−.13†	.07	.05	.07	.18*	.07
Education	.31	.31	.15	.25	−.09	.28
Age	−.19	.19	−.41*	.18	−.39*	.20
Income	−.06	.19	.09	.16	−.43**	.16
Married	.15†	.09	−.08	.08	−.03	.09
Employed	−.01	.08	−.02	.07	.03	.09
Metropolitan residence	−.05	.11	.09	.11	.15	.11
Catholic	−.005	.09	.08	.09	−.10	.10
Household size	.07	.23	−.20	.22	.51*	.23
N	1,686		1,689		1,687	

Note: Coefficients estimated using ordered probit. Data are weighted. All variables are rescaled to run from 0 to 1. †$p \leq .10$, *$p \leq .05$, **$p \leq .01$, and ***$p \leq .001$, two-tailed.
Source: 2013/14 US Group Empathy Two-Wave Study (GfK)

perceived threat of Arabs and SDO, thereby strongly corroborating H1a ($p \leq .001$). The probability of being highly cognizant of such a stereotype increases from 25 to 47 percent as one moves from low to high scores on the GEI.

Awareness of criminalizing stereotypes about Arabs does not guarantee that one will display policy support for Arabs. In fact, the results show that perceiving Arabs as a security threat is positively associated with such awareness, just like group empathy, but it depresses favorable attitudes toward Arabs. The effect of group empathy should go beyond simple awareness. It should also be associated with opposition to discriminatory security policies targeting Arabs (H1b). We asked our respondents: "Assuming it could help improve national security, how strongly do you support or oppose police and other law enforcement officials (such as border patrol and airport security) stopping and questioning [Arabs] simply on the basis of their appearance?" Response options ranged from "strongly support" to "strongly oppose" on a 5-point scale. The results, presented in the second set of columns in Table 5.1, indicate that group empathy is a predictor of policy opinion on the racial profiling of Arabs, although the level of statistical significance is marginal ($p \leq .10$). The probability of strongly opposing the racial profiling of Arabs decreases from 26 to 18 percent as one moves from low to high scores on the GEI. However, keep in mind that we fitted a very conservative model that includes personal experience of discrimination by law enforcement (along with a large set of key political predispositions), so the fact that the GEI retains its significance is notable. These results are thus supportive of H1b.

We also find empirical support for H1c, which predicted that group empathy would be linked with higher opposition to punitive immigration policies aimed at capturing and deporting undocumented Arab immigrants. The third set of columns in Table 5.1 shows that the GEI is indeed one of the top three predictors in the model, alongside perceived threat of Arabs and threat of immigration ($p \leq .01$). The predictive power of the GEI even surpasses party identification and ideology. The substantive effect of group empathy is large. Moving from low to high scores on the GEI, the probability of strongly supporting the capture and deportation of undocumented Arab immigrants drops from 40 to 24 percent.

All in all, these patterns provide evidence that group empathy – above and beyond political predispositions, perceptions of threat, and socio-demographic factors – powerfully predicts who is willing to accept punitive policies aimed at Arabs and who is not. Besides the main effects of group empathy, we also expect that this dimension will help explain the observed racial/ethnic group differences. As Figure 5.1 illustrates, compared to whites in the sample, African Americans and Latinos are on average less likely to support discriminatory security and immigration policies targeting Arabs. We suspect these differences are at least partly because of the higher levels of empathy minorities display for stigmatized outgroups.

To test this hypothesis, we use generalized structural equation modeling (GSEM). We control for all of the variables included in the previous models and employ a bootstrapping procedure with bias-corrected confidence intervals to estimate and test the significance of indirect effects. Figure 5.2 presents the path coefficients obtained via GSEM. The results indicate that, for all of the dependent

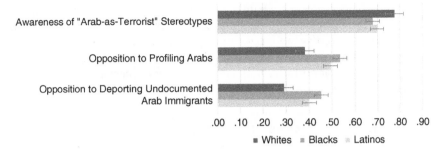

FIGURE 5.1 Racial/ethnic differences in attitudes about Arabs
Note: The bars represent marginal means. The lines represent 95 percent confidence intervals. Data are weighted. All variables are rescaled to run from 0 to 1. Estimates from full model available in the online appendix.
Source: 2013/14 US Group Empathy Two-Wave Study (GfK)

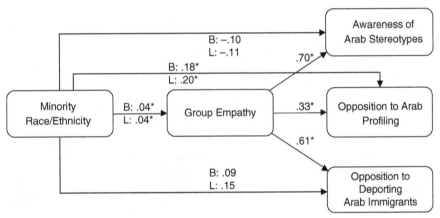

FIGURE 5.2 The role of group empathy in explaining racial/ethnic differences in attitudes about Arabs
Note: Path coefficients estimated using generalized structural equation modeling based on the full models. "B" denotes blacks and "L" denotes Latinos. White respondents constitute the baseline category. All indirect paths are statistically significant. Data are weighted. All variables are rescaled to run from 0 to 1. *p ≤ .05, one-tailed.
Source: 2013/14 US Group Empathy Two-Wave Study (GfK)

variables examined, the indirect effects via group empathy are statistically significant for both blacks and Latinos (p ≤ .05), thereby corroborating H2.[8] Surprisingly, whites on average appear to be the most cognizant of the "Arab-as-terrorist" stereotype (as shown in Figure 5.1). But, because minorities display

[8] The full estimates from these GSEM analyses are available in the online appendix.

significantly higher group empathy, and because, in turn, group empathy significantly increases one's recognition of such criminalizing stereotypes, the indirect path is positive and significant. As for policy opinion, the results confirm that group empathy significantly helps explain the minority–majority differences in opposition to discriminatory law enforcement practices targeting the Arab community.

THE "FLYING WHILE ARAB" EXPERIMENT

In the second wave of the 2013/14 US Group Empathy Two-Wave Study, we explored experimentally how whites and nonwhites reacted to news stories involving potential terror threats. A total of 673 respondents (244 whites, 217 blacks, and 212 Latinos) from the first wave took part in what we refer to as the "Flying While Arab" experiment in the second wave. We expected that nonwhites would be more resistant to profiling Arabs even in an ambiguous, potentially threatening situation. We employed a between-groups factorial design by randomly assigning participants to different experimental conditions in which they were exposed to a hypothetical news report.[9] The news report depicted the detention and search of a passenger behaving somewhat ambiguously at an airport security checkpoint. The news report was accompanied by a photograph of a fictitious person, and our experimental manipulation was to alter the race/ethnicity of the individual to appear white or Arab.[10] The text of the news report was held constant across all conditions. A caption under the picture read: "Passenger pulled out of security line at New York's JFK International Airport."

This experimental design carries the important feature that all passengers, by definition, are equally vulnerable to an individual who might hijack an airplane they are about to board. By keeping the existential threat constant and altering only the visible race/ethnicity of the passenger, we can determine (1) whether racial/ethnic cues affect participants' perceptions of the two parties in dispute (i.e., whether the passenger or the airport security officer were correct to act as they did); and (2) judgments about the behavior of the authorities (i.e., whether there is reasonable cause for additional screening). We followed Peffley and Hurwitz's (2010) strategy in developing our experimental scenario by presenting an ambiguous incident such that for some, additional search and questioning of the passenger would seem reasonable, while for others it might suggest unfair racial profiling. The news report read as follows:

---

[9] As we mentioned in the Prologue, the experimental vignette was designed to resemble a real-life incident at an airport that appeared in the news in October 2011. See Kate Auletta (2011), "Misheard Words Prompt Southwest to Remove Muslim Woman from Flight," *HuffPost*, www .huffpost.com/entry/southwest-muslim-student_n_836815.

[10] The experiment originally contained conditions for black and Latino passengers, in addition to white and Arab. For the purpose of this chapter, we review only the white and Arab conditions.

Controversy at the Airport: "It's a go!" or "I've got to go!"?(News Report)

Recently, a passenger was flying from New York to Chicago when he was pulled out of a security line, searched, and questioned. The passenger was talking on his cell phone while waiting in line to board his flight. One of the airport security officers standing nearby said that he heard the passenger say, "It's a go!" which qualifies as suspicious behavior according to the Transportation Security Administration (TSA) guidelines. In response, the airport security officer took the passenger aside for further screening. The passenger, however, claimed that when it was his turn to board the plane, he told the person on the phone, "I've got to go!" and hung up. Amid the controversy, the airport security officer said that he had a reasonable cause to search and question the passenger. The passenger, on the other hand, said that the additional screening was unwarranted.

> Photo with nonverbal racial/ethnic cue

> **Passenger pulled out of security line at New York's JFK International Airport**

To manipulate racial/ethnic cues in a subtle way that would not overtly sensitize participants to the intent of the study, we altered only the photo accompanying the report, without openly referring to the targeted person's race/ethnicity or national origin. We chose photos that reflected the intended race/ethnicity while holding other traits as constant as possible. This was accomplished by selecting pictures from a pool of forty photos based on ratings provided by an independent panel of eight judges naive to our hypotheses.[11] The judges rated how much each person appeared white or Arab, as well as scoring how friendly, attractive, wealthy, law-abiding, educated, and trustworthy they appeared. We used pictures judged to be significantly different from one another on the race/ethnicity dimension – with perceptions of the race/ethnicity of the person in the picture matching the intended racial/ethnic cue for each condition – but statistically indistinct across all other traits, thereby ensuring the internal validity of our experimental manipulation.[12] The result is a highly conservative test of our hypotheses, narrowly manipulating visual racial/ethnic cues without introducing potential confounds.

As an additional manipulation check, we conducted an online survey via MTurk with a convenience sample of 125 participants naive to the objectives of

---

[11] A graduate research assistant who was an amateur photographer with sophisticated camera equipment walked around the University of Michigan campus for several days asking individuals if they would mind having their picture taken as part of our study. They each signed a release so that their image could be used in our publications. The initial pool consisted of 119 pictures rated by judges, 40 of which matched the intended race/ethnicity cues that we then tested to identify the photos we used in our experimental conditions.

[12] Across the six other trait dimensions, mean differences between any two pictures did not exceed .4 points nor approach statistical significance.

our experiment to further ensure that the pictures we used were representative of the intended racial/ethnic cues.[13] For each of the pictures, we asked our participants: "If you had to guess, which racial/ethnic group do you think this person belongs to?" All participants identified the white-cue photo accurately as white, while 85 percent of participants identified the person in the Arab-cue photo as Arab. These results further confirm the internal validity of our experimental manipulation.[14]

Neither the pictures nor the text contained religious identity cues. This is especially important for the Arab condition, since scholars have found that a majority of Americans generally treat as synonyms the terms "Arab," "Muslim," and "Middle Eastern" (Jackson 1996). Another important dynamic to acknowledge is that most non-Arab Muslims living in the United States are African Americans, and Islam has been historically perceived as a positive force in the African American community (Davis 2006, 210). With these considerations in mind, the photo of the person we selected for the Arab condition contained no Muslim clothing or other Muslim identity cues to ensure the image would primarily trigger the salience of the person's race/ethnicity rather than his religious identity.[15]

After exposure to the news report, participants were asked: "Who are you more likely to agree with in this case – the airport security officer or the passenger?" We assigned a code of "1" for siding with the passenger and "0" for taking the airport security officer's side. Participants reported whether they thought the airport security officer had reasonable cause to conduct an additional search of the passenger. We then compared those who perceived the search to be unreasonable ("definitely" and "probably") versus otherwise.

The experiment also included key measures of civil rights policy preferences pertaining to the terrorism and national security context. Specifically, we asked participants how strongly they supported or opposed: (1) more intensive security checks for passengers at US airports; (2) policies to protect airport security officials from being sued by passengers claiming they have been mistreated; (3) airport security officials holding passengers for questioning even if not charged with a specific crime; and (4) law enforcement officials monitoring people's telephone calls, e-mail accounts, and other forms of communication. The results of Cronbach's alpha tests justify an additive index of terrorism-related civil rights policy preferences ($\alpha = .77$).

We also included measures to capture participants' behavioral intentions to support the civil rights of the targeted persons in situations like the one depicted

---

[13] See the "2015 US Group Empathy Study (MTurk)" section in the Appendix for further details.

[14] These manipulation checks and additional sensitivity analyses are available in the online appendix.

[15] Black Muslims might still identify with Arabs not as an outgroup but as fellow Muslims. This would call into question the presumption that outgroup empathy is at the root of any distinct reactions to terrorist threats. However, there were only a total of 7 Muslims out of 1,799 respondents in our whole dataset (the first and second waves combined). In addition, controls for respondents' religious affiliations did not diminish racial/ethnic differences in reactions to the vignettes.

in the news report. Specifically, we asked participants how likely they were to: (1) request more information about how to protect the rights of passengers; (2) sign an electronic petition to prevent the profiling of passengers at US airports; and (3) attend a public meeting to defend the rights of passengers. These were combined to generate a single summative index ($\alpha = .61$).

EXPERIMENTAL RESULTS

Before analyzing the results, we first checked to ensure our experimental conditions were balanced across ideological orientation and key socio-demographic controls (age, education, gender, income, metropolitan residence, and religion). To do so, we conducted a MANCOVA with Bonferroni adjustment for multiple comparisons. None of the pairwise comparisons across these covariates are statistically significant at the .05 level, thereby confirming balance across conditions and the effectiveness of random assignment. Our goal is first to see if the three racial/ethnic groups respond differently to experimental vignettes as predicted. We then conduct GSEM analyses to determine if group-based empathic reactions to the vignettes indeed help explain any of these intergroup differences while controlling for all of the political and socio-demographic factors included in the previous models.

Siding with the Immigrant Detainee and Perceptions of Reasonable Cause

Figure 5.3 illustrates the predicted probabilities for siding with the passenger and for perceiving the additional search of the passenger to be unreasonable across white versus Arab passenger experimental conditions.[16] We found no significant differences between our three racial/ethnic respondent groups with regards to one's willingness to side with the white passenger. In the Arab passenger condition, however, support dropped off dramatically among white respondents, from 46 to 20 percent, but remained essentially unchanged among African Americans and Latinos. The results therefore indicate significant differences between majority and minority respondent groups in their reactions to the white versus Arab cues. Overall, the results corroborate H3a.

The same basic pattern emerges when respondents consider whether security officials had reasonable cause to conduct the additional search and questioning of the passenger. Whites reported much lower rates of concern that the search was unreasonable in the case of the Arab passenger compared to the white passenger condition. While Latino perceptions of the search as unreasonable were somewhat lower in the Arab passenger condition, they remained

---

[16] As previously mentioned, because the primary stigmatized group in the context of airport security is Arabs, we focus our discussion of the results on reactions to the vignette featuring this group in comparison to the white passenger condition as the baseline. Full results (with coefficients and standard errors for all experimental conditions) are available in the online appendix.

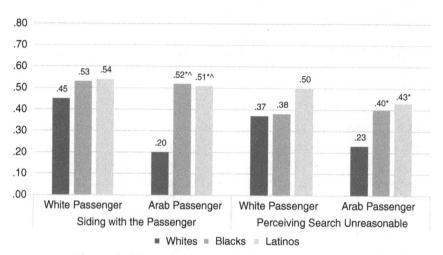

FIGURE 5.3 The probability of siding with the passenger and perceiving search unreasonable upon exposure to white versus Arab passenger vignettes, by respondents' race/ethnicity

Note: Predicted probabilities calculated using the observed-value approach after fitting probit models with robust standard errors. The asterisk denotes which coefficients for blacks and Latinos are statistically distinct from the ones for whites *within* each experimental condition (*p ≤ .05, one-tailed). The symbol ^ denotes whether the comparative effect of exposure to the white versus Arab passenger condition on the outcome is statistically different among blacks or Latinos compared to whites (^p ≤ .05, one-tailed).

Source: 2013/14 US Group Empathy Two-Wave Study (GfK)

significantly higher compared to white respondents. African Americans also perceived the search as unreasonable at significantly higher levels than whites in the Arab condition. We thus find support for H3b.

Support for Civil Rights Policies and Pro–Civil Rights Behavior

Figure 5.4 displays the impact of our racial/ethnic cue manipulation on support for civil rights policies and pro–civil rights behavior concerning terrorism and security issues.[17] As mentioned, the index of civil rights–related policy

---

[17] For ease of presentation, in calculating the predicted probabilities of support for civil rights policies and pro–civil rights behavior, we transformed these measures into a binary format by coding scores 0 through .5 as "0" and scores over .5 to 1 as "1" to differentiate between low and high levels of support for civil rights policies and pro–civil rights behavior. Because these measures consist of multiple scores, presenting predicted probabilities for each score in a graph would not be feasible (particularly since we need to report these for each of the three racial/ethnic respondent groups across all experimental conditions). Analyses with the original ordinal-level variables yield results consistent with those obtained by employing the binary

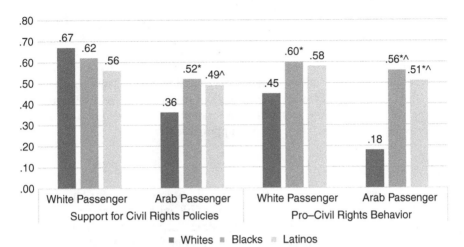

FIGURE 5.4 The probability of support for civil rights policies and pro–civil rights behavior upon exposure to white versus Arab passenger vignettes, by respondents' race/ethnicity
Note: Predicted probabilities calculated using the observed-value approach after fitting probit models with robust standard errors. The asterisk denotes which coefficients for blacks and Latinos are statistically distinct from the ones for whites *within* each experimental condition (*p ≤ .05, one-tailed). The symbol ^ denotes whether the comparative effect of exposure to the white versus Arab passenger condition on the outcome is statistically different among blacks or Latinos compared to whites (^p ≤ .05, one-tailed).
Source: 2013/14 US Group Empathy Two-Wave Study (GfK)

preferences included one's opposition to: (1) more intensive security checks; (2) more protection for airport security officers; (3) greater leeway for questioning a passenger not charged with a specific crime; and (4) heightened law enforcement surveillance. In the white condition, all three racial/ethnic groups were resistant to trading civil rights for security. In the Arab condition, however, opposition to these policies dropped by over 30 percentage points among whites, from 67 to 36 percent, but fell far less among African Americans and Latinos. Therefore, minorities reacted differently to the white versus Arab cues than did whites. These results support H4a.

We found a very similar pattern regarding the effects of the racial/ethnic cue manipulation on pro–civil rights behavioral intentions. As mentioned earlier, this measure consisted of one's likelihood to: (1) request more information; (2)

forms. As an alternative method, we conducted OLS regression analyses and created graphs with regression coefficients (instead of predicted probabilities) for each of the three racial/ethnic respondent groups across experimental conditions. These regression results are also consistent with the results of the probit analyses.

sign a petition; and (3) attend a public meeting in order to protect passenger rights in cases like the one in the vignette. African Americans and Latinos were much more likely to engage in such actions across both the white and Arab passenger conditions. However, whites were even less likely to engage in these acts if exposed to the Arab passenger vignette (18 percent) instead of the white passenger one (45 percent). This once again produced statistically significant differences between white versus minority respondent groups in reactions to the white versus Arab cues. These results support H4b.

A REPLICATION

We also analyzed data from another national survey experiment, the 2012 US Group Empathy Pilot Study, conducted via GfK with a separate pool of 621 randomly selected participants, including 221 whites, 193 African Americans, and 207 Latinos. This survey experiment included the same experimental vignette and the same photos used in the 2013/14 two-wave study to manipulate the racial/ethnic cues along with two key dependent variables – siding with the passenger and perceiving the search unreasonable. The results of this pilot study are consistent with our main findings, demonstrating that African Americans and Latinos are much more likely than whites to side with the Arab passenger and to perceive the search as unreasonable (see Figure 5.5).

An alternate explanation for these results that does not depend on outgroup empathy lies in the concept of linked fate. What if African Americans and Latinos simply think their fates are linked with Arabs as part of a larger stigmatized minority community? If so, ingroup interest - not outgroup empathy - might be driving these reactions across racial/ethnic groups in the sample. To address this possibility, the survey portion of the pilot study included a measure of linked fate to gauge this alternative causal mechanism for explaining divergent group reactions to the experimental vignette. However, as demonstrated in Chapter 3, African Americans and Latinos felt no more linked fate toward Arabs than they did toward whites. So linked fate toward Arabs – or feeling disconnected from whites – cannot explain these findings.

In addition to the reactions to the experimental vignette, we also measured respondents' preexisting attitudes about the racial profiling of Arabs and the civil rights–security trade-off, as well as respondents' emotional reactions – anger, anxiety, fear, and sadness – in response to terrorism threats. Previous research suggests that distinct emotional experiences lead to different policy preferences. For instance, Skitka et al. (2006) find that anger was strongly linked to support for expanding the "War on Terror" beyond Afghanistan, whereas fear predicted support for the deportation of Arabs, Muslims, and first-generation immigrants. On a parallel basis, Huddy et al. (2005, 2009) find that high levels of anxiety induced by the 9/11 attacks reduced support for aggressive military action against terrorism. Given these

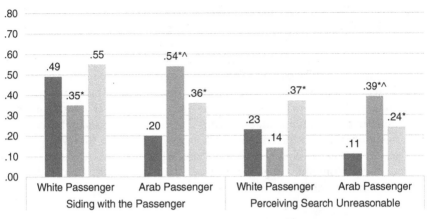

FIGURE 5.5 The probability of siding with the passenger and perceiving search unreasonable upon exposure to white versus Arab passenger vignettes, by respondents' race/ethnicity – a replication
Note: Predicted probabilities calculated using the observed-value approach after fitting probit models with robust standard errors. The asterisk denotes which coefficients for blacks and Latinos are statistically distinct from the ones for whites *within* each experimental condition (*p ≤ .05, one-tailed). The symbol ^ denotes whether the comparative effect of exposure to the white versus Arab passenger condition on the outcome is statistically different among blacks or Latinos compared to whites (^p ≤ .05, one-tailed).
Source: 2012 US Group Empathy Pilot Study (GfK)

findings, Huddy et al. (2009, 306) conclude: "If fear-mongering heightens a sense of national threat without increasing public anxiety, it is likely to increase support for aggressive government anti-terrorist policies." The pilot study allowed us to conduct sensitivity analyses with extended models that control for these key emotional states.

The survey experiment also included an alternative measure, group-specific sympathy, as a more limited, affective correlate of group empathy.[18] As discussed in Chapter 2, we do not treat group empathy and sympathy interchangeably. Instead, we consider sympathy as one of the key emotional consequences of empathy. Both African American and Latino respondents expressed higher levels of sympathy for the Arab community than white respondents did, aligned with their reactions to the experimental stimuli and responses to the posttest attitudinal questions. Sympathy for Arabs had

---

[18] The alternative measure focused on sympathy felt for several groups in society, including Arabs. Specifically, we asked respondents: "How often have you felt sympathy toward each of the following groups?" with response options ranging from "not at all" to "very much."

a significant effect on one's opposition to their racial profiling (p ≤ .05).[19] The probability of perceiving the racial profiling of Arabs for security purposes as never justifiable doubles from 7 to 14 percent as one moves from the lowest to the highest level of sympathy for Arabs. Similarly, one's concern for the violation of individual rights and liberties in exchange for national security was also significantly influenced by one's level of sympathy for Arabs (p ≤ .001). The probability of being very concerned surges from 17 to 50 percent moving from the minimum to maximum value on sympathy for Arabs. In short, the results of the pilot study were consistent with those of the two-wave survey experiment reported earlier and remained robust even when controlling for a host of emotional reactions (i.e., anger, anxiety, fear, and sadness) triggered by the possibility of a terrorist attack on US soil.

EXPLAINING MINORITY–MAJORITY DIFFERENCES
IN REACTIONS VIA GROUP EMPATHY

In Chapter 2 we theorized that those high in group empathy – particularly minorities – would react much more strongly to incidents that involve the suffering and discriminatory treatment of marginalized communities and that these stronger empathic reactions would alter political responses. In Chapter 3 we found that the GEI significantly predicted empathic reactions to the targeted persons featured in our experimental vignettes across both the airport security and immigrant detention contexts. In Chapter 4 we found in a nationally representative sample that whites, African Americans, and Latinos differed significantly on all indicators of group empathy. And in this chapter we found that these groups indeed reacted differently to specific threats based on the race/ethnicity of the individual target (i.e., white versus Arab passengers) in an experimental setting. This is a lot of circumstantial evidence in support of our causal model. Still, we can tie these findings together to test whether the intergroup variation in policy reactions is really a function of differences in group-based empathy. To do so, we conduct GSEM analyses. The outcomes we are most interested in here are the same as what we have focused on thus far: reactions to search and questioning decisions in the context of airport security, support for civil rights policies, and behavioral intentions to protect people targeted by law enforcement and security personnel.

Figure 5.6 presents the results of path analyses of the experimental data. The bootstrap tests indicate that group-based empathic reactions to the experimental vignettes significantly mediate intergroup differences we observe in all of our outcome variables, even after controlling for party identification, ideology, SDO, ethnocentrism, authoritarianism, perceived threats, political trust, and a host of socio-demographic factors. As Group

---

[19] See the online appendix for full results.

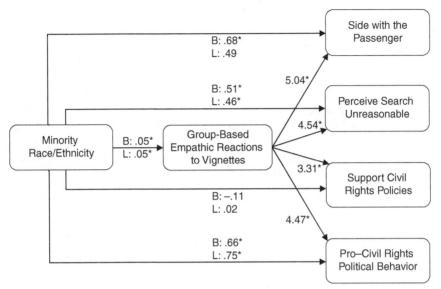

FIGURE 5.6 The role of group empathy in explaining racial/ethnic differences in reactions to the "Flying While Arab" experiment
Note: Path coefficients estimated using generalized structural equation modeling based on the full models. "B" denotes blacks and "L" denotes Latinos. White respondents constitute the baseline category. All indirect paths are statistically significant. All variables are rescaled to run from 0 to 1. *p ≤ .05, one-tailed.
Source: 2013/14 US Group Empathy Two-Wave Study (GfK)

Empathy Theory would predict, African Americans and Latinos react much more empathically to an ambiguous situation where the person under scrutiny is potentially unfairly targeted, regardless of their race/ethnicity, and these empathic reactions in turn affect the outcomes of interest, providing strong empirical support for H5.[20]

A leading alternative explanation for the distinct intergroup reactions to such ambiguous situations is simply that whites perceive them to be more threatening than do minority groups. On its face, this alternative seems improbable, because minorities are significantly more likely than whites to feel vulnerable to terrorist attacks (Davis 2006; Eisenman et al. 2009). Nevertheless, we tested this alternative mechanism using perceived threat of terrorism as a possible explanation for the racial/ethnic group differences in all of the outcomes we have discussed in this chapter. Under the existential threat hypothesis, the racial/ethnic groups who perceive themselves at higher risk from terrorism should be *less* likely to side with the Arab passenger; *more* likely to perceive

---

[20] See the online appendix for full estimates of these analyses.

the additional search as reasonable; and *more* supportive of policies and actions to increase security at the expense of civil rights and liberties.

We first conducted ANCOVA with Bonferroni correction to compare the differences in group means vis-à-vis the preexisting levels of perceived threat for terrorism as measured in our first-wave survey. Whites, African Americans, and Latinos all perceived the nation to be at high risk for another terrorist attack at the time of our study (fielded in December 2013–January 2014), but there were no significant racial/ethnic group differences in these perceptions (M_{White} = .66, M_{Black} = .67, and M_{Latino} = .68, p > .10). On the other hand, African Americans and Latinos perceived themselves to be at significantly *higher* personal risk from terrorism than whites in our sample (M_{White} = .44, M_{Black} = .52, and M_{Latino} = .50; p ≤ .05). The size and direction of these group differences suggest that it cannot be whites' perceptions of threat that drive the pattern of results we report. African Americans and Latinos were either equally or more concerned about terrorism compared to whites. Therefore, something else must explain minorities' significantly higher levels of support for the Arab passenger in the airport security vignette, as well as their stronger commitment to pro-civil rights policies and actions in this domain.

To be sure, we once again ran GSEM analyses with bootstrapping. The results demonstrate that, while perceived threat directly reduces support for the passenger and civil rights policies, it does not have a significant mediating effect on any of our dependent variables.[21] Racial/ethnic differences in perceptions of terrorism threat, then, do not explain the concomitant differences in support for individuals subjected to discrimination for the benefit of national security, nor do they explain intergroup differences in civil rights–related policy views or political action tendencies.

CONCLUSION

This chapter tested Group Empathy Theory in the context of homeland security. We found that, compared to whites, African Americans and Latinos exhibit more favorable attitudes toward Arabs and higher opposition to discriminatory practices targeting this group. Our experimental findings further corroborate these survey results by demonstrating that African Americans and Latinos are more cognizant of the profiling of Arabs in airport security and are thus more likely to side with an Arab passenger targeted by TSA officers even when their perceived threat of terrorism is similar to and at times higher than that of whites.

---

[21] See the online appendix for full results.

These findings encourage longitudinal explorations of group empathy and its consequences going forward. The same potential threat triggers very different reactions across groups and that those different reactions are explained by outgroup empathy. An important hint comes from results in a study by Davis (2006), who set out to explain public reactions in the wake of an existential security threat – the attacks of September 11, 2001 (see also Davis & Silver 2004). Analyzing data collected in the first three years after the 9/11 attacks, Davis found that sociotropic threat perceptions were initially the strongest determinants of the public's willingness to concede civil liberties for security. Whites and Latinos were much more willing than African Americans to make this trade-off. Furthermore, analyses of feeling thermometer ratings indicated that Latinos viewed Arabs more negatively even than did whites, while no statistically significant differences existed between African Americans and whites at the time (Davis 2006, 211). Davis also found that higher levels of perceived threat among African Americans and Latinos caused them to reject Arabs. However, he suggested that such group differences might be subject to change as the public's anxiety about terrorism wanes over time or if another major terrorist attack were to occur. Davis suggested that this change was related to declining trust in political authorities in the years following the attacks. We suspect changes in outgroup empathy may have also played an important role.

Immediately after 9/11, nearly every non-Arab US citizen might have felt high levels of terror threat and distrust of Arabs. Over time, having observed the plight of Arabs as victims of racial profiling and stigmatization, non-whites may have moderated their policy views as a result of higher levels of outgroup empathy. In a national survey conducted in 2004, Shildkraut (2009) found that both blacks and Latinos more strongly opposed racial profiling not only toward their own groups but also toward Arabs and people who looked Middle Eastern. According to Alsultany (2006, 141), "Prior discussions on racial profiling focused on 'DWB' (Driving While Black/Brown), and shifted to 'FWA' (Flying While Arab), creating a parallel experience shared by African Americans, Latinos, and now Arabs in being racialized and criminalized." Just such a process of empathizing with Arabs may thus have occurred among African Americans and Latinos in the months and years after 9/11.

The evolution of group empathy for Arabs, especially among minority citizens, may be further triggered by witnessing anti-Muslim/anti-Arab rhetoric and policies in the Trump era. After all, African Americans and Latinos have also been targeted by Trump's racialized discourse and policy enactments on matters of immigration, national security, law enforcement, and criminal justice, among others. Contemporary rhetoric also fuses threats of Latinx immigration and Middle Eastern terrorism. For instance, on October 22, 2018, Trump tweeted that "criminals and unknown Middle

Easterners are mixed in" what he called the "caravan" of Central American immigrants who were headed on foot toward the United States.[22] He then declared the situation a national emergency and dispatched US troops to the southern border. Later, Trump repeated his claim to White House reporters by stating: "You're going to find MS-13, you're going to find Middle Eastern. You're going to find everything. And guess what? We're not allowing them in our country. We want safety."[23] Such claims are not only unsubstantiated – a fact Trump himself later momentarily acknowledged before re-denying – but they also stigmatize both Latino immigrants and people of Middle Eastern descent.[24] In reaction to Trump's remarks, Abed Ayoub, legal and policy director of civil rights organization the American-Arab Anti-Discrimination Committee, noted: "It's playing on people's fears. It is looking at our community, the brown communities, the black communities, the Arab communities – all of us – through the same lens – as a threat to our national security."[25] The institutionalization of discrimination represented by racial profiling cases like the "Flying While Arab" phenomenon along with Trump's Islamophobic, anti-Arab discourse and executive actions may thus remind African Americans and Latinos of what they perceive to be arbitrary law enforcement scrutiny and discriminatory government policies, triggered primarily by the color of their skin and spelling of their name.

We do not conceptualize group empathy as a trait exclusive to minorities. Our findings demonstrate quite compellingly that group empathy has a strong, reliable, and direct effect on policy preferences and political behavior *regardless* of one's race/ethnicity. Even though whites may not have the first-hand experience of racial profiling and discrimination, they still have the capacity to develop reactive empathy for the plight of others, by witnessing and becoming informed about the injustices inflicted on various groups. There are indeed many inspiring stories of whites acting empathically and in solidarity with Arabs and Muslims in the post-9/11 era, such as a white Christian woman from Illinois, Jessey Eagan, who decided to wear hijab for forty days during the Lent season of 2015. In an interview, Eagan

---

[22] See https://twitter.com/realdonaldtrump/status/1054351078328885248?lang=en.

[23] Scott Horsley (2018), "Fact Check: President Trump's False Claims on Migrant Caravan, Tax Cuts," NPR, www.npr.org/2018/10/23/659917659/fact-check-president-trumps-false-claims-on-migrant-caravan-tax-cuts.

[24] After being repeatedly asked by reporters to provide evidence for his claims on Middle Easterners hiding in the migrant caravan, Trump conceded that "there's no proof of anything" while adding that "there very well could be." See Jennifer Epstein and Justin Sink (2018), "President Trump Admits He Has 'No Proof' Terrorists Are in the Migrant Caravan," *Time*, http://time.com/5432702/trump-no-proof-terrorists-migrant-caravan/.

[25] Rowaida Abdelaziz (2018), "Trump's 'Unknown Middle Easterners' Tweet is Both False and Racist," *HuffPost*, www.huffpost.com/entry/trump-twitter-unknown-middle-easterners_n_5bc f652ae4b0d38b587d11c5.

said she wanted to practice hospitality "by stepping into the shoes of another person, just to kind of get a glimpse into what their public life is like, and I wanted to do that to remind myself what it feels like to be on the margins of society."[26] It is this kind of active, empathic engagement that would benefit society as a whole and help facilitate civil rights protections without undermining national security.

[26] See www.cnn.com/videos/us/2015/03/08/newsroom-christian-woman-wears-hijab-for-lent.cnn.

6

Group Empathy and the Politics of Immigration

> Not like the brazen giant of Greek fame,
> With conquering limbs astride from land to land;
> Here at our sea-washed, sunset gates shall stand
> A mighty woman with a torch, whose flame
> Is the imprisoned lightning, and her name
> Mother of Exiles. From her beacon-hand
> Glows world-wide welcome; her mild eyes command
> The air-bridged harbor that twin cities frame.
> "Keep, ancient lands, your storied pomp!" cries she
> With silent lips. "Give me your tired, your poor,
> Your huddled masses yearning to breathe free,
> The wretched refuse of your teeming shore.
> Send these, the homeless, tempest-tost to me,
> I lift my lamp beside the golden door!"
>
> Emma Lazarus, "The New Colossus" (1883)

On July 4, 2018, a black woman made national news headlines for scaling the Statue of Liberty in protest of the Trump administration's family separation policy at the USA–Mexico border. A naturalized American citizen who arrived from Congo twenty-four years ago, Therese Patricia Okoumou told the police who surrounded her that she would not come down until they released all of the immigrant children in cages. Taking shelter in the green metal folds of Lady Liberty's robes on Independence Day, Okoumou feared that the police on the ground or in the law enforcement helicopters flying around would shoot or tranquilize her, but nevertheless she persisted in shouting: "My life doesn't matter to me now – what matters to me is that in a democracy we are holding children in cages."[1] She was

---

[1] Joanna Walters (2018), "'Are They Going to Shoot Me?': Statue of Liberty Climber on Her Anti-Trump Protest," *The Guardian*, www.theguardian.com/us-news/2018/jul/07/statue-of-liberty-protester-patricia-okoumou-interview?CMP=twt_gu.

apprehended after a four-hour standoff. Okoumou faced up to eighteen months in prison, though in the end she was sentenced to five years' probation and 200 hours of community service. In an interview, Okoumou said she experienced a strange tranquility as she spent the night in federal custody: "I felt peaceful, that I was with those children in spirit. I could feel their isolation and their cries being answered only by four walls."[2]

What compelled Okoumou to risk her freedom and life to stand against the separation of mostly Central American immigrant children from their families at the USA–Mexico border? Since she was protesting Trump's policies, one might guess it was party identification and ideology. Considering she was donning a "White Supremacy is Terrorism" t-shirt in front of the federal courthouse where she was tried, others might suspect it was a reaction against racial hierarchy in general. As an immigrant herself, perhaps identification with other immigrants drove her. Even though any individual act can have myriad causes, we think outgroup empathy plays a key role in reactions like these. While Okoumou was African American, the child separation policies she was protesting mostly impacted the Latinx community. We suspect group empathy can be a powerful determinant of decisions like Okoumou's to rally on behalf of the rights of others.

In this chapter we explore the effects of group empathy on immigration policy preferences and attitudes toward newcomers using data from the 2013/14 US Group Empathy Two-Wave Study. Our experimental vignette was a news story about an undocumented immigrant at a detention center who asked for, but was denied, medical attention. The pattern of results is very similar to those discovered in Chapter 5, when our focus was national security and terror threat. But first, let us discuss contemporary US immigration rhetoric and policies, as well as public reactions.

A NATION OF, OR AGAINST, IMMIGRANTS?

Globalization poses both opportunities and challenges for any nation. International labor flows create opportunities for the poorest of the world in ethnically and culturally distant lands. Accommodating newcomers often challenges nations trying to build social welfare programs to adequately serve their own citizens. Immigration openness also often carries some security risk to the receiving nations. As the international reach of terrorist organizations grows, and as drug and human trafficking by violent cartels continues, the debate over the proper balance between welcoming newcomers and protecting citizens intensifies.

Against this backdrop, understanding the causal dynamics of public opinion about immigration is important. When the issue of immigration is framed along the lines of threat and fear, the ensuing public animosity toward immigrants

---

[2] Ibid.

may fuel scapegoating, discriminatory practices, and hate crimes. This in turn paves the way for extreme policies, as political elites sense they have the public's backing to clamp down. The Trump administration's immigration platform may represent a cultivation of such negative frames. In his presidential announcement speech on June 16, 2015, Donald Trump asserted: "When Mexico sends its people, they're not sending their best. They're not sending you. They're not sending you. They're sending people that have lots of problems, and they're bringing those problems with [them]. They're bringing drugs. They're bringing crime. They're rapists. And some, I assume, are good people."[3] While most political pundits suspected that Trump's hostile rhetoric about immigration and national security would hold limited appeal, he nonetheless dominated the Republican primary process against sixteen more mainstream conservative opponents and eventually became the forty-fifth president of the United States by defeating Hillary Clinton through the Electoral College.

If diverse public reactions to the current immigration rhetoric and policies in the United States are simply a product of partisan divides, we would not need to look to group empathy as an explanation. There is no doubt that Democrats and Republicans deeply disagree, on average, in this policy area. Yet there are some immigration policies where partisan polarization is stronger than others. For instance, according to a 2018 PRRI poll, 74 percent of Republicans think immigrants "burden local communities by using more than their share of social services," while only 35 percent of Democrats feel the same way.[4] By comparison, a 2018 CBS News poll shows that nearly eight out of ten Republicans and nine out of ten Democrats favor "allowing immigrants who were brought to the US illegally as children to stay."[5] Party identification is not the only driver of immigration policy views.

Alternatively, the perceived severity of threats due to immigration may drive opinions on these policies. Some Americans may simply buy into the "criminal immigrant" stereotype, even if the facts undermine such beliefs. Those misperceptions may lead to concerns about their own safety and the nation's security, which in turn drive anti-immigrant policy support. Perceived economic threats, bolstered by the discourse that immigrants are "stealing American jobs" and straining US resources, could also be central to opinions about these policies.

If perceived threats – be they existential or economic – drive immigration policy opinion, African Americans should display the strongest opposition

---

[3] For the full text of Trump's presidential campaign announcement, see http://wapo.st/1HPABjR?tid=ss_mail.

[4] See https://immigrationforum.org/article/american-attitudes-on-immigration-steady-but-showing-more-partisan-divides/.

[5] Jennifer De Pinto, Fred Backus, Kabir Khanna, and Anthony Salvanto (2018), CBS News, "Most Americans Support DACA, But Oppose Border Wall – CBS News Poll," www.cbsnews.com/news/most-americans-support-daca-but-oppose-border-wall-cbs-news-poll/.

to newcomers. After all, they are more likely to be victims of violent crime (Harrell 2007) and to suffer from wage declines and unemployment due to increases in the size of the low-skilled workforce (Borjas et al. 2010). But that is not what we observe. According to the 2018 General Social Survey, while 41 percent of whites want a decrease in immigration, only 24 percent of blacks agree. They are in near perfect agreement with Latinos, of whom only 22 percent support decreased immigration.[6] As mentioned in the Prologue, a 2018 Quinnipiac poll indicated that nearly nine out of ten African Americans oppose Trump's border wall. This is the highest opposition among all racial/ethnic groups, surpassing even Latinos, at 71 percent.[7]

Group Empathy Theory predicts that variation in public attitudes about immigration arises largely from an empathy gap between different groups in society. Those higher in group empathy are likely to be much more reactive to anti-immigrant rhetoric and policies. Group empathy can even override partisan allegiances, especially for certain issues like DACA, which involves children and young adults and thus is particularly prone to activate empathic responses.[8] And because of their own history of stigmatization, we expect minorities to display the highest tendency to side with immigrants. In the next section, we present hypotheses for the effects of group empathy on general attitudes toward undocumented immigrants along with our predictions regarding intergroup differences in reactions of white, black, and Latino respondents to the immigrant detention experiment.

HYPOTHESES AND DATA

Public opinion about immigration is often assumed to be monolithic, and little is known about the size or explanation for differences across racial or ethnic group lines. However, many public opinion domains appear to be group-centric: the media often discuss policies, and the public often thinks about them, in terms of who gets what and whether they deserve it (Nelson & Kinder 1996). Large racial and ethnic opinion gaps persist in many policy domains. Policies closely linked to racial redistribution, for example, often receive much less support from whites than from blacks (Kinder & Winter 2001). There is reason to believe that immigration opinions might display similar contours, and Group Empathy Theory might explain intergroup differences in political attitudes and behavior toward immigrants.

---

[6] Amy Taxin (2019), "Poll: More Americans Want Immigration to Stay the Same," AP News, www.apnews.com/fd35d6b9eba64f8e884168ef064be080.

[7] See https://poll.qu.edu/images/polling/us/us04112018_ugnt28.pdf/.

[8] The results in Chapter 8 demonstrate that group empathy is indeed the best predictor of support for DACA, above and beyond other predispositions including party identification and ideology.

Based on the premises of our theory, we hypothesize that group empathy significantly increases perceived discrimination against undocumented immigrants (H1a) and opposition to the racial profiling of undocumented immigrants by law enforcement (H1b). Those who score high in group empathy are also more likely to oppose deportations targeting immigrants of Latino descent (H1c).

We also anticipate significant intergroup differences in opinion arising from group empathy. The race/ethnicity of an undocumented immigrant was experimentally manipulated in a news story about an ambiguous incident at a detention center. African Americans and Latinos should be more likely to side with nonwhite detainees over detention center officials (H2a). Minority respondents should also perceive law enforcement decisions targeting immigrant detainees to be unreasonable (H2b), even when the detainees are from a different racial/ethnic group than their own. The theory also predicts that African Americans and Latinos will exhibit higher support for civil rights protections (H3a) and stronger commitments to political action for addressing the plight of undocumented immigrants (H3b). Upon exposure to experimental vignettes, African Americans and Latinos should also exhibit stronger opposition to deportation policies, particularly those targeting nonwhite groups and especially if the racial/ethnic cue matches the race/ethnicity of the group targeted by such policies (H4). Last, differences in group-based empathic reactions between whites and nonwhites should explain gaps in policy opinions and political action tendencies (H5).

To test these hypotheses, we employ data from the 2013/14 US Group Empathy Two-Wave Study, fielded nationally by GfK with 1,799 randomly selected respondents (633 whites, 614 African Americans, and 552 Latinos). Our focus in the second-wave portion of the data is on the immigrant detention experiment, conducted with a total of 671 participants (244 whites, 217 African Americans, and 210 Latinos) from the first wave. We next describe in detail our experimental design.

THE IMMIGRANT DETENTION EXPERIMENT

This experiment employs a between-subjects design, which manipulated an ambiguously threatening news vignette about an undocumented immigrant held at a US detention center. As in the "Flying While Arab" experiment detailed in Chapter 5, we carefully altered only the race/ethnicity of the immigrant detainee featured in the vignette. The experimental design consists of four conditions, with the same vignette featuring an immigrant of either white, Arab, black, or Latino descent.[9] This design allows us to compare reactions to each racial/ethnic cue across whites, African Americans, and Latinos.

---

[9] The experimental conditions are statistically balanced in ideological orientation and all major socio-demographic factors, thereby indicating effective random assignment.

The news vignette depicted an ambiguous incident in which a detainee claimed he was suffering from a serious health condition. Treatment would have necessitated transportation to a hospital outside the detention facility, but detention center officials denied the request because they considered him a flight risk.[10] A caption under the picture read: "Detainee denied medical attention due to alleged flight risk." The news report read as follows:

Controversy at the Detention Center: Medical Negligence or Flight Risk?

Recently, there have been several investigative reports regarding the condition of undocumented immigrants being held in detention centers around the United States. The reports indicate that some detainees are held for long periods of time under inhumane conditions, lacking sufficient nutrition, proper sanitary facilities, access to legal counseling, or even contact with family members. The reports also discuss cases of medical negligence concerning the treatment of detainees with serious health problems. In one case, a detainee told authorities he was suffering from severe chest pain, profound shortness of breath, and dizziness and asked for immediate medical attention. However, these situations require supervised transportation to a hospital several miles away from the detention center. In response, detention center officials denied the detainee this medical service because they considered him to be

Photo with nonverbal racial/ethnic cue
Detainee denied medical attention due to alleged flight risk

a flight risk. The officials said they had a reasonable cause to deny medical attention outside the facility. The detainee, on the other hand, said that the denial of medical attention was unwarranted and that his health was continuing to deteriorate.

After reading the vignette, it was up to participants to decide how to interpret the incident. For some, the denial of medical attention was reasonable considering the potential threat posed by the detainee, while others thought it was unfair and inhumane to deny treatment in this circumstance.[11] In the posttest, similar to the "Flying While Arab" experiment, participants indicated whether they sided more with the detainee or with the detention center officials, as well as whether they thought the conduct of the officials was reasonable. The posttest questionnaire also included measures of participants' civil-rights policy preferences pertaining

---

[10] This experimental scenario was inspired by an actual incident as well as official reports on the conditions of immigrants held in detention centers. See Nina Bernstein (2009), "Immigrant Detainee Dies, and a Life is Buried, Too," *New York Times*, www.nytimes.com/2009/04/03/nyregion/03detain.html?_r=1&. See also Dora Schriro (2009), "Immigration Detention Overview and Recommendations," Immigration and Customs Enforcement (ICE), www.ice.gov/doclib/about/offices/odpp/pdf/ice-detention-rpt.pdf.

[11] In designing this scenario, we once again followed Peffley and Hurwitz's (2010) strategy of depicting a controversial incident in an ambiguous manner that allows for open interpretation by respondents.

to undocumented immigrants. Specifically, we asked participants how strongly they supported or opposed: (1) more intensive immigration policies aimed at capturing and deporting undocumented immigrants; (2) policies to protect immigrant detention center officials from being sued by detainees claiming mistreatment; (3) law enforcement officials detaining anyone who cannot verify their legal status even if not charged with a specific crime; and (4) giving undocumented immigrants a chance to keep their jobs and apply for legal status. Using these items, we generated a reliable additive index of immigration-related civil-rights policy preferences ($\alpha = .75$).

We also measured participants' commitment to political action in defense of the rights of undocumented immigrants by asking how likely they were to: (1) request more information about how to protect the rights of detainees; (2) sign an electronic petition to improve the conditions in immigrant detention centers; and (3) attend a public meeting to defend the rights of detainees. We then generated an additive index of pro–civil rights behavior ($\alpha = .73$). Participants also reported how strongly they supported or opposed more intensive immigration policies aimed at capturing and deporting undocumented immigrants of white, Latino, black, and Arab descent. Response options ranged from "very strongly support" to "very strongly oppose" on a 5-point scale, with higher values thus indicating higher opposition to deportation policies targeting these groups.

SURVEY RESULTS

We first analyze the Wave I survey data to test our hypotheses about the effects of group empathy on general attitudes concerning undocumented immigrants (H1a–H1c). Ordered logistic regression analyses with sample weights were conducted. All models include controls for a host of socio-demographic factors, as well as partisanship, ideology, SDO, ethnocentrism, authoritarianism, and trust in political authorities. We also control for not only general perceptions of threat concerning immigration and terrorism but also perceptions of threat specifically directed at undocumented immigrants as an outgroup. The models even control for personal experience of discrimination to show that the effects of group empathy are not only a reflection of encounters with law enforcement, though such experiences may help cultivate group empathy over time, as theorized in Chapter 2 and empirically demonstrated in Chapter 4. These are conservative tests of Group Empathy Theory. If the effect of group empathy is robust even with other competing explanatory factors of immigration attitudes controlled, it will increase confidence that this dimension is independently important for explaining political attitudes and behavior.

Perceptions of discrimination against undocumented immigrants were measured by asking respondents how fairly they think law enforcement officials treat undocumented immigrants on a 4-point scale ranging from "very fairly" to "very unfairly." To measure opposition to racial profiling practices targeting undocumented immigrants, we asked respondents: "Assuming it could help improve national security, how strongly do you support or oppose police and other law enforcement officials (such as border patrol and airport security) stopping and questioning [undocumented immigrants] simply on the basis of their appearance?" Response options ranged on a 5-point scale from "strongly support" to "strongly oppose." We also inquired about respondents' opposition to strict deportation policies targeting undocumented immigrants of Latino descent – the primary group affected by such punitive measures. The response options again ranged on a 5-point scale.

Once again, group empathy, as measured by the Group Empathy Index (GEI), is a statistically significant and substantively large predictor of a variety of policy views concerning undocumented immigrants (see Table 6.1). Regardless of how we measure opinions about undocumented immigrants, group empathy powerfully predicts more favorable attitudes even after controlling for a large set of alternative factors. The effect of group empathy on perceived discrimination against undocumented immigrants is statistically significant and substantively larger than several key alternative factors, including party identification, ideology, authoritarianism, and perceptions of threat regarding undocumented immigrants and terrorism. More specifically, the probability of deeming the treatment of undocumented immigrants as very unfair increases from 19 to 35 percent as the GEI moves from its minimum to maximum value. Those who have higher group empathy are also significantly more likely to oppose racial profiling of undocumented immigrants. The magnitude of this effect is larger than many competitive explanatory factors, once again surpassing the effects of party identification and ideology, among others. The probability of strongly supporting racial profiling of undocumented immigrants drops from 31 to 19 percent as the GEI moves from its lowest to highest score. Group empathy also has a significant effect on one's opposition to stricter immigration policies aimed at capturing and deporting undocumented immigrants of Latino descent. The probability of strongly supporting such policies decreases from 32 to 21 percent as the GEI moves from low to high scores. Overall, these results corroborate our first set of hypotheses.

EXPERIMENTAL RESULTS

Siding with the Immigrant Detainee and Perceptions of Reasonable Cause

Figure 6.1 illustrates the predicted probabilities for siding with the immigrant detainee, calculated using the observed-value approach after fitting probit models. Of the three racial/ethnic respondent groups, African Americans displayed the most support for nonwhite detainees, particularly blacks and Latinos – the latter providing the strongest evidence in line with Group Empathy Theory. When the immigrant detainee in the vignette was black, African Americans were significantly more likely to take his side (75 percent),

TABLE 6.1 *The relationship between group empathy and attitudes about undocumented immigrants*

	Perceived discrimination against undocumented immigrants		Opposition to profiling undocumented immigrants		Opposition to deporting undocumented Latino immigrants	
	β	S.E.	β	S.E.	β	S.E.
Group empathy	1.00**	.39	.91**	.35	.77*	.36
Experience of discrimination	.95***	.26	.88***	.27	.96***	.22
SDO	−2.02***	.42	−1.43***	.43	−1.14**	.41
Ethnocentrism	1.36**	.54	−1.51***	.47	.30	.54
Authoritarianism	−.40†	.24	−.39	.25	−.69**	.23
Political trust	−1.02***	.29	−.09	.31	.32	.28
Threat of undocumented immigrants	−.35	.29	−1.76***	.30	−1.84***	.27
Terrorism threat	.02	.30	−.78***	.26	−.25	.26
Immigration threat	−1.43***	.31	−1.43***	.30	−1.92***	.28
Party ID	−.91***	.26	−.71***	.24	−.74***	.24
Ideology	−.28	.32	.17	.32	.12	.33
Black	.22	.17	.46**	.18	.16	.17
Latino	.29	.19	.47**	.18	.30	.19
Female	.15	.12	.17	.12	.28*	.12
Education	−.03	.47	−.70	.46	−1.34**	.48
Age	−.03	.35	−1.30***	.32	−.54	.34
Income	−.04	.29	−.13	.30	−.31	.27
Married	−.22	.15	−.03	.14	.04	.14
Employed	−.11	.14	−.07	.13	−.03	.14
Metropolitan residence	.07	.19	.20	.21	.18	.17
Catholic	.21	.16	.02	.16	.09	.16
Household size	.31	.43	−.35	.38	.50	.37
N	1,673		1,685		1,687	

Note: Coefficients estimated using ordered logistic regression. Data are weighted. All variables are rescaled to run from 0 to 1. †p ≤ .10, *p ≤ .05, **p ≤ .01, and ***p ≤ .001, two-tailed.
Source: 2013/14 US Group Empathy Two-Wave Study (GfK)

while white respondents were less so (37 percent). Comparing the results between the white detainee and black detainee conditions, one sees that African American support rose by 28 percentage points, while white support declined by

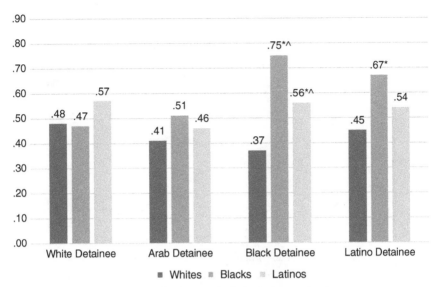

FIGURE 6.1 The probability of siding with the immigrant detainee upon exposure to white versus nonwhite detainee vignettes, by respondents' race/ethnicity

Note: Predicted probabilities calculated using the observed-value approach after fitting probit models with robust standard errors. The asterisk denotes which coefficients for blacks and Latinos are statistically distinct from the ones for whites *within* each experimental condition (*p ≤ .05, one-tailed). The symbol ^ denotes whether the comparative effect of exposure to the white versus nonwhite detainee condition on the outcome is statistically different among blacks or Latinos compared to whites (^p ≤ .05, one-tailed).

Source: 2013/14 US Group Empathy Two-Wave Study (GfK)

11 percentage points, an obviously significant polarizing effect. Of course, this pattern is consistent with ingroup affinity, not necessarily group empathy. However, when the immigrant detainee was Latino, African Americans were still more likely to take his side (67 percent) compared to whites (45 percent), representing both a significant difference between African American and white reactions *within* the Latino detainee condition as well as a significant difference in such reactions *across* white versus Latino detainee conditions.

The findings show that Latino support for the detainee – while consistently higher than white support – was unchanged by the race/ethnicity of the individual featured in the vignette. Interestingly, Latinos did not even support the Latino detainee more than they did the white detainee (54 percent compared to 57 percent). In this case, Latinos did not seem to be driven by a desire to protect an ingroup member in trouble. On the other hand, Latino support for the black detainee (56 percent) was significantly higher than among whites (37 percent), a group difference we think may be driven by their higher overall level of empathy for marginalized outgroups. Nevertheless, we do not find that Latinos react much

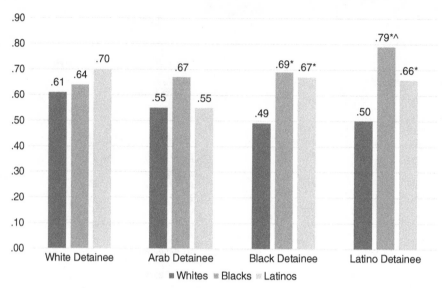

FIGURE 6.2 The probability of perceiving denial of medical attention unreasonable upon exposure to white versus nonwhite detainee vignettes, by respondents' race/ethnicity

Note: Predicted probabilities calculated using the observed-value approach after fitting probit models with robust standard errors. The asterisk denotes which coefficients for blacks and Latinos are statistically distinct from the ones for whites *within* each experimental condition (*$p \leq .05$, one-tailed). The symbol ^ denotes whether the comparative effect of exposure to the white versus nonwhite detainee condition on the outcome is statistically different among blacks or Latinos compared to whites (^$p \leq .05$, one-tailed).

Source: 2013/14 US Group Empathy Two-Wave Study (GfK)

differently than white respondents with respect to the direction of support for white versus nonwhite detainees. In short, the findings are supportive of H2a for African Americans but mixed for Latinos.

Next we examine the impact of racial/ethnic cues in these vignettes on opinion about whether the immigration officials had reasonable cause to deny the detainee's request for medical treatment. A familiar pattern emerges. Figure 6.2 illustrates that, in the white detainee condition, there were no statistically significant differences between the reactions of the three racial/ethnic respondent groups. In the Arab condition, perceiving the officials' decision as unreasonable somewhat increased among African Americans and declined among whites, which is in line with our expectations. This pattern was enhanced when the detainee was depicted as black: support rose for African American respondents to 69 percent and declined among white respondents to 49 percent, producing a significant racial/ethnic gap in support within the black detainee condition. More impressively, when the detainee was Latino, support among African Americans was maximized (79 percent) while remaining substantially lower among white respondents (50 percent). This not only produced a statistically significant difference *within* the Latino detainee condition between black and white respondents but also suggested that blacks reacted significantly differently than whites to a white versus Latino detainee. This latter result provides particularly strong evidence for Group Empathy Theory, because African American respondents displayed even more support for Latino immigrant detainees, a competitive outgroup, than they showed for a member of their *own* racial group.

Latino respondents in the nonwhite detainee conditions did not differ from Latinos in the white detainee condition in their evaluations of the decision to deny the detainee medical attention. Nevertheless, Latinos still displayed significantly higher perceptions of unreasonable cause in reaction to the black and Latino detainee vignettes than did white respondents. Most notably, Latino perceptions of unreasonable cause for the black detainee (67 percent) were significantly higher than those among whites (49 percent), suggesting Latino outgroup empathy for black detainees. At the same time, we find no significant difference in the direction of Latino versus white reactions to the white versus Latino detainee conditions. Overall, the results for African Americans corroborate H2b. By comparison, we find once again mixed support as it pertains to Latinos. We will speculate about why our findings seem consistently stronger for African Americans compared to Latinos in the concluding section of this chapter.

Support for Civil Rights Policies and Pro–Civil Rights Behavior

Next we examine the impact of group empathy on more general views about immigration policy. Here we employ the index of civil rights policies, which measures opposition to (1) restrictive immigration policies; (2) protection for detention center officials; (3) greater leeway for detaining anyone who cannot verify their legal status; and support for (4) giving undocumented immigrants a chance to keep their jobs and apply for legal status. Across all four experimental conditions, African Americans and Latinos were significantly more likely than whites to support the civil rights of immigrants, regardless of the race/ethnicity of the detainee portrayed in the vignette (see Figure 6.3).[12]

Once again we see that African Americans consistently displayed higher support for civil rights policies when the undocumented immigrant featured in the vignette was nonwhite. African Americans expressed more pro–civil rights views when the detainee was Arab (67 percent), black (63 percent), and Latino (60 percent)

---

[12] As in Chapter 5, for ease of presentation, we transformed these measures into a binary format by coding scores 0 through .5 as "0" and scores over .5 to 1 as "1." OLS and ordered logistic regression analyses with original ordinal measures yield results consistent with those obtained via employing the binary forms.

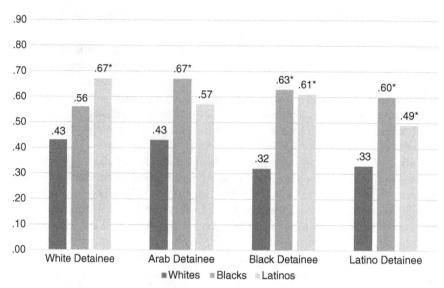

FIGURE 6.3 The probability of support for civil rights policies upon exposure to white versus nonwhite detainee vignettes, by respondents' race/ethnicity
Note: Predicted probabilities calculated using the observed-value approach after fitting probit models with robust standard errors. The asterisk denotes which coefficients for blacks and Latinos are statistically distinct from the ones for whites *within* each experimental condition (*p ≤ .05, one-tailed).
Source: 2013/14 US Group Empathy Two-Wave Study (GfK)

compared to the white detainee condition (56 percent). Meanwhile, white respondents displayed much lower levels of support for these policies, particularly upon exposure to the black and Latino detainee vignettes. The result is a significant difference between African American versus white respondent reactions *within* each nonwhite detainee condition. By comparison, the level of support Latinos displayed for pro–civil rights policies in the nonwhite detainee conditions was not statistically distinct from that in the white detainee condition, which was actually the highest of all conditions among Latinos, at 67 percent. Nevertheless, Latino support for civil rights policies was once again significantly higher than among white respondents in the black (61 versus 32 percent) and Latino (49 versus 33 percent) detainee conditions. Latino respondents seemed to exhibit high empathy for minorities here. In fact, their support was 12 percentage points higher in the black detainee condition – their economic competitor – than in the Latino detainee condition.

Last, Figure 6.4 displays the results for pro–civil rights behavior, in this case: (1) requesting more information; (2) signing a petition; and (3) attending a public meeting in order to protect undocumented immigrants. Whites were far less likely to commit to these actions across the board, but especially when the detainee was black or Latino. African Americans also reacted consistently with theoretical

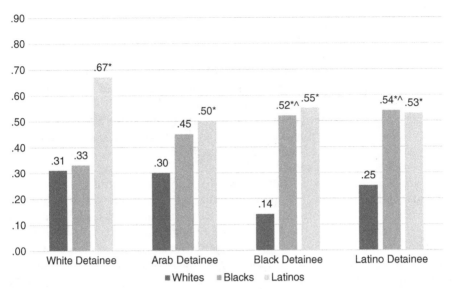

FIGURE 6.4 The probability of willingness to engage in pro–civil rights behavior upon exposure to white versus nonwhite detainee vignettes, by respondents' race/ethnicity
Note: Predicted probabilities calculated using the observed-value approach after fitting probit models with robust standard errors. The asterisk denotes which coefficients for blacks and Latinos are statistically distinct from the ones for whites *within* each experimental condition (*p ≤ .05, one-tailed). The symbol ^ denotes whether the comparative effect of exposure to the white versus nonwhite detainee condition on the outcome is statistically different among blacks or Latinos compared to whites (^p ≤ .05, one-tailed).
Source: 2013/14 US Group Empathy Two-Wave Study (GfK)

expectations across all conditions. When the detainee was white, African Americans were about as motivated as whites (33 versus 31 percent) to engage in these pro–civil rights acts. However, African Americans' commitment to act was substantially higher than whites' when the detainee was Arab (45 versus 30 percent), black (52 versus 14 percent), and Latino (54 versus 25 percent). These differences were so large that they suggest African Americans and whites react very differently to white versus nonwhite detainees.

The commitment to defend the civil rights of undocumented immigrants was consistently high among Latinos regardless of the race/ethnicity of the detainee. As a result, the pattern for Latinos was distinct from that of African Americans, perhaps because the issue is so powerfully linked to Latinx collective experiences that the vignettes activated thoughts of the ingroup and triggered protective reactions on that basis. Overall, these results corroborate our third set of hypotheses, particularly among African Americans.

Opposition to Deportation Policies

Next we test our fourth hypothesis (H4) regarding opinions on punitive immigration policies targeting specific racial/ethnic groups.[13] We asked respondents to what extent they supported/opposed the capture and deportation of undocumented immigrants of white, Arab, black, and Latino descent. We expected that African Americans and Latinos would exhibit stronger opposition to deportation policies, particularly those targeting nonwhite groups, and especially if the racial/ethnic cue provided in the experimental vignette matched the race/ethnicity of the immigrant group specifically inquired about in the posttest as the target of such policies (H4).

We first focus on attitudes toward Latino immigrants as the main disadvantaged group in this particular context. The results show significant between-group differences, $F(2, 666) = 12.452$, $p \leq .05$. Pairwise comparisons of group means with Bonferroni adjustment indicate that both African Americans and Latinos overall expressed higher levels of opposition to immigration policies aimed at capturing and deporting Latino undocumented immigrants compared with white respondents ($M_{Black} = .44$; $M_{Latino} = .47$; $M_{White} = .30$). Furthermore, African Americans did not significantly differ from Latinos with regard to their policy stance concerning Latino immigrants ($p > .10$).

The interaction between the race/ethnicity of the respondents and race/ethnicity of the immigrant detainees is in the expected direction, although only marginally significant, $F(6, 666) = 1.583$, $p \leq .10$. As the first panel of Figure 6.5 illustrates, compared with African American and Latino respondents, white respondents expressed the lowest opposition to deportation policies targeting Latinos across all experimental conditions, and their opposition in the Latino detainee condition was even lower ($M_{White} = .29$) than in the white detainee condition ($M_{White} = .34$). In contrast, African Americans more strongly opposed punitive policies targeting Latinos when exposed to the vignette featuring a Latino detainee ($M_{Black} = .46$) compared with the level of support they expressed for Latinos following exposure to the white detainee vignette ($M_{Black} = .38$). Therefore, compared to the levels observed in the white detainee condition, being exposed to the vignette featuring a Latino immigrant in distress increased policy support to help undocumented immigrants of Latino descent among black respondents while it somewhat suppressed support for Latino immigrants among white respondents. Indeed, in the Latino detainee condition, African Americans did not significantly differ from Latino respondents concerning their policy support for Latino immigrants ($M_{Black} = .46$; $M_{Latino} = .47$). By comparison, Latinos expressed similar levels of support for Latino immigrants across both the white and Latino detainee conditions.

---

[13] Full results are available in the online appendix.

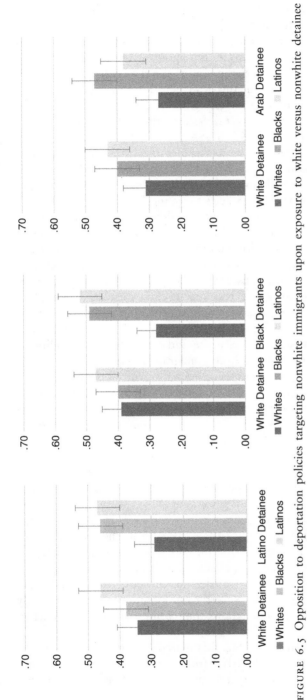

FIGURE 6.5 Opposition to deportation policies targeting nonwhite immigrants upon exposure to white versus nonwhite detainee vignettes, by respondent's race/ethnicity

Note: The bars represent estimated marginal means per each racial/ethnic respondent group. The lines represent 95 percent confidence intervals.

Source: 2013/14 US Group Empathy Two-Wave Study (GfK)

We next compare racial/ethnic respondent groups' policy judgments concerning black immigrants upon exposure to the experimental vignette featuring the black detainee versus the white detainee. The pattern is similar to policy judgments concerning Latino immigrants. Once again there is a significant main effect of the race/ethnicity of the respondent, $F(2, 666) = 8.613$, $p \le .05$. Specifically, African Americans and Latinos expressed higher opposition to deportation policies targeting blacks compared with whites ($M_{Black} = .45$; $M_{Latino} = .47$; $M_{White} = .34$). Second, there is again a marginally significant interaction effect, $F(6, 666) = 1.476$, $p \le .10$. As the second panel of Figure 6.5 illustrates, whites in the black detainee condition expressed significantly lower opposition to deporting black immigrants ($M_{White} = .28$) compared to white respondents in the white detainee condition ($M_{White} = .39$). Latinos' opposition to deportation policies targeting blacks, by comparison, was higher than not only that of whites but also that of African Americans in both the white detainee ($M_{Black} = .40$; $M_{Latino} = .47$) and the black detainee ($M_{Black} = .49$; $M_{Latino} = .52$) conditions, although the Latino–black differences within experimental conditions are not statistically significant as the confidence intervals overlap. To sum up, considering the policy views expressed in the white detainee condition as the baseline levels, exposure to the black detainee cue significantly *decreased* support for black undocumented immigrants among white respondents, whereas Latinos' support for black immigrants remained consistent across white and black detainee conditions.

Regarding policy attitudes toward Arab immigrants, once again, the results indicate significant between-group differences regarding the race/ethnicity of the respondent, $F(2, 666) = 8.361$, $p \le .01$. Compared with whites, both African Americans and Latinos expressed much higher opposition to deportation policies targeting Arabs ($M_{Black} = .43$; $M_{Latino} = .42$; $M_{White} = .28$). The interaction effect is also highly significant at the .01 level. As illustrated in the third column of Figure 6.5, similar to the results concerning policy attitudes toward Latino and black immigrants, whites in the Arab detainee condition expressed lower opposition to deportation policies targeting Arabs ($M_{White} = .27$) than whites who were exposed to the white detainee vignette ($M_{White} = .31$). In contrast, African Americans showed higher policy support for Arab immigrants in the Arab detainee condition ($M_{Black} = .47$) than they did in the white detainee condition ($M_{Black} = .40$). By comparison, the direction of change in Latinos' policy stance was similar to white respondents as their opposition to deporting Arabs was lower upon exposure to the Arab detainee vignette ($M_{Latino} = .38$) than the white detainee one ($M_{Latino} = .43$). Nevertheless, Latinos showed significantly higher policy support for Arab immigrants than whites in both experimental conditions.

Overall, these results corroborate H4. Compared with the members of the majority group, minorities – particularly African Americans – express higher opposition to deportation policies targeting undocumented immigrants *even if they do not share the same racial/ethnic background.* These findings further corraborate the main tenets of Group Empathy Theory.

EXPLAINING MINORITY–MAJORITY DIFFERENCES IN REACTIONS VIA GROUP EMPATHY

We next explore if differences in group empathy help explain the gaps we observe across racial/ethnic groups in both preexisting policy views and reactions to our experimental vignettes. As in the previous chapter, generalized structural equation modeling (GSEM) is used to estimate path coefficients. We then examine the indirect effects of race/ethnicity through group empathy using a bootstrap procedure that yields bias-corrected confidence intervals.

We first revisit the findings from the first-wave survey data. Figure 6.6 shows that blacks and Latinos, on average, substantively differ from whites on all three of the policy variables: mainly, perceptions of discrimination against undocumented immigrants, opposition to racial profiling practices targeting undocumented immigrants, and opposition to the deportation of Latino immigrants. Recall that group empathy is strongly associated with those outcomes, even after controlling for a wide range of other explanations (refer back to Table 6.1). The results of the GSEM analyses, presented in Figure 6.7, now fill in the last step: Group empathy indeed helps explain the racial/ethnic group differences we see in all three outcomes of interest given the statistically significant indirect effects confirmed by bootstrapping. These results are supportive of H5 for the survey portion of the data.

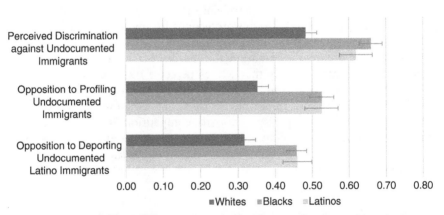

FIGURE 6.6 Racial/ethnic differences in attitudes about undocumented immigrants
Note: The bars represent estimated marginal means per each racial/ethnic respondent group. The lines represent 95 percent confidence intervals. Data are weighted. All variables are rescaled to run from 0 to 1.
Source: 2013/14 US Group Empathy Two-Wave Study (GfK)

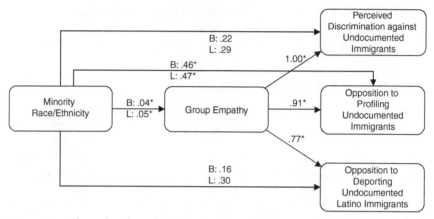

FIGURE 6.7 The role of group empathy in explaining racial/ethnic differences in attitudes about undocumented immigrants
Note: Path coefficients estimated using generalized structural equation modeling based on the full models. The significance of indirect effects tested via bootstrapping with bias-corrected confidence intervals. "B" denotes blacks and "L" denotes Latinos. White respondents constitute the baseline category. All indirect paths are statistically significant. Data are weighted. All variables are rescaled to run from 0 to 1. *$p \leq .05$, one-tailed.
Source: 2013/14 US Group Empathy Two-Wave Study (GfK)

We also conduct path analyses with the second-wave experimental data. The results illustrated in Figures 6.8 show that group-empathic reactions to the experimental vignettes significantly explain minority–majority differences in siding with the detainee, perceiving the denial of medical attention unreasonable, supporting civil rights protections for undocumented immigrants, and proclivity for political action to help undocumented immigrants.[14]

A leading alternative explanation for the distinct intergroup reactions to immigration threats is simply that whites perceive these threats to be larger than do African American and Latino respondents. On its face, this alternative seems improbable because minorities are more likely than whites to experience direct downward wage pressure due to competition with undocumented immigrants (Borjas 2001; Gay 2006). Under this material threat hypothesis, those who perceive higher immigration threat should be *least* likely to side with an immigrant detainee. As illustrated in Figure 6.9, we observe no significant

---

[14] In addition to the experimental measure of group empathy we use to test the mediational path concerning intergroup reactions to the experimental treatments, we also conduct alternative path analyses using our general group empathy measure, the GEI, as well as our more targeted measure of group empathy specific to the outgroup of concern – here, empathy for undocumented immigrants. The results (available in the online appendix) are generally consistent across these different measures of group empathy.

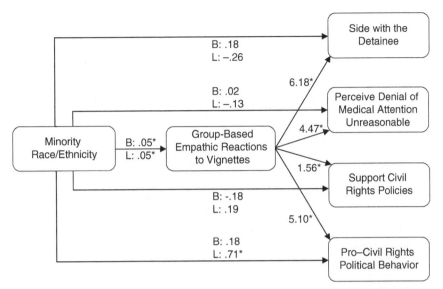

FIGURE 6.8 The role of group empathy in explaining racial/ethnic differences in reactions to the immigrant detention experiment
Note: Path coefficients estimated using generalized structural equation modeling based on the full models. The significance of indirect effects tested via bootstrapping with bias-corrected confidence intervals. "B" denotes blacks and "L" denotes Latinos. White respondents constitute the baseline category. All indirect paths are statistically significant. All variables are rescaled to run from 0 to 1. *p ≤ .05, one-tailed.
Source: 2013/14 US Group Empathy Two-Wave Study (GfK)

differences between whites, blacks, and Latinos in the sample with respect to perceptions of personal immigration threat.[15] Perceived personal threat of immigration, therefore, cannot explain intergroup differences in the outcomes we examine. However, whites perceive significantly higher levels of national immigration threat, which could potentially explain these differences. That said, Figure 6.9 also indicates that African Americans display significantly higher concerns about economic competition with other groups, including immigrants, than do whites. This makes sense, since an influx of low-skilled foreign workers could pose an *actual* threat to African American jobs (Borjas et al. 2010). Nonetheless, in line with our theory and contrary to the material threat hypothesis, African Americans not only show greater support than whites for all undocumented immigrant groups but also demonstrate particularly high support for Latino immigrants – their *primary* economic competitor.

---

[15] The operationalization of immigration threat comprises economic and cultural elements (adopted from Brader et al. 2008).

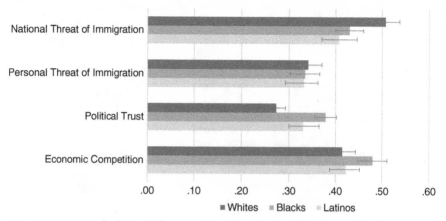

FIGURE 6.9 Racial/ethnic differences in perceptions of threat, political trust, and economic competition
Note: The bars represent estimated marginal means per each racial/ethnic respondent group. The lines represent 95 percent confidence intervals. Data are weighted. All variables are rescaled to run from 0 to 1.
Source: 2013/14 US Group Empathy Two-Wave Study (GfK)

As in the "Flying While Arab" experiment, GSEM analyses already control for threat perceptions along with other key explanatory factors, including party identification, ideology, SDO, ethnocentrism, and authoritarianism. The results demonstrate that, while perceived immigration threat has a significant direct effect, it is much smaller than that of group-based empathic reactions on each outcome of interest, and it does not negate any of the observed indirect effects.

Alternatively, minorities may trust the government less and therefore be less likely to side with law enforcement officials or concede civil rights amid political threats (Davis 2006). However, Figure 6.9 illustrates that, while political trust was low among each racial/ethnic group in the sample, it was actually *highest* among African Americans and *lowest* among whites. This may seem unusual at first glance, yet one must remember that the sitting president at the time of this survey experiment (December 2013–January 2014) was Barack Obama. Trust in government rose among African Americans after Obama's election, eclipsing that among whites (Nunnally 2012). In any case, political trust generally yields no significant direct or indirect effects in these analyses.

Even though minorities reported higher trust in government at that particular political moment, this may not necessarily translate into positive perceptions of law enforcement. So, another competing explanation for these findings is that minority–majority differences in reactions to the experimental vignettes are the result of higher *antipathy* toward law enforcement officials among minority groups. While there was no reference to the race/ethnicity of the detention center officials in our vignettes, it is possible that the race/ethnicity of these officials is assumed to be white, triggering minority respondents to react defensively in ways that look like empathy for nonwhite groups. To test this alternative hypothesis, we examined between-group differences in sympathy expressed toward detention center officials upon exposure to the experimental vignettes. The results of pairwise comparisons with Bonferroni adjustment indicate no significant differences between whites, African Americans, and Latinos (M_{White} = .33; M_{Black} = .31; M_{Latino} = .32), $F(2, 654)$ = .180, p > .10. Accordingly, differences between racial/ethnic groups in antipathy toward detention center officials do not explain the gaps we observe.

CONCLUSION

In this chapter we examined the effect of group empathy on public perceptions and attitudes regarding undocumented immigration. We also experimentally explored intergroup reactions to undocumented immigrants of different racial/ethnic descent and whether group-based variation in empathic reactions helps explain differences in such responses. To date, few empirical studies have offered systematic explanations for variation across racial/ethnic groups in response to the issue of undocumented immigration. Large racial/ethnic gaps in opinion about immigration confound threat-based or ingroup interest explanations because native minority groups often express high levels of policy support for undocumented immigrants even though these groups are in direct competition for resources. Group Empathy Theory helps us better understand why one minority group could display high levels of support for another – in this case, undocumented immigrants from various racial/ethnic backgrounds – even in situations of direct material conflict or perceived threat.

Our central findings are clear. First, the survey results demonstrate that trait-level group empathy, measured by the GEI, is significantly linked to political views and attitudes about undocumented immigrants, even after controlling for a variety of other major explanatory factors including partisanship, ideology, SDO, threat, and more. While the significant main effects of group empathy apply to all racial/ethnic groups, minorities display higher levels of group empathy than do whites, and such intergroup differences in turn significantly mediate the indirect path between race/ethnicity and opinions about undocumented immigration.

The experimental findings further reveal substantial intergroup differences. African Americans and Latinos were far more likely to side with any immigrant detainee in distress than were white respondents. For African Americans, these gaps were largest when the detainee was nonwhite. African Americans and Latinos were also more supportive of pro–civil rights policies and actions compared to whites. White respondents who viewed a nonwhite immigrant vignette were less opposed to deportation policies as compared to white respondents in the white detainee condition. In contrast, black respondents displayed higher levels of opposition when the immigrant was depicted as nonwhite. Latinos, likely as a result of their strong ingroup association with the issue of immigration, were the most opposed to deportation policies regardless of the race/ethnicity of the immigrant. Finally, we confirm that differences in group-based empathic reactions (rather than perceived threat of immigration) powerfully helped explain these racial/ethnic gaps in policy opinions, attitudes, and political action tendencies concerning undocumented immigrants.

In all, the strongest evidence of group empathic reactions comes from African American respondents, since they were much more likely to empathize with nonwhite immigrants. Surprisingly, Latino respondents' reactions to minority detainees were often not different than their reactions to the white detainee. Latinos in some cases expressed a great deal more empathy for white immigrants than did African American respondents and even whites. This is an interesting pattern, because it implies that Latinos may simply empathize with all immigrants as a result of their group's attachment to the immigrant community. In other words, given their own experiences with stigmatization as immigrants, Latinos are highly sensitive to inhumane treatment in the immigrant detention context *regardless* of the detainees' racial/ethnic origin. This is consistent with Masuoka and Junn's (2013) experimental findings that racial primes do not have an additive effect on Latino attitudes given their generally positive views on immigration.

Consistent with our results in Chapter 4, these findings suggest that Latinos fall between whites and African Americans with respect to levels of group empathy. As previously mentioned, the process of acculturation and assimilation may set the political attitudes and behavior of some Latinos closer to those of whites rather than other minority groups (de la Garza et al. 1996). This is in line with research that finds Latino prejudice against blacks can be politically consequential (Krupnikov & Piston 2016). All groups can exhibit prejudice toward others, and ethnocentrism is not restricted to whites as a group (Kinder & Kam 2010). Nevertheless, because of their ethnic consciousness as a minority group, Latinos may still be critical of the political system (Davis 2006), and they may empathize with the plight of other minority groups more often than whites on average.

Further, the Latinx community is substantially more heterogeneous in terms of its politics, culture, and history than the African American community. As descendants of immigrants hailing from many nations and backgrounds, Latinos may not uniformly experience empathy for other oppressed groups. Indeed, analyzing the first-wave survey data for Latinx subgroups indicates differences in group empathy between Mexican, Puerto Rican, Cuban, and other Latino respondents. Future research might conduct experiments with randomized oversamples of Latinx subgroups and vignettes that include more nuanced differentiations of the Latino cue at the subgroup level. Considering the generational status of respondents and offering the option to participate in the experiment in Spanish could also further help unveil empathy-driven attitudes of Latinos at different levels of acculturation and ingroup affinity.

What should we take away from all this? Although disadvantaged minority groups are in more direct competition for rights and resources, they are nevertheless more likely than the majority to extend policy support to those in need. That said, we would not want to leave readers with the impression that whites do not show empathy for outgroups in distress or that empathic reactions among whites have no political consequences. Whites who empathize with the immigrant detainees in our vignettes are far more likely to oppose deportation practices and support pro–civil rights policies and actions. The results nonetheless reveal important intergroup differences, on average, depending on whether respondents belong to groups in society that have experienced systemic discrimination. When discrimination becomes embedded in a group's collective memory, and stories of how to manage that discrimination (coupled with personal encounters of unfair treatment) become a regular part of the socialization of young people, awareness of injustices faced by other groups in comparable circumstances may also grow. Hurwitz et al. (2015) discovered exactly this pattern between blacks and Latinos in the domain of criminal justice. They suggest that perceived outgroup discrimination is more likely among disadvantaged minorities who feel a heightened sense of linked fate with their ingroup and in non-zero-sum environments (where one group's gain does not amount to another's loss). Our findings regarding black and Latino reactions suggest that high levels of outgroup empathy would trigger similar outcomes even in a zero-sum policy domain as undocumented immigration.

Another provocative claim supported by these data is that groups do not need to identify with each other in any direct way for rights and privileges to be extended. The empathic process is more or less an automatic reaction to situations that resonate with one's own personal and cultural experiences with discrimination. As a result, large gaps in policy support can emerge that seem to defy simple explanations based on economic or security threats, in this case the threats supposedly posed by undocumented immigrants entering the country.

Future studies may examine these processes among other key communities, particularly Asian Americans. Asian Americans are, on average, economically better off than African Americans and Latinos (Lai & Arguelles 2003), which may set their socio-economic experiences closer to those of whites. At the same time, their immigration experiences are closer to Latinos, since both groups together constitute the majority of current immigration flow to the United States and both are perceived as non-English-speaking newcomers even when they are native-born, English-speaking Americans (Hetherington & Weiler 2018; Masuoka & Junn 2013). Asian Americans have thus been branded as "perpetual foreigners," suffering from racial stereotypes and discrimination generation after generation (Masuoka & Junn 2013, 61; see also Uhlaner 1991). As mentioned earlier, Chong and Kim (2006) find a common process affecting all minorities: even affluent minority individuals support policies to redress racial/ethnic inequality if they experience discrimination. Accordingly, as with African Americans and Latinos, we expect Asian Americans – especially those who personally encounter unfair treatment – will react with heightened empathy toward immigrants from other groups despite their generally higher economic status (see Lopez & Pantoja 2004; Ramakrishnan 2014).

Another potential avenue of research is to replicate our experiment in different cultural and national settings. One could investigate whether minority immigrant groups in Europe also feel more empathic toward one another and can build intergroup coalitions around common policy concerns amid the animosity and discrimination they collectively face as "the perpetual other" in many European nations (Dancygier 2010). The current political climate concerning Arab and Muslim immigrants in Europe provides fertile ground for such a test.

Blacks and Latinos expressing empathy toward undocumented immigrants does not mean they believe they hold common values or political goals. For instance, Latinos have an inherent connection to the issue of bilingual education that African Americans do not share (Falcon 1988). Despite such issue-specific differences, and the more general differences in socio-economic interests that could trigger conflict (Jones-Correa 2005; McClain & Karnig 1990), empathy in reaction to the mistreatment of others can still bring groups together. It is quite noteworthy that, in reaction to the experimental vignettes, African Americans displayed such high levels of support for undocumented immigrants, particularly for Latino detainees (even more than for black detainees). This stands in contrast to the long-standing presumption of African American aversion to immigrants postulated by the inter-minority conflict perspective. Instead, common contemporary political contexts prompt both blacks and Latinos to side with other minorities experiencing discrimination even when they may perceive such outgroups to be a significant threat to their socio-economic and political interests. As Hurwitz et al. (2015, 517) put it: "To the extent that empathy fosters awareness and awareness fosters action, the shared understanding among blacks and Latinos ultimately may function as a valuable political resource." This opens the door for more coalition-building between African Americans and Latinos on immigration and other policy issues affecting disadvantaged groups.

7

Group Empathy and Foreign Policy

> They only see us when we do something they don't want us to do, Mahmoud realized. The thought hit him like a lightning bolt. When they stayed where they were supposed to be – in the ruins of Aleppo or behind the fences of a refugee camp – people could forget about them. But when refugees did something they didn't want them to do – when they tried to cross the border into their country, or slept on the front stoops of their shops, or jumped in front of their cars, or prayed on the decks of their ferries – that's when people couldn't ignore them any longer.
>
> Mahmoud's first instinct was to disappear below decks. To be invisible. Being invisible in Syria had kept him alive. But now Mahmoud began to wonder if being invisible in Europe might be the death of him and his family. If no one saw them, no one could help them. And maybe the world needed to see what was really happening here.
>
> Alan Gratz, *Refugee* (2017)[1]

Great powers seek to maintain global influence by intervening in international conflicts, both for military and humanitarian purposes. However, risk-averse publics often constrain leaders, keeping them from taking military risks or making expensive promises of aid (Jentleson & Britton 1998; Stam 1996). In fact, the role of public opinion as a brake on international interventions has often been cited as a primary distinction between democratic and nondemocratic regimes.

A central assumption of Democratic Peace Theory, one of the most influential ideas in International Relations, dates back to the philosophy of Immanuel Kant. His conjecture was that a democratic citizenry restricts an elected leader's policy options (Doyle 1986; Russett 1993). To this date, it remains widely accepted that democratic citizenries do constrain leaders in

---

[1] Alan Gratz (2017), *Refugee*, New York: Scholastic Press.

the foreign policy realm (see Gowa 2011; Tomz & Week 2013). Within that scope, understanding the role of group empathy in shaping public opinion dynamics with regard to the foreign policy domain is essential.

Civil wars and ethnic insurgencies constitute the most common, and often the most violent, forms of large-scale political conflict in the world (Hoeffler 2014). Conventional wisdom suggests that timely intervention by the international community can help reduce the loss of innocent lives in such humanitarian crises. However, scholars find that, when it comes to military interventions, the US public is often quite risk averse (Jentleson & Britton 1998; Russett & Nincic 1976). The public is particularly sensitive to the potentially high costs involved with strictly humanitarian military interventions that carry no obvious or direct national security benefits.

The US public is also often reluctant to extend monetary foreign aid to countries in distress. Although support for foreign aid has generally been higher than support for humanitarian military interventions, it has not been popular (Kinder & Kam 2010). Scholars suggest such low levels of public support reduce not only the quantity of aid but also its quality and effectiveness (Paxton & Knack 2012). Nevertheless, research on the determinants of public opinion regarding foreign aid in donor countries has been scarce (see Chong & Gradstein 2008; Kinder & Kam 2010; Milner & Tingley 2010).

Studies in this area of research generally assume that a uniform opinion dynamic will operate for all racial/ethnic groups (see Berinsky 2007). This is a reasonable starting point. Given the heightened salience of national identity in the foreign policy domain (Transue 2007), one might expect all native groups to react similarly to foreign policy actions. US citizens, regardless of their own racial/ethnic background, might balance sociotropic domestic priorities with foreign policy goals and come to the same opinion about whether to support humanitarian action. However, this assumption is not corroborated by empirical evidence.

Large opinion gaps exist along racial/ethnic lines regarding military interventions overseas (Burris 2008). On the one hand, African Americans were substantially less supportive of the Korean, Vietnam, and Gulf wars compared to whites (Mueller 1973, 1994; Nincic & Nincic 2002). On the other hand, they were substantially more supportive of the intervention in Somalia (Burris 2008) than whites and were more likely to side with Ethiopia following the Italian invasion during World War II (Gramby-Sobukwe 2005). African Americans were also more supportive than whites of humanitarian efforts in Haiti and South Africa (Henry 2010).

One common explanation offered for these differences involves shared group identity. People may be more likely to support interventions to protect the lives and human rights of victims of violent conflicts or genocides when the victims are like them, ethnically or otherwise (Bass 2008). Aristotle wrote that men pity most of all the suffering of "their equals and contemporaries, by character, by habit, by esteem and by birth; for in all these cases it seems more likely that it could happen to them" (Aristotle 1991, 164). Speaking to students at Emory University in 1996, former president Jimmy Carter worried that "we concentrate our effort and our troops on Bosnia and we don't pay any attention to Liberia and Rwanda and Burundi and Sudan because they're African countries. They're black people and they're poor people and we concentrate our efforts on white people in Europe."[2] Religious similarities may also play a role in decisions to intervene. According to some, the conflict in what is now South Sudan received increased attention from the Bush administration mainly because American evangelicals pressured the United States to intervene to halt the violence directed against Sudan's Christian minority.[3]

Explanations based on material and existential threats have also been forwarded in this domain. Since minorities bear a disproportionate share of the human costs of war (Kriner & Shen 2010), African Americans and Latinos might be more strongly opposed to military interventions in general. For instance, the racial/ethnic opinion gaps in support for the Iraq war could have been driven by the belief among African Americans that they would be disproportionately called upon to do the fighting and the dying (Rohall & Ender 2007; Westheider 1997). Alternatively, these groups might believe costly foreign wars would draw the country's resources away from domestic social welfare programs upon which they depend (Wilcox et al. 1993). However, these explanations have not performed very well empirically, especially when the issue involves humanitarian considerations.

Minorities in the United States are often willing to extend policy benefits to groups other than their own, even when those outgroups are perceived as threatening or in competition with their ingroup. For example, Gartner and Segura (2000) found that African American citizens were not necessarily more sensitive to black than to white casualties when it came to predicting support for the Vietnam War. African Americans are also, ceteris paribus, more likely to support international humanitarian aid around the world for those in need, not just for Africa (Este-McDonald 2011). Further challenging group interest and external threat explanations, African Americans were more protective of the rights of Arab Americans after 9/11, even though they perceived themselves to be at higher risk from terrorism (Davis 2006). As mentioned before, African Americans are also significantly more tolerant of Latino immigration than are whites, despite the fact that blacks, on average, experience higher levels of economic competition with newcomers (Brader et al. 2010). Even Latino Americans' support for immigration is not unambiguous evidence of ingroup interest, since native Latinos, like African

[2] *Washington Post* (1996), "Countries Blocking Plans on Burundi Intervention," January 27: A15, print.
[3] Steve Mufson (2001), "Christians' Plight in Sudan Tests a Bush Stance: Evangelicals Urge Intervention," *Washington Post*, March 24: A1, print.

Americans, are also vulnerable to downward wage pressures from an influx of new immigrant workers (Borjas 2001; Gay 2006). While systematic research on Latinos' foreign policy attitudes is scant, several public opinion polls indicate that Latino Americans show high support for accepting refugees into the United States, even those who are of non-Latino descent. For instance, while a majority of Americans opposed granting asylum to Syrians in the wake of the 2015 ISIS attacks in Paris, many Latino immigrant groups advocated for Syrian refugees.[4]

Group Empathy Theory predicts African Americans and Latinos will be more likely to support foreign aid and other forms of humanitarian intervention compared to whites, not because of their identification with specific racial/ethnic groups abroad but because they possess on average higher levels of empathy in general for outgroups in distress. Note the strength of this claim. We suspect African Americans and Latinos may support humanitarian aid and military interventions on behalf of foreign groups in distress *even when they share no racial/ethnic ties and even if they perceive themselves and the nation vulnerable to security threats and costly wars.*

We therefore expect that empathy for outgroups experiencing human rights violations, oppression, and discrimination should override economic or security concerns associated with helping these people from other places. This hypothesis is in line with prior social psychological work that shows the potential of empathy for evoking altruistic motivations, which may counterbalance one's egoistic, competitive desire to maintain relative group advantage and avoid personal sacrifice (Batson et al. 1997). If the theory holds, we would have evidence that group empathy powerfully counteracts negative reactions to existential and material threats. This would also help account for significant racial/ethnic gaps in foreign policy attitudes and behavior that have been heretofore largely unexplained.

To effectively test these predictions, we conducted a national survey experiment in 2016 with representative samples of whites and representative oversamples of African Americans and Latinos. We first examine the survey results regarding general foreign policy attitudes about the US responsibility to protect other nations in distress, foreign aid, the US response to the Syrian civil war (including the refugee resettlement and military options on the table), and the Muslim ban proposed by then-presidential candidate Donald Trump. We then examine whether racial/ethnic groups in the United States react differently to a news vignette depicting a humanitarian crisis abroad depending on the race or ethnicity of the people in need of assistance. As in previous chapters, we explore whether group empathy helps explain intergroup differences in these reactions.

---

[4] Cedar Attanasio (2015), "Latino Immigrant Groups Support Syrian Refugees at Pro-DAPA, DACA Rallies," *Latin Times*, www.latintimes.com/latino-immigrant-groups-support-syrian-refugees-pro-dapa-daca-rallies-354964.

HYPOTHESES

This chapter explores whether empathy for the suffering of foreign racial/ ethnic outgroups explains variation in foreign policy opinions among domestic racial/ethnic groups in the United States. We expect that native groups who have experienced various forms of deprivation, oppression, discrimination, and criminalization in the United States may support policy actions on behalf of foreign groups in need of help as a result of their empathic understanding of those circumstances. This should occur even when a foreign racial/ethnic group is seen as threatening, either economically, culturally, or existentially.

Based on the premises of Group Empathy Theory, African Americans and Latinos should display significantly different foreign policy attitudes compared to whites. Specifically, compared to whites, African Americans and Latinos should attribute higher responsibility to the United States to protect people from other countries in need, all else equal, particularly during times of war and natural disasters (H1a). In addition, African Americans and Latinos should be more supportive of increasing the portion of the US budget allocated to foreign aid (H1b). Both minority groups should also be supportive of a more proactive US foreign policy in dealing with the Syrian civil war – including providing aid, asylum, and military assistance to help the victims of this violent strife (H1c). And when it comes to exclusionary foreign policy propositions under the guise of homeland security, as is the case with Trump's Muslim ban, African Americans and Latinos should display stronger opposition (H1d). As in previous chapters, we once again expect minority groups to have higher levels of general group empathy and more empathy for stigmatized outgroups including refugees, Muslims, and Arabs than do whites (H2).

Group Empathy Theory also predicts that African Americans and Latinos, compared to whites, will react differently to news depicting civilians suffering under an oppressive regime. Specifically, African Americans and Latinos should be more likely than whites to support foreign policy actions including military intervention, humanitarian aid, and asylum (H3a). They should also exhibit higher engagement in empathy-driven political behavior – such as requesting more information, donating money, and signing a petition to help the victims (H3b). African Americans' and Latinos' support for policy actions to help a foreign nation in distress should remain significantly higher than that of whites even for victim groups that may be seen as threatening to the United States (H3c). In particular, African Americans and Latinos will be more supportive of humanitarian action in an Arab country compared to a predominantly white European one. They will also be more accepting of the refugees seeking asylum due to their higher group empathy even for outgroups who are generally stigmatized and labeled as a source of threat. To test these hypotheses, we perform an experiment by randomly assigning respondents to two different versions of an experimental vignette – one featuring a European nation and the other an Arab nation – in need of humanitarian action.

This chapter provides a clear discriminating test between ingroup interest and outgroup empathy as drivers of intergroup differences in policy opinion. Under the group interest hypothesis, those who perceive higher costs and greater risk should be *least* likely to support humanitarian interventions. If there are differences between racial/ethnic groups in terms of perceptions of personal or national costs and risks, those who perceive the highest costs/risks should react most strongly against foreign policy assistance for outgroups in need. Group Empathy Theory predicts that there is no simple ingroup interest mechanism at work. Instead, foreign policy attitudes related to humanitarian rights, needs, and emergencies abroad should be mostly driven by differences in group empathy (H4).

RESEARCH DESIGN

To test these hypotheses, we designed a national survey experiment set in the foreign policy domain. The project was funded by Time-sharing Experiments for the Social Sciences (TESS) and fielded by GfK in September/October 2016. Overall, a representative sample of 508 respondents participated, consisting of 173 whites, 172 African Americans, and 163 Latinos.

The pretest survey measured general group empathy using the fourteen-item Group Empathy Index (GEI). As with other surveys we performed, the Cronbach's alpha for the GEI proved to be very high ($\alpha = .85$), and consistent across racial/ethnic respondent groups ($\alpha_{White} = .87$; $\alpha_{Black} = .81$; $\alpha_{Latino} = .86$). Confirmatory factor analyses supported the generation of a factor-based measure.

This survey also included group-specific measures of empathy. To measure this targeted form of empathy for key groups of interest, we first asked respondents how concerned they were about the challenges refugees, Arabs, and Muslims face these days. Respondents placed themselves on a 5-point scale ranging from "not at all concerned" to "very concerned." To measure group-specific perspective-taking abilities without triggering social desirability biases, the survey reassured respondents: "Regardless of the challenges another group faces, sometimes it is easier and other times more difficult to understand what members of a given group are going through." We then asked respondents how easy it is for them to put themselves in the shoes of each group. Response options ranged from "not easy at all" to "very easy" on a 5-point scale. By combining these empathic concern and perspective taking submeasures, we generated group-specific empathy measures for refugees, Arabs, and Muslims.

For our dependent variables, we inquired about participants' preexisting foreign policy views, particularly regarding protecting citizens of other countries in distress and foreign aid. Participants also indicated how they felt the United States should respond to the Syrian civil war, including whether the country should accept Syrian refugees, provide humanitarian aid for Syrian civilians, and intervene militarily by conducting airstrikes and/or sending ground troops to stop the civil war. We also asked participants whether they supported or opposed then-candidate Trump's Muslim ban campaign proposal.[5]

For the experiment, we randomly assigned half of each of the three racial/ethnic groups to one of two conditions. Participants first read a short fictitious news report about the violent actions of an oppressive government in an island nation abroad, located either in the Balkans or in the Arabian Peninsula. The story was accompanied by a photograph of a young man, which carried the racial/ethnic cue. The individual appeared to be either European or Arab and was identified in the story as one of many victims who died as a result of government oppression and police brutality.

To manipulate racial/ethnic cues, we used the same two photos representing white and Arab race/ethnicity that our previous survey experiments employed. Using the same photos allows us to achieve more control over exactly which cues might be driving differences in reactions. We are thus better able to compare results across these studies.

The vignette reported that the said authoritarian government was severely violating human rights and engaging in extremely violent acts against civilians. The young person in the photo accompanying the vignette was identified as a college student who was killed by the police for posting messages on a social network site about what was going on in his country.[6]

Violent Repression in [Kornati/Farasan]: Government Clamps Down on Civilians to Line Its Pockets
The country of [Kornati/Farasan] is an independent island located in [the Balkans in Europe/the Arabian Peninsula in the Middle East]. The island nation is composed of an ethnically homogenous population of 4.5 million living under an authoritarian, non-democratic government. [Kornati/Farasan] has recently become destabilized, and human rights violations are now occurring across the country. The discovery of gold on the

[5] After answering these survey questions, participants were given a distractor task in an attempt to clear their minds a bit before they read the experimental vignettes. The task consisted of a battery of questions asking about pop culture and technology: "Below are four things that happened in pop culture and the technology world in 2015. For each one, please indicate to what extent you thought it was memorable or forgettable." The items were: (1) *Late Show with David Letterman* airs its final episode; (2) Apple Watch is launched in stores; (3) *Star Wars: The Force Awakens* is released in theaters; and (4) Tesla auto company delivers an autopilot mode that allows its cars to "drive themselves."

[6] To make the scenario more realistic, real place names were used. Kornati is a Croatian island in the Mediterranean Sea and Farasan is an island in the Red Sea and belongs to Saudi Arabia. That said, the incidents depicted in the news report were fictitious, and we debriefed all subjects to this effect at the end of the survey.

island proved to be a curse rather than a blessing for the people of this small country. The government has claimed absolute control over all natural resources and has begun to force its citizens to help extract these minerals with extremely low wages and without any concern for their health. There are reports that, despite public opposition, the government is using significant amounts of arsenic for gold mining, which has contaminated the island's water and soil, leading to illness and many deaths among workers and their families.

In reaction to peaceful protests, there has been a surge of government-sponsored violence on the island in recent weeks. Government forces have targeted civilians participating in demonstrations with live ammunition in order to clear the streets. The government is also tracking social media accounts and imprisoning without trial any citizens attempting to raise international awareness and call for help. Families of many of these activists claim their loved ones have "disappeared" while under police custody. United Nations observers estimate that thou-
sands *of civilians have been killed over the last few weeks, and the number of casualties is expected to rise.*

Photo of the (white/Arab) victim
Unarmed college student (pictured above), who was posting Facebook messages about the ongoing government oppression, was recently beaten to death on his way to school by police forces.

After reading the vignette, participants responded to several items inquiring about their reaction. The posttest questionnaire included measures of several relevant policy preferences. We asked participants about how strongly they supported or opposed: (1) using US military force against the oppressive government of [Kornati/Farasan] in order to help the people experiencing violence; (2) the United States providing financial aid to the victims of this violent repression; and (3) granting asylum to refugees attempting to escape from [Kornati/Farasan] to the United States.

We also captured participants' proclivity for engaging in relevant political behavior. Specifically, participants indicated their willingness to: (1) receive more information about the situation in [Kornati/Farasan]; (2) donate to a nongovernmental organization that works to help the victims; and (3) sign an electronic petition to be sent to Congress indicating their support for humanitarian aid. All of these measures were designed to capture participants' *actual* behavioral intentions rather than their self-reported *potential*. More specifically, participants were asked: "Would you like to receive more information about the situation in [Kornati/Farasan]? If yes, please click on the box next to the statement 'Yes, I would like to receive more information.' At the end of the survey, you will be provided a link to the key news feeds and updates about this conflict. If no, please click 'No, I prefer not to receive more information.' In either case, your response will remain anonymous to the researchers who prepared this survey." To measure donation behavior, participants were given an extra dollar in addition to their regular fee for their participation in our experiment. In the posttest, they were told: "As mentioned before, for your valuable participation in this survey, you will receive an extra $1.00 credited to your GfK account. You can donate any part of this $1.00 to a nongovernmental organization that works to help the victims of the violent conflict in [Kornati/Farasan]. Please specify the amount of money you would like to donate. You can enter any amount from $0.00 to $1.00." We also asked participants: "Would you like to sign an electronic petition to be sent to Congress indicating your support for humanitarian aid to help the victims of the violent conflict in [Kornati/Farasan]? If yes, please click on the 'Yes, I would like to sign the petition to help' box below and you will be directed to the petition website. If no, please click 'No, I prefer not to sign the petition to help.' In either case, your response will remain anonymous to the researchers who prepared this survey." At the end of the experiment, participants were fully debriefed about the fictitious nature of the experimental setup and compensated for their time.

RESULTS

We first look at the survey results concerning foreign policy attitudes related to humanitarian interventions and aid. In analyzing the survey data, we employ poststratification sampling weights provided by GfK on racial/ethnic group strata to bring the oversampled groups to their population proportions.[7]

To measure opinions about protecting other nations in distress, participants assessed a pair of statements about the role the United States should play in international politics. The first statement read: "As the leader of the world, the United States has a responsibility to help people from other countries in need, especially in cases of war and natural disasters." The second statement was the opposite of the first, rejecting the US's responsibility to protect. Respondents indicated which statement came closer to their own point of view and how strongly they felt that way. Response options ranged from "very strongly" agreeing with the first statement to "very strongly" agreeing with the second one on a 6-point scale. The results of an ordered probit analysis, displayed in Table 7.1, Model 1, show that African Americans and Latinos attributed to the United States a higher responsibility for protecting people of other countries in need as compared to whites. For instance, the predicted probability of whites very strongly agreeing with the first statement that ascribes the United States responsibility to protect other nations was 8 percent, whereas it was 17 percent for both African Americans and Latinos.

Participants also indicated whether the amount the United States allocates for foreign aid to help alleviate the suffering of people overseas should be

---

[7] As a robustness check, we conducted the analyses again, without sampling weights, and the results are consistent with those of the stratified models.

TABLE 7.1 *The relationship between group empathy and the responsibility to protect citizens of other nations in distress*

	Model 1		Model 2		Model 3	
	β	S.E.	β	S.E.	β	S.E.
Group empathy			1.12***	.34	.86*	.37
Race/ethnicity						
Black	.45**	.14	.34*	.15	−.01	.18
Latino	.44**	.14	.32*	.15	.23	.16
Political factors						
National threat of terrorism					.50†	.30
Personal threat of terrorism					.27	.32
Threat of high-casualty war					−.16	.42
Threat of costly war					−.59	.43
Trust in Congress					.16**	.30
Trust in president					.73	.29
Trust in military					.20	.26
Party ID					−.41	.25
Ideology					−.18	.31
Socio-demographic factors						
Female	.01	.12	−.10	.12	−.20†	.12
Education	1.21**	.43	1.01*	.44	1.02*	.44
Age	.85**	.31	.81**	.32	.84**	.33
Income	−.39	.29	−.49†	.29	−.51†	.31
Married	−.03	.14	.04	.15	.04	.14
Employed	.06	.13	.02	.13	−.04	.13
Metropolitan residence	−.14	.16	−.10	.17	−.15	.17
Catholic	.03	.13	.04	.13	−.11	.13
Household size	.41	.48	.36	.51	.55	.50
N	498		486		477	

Note: Coefficients estimated using ordered probit. Data are weighted. All variables are rescaled to run from 0 to 1. †p ≤ .10, *p ≤ .05, **p ≤ .01, and ***p ≤ .001, two-tailed.
Source: 2016 US Group Empathy TESS Study (GfK)

increased, reduced, or kept about the same.[8] Ordered probit results, displayed in Table 7.2, Model 1, indicate that African Americans and Latinos were more

[8] We also asked participants: "How often do you think the foreign aid the US provides actually helps the victims of wars and natural disasters abroad rather than simply going into the pockets of the rich and powerful in those countries?" This item was to ensure that intergroup differences in support for foreign aid do not emerge from any potential differences in these groups' worldview

TABLE 7.2 *The relationship between group empathy and support for foreign aid*

	Model 1		Model 2		Model 3	
	β	S.E.	β	S.E.	β	S.E.
Group empathy			1.23***	.34	.91**	.36
Race/ethnicity						
Black	.40**	.14	.32*	.15	.08	.18
Latino	.50***	.14	.38*	.15	.38*	.17
Political factors						
National threat of terrorism					.01	.33
Personal threat of terrorism					.14	.30
Threat of high-casualty war					.50	.46
Threat of costly war					−1.03*	.47
Trust in Congress					.21	.29
Trust in president					.80**	.28
Trust in military					−.28	.28
Party ID					−.15	.26
Ideology					1.28***	.32
Socio-demographic factors						
Female	.20†	.12	.09	.12	.04	.13
Education	1.42***	.44	1.21**	.44	1.07**	.43
Age	.13	.33	.01	.35	.46	.36
Income	−.39	.27	−.54*	.27	−.38	.29
Married	−.04	.14	.07	.14	.13	.14
Employed	.07	.13	.02	.14	.01	.13
Metropolitan residence	.06	.17	.09	.18	.03	.18
Catholic	−.06	.14	−.04	.15	−.18	.14
Household size	.11	.48	.03	.47	.53	.49
N	496		483		474	

Note: Coefficients estimated using ordered probit. Data are weighted. All variables are rescaled to run from 0 to 1. †p ≤ .10, *p ≤ .05, **p ≤ .01, and ***p ≤ .001, two-tailed.
Source: 2016 US Group Empathy TESS Study (GfK)

strongly in favor of increasing foreign aid than whites. With respect to marginal effects, the predicted probability of whites to support a policy to greatly reduce foreign aid was 16 percent, whereas it was about 8 percent for African Americans and 7 percent for Latinos.

on the effectiveness of foreign aid. There are no statistically significant differences in perceptions of foreign aid effectiveness across the three racial/ethnic groups.

The pretest survey also included a battery of questions about the civil war in Syria. Subjects read the following statement: "As you may know, there has been a violent conflict in Syria between the authoritarian government forces and rebel groups, which has caused thousands of civilian casualties, including many women and children. How strongly would you support or oppose the United States taking each of the following actions with respect to Syria?" The results presented in Table 7.3, Model 1, show that African Americans and Latinos were significantly more likely to support accepting Syrian refugees into the United States. The predicted probability to strongly support the United States allowing Syrian refugees into the country was 22 percent for African Americans and 25 percent for Latinos, whereas it was only 13 percent for whites. As for sending humanitarian aid and supplies to civilians in Syria, only Latino minorities were significantly more supportive than whites (p ≤ .05). The predicted probability of choosing the "strongly support" response was 38 percent for Latinos, 26 percent for whites, and 32 percent for African Americans. As Table 7.4, Model 1, shows, when it comes to the military option of "enforcing a no-fly zone over civilian areas in Syria, which may require bombing Syrian air defenses," all three racial/ethnic groups displayed somewhat similar levels of support, although the coefficient is marginally significant for Latinos (p ≤ .10). African Americans and Latinos were both significantly more supportive of "sending ground troops to Syria to protect innocent civilians from violent attacks" than whites. For instance, the predicted probability for strongly opposing the military option of sending ground troops to Syria was 28 percent for whites, whereas it was 16 percent for African Americans and 20 percent for Latinos.

We further examine potential group-based differences in policy attitudes regarding Trump's controversial Muslim ban proposition, which called for "a total and complete shutdown of Muslims entering the United States."[9] At the time of the survey (which was conducted several weeks before the election in November 2016), this proposition was among Trump's flagship campaign promises during his presidential bid.[10] As Table 7.5, Model 1, shows, both African Americans and Latinos indicated significantly higher opposition than whites to such an exclusionary policy proposal targeting a specific group solely based on that group's religious characteristic. The predicted probability of strongly opposing Trump's Muslim ban proposal was 48 percent for African Americans and 35 percent for Latinos as compared to 22 percent for whites.

There is strong support for our first set of hypotheses (H1a–H1d) regarding intergroup differences in foreign policy attitudes. But do these differences between white and nonwhite respondents emanate from differences in group

---

[9] See www.washingtonpost.com/news/post-politics/wp/2015/12/07/donald-trump-calls-for-total -and-complete-shutdown-of-muslims-entering-the-united-states/.

[10] The issue of the Muslim ban is revisited in Chapter 8, which presents the results of our 2018 national survey that examines public attitudes about key policy issues in the era of the Trump presidency.

TABLE 7.3 *The relationship between group empathy and attitudes about victims of the Syrian civil war*

| | Accepting Syrian refugees into the United States | | | | | | Humanitarian aid to Syrian civilians | | | | | |
| | Model 1 | | Model 2 | | Model 3 | | Model 1 | | Model 2 | | Model 3 | |
	β	S.E.	β	S.E.	β	S.E.	β	S.E.	β	S.E.	β	S.E.
Group empathy			1.56***	.34	1.23***	.35			1.88***	.40	1.59***	.44
Race/ethnicity												
Black	.37**	.14	.25†	.15	-.11	.18	.19	.14	-.01	.15	-.11	.17
Latino	.47***	.14	.30†	.16	.30†	.16	.35*	.16	.15	.17	.21	.18
Political factors												
National threat of terrorism					-.96**	.35					-.12	.33
Personal threat of terrorism					-.12	.28					-.62†	.35
Threat of high-casualty war					.62	.46					.44	.43
Threat of costly war					-1.06*	.43					-.29	.46
Trust in Congress					.13	.30					.11	.30
Trust in president					1.61***	.26					.35	.28
Trust in military					-.56*	.27					.25	.29
Party ID					-.42†	.25					-.30	.27
Ideology					-1.75***	.35					-.87*	.39
Socio-demographic factors												
Female	.33**	.12	.21	.13	.22†	.13	.27*	.13	.10	.13	.18	.14
Education	2.01***	.45	1.82***	.47	1.60***	.41	2.13***	.48	1.94***	.49	1.85***	.50

(continued)

TABLE 7.3 (continued)

	Accepting Syrian refugees into the United States						Humanitarian aid to Syrian civilians					
	Model 1		Model 2		Model 3		Model 1		Model 2		Model 3	
	β	S.E.	β	S.E.	β	S.E.	β	S.E.	β	S.E.	β	S.E.
Age	.02	.32	-.16	.34	.79*	.34	1.00**	.32	.84**	.33	1.37***	.34
Income	-.09	.30	-.29	.30	.13	.30	-.03	.31	-.24	.30	-.08	.30
Married	-.25†	.14	-.12	.14	-.07	.14	-.26†	.14	-.11	.14	-.16	.14
Employed	.04	.14	-.005	.14	.01	.13	.19	.14	.16	.14	.28†	.15
Metropolitan residence	.07	.20	.13	.21	.04	.21	-.02	.19	.05	.19	-.04	.20
Catholic	-.08	.13	-.05	.14	-.26†	.15	.09	.15	.12	.15	.05	.17
Household size	.48	.48	.44	.47	1.70***	.50	.66	.48	.63	.46	1.13*	.48
N	498		485		477		494		482		474	

Note: Coefficients estimated using ordered probit. Data are weighted. All variables are rescaled to run from 0 to 1. †p ≤ .10, *p ≤ .05, **p ≤ .01, and ***p ≤ .001, two-tailed.

Source: 2016 US Group Empathy TESS Study (GfK)

TABLE 7.4 *The relationship between group empathy and support for US military intervention in the Syrian civil war*

	US airstrikes						US ground troops					
	Model 1		Model 2		Model 3		Model 1		Model 2		Model 3	
	β	S.E.	β	S.E.	β	S.E.	β	S.E.	β	S.E.	β	S.E.
Group empathy	.15	.13	.87**	.35	.90*	.39			.44	.35	.66†	.38
Race/ethnicity												
Black	.15	.13	.05	.14	-.09	.15	.41**	.14	.38**	.15	.46*	.19
Latino	.24†	.15	.14	.15	.10	.16	.27†	.15	.22	.16	.30†	.18
Political factors												
National threat of terrorism					.004	.39					-.17	.42
Personal threat of terrorism					.32	.30					.50†	.30
Threat of high-casualty war					-.56	.46					.32	.37
Threat of costly war					.001	.41					-.62†	.36
Trust in Congress					.36	.31					1.04***	.28
Trust in president					-.01	.26					-.22	.27
Trust in military					.49†	.30					.27	.28
Party ID					-.13	.24					.53*	.24
Ideology					-.07	.30					-.68*	.34
Socio-demographic factors												
Female	-.13	.12	-.22†	.13	-.25*	.13	.20	.13	.16	.13	.16	.14

(continued)

TABLE 7.4 (*continued*)

| | US airstrikes | | | | | | US ground troops | | | | | |
| | Model 1 | | Model 2 | | Model 3 | | Model 1 | | Model 2 | | Model 3 | |
	β	S.E.	β	S.E.	β	S.E.	β	S.E.	β	S.E.	β	S.E.
Education	.56	.47	.46	.47	.46	.46	-.75†	.46	-.76†	.46	-.54	.46
Age	1.23***	.34	1.22***	.35	1.12**	.36	-.14	.33	-.17	.34	-.26	.34
Income	.40	.29	.32	.29	.28	.33	.27	.28	.20	.28	.10	.30
Married	-.11	.14	-.06	.14	-.09	.14	-.04	.14	.02	.15	.01	.15
Employed	-.18	.13	-.20	.13	-.27*	.14	.12	.13	.11	.13	.02	.13
Metropolitan residence	-.12	.19	-.08	.19	-.07	.18	.13	.19	.15	.20	.17	.19
Catholic	-.12	.14	-.12	.14	-.18	.14	.04	.14	.05	.14	.04	.14
Household size	.96*	.47	.98*	.47	.87†	.49	.41	.47	.42	.47	.07	.48
N	495		483		475		496		484		476	

Note: Coefficients estimated using ordered probit. Data are weighted. All variables are rescaled to run from 0 to 1. †p ≤ .10, *p ≤ .05, **p ≤ .01, and ***p ≤ .001, two-tailed.

Source: 2016 US Group Empathy TESS Study (GfK)

TABLE 7.5 *The relationship between group empathy and opposition to the Muslim ban*

	Model 1		Model 2		Model 3	
	β	S.E.	β	S.E.	β	S.E.
Group empathy			1.92***	.35	1.91***	.38
Race/ethnicity						
Black	.77***	.15	.60***	.16	.25	.20
Latino	.42**	.15	.22	.17	.19	.19
Political factors						
National threat of terrorism					−.99**	.33
Personal threat of terrorism					−.66*	.32
Threat of high-casualty war					.23	.46
Threat of costly war					−.52	.43
Trust in Congress					−.21	.32
Trust in president					1.44***	.28
Trust in military					−.45	.28
Party ID					−.79**	.26
Ideology					−1.67***	.35
Socio-demographic factors						
Female	.03	.13	−.13	.13	−.23†	.14
Education	1.78***	.48	1.49**	.52	1.13*	.55
Age	−.38	.34	−.58	.36	.32	.35
Income	−.01	.31	−.20	.31	.32	.31
Married	−.21	.16	−.08	.16	.004	.16
Employed	.13	.14	.06	.15	.19	.14
Metropolitan residence	.09	.19	.14	.19	.10	.22
Catholic	.08	.14	.09	.14	−.07	.16
Household size	−.80	.51	−.94†	.50	−.09	.54
N	500		487		478	

Note: Coefficients estimated using ordered probit. Data are weighted. All variables are rescaled to run from 0 to 1. †$p \leq .10$, *$p \leq .05$, **$p \leq .01$, and ***$p \leq .001$, two-tailed.
Source: 2016 US Group Empathy TESS Study (GfK)

empathy or are they the result of perceptions of threat or other political predispositions?

Our next set of analyses indicates that these racial/ethnic gaps are unlikely to be driven by perceptions of threat. As shown in Figure 7.1, whites and nonwhites do not significantly differ in their perceptions of (1) the possibility of a terrorist attack on US soil in the near future (*perceived national threat of*

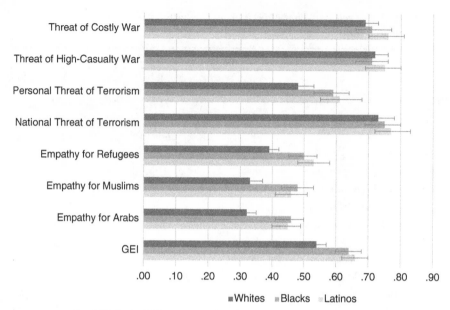

FIGURE 7.1 Racial/ethnic differences in threat/cost perceptions and group empathy
Note: The bars represent predictive margins calculated after OLS regression. The lines represent 95 percent confidence intervals. Models control for gender, education, age, income, marital status, household size, employment status, metropolitan residence, and religion (Catholic). Data are weighted. All variables are rescaled to run from 0 to 1. Estimates from full model available in the online appendix.
Source: 2016 US Group Empathy TESS Study (GfK)

terrorism); (2) the possibility of the United States getting involved in a high-casualty war overseas that costs the lives of American soldiers (*perceived threat of high-casualty war*); and (3) the possibility of getting involved in a costly war that would hurt the US economy (*perceived threat of costly war*). But when asked about the possibility that they or their friends might be the victim of a terrorist attack in the near future (*perceived personal threat of terrorism*), African Americans and Latinos report substantively higher concern (p ≤ .01) compared to whites (M_{Black} = .59; M_{Latino} = .61; M_{White} = .48).[11]

We then calculated group means for general and group-specific empathy among participants across the three racial/ethnic groups. The results are also displayed in Figure 7.1. Similar to previous findings, African Americans and Latinos both display significantly higher levels of group empathy in general compared to whites (M_{White} = .54; M_{Black} = .64; M_{Latino} = .66). African Americans and Latinos are also significantly more empathic toward refugees

---

[11] We employ Bonferroni correction for multiple comparisons of marginal means across the three racial/ethnic categories to discern which group means are statistically different from one another.

(M_{White} = .39; M_{Black} = .50; M_{Latino} = .53), Arabs (M_{White} = .32; M_{Black} = .46; M_{Latino} = .45), and Muslims (M_{White} = .33; M_{Black} = .48; M_{Latino} = .46).[12] In other words, African Americans and Latinos score higher on group-specific empathy toward refugees, Arabs, and Muslims – key outgroups stereotypically associated with terror threat – despite perceiving themselves and their loved ones to be more vulnerable. These results support Hypothesis 2.

While minorities appear to have higher levels of group empathy, this does not necessarily mean that group empathy is the driver of intergroup variation observed in the outcomes of interest. To systematically test this, we include the GEI in the second set of models in Tables 7.1 through 7.5. We also include alternative factors that might explain these group differences: perceptions of threat and political trust, as well as partisanship and ideology.[13] These are in Model 3 of Tables 7.1 through 7.5. Finally, generalized structural equation modeling (GSEM) helps explore if group empathy significantly accounts for these racial/ethnic differences on foreign policy attitudes.

In line with our theory, group empathy powerfully predicts foreign policy attitudes on every dependent variable examined, including attitudes concerning the US responsibility to protect, foreign aid, the US response to Syrian civil war, and the Muslim ban. This holds even after controlling for a host of political variables representing alternative explanations. In fact, the impact of group empathy is larger than that of any other political covariate on most of the outcomes of interest. To illustrate, moving from the lowest to highest levels of the GEI more than quadruples one's probability of attributing responsibility to the United States to protect other nations in need – an increase from 4 to 17 percent. The predicted probability of opposition to foreign aid decreases from 25 to 7 percent when the GEI moves from its lowest to highest level. Group empathy also substantively affects attitudes toward the civil war in Syria. Moving from low to high scores on the GEI is associated with a substantial decrease in opposition to the resettlement of the Syrian refugees in the United States from 38 percent down to only 13 percent. As for the predicted probability of supporting US financial aid for the victims of the Syrian civil war, shifting from the lowest to highest level of the GEI results in more than a six-fold increase: 8 to 50 percent. Regarding support for potential military options to intervene in this civil war, the predicted probability of very strongly supporting US airstrikes increases from 7 to 25 percent with group empathy, whereas very strongly opposing the deployment of US ground troops in Syria decreases from 38 to 18 percent.

---

[12] Pairwise comparisons with Bonferroni adjustment indicate that the levels of general and group-specific empathy that African Americans and Latinos display do not statistically differ from one another.

[13] Due to space restrictions, this survey experiment did not include measures of social dominance orientation, ethnocentrism, and authoritarianism, all of which involve multi-item indexes. We have already shown in previous chapters that the results are robust to model specifications that include these measures.

Group empathy also substantively affects one's likelihood to oppose then-presidential candidate Trump's Muslim ban proposal, even with controls for perceived threat of terrorism, political trust, party identification, ideology, and key socio-demographic factors. For those who score lowest in the GEI, the predicted probability of very strongly opposing the Muslim ban proposal is only 9 percent compared to 44 percent for those scoring highest. We revisit this issue in Chapter 8 with new national data collected after Trump became president and turned his controversial campaign proposal into actual government policy.

These results demonstrate that, across all three racial/ethnic groups, group empathy substantively increases support for foreign policies designed to help other nations in distress. The last set of analyses explores whether the racial and ethnic differences in opinion on these policy variables are explained by differences in group empathy. We conduct GSEM analyses to systematically test this possibility. The results suggest that group empathy does in fact help explain the intergroup differences we observe. The bootstrap procedures demonstrate that, other than support for deploying US ground troops to Syria, the indirect effects are statistically significant for all of the outcomes of interest discussed in the chapter thus far.[14]

Experimental Findings

We next analyze the experimental data. The initial results, illustrated in Figure 7.2, confirm the presence of racial/ethnic group variation in reactions to the international humanitarian crisis scenario. African Americans and Latinos overall displayed significantly higher support than whites for a US military intervention against the oppressive regime depicted in the vignette. Nonwhite respondents – particularly Latinos – were also more favorable toward the US providing financial aid to the victims on average. On the other hand, there were no significant racial/ethnic group differences in support for granting asylum to the refugees of this conflict. Finally – and this was something of a surprise to us – the race/ethnicity of the foreign nation in need did not seem to have any effect on the policy reactions of any racial/ethnic group of respondents in the sample. In other words, respondents of all races and ethnicities generally reacted similarly toward the Arab nation as they did toward the European nation.

We found racial/ethnic group differences in prosocial behavior, also illustrated in Figure 7.2, measured by respondents' propensity to request more information, donate money, and sign a petition to help the nation depicted in the vignettes. Keep in mind that only in the final, debriefing section did we tell participants: "Because this was a fictional conflict, there is no additional

---

[14] The full estimates of these GSEM analyses are available in the online appendix.

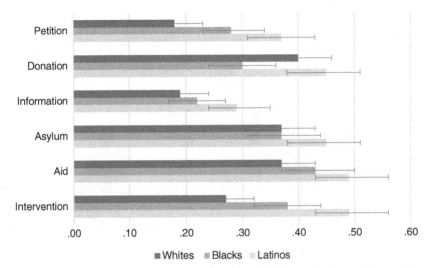

FIGURE 7.2 Racial/ethnic differences in reactions to the humanitarian crisis experiment
Note: The bars represent predicted probabilities calculated after logistic regression. The lines represent 95 percent confidence intervals. All variables are rescaled to run from 0 to 1. Estimates from full model available in the online appendix.
Source: 2016 US Group Empathy TESS Study (GfK)

information or electronic petition, and you will receive the full $1.00 bonus for your valuable contribution to this research." So, up until the last section of the survey experiment, participants thought they were really invited to sign up for news updates, donate money, and sign a petition to help the victims of a real conflict. As mentioned, this is important because the experimental design tests participants' *actual* political behavior rather than their self-reported intentions. On average, Latinos were significantly more interested in receiving further information about the conflict than whites. African Americans were least likely to donate money for the victims, although they were more likely to donate money to Arab victims than were white respondents. Compared to whites, both African Americans and Latinos showed a much stronger tendency to sign a petition urging the federal government to take humanitarian action. This is especially remarkable given that minorities are often perceived to be more cautious about their dealings with government agencies, partly due to being targeted or unfairly treated by law enforcement. However, they do not shy away from putting their names down for the record and signing a petition to help a foreign nation.

Besides average group differences regarding these behavioral outcome measures, there was interesting intergroup variation across experimental conditions, as illustrated in Figure 7.3. In reaction to the manipulation of the racial/ethnic cues, whites displayed less interest in obtaining further

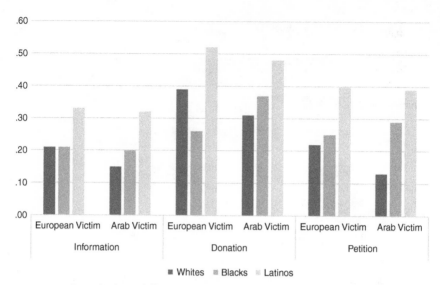

FIGURE 7.3 Racial/ethnic differences in political behavior upon exposure to European versus Arab victim vignettes
Note: The bars represent estimated group means calculated using MANCOVA. Models control for gender, education, age, income, marital status, household size, employment status, metropolitan residence, and religion (Catholic). All variables are rescaled to run from 0 to 1. Estimates from full model available in the online appendix.
Source: 2016 US Group Empathy TESS Study (GfK)

information in the Arab nation condition (.15) compared to the European one (.21). By comparison, the mean levels of interest in more information about the conflict were stable among African Americans (.21 in the European vignette and .20 in the Arab one) and Latinos (.33 in the European vignette and .32 in the Arab one) across both experimental conditions.

Whites were much more likely to donate their extra dollar in the European nation condition (.39) than the Arab condition (.31). We observed the opposite trend for African Americans: the marginal mean for African Americans was .26 in the European condition, while it was .37 in the Arab one. Latinos' donation tendency somewhat parallels that of whites: the marginal mean for Latinos was .52 in the European condition, and it was down to .48 in the Arab condition. However, across both conditions, Latinos displayed the highest propensity to donate money to the victims of the conflict as compared to both African Americans and whites.

The third measure of political behavior was signing a petition for humanitarian action. Here we observe a pattern across conditions similar to the one in the donation behavior. In the European condition, the marginal mean for whites was .22; however, it was .13 in the Arab condition. African Americans' reaction to the petition invitation was once again opposite to that of whites across the two conditions: the marginal mean for African Americans in the Arab condition was .29, somewhat higher than the .25 observed in the European condition. The marginal mean for Latinos was .40 in the European condition and .39 in the Arab condition, so Latino reactions were almost identical in both conditions.

We further analyze the posttest data by including group empathy in the models along with party identification, ideology, and all of the socio-demographic controls we included in the pretest survey analyses. The results consistently demonstrate that group empathy generally comes out as the most statistically and substantively significant factor in explaining participants' reactions to the experimental vignettes.[15] GSEM analyses further confirm the fact that group empathy substantially explains the racial/ethnic group differences observed earlier. More specifically, the bootstrap results indicate the significance of indirect effects for all of the posttest measures with group empathy as the mediator. These results are illustrated in Figure 7.4.

Overall, these findings corroborate Group Empathy Theory in the foreign policy context. The results also reveal some differences between the domestic- versus foreign-policy domains with respect to white, African American, and Latino political attitudes and behavior. In the domestic policy context, our survey and experimental data indicated that African Americans show the highest empathy for stigmatized groups and display the strongest support for policies intended to help them. By comparison, Latinos turn out to be the most responsive and empathic – surpassing African Americans – when it comes to various foreign policy issues. This was particularly the case for reactions to the experimental vignettes. Latinos were the racial/ethnic group most likely to support policies for undertaking a military intervention, providing aid, and granting asylum. Latinos also demonstrated the highest proclivity to request more information, donate money, and sign a petition in support of the victims across both European and Arab conditions.

Can it be that, because Latinx citizens are still stereotypically perceived as "foreigners" in American society (Johnson 1998), they display such high outgroup empathy for people of foreign nations? Perhaps most particularly, those Latinos who still retain transnational ties to their home countries and practice a bilingual, bicultural way of life may have an increased sensitivity and responsiveness toward other cultures outside the United States. Indeed, Sanchez (2006) shows that Latinos who are foreign-born and less proficient in English have less restrictive attitudes toward Latino-salient policy areas (immigration and bilingual education) as well as other political issues (abortion and death penalty) that are not directly tied to Latinos. Similarly, Branton (2007, 300) finds that "less acculturated Latinos are more likely to support policy positions that

---

[15] Full results of these analyses are available in the online appendix.

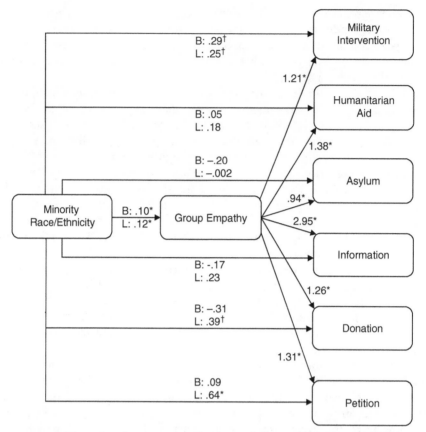

FIGURE 7.4 The role of group empathy in explaining racial/ethnic differences in reactions to the humanitarian crisis experiment

Note: Coefficients estimated using generalized structural equation modeling based on the full models. "B" denotes blacks and "L" denotes Latinos. White respondents constitute the baseline category. Estimates from full models available in the online appendix. All indirect paths are statistically significant. Data are weighted. All variables are rescaled to run from 0 to 1. *p ≤ .05, one-tailed.

Source: 2016 US Group Empathy TESS Study (GfK)

distribute benefits to immigrants, the needy, and minority groups in general than when compared to 'fully' acculturated Latinos." But even Latinos who are born in the United States and do not have bilingual skills may nevertheless still be exposed (via their first-generation family members) to the Latinx collective memory that contains stories and experiences of people who are forced to leave their countries due to oppression and/or financial impasse, seeking asylum in foreign lands. Moreover, native-born and English-proficient Latinos are not necessarily immune to the stigmatization of the Latinx community as "foreigners" due to the color of their skin and/or their family names no matter how acculturated they might feel. In all, the experience of discrimination that contributes to Latino group consciousness and identification (Sanchez 2006) may lead to higher group empathy for foreign nations and may thus help explain our findings in this policy domain.

THE CURRENT DIRECTION OF US FOREIGN POLICY AND PUBLIC OPINION

The Trump administration's foreign policies bring the relevance of our theory and findings into sharp focus. Since entering the White House, Trump has withdrawn the United States from several United Nations organizations with humanitarian missions such as the International Criminal Court and the UN Human Rights Council. Trump also officially quit the UN Educational, Scientific, and Cultural Organization (UNESCO) – effectively moving the status of the United States from that of full member to that of observer.[16] Furthermore, Trump ended the Iran nuclear deal brokered under the Obama administration and reimposed economy-crippling sanctions on the nation of Iran.[17] Trump also pulled the country out of the Paris Climate Accord, making it officially the only nation in the world to reject this agreement, even though the United States stands as one of the top two largest global emitters of greenhouse gases.[18] The Trump administration also exited the negotiation and adoption process of the Global Compact for Migration – the first-ever UN global agreement on reaching a common approach to international migration.[19]

The Trump administration also severely restricted the number of refugees offered protection in the United States, which disproportionately affected refugees from predominantly Muslim countries. The annual refugee admissions

[16] Maya Finoh (2018), "Five Ways the Trump Administration Has Attacked the UN and International Human Rights Bodies," American Civil Liberties Union (ACLU), www.aclu.org /blog/human-rights/five-ways-trump-administration-has-attacked-un-and-international-human -rights.

[17] Brian Naylor and Ayesha Rascoe (2018), "Trump: US 'Will Withdraw' From Iran Nuclear Deal," NPR, www.npr.org/2018/05/08/609383603/trump-u-s-will-withdraw-from-iran-nuclear-deal.

[18] Trevor Nace (2017), "America Is Officially the Only Nation on Earth to Reject the Paris Agreement," *Forbes*, www.forbes.com/sites/trevornace/2017/11/07/america-is-officially-the-only-nation-on-earth-to-reject-the-paris-agreement/#bc3ed644dc46.

[19] See Megan Specia (2018), "UN Agrees on Migration Pact, but US Is Conspicuously Absent," *New York Times*, www.nytimes.com/2018/07/13/world/europe/united-nations-migration-agreement.html. On a separate but related note, the United States remains the sole UN member that failed to ratify the Convention of the Rights of the Child – a landmark agreement adopted in 1989 that became the most widely ratified human rights treaty in history (see http:// indicators.ohchr.org). The United States also remains nonsignatory to the 1999 Ottawa Treaty (also known as the Mine Ban Treaty), which aims at eliminating antipersonnel landmines around the world. See www.armscontrol.org/factsheets/ottawa.

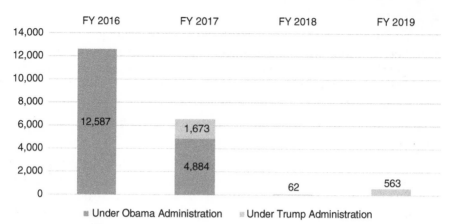

FIGURE 7.5 Syrian refugee admissions to the United States in fiscal years 2016–19
Note: Each fiscal year runs from October 1 of the previous calendar year to September 30
of the following calendar year.
Source: The Refugee Processing Center (RPC)

ceiling became substantively lower with each fiscal year that Trump was in office.
The ceiling was reduced down to only 30,000 in FY 2019 and then a scant 18,000
in FY 2020 – the lowest numbers in the history of the US refugee admissions
program.[20] The ceiling represents the maximum number of refugees to be
allowed, rather than a goal to achieve, and the actual admissions typically fall
far below the ceiling.

Figure 7.5 presents data from the US Refugee Admissions Report for FY
2016–19. The number of Syrian refugees admitted under the Obama
administration for FY 2017 were calculated based on data for the months of
October 2016–January 2017, whereas those admitted from February to
September 2017 were counted under the Trump administration. It should be
noted that most of the refugees admitted during FY 2017 after Trump took
office were the ones who were already vetted and processed during the Obama
administration. Therefore, the data points for FY 2018 and FY 2019 are more

[20] See https://fas.org/sgp/crs/homesec/IN11196.pdf. The refugee ceiling was set above 230,000 in
1980 – the year the Refugee Act was signed into law. The average ceiling throughout the Reagan
administration was around 90,000 and fluctuated between 125,000 and 142,000 during the
presidency of George H. W. Bush. President Clinton continued this trend for which refugee
resettlement surpassed 100,000 per year. The ceiling ranged between 70,000 and 85,000
throughout the second Bush administration, and Barack Obama raised it to 110,000 in the
last two years of his presidency. See Stuart Anderson (2018), "Here's What Trump's New Limits
on Refugees Mean," *Forbes*, www.forbes.com/sites/stuartanderson/2018/09/20/trump-official-
announces-controversial-new-limits-on-refugees/#7abc1ffb410a.

representative of the Trump-era policy toward resettling Syrian refugees in the United States. As the figure illustrates, the number of Syrian refugees plummeted to merely 62 in FY 2018 and 563 in FY 2019 under Trump, compared to 12,587 refugees admitted under the Obama presidency in FY 2016.

Given its status as the world's only remaining superpower and perceived leading nation, critics may view the United States as falling short of doing its fair share in resettling refugees. This is also the case for many other developed, wealthy nations. According to the UN Refugee Agency's 2017 Global Trends Report, 85 percent of the world's refugees are hosted by developing nations, and the poorest nations of the world have provided asylum to one-third of the global total.[21] To put these figures in perspective, the number of registered Syrian refugees granted asylum in Turkey as of November 2018 was 3,591,714 (63.8 percent of total persons of concern), with the next largest numbers in Lebanon (952,562) and Jordan (672,578). Including the Palestine refugees under the UN Relief and Works Agency (UNRWA) alongside Syrians, one in four people in Lebanon and one in three in Jordan were refugees, according to the 2017 data. Despite the high number of refugees these countries host, the majority of the financial burden has been left to these developing nations rather than being taken on more universally by the international community, led by the United States.

Trump has also significantly cut humanitarian assistance to troubled regions around the world. For instance, in August 2018, Trump declared that the United States will no longer provide aid to the UNRWA for Palestine Refugees. Given that the United States was its largest funder, this suddenly left the UNRWA with a budget deficit of over $270 million.[22] This abrupt and drastic funding cut was followed by many other cuts to humanitarian programs, perhaps most notably the $200 million in cuts from the US Agency for International Development (USAID) – the primary agency for administering foreign aid and developmental assistance to other countries.[23] In his speech to the United Nations General Assembly on September 25, 2018, Trump said: "Moving forward, we are only going to give foreign aid to those who respect us and, frankly, are our friends."[24] Part of this policy, Trump remarked, would also involve trimming back US contributions to UN peacekeeping operations around the world.

Perhaps the most remarkable slogan in Trump's UN speech in September 2018 was his proclamation that "We reject the ideology of globalism, and we embrace

---

[21] The full report is available at www.unhcr.org/5b27be547.pdf.
[22] See Finoh (2018) at note 16.
[23] Karim Doumar (2018), "Cities Will Bear the Brunt of Trump's Aid Cuts to Palestine," *Bloomberg*, www.citylab.com/equity/2018/10/cities-will-bear-the-brunt-of-trumps-aid-cuts-to-palestine/573340/.
[24] Trump's UN speech can be accessed at www.whitehouse.gov/briefings-statements/remarks-president-trump-73rd-session-united-nations-general-assembly-new-york-ny/.

the doctrine of patriotism."[25] At a rally a few weeks later, Trump made clear that what he actually means by patriotism is nationalism:

A globalist is a person that wants the globe to do well, frankly, not caring about our country so much. And you know what? We can't have that. You know, they have a word – it's sort of became old-fashioned – it's called a nationalist. And I say, really, we're not supposed to use that word? You know what I am? I'm a nationalist, okay? I'm a nationalist. Nationalist! Nothing wrong. Use that word. Use that word![26]

This declaration marked an end to the United States' long-standing foreign policy stance on globalism and unsettled many US allies. At the gathering of world leaders in Paris on November 11, 2018, for Armistice Day, marking 100 years since the end of World War I, French President Emmanuel Macron rebuked Trump's discourse by asserting: "Patriotism is the exact opposite of nationalism."[27] He continued his remarks by stating: "Nationalism is a betrayal of patriotism. By saying 'our interests first, who cares about the others,' we erase what a nation holds dearest, what gives it life, what makes it great, and what is essential: its moral values."

Even prior to Trump's election, experts noted the challenges of securing funding for humanitarian projects and interventions despite considerable returns on security and human rights in receiving countries. As Kull (2011, 53) puts it: "A central question facing the US aid and development community is whether, with increasing pressures on all forms of spending in the current fiscal environment, the levels of US spending on development and humanitarian aid can be sustained." But, in the current context, the issue is more about the willingness of the US leadership to embrace its humanitarian responsibilities rather than a matter of financial sustainability.[28] Even within the broadest definition of aid (including military and security assistance provided partly for national security purposes), foreign aid accounted for about 1.2 percent of the federal budget in FY 2016. Therefore, strictly humanitarian aid – which amounted to only 14 percent of the foreign assistance activities – constituted much less than 1 percent of the total federal budget in that fiscal year under the Obama administration.[29] With the new cuts to humanitarian aid under Trump,

---

[25] Ibid.

[26] Peter Baker (2018), "'Use That Word!': Trump Embraces the 'Nationalist' Label," *New York Times*, www.nytimes.com/2018/10/23/us/politics/nationalist-president-trump.html.

[27] Kevin Liptak (2018), "Macron Rebukes Nationalism as Trump Observes Armistice Day," CNN, www.cnn.com/2018/11/11/politics/donald-trump-armistice-day-paris/index.html.

[28] On the legislative leadership side, Trump's proposed budget cuts to USAID received bipartisan backlash in the US Senate. See Lesley Wroughton and Patricia Zengerle (2018), "US Senators Pledge to Fight Trump Push to Cut Aid Funding," Reuters, www.reuters.com/article/us-usa-trump-aid/u-s-senators-pledge-to-fight-trump-push-to-cut-aid-funding-idUSKBN1L12F3.

[29] See James McBride (2018), "How Does the US Spends Its Foreign Aid?" Council on Foreign Relations, www.cfr.org/backgrounder/how-does-us-spend-its-foreign-aid; Curt Tarnoff and Marian L. Lawson (2018), "Foreign Aid: An Introduction to US Programs and Policy," Congressional Research Services, https://fas.org/sgp/crs/row/R40213.pdf.

the percentage approached an all-time record low in 2020, as Trump further crippled USAID funding while also cutting ties with the World Health Organization (WHO) as part of a blame-shifting strategy for the delayed response to the COVID-19 pandemic.[30]

Beyond the willingness of leadership, humanitarian foreign policy actions also rely on the willingness of the public. Part of this willingness is tied to how informed the public is about these issues. According to a Kaiser Family Foundation (KFF) poll conducted in December 2014, when asked about how much of the federal budget goes to foreign aid, only 5 percent of the 1,505 respondents knew the correct answer was about 1 percent; the average respondent estimated that foreign aid occupies 26 percent of the federal budget.[31] In a later KFF poll conducted in January 2018, 49 percent of respondents thought the United States spends too much on foreign aid.[32] However, once informed that only about 1 percent of the federal budget goes to assisting other nations, those who continued to think it was too much dropped by 20 percentage points, down to 29 percent. While one's level of political information is an important factor, our findings suggest that public opinion dynamics regarding such policies are also very much tied to group empathy for those experiencing repression, violence, famine, and natural disasters abroad. In other words, even when members of the public may be aware of the facts, they may simply not care.

The public's general lack of outgroup empathy may represent for like-minded leaders a blank check to formulate and execute policies that could seriously undermine humanitarian and egalitarian norms. By contrast, even when only a portion of the public does care, it can be a powerful force that sets the cogs of checks and balances in motion. For instance, on January 27, 2017, the night Trump issued the first iteration of the Muslim ban, mass protests – involving people from all walks of life – immediately broke out across the United States as reports started coming in detailing how even patients in need of urgent medical attention and US legal permanent residents were not being allowed to enter the country.

One such report involved a four-month-old Iranian baby girl with a serious heart condition who was scheduled to meet with doctors in Portland, Oregon, for life-saving surgery. Her family was denied visas due to Trump's executive order. To bring attention to the predicament of the baby, Representative Suzanne Bonamici addressed her colleagues in the House of Representatives by standing next to an easel with a large photograph of the infant, pleading: "This is Fatemeh.

---

[30] Nahal Toosi (2020), "Trump Hobbles Foreign Aid as Coronavirus Rips around the World," *Politico*, www.politico.com/news/2020/04/15/trump-foreign-aid-coronavirus-188659.

[31] Poncie Rutsch (2015), "Guess How Much of Uncle Sam's Money Goes to Foreign Aid. Guess Again!" NPR, www.npr.org/sections/goatsandsoda/2015/02/10/383875581/guess-how-much-of-uncle-sams-money-goes-to-foreign-aid-guess-again.

[32] See http://files.kff.org/attachment/Topline-Kaiser-Health-Tracking-Poll%E2%80%93January-2018.

She is not a terrorist. She's a four-month-old baby girl who is in immediate need of open-heart surgery."[33] Bonamici further condemned the Muslim ban by saying: "Keeping four-month-old babies out of our country doesn't make us safer. It puts her life in danger and diminishes the United States in the eyes of the world." Fortunately, Fatemeh and her family were granted waivers to travel to the United States where she finally underwent a successful operation that repaired her life-threatening heart defect. A Portland immigration attorney, Jennifer M. Morrisey, who represents the family said: "I think Fatemeh's case is one of generosity and compassion on a great number of individuals. And I hope that we'll see other cases of that kind of compassionate concern coming forward in the times to come in the immigration realm."[34] Empathic reactions among the members of the public and media attention to stories like this may help increase the salience of policy issues tied to humanitarian and social justice concerns about targeted outgroups (foreign and domestic) among state and federal lawmakers, government officials, and the judiciary.

CONCLUSION

Public opinion often serves as a major constraint on decision makers, particularly when it comes to military interventions and other salient foreign policy issues, setting the limits within which policy makers may operate (e.g., Foyle 1999; Sobel 2001). Such a constraining role of the public in the foreign policy domain has been demonstrated prominently in studies examining audience costs (Fearon 1994) and the structural explanations of the democratic peace phenomenon (e.g., Bueno de Mesquita & Lalman 1992; Maoz & Russett 1993).

One of the key strategies for the United States to project its influence and maintain its superpower status in the global arena lies in assuming leadership in international crises and providing assistance to countries in need. Such actions are also vital for fulfilling the leading role of the United States in honoring the "Responsibility to Protect" principle, which relegates the international community the responsibility to protect those people in need when their own governments are unwilling or unable to do so (Evans 2008). However, prior research shows that public opposition to the costs of military interventions and other foreign policy actions may force US presidents to avoid involvement in an international crisis all together or – in the case that an intervention is already in progress – prematurely terminate the mission (see Jentleson & Britton 1998). This is not only an important concern for US foreign policy and national security but is also disconcerting from a humanitarian perspective.

---

[33] Amy Wang (2017), "'She Is Not A Terrorist': Iranian Baby Caught in Travel Ban Is Granted Entry for Heart Surgery," *The Gazette*, https://gazette.com/health/she-is-not-a-terrorist-iranian-baby-caught-in-travel/article_bd1d9708-c4bd-57f3-aa83-ac61ed515210.html.

[34] Darran Simon (2017), "First Barred by Travel Ban, Iranian Baby Now Recovering After Surgery in US," CNN, www.cnn.com/2017/02/27/health/travel-ban-iranian-baby-surgery/index.html.

If a president misperceives the US public as unconditionally cost-averse, this may result in poor decision making that undervalues the long-term goals of foreign policy and jeopardizes mission accomplishments (Burk 1999; Filson & Werner 2002; Goemans 2000; Slantchev 2004; Sullivan 2008; Wagner 2000). In addition to adversely affecting US foreign policy, such misperceptions may exacerbate humanitarian emergencies. This was the case with President Bill Clinton prematurely terminating the humanitarian mission in Somalia following the deaths of nineteen US soldiers in October 1993. The Clinton administration's refusal to intervene in the Rwandan genocide in April 1994 and belated response to the Bosnian war (only after the Srebrenica massacre in 1995) may also be partly attributed to such misperceptions about the cost sensitivity of the public. Our findings, however, suggest that the public does not react homogenously to foreign policy threats. Some groups may be more supportive of humanitarian interventions and monetary aid due to higher group empathy, regardless of perceived costs and benefits.

Further theory-based investigations in this line of research are warranted for improving our understanding of the dynamics of public opinion in the foreign policy domain. Given the influence of the public in steering leadership decisions, investigating the role group empathy plays in public responses to humanitarian emergencies has important broader implications, particularly concerning US foreign policy, as well as national and international security. We thus expect these findings are relevant not only for the research community but also for policy makers.

8

Group Empathy in the Era of Trump

> You got your ideas and your visions / And you say you sympathize / You look but you don't listen / There's no empathy in your eyes / You make deals and promises / And everybody bows down / And now you wanna come shake my hand / On the east side of town
>
> Lucinda Williams, "East Side of Town," from the album *Down Where the Spirit Meets the Bone* (2014)[1]

Three hot pink seesaws bounced up and down as children on the opposite ends giggled with joy. Yet the kids playing together were not just on opposite sides of the seesaws; they were on opposite sides of the border between the United States and Mexico, with a wall separating them down the middle. The seesaws were installed on the steel slats of a section of the border wall in Sunland Park, New Mexico, where, only a couple of months before, members of a far-right armed militia attempted to detain migrant families crossing over while another group was erecting crowd-funded border fencing on private land. One of the artists who designed the "Teeter-Totter Wall," Ronald Rael, said the installation represented the idea that "actions that take place on one side have a direct consequence on the other side."[2]

The juxtaposition of children playing and anti-immigrant vigilante groups guarding the border is a metaphor for the age-old civil rights versus security debate. On one side of the seesaw, public criticism in response to Donald Trump's rhetoric and policies often invoke the concept of empathy. The border wall, family separations, the Muslim ban, retrenchment on the civil rights of the LGBTQ community, and so on are described as heartless and cruel by Democrats and many mainstream news editorials. They often

---

[1] "East Side of Town," written by Lucinda Williams. Published by Highway Twenty Music (BMI).
[2] Simon Romero (2019), "Seesaws Straddle the Mexico Border, and Smiles Shine Through," *New York Times*, www.nytimes.com/2019/07/30/us/seesaws-border-wall.html.

implore Trump's supporters to put themselves in the shoes of those negatively affected.

As we discuss throughout this book, empathy for groups very different than ours is not as common as empathy for one's own group. Interpersonal empathy is often conceived as an evolutionarily adaptive mechanism for protecting our family, close friends, and members of our own tribe from threats. In fact, on the other side of the seesaw, some view Trump's harsh immigration policies as a protectionist response prioritizing Americans and their interests against perceived attacks from hostile foreigners. When ingroup bonds are strong and there is a powerful sense of external threat, such protectionist, Machiavellian-like policies might strategically cater to ingroup-oriented empathy that puts one's co-ethnics first at the expense of others and at all costs. However, empathy for outgroups does emerge even in these situations – and when it does, it powerfully constrains support for the exclusionary, ethnonationalist, anti-immigrant policies ascendant in the United States and in many other nations.

TRUMP AND THE POLITICS OF EXCLUSION

The Trump era provides a natural experimental setting to test the power of group empathy versus threat, ingroup interests, and symbolic politics on public opinion. To illustrate, a primary target of Trump's politics of exclusion has been undocumented immigrants. After taking office, Trump continued the anti-immigrant rhetoric he initiated during his campaign, and he soon enacted a series of punitive immigration policies. In his rallies and tweets, Trump often told anecdotes about undocumented immigrants allegedly committing violent crimes against American citizens. He would host families of crime victims at his rallies and White House events, and retweet news stories in which undocumented immigrants were the alleged perpetrators. He blamed Democrats for the human tragedy caused by his own family separation policy, tweeting: "They don't care about crime and want illegal immigrants, no matter how bad they may be, to pour into and infest our country, like MS-13."[3] In reality, however, crime rates are substantially lower in communities where immigrants are concentrated, and immigrants are less likely to commit crimes than natives of similar class status (Adelman et al. 2018; Light & Miller 2018).

Trump framed undocumented immigration as not only a security threat but also an economic one. In his 2019 State of the Union address, he asserted that "working-class Americans are left to pay the price for mass illegal immigration, reduced jobs, lower wages, overburdened schools, hospitals that are so crowded

---

[3] See https://twitter.com/realdonaldtrump/status/1009071403918864385?lang=en.

you can't get in, increased crime, and a depleted social safety net."[4] Aiming to turn the tables on those who side with undocumented immigrants, he added: "Tolerance for illegal immigration is not compassionate, it is actually very cruel."[5] Here, too, the evidence contradicts the arguments. Studies routinely suggest that, at worst, undocumented immigrants have a net-neutral impact on the overall economy and there is in fact good reason to be more optimistic than that (e.g., Hanson 2007; see also Blau & Mackie 2017).

While solidifying his base, Trump's discourse also triggered strong public opposition. Citizens around the country began to actively organize and protest against the rise of xenophobia in the United States. The reactions ranged from responding publicly to Trump's posts on Twitter – noting the dehumanizing use of a term commonly used for disease-carrying pests, "infestation," in reference to undocumented immigrants – all the way to climbing up the Statue of Liberty in defense of immigrant children housed in cages, as Patricia Okoumou did. What prompts some people to reject populist, exclusionary appeals and even take risky political actions in defense of outgroups, while others remain on the sidelines or embrace punitive policies that target such groups?

In this chapter we examine the effects of group empathy on a host of policies pursued by the Trump administration using data from (1) the 2018 US Group Empathy Study and (2) the 2018 ANES Pilot Study, both fielded by YouGov using national samples. In line with our theory, group empathy is closely linked to public opinion about a wide range of Trump's policy initiatives. Differences in group empathy also help explain opinion gaps between racial and ethnic groups on these policies. Nonwhite respondents generally display higher levels of group empathy than whites, and they also support policies that protect stigmatized, disadvantaged groups even when they are in competition with those groups for jobs and resources.

The next section presents our hypotheses and research design. We then provide a contextual overview of the policies and issues central to the Trump administration. In addition to the direct predictive power of group empathy on policy views above and beyond standard political predispositions, we also examine its power to explain intergroup differences. The findings reveal important policy implications, especially in an era where partisan polarization and societal divisions run high. On the positive side, normatively speaking, group empathy represents a countervailing force that can bring competing groups together, serving as an antidote to contemporary discourses of threat, dehumanization, scapegoating, and xenophobia.

---

[4] The full transcript can be accessed at www.whitehouse.gov/briefings-statements/remarks-president-trump-state-union-address-2/?utm_source=link.
[5] Ibid.

HYPOTHESES AND DATA

We anticipate that group empathy drives reactions to many of the Trump administration's policies targeting stigmatized groups (H1). Specifically, the issues of interest include opinions about the border wall, family separation, DACA, the Muslim ban, hurricane relief for Puerto Rico, the removal of symbols offensive to minorities (specifically, the use of Native American symbols in sports and symbols of Confederacy), the Black Lives Matter and #MeToo movements, and LGBTQ rights.

While group empathy should structure opinions across all racial/ethnic groups, our theory suggests racial/ethnic differences of opinion will be explained by differences in group empathy. If that is so, key minority–majority differences in group empathy should appear (H2) and those differences should help explain why some groups take more progressive positions on the Trump-era policies targeting stigmatized communities (H3).

We use two datasets to test these hypotheses. The 2018 US Group Empathy Study interviewed a total of 1,050 respondents – 350 whites and stratified oversamples of 350 African Americans and 350 Latinos – in October 2018. The 2018 ANES Pilot Study was conducted in December 2018 with a total of 2,500 respondents, of which 1,854 were white, 255 were African American, and 247 were Latino. Asians, Native Americans, and other racial/ethnic minorities constituted about 6 percent of the observations. The models included survey weights to reflect several demographic dimensions of the US public in order to obtain more accurate estimates of the population parameters of interest.[6]

The 2018 US Group Empathy Study and the 2018 ANES Pilot Study both employ the same four-item version of the Group Empathy Index (GEI) introduced in Chapter 3.[7] In addition to the main GEI measure, common controls include party identification, ideology, and key socio-demographic factors. The 2018 US Group Empathy Study also included measures for social dominance orientation (SDO) and ethnocentrism.[8] We also control for

---

[6] We employ unweighted data for sensitivity analyses that compare the reactions of whites, African Americans, and Latinos, and for within-group analyses. The results are nearly always identical across these different model specifications using weighted and unweighted data.

[7] Refer back to Table 3.5 in Chapter 3 that lists the items selected for the short GEI. In both datasets, the Cronbach's alpha reliability coefficient between the four GEI items is very high (.88 for the ANES study and .86 for our national survey). As discussed in Chapter 3, about half of respondents in the ANES survey were randomly given different question wordings in a couple of the GEI items. We reran the models with only the portion of the ANES data that uses the same question wording as our own national survey. These sensitivity analyses yield consistent results (available in the online appendix).

[8] Due to space limitations, we measure ethnocentrism in this study with only one of the six items previously employed (adopted from Bizumic et al. 2009). The item is "No matter what happens, I will ALWAYS support my cultural or ethnic group and never let it down" on a 5-point scale ranging from "strongly disagree" to "strongly agree." It is one of the top two items with the

perceptions of immigration and terror threats, where relevant and available, in order to compare the two forces – group empathy versus threat – directly. The 2018 ANES Pilot Study did not measure SDO, but it includes the racial resentment scale, which allows us to examine the role of group empathy above and beyond this consistently powerful measure of racial animus. Both surveys also provided data on church attendance. Controlling for this allows us to help separate the association of group empathy from that of religious belief systems, such as the moral obligation to do charity work or reject LGBTQ rights. We also included a measure of how closely respondents followed news on government and public affairs, to see if that exposure contributes to group empathy and, also, to check if group empathy's effect remains even after controlling for it. Next we explore public opinion about the border wall and family separation policies using the ANES data. The rest of the analyses are conducted with data from the 2018 US Group Empathy Study.

THE BORDER WALL

One of Trump's hallmark campaign promises was to build a wall on the US southern border and that Mexico would pay for it. His promise was riddled with financial, diplomatic, geological, environmental, and property-rights obstacles. Yet its simple populist appeal among certain segments of the public was indisputable. It offered a seemingly tangible and simple solution to the complicated issue of undocumented immigration, which he repeatedly termed an "invasion."[9] Less than a week after his inauguration, Trump signed an executive order to begin construction on the wall, despite having no budget to pay for it.[10]

With Mexico plainly unwilling to pay for Trump's wall, he turned predictably to the US taxpayer. Trump's attempt to convince Congress to allocate $5.7 billion for construction costs, which would cover the cost for building a wall on less than 12 percent of the total 2,000-mile southern border, failed. The legislature's unwillingness to fund the project led to the longest government shutdown in US history, leaving hundreds of thousands of federal workers on furlough without a paycheck for thirty-four days. The saga finally ended on January 25, 2019, when Trump relented and reopened the

---

highest factor loadings (.72), and we picked this one because we considered it as the most representative of the concept compared to others. Excluding ethnocentrism from the models does not change the results reported in this chapter (see the online appendix for the results of these sensitivity analyses).

[9] Thomas Kaplan (2019), "How the Trump Campaign Used Facebook Ads to Amplify His 'Invasion' Claim," *New York Times*, www.nytimes.com/2019/08/05/us/politics/trump-campaign-facebook-ads-invasion.html.

[10] Joseph W. Kane (2019), "Shutdown Watch: How the US Pays for Trump's Border Wall May Leave a Costly Legacy," Brookings, https://brook.gs/2FqkoYf.

government.[11] However, when Congress approved only $1.375 billion, to be used for 55 miles of "pedestrian fencing," Trump declared a national emergency in February 2019 in order to redirect money from various government programs without congressional consent. At the news conference announcing the emergency declaration, Trump invoked the word "invasion" seven times. He claimed: "We're talking about an invasion of our country with drugs, with human traffickers, with all types of criminals and gangs."[12] Several courts challenged Trump's reappropriation of military funding without congressional approval and halted construction of the wall. Yet, in July 2019, in a 5–4 split along ideological lines, the Supreme Court allowed the Trump administration to continue building the wall while litigation was ongoing.[13]

The idea of a border wall to "protect" natives from perils associated with newcomers is not new. Over the past few decades, multiple polls have tracked US public opinion on this issue. A slim majority of Americans supported building a wall on the USA–Mexico border from 2007 up until 2015, when Trump launched his presidential bid.[14] Since then, there has been growing public disapproval. By 2019, polls indicated a solid majority (over 60 percent) opposed the wall and that opposition was especially intense among minorities.[15] Of course, partisanship and ideology are important factors shaping public opinion on this matter, since the border wall has been highly politicized. However, if opinions about the border wall simply reflected partisan and ideological divisions, there would not have been such dramatic changes over the last few years. Other forces must be at work. Trump's narrative of the border wall as a fortress against a foreign "invasion" essentializes it as a symbol of protection against outsiders who are racially and ethnically distinct. If so, racial animus might be a powerful driver of support, while outgroup empathy might substantially undermine it.

The 2018 ANES Pilot Study includes a measure of opinions about the border wall. Specifically, respondents were asked: "Do you favor, oppose, or neither favor nor oppose building a wall on the US border with Mexico?" with response

---

[11] Andrew Restuccia, Burgess Everett, and Heather Caygle (2019), "Longest Shutdown in History Ends after Trump Relents on Wall," *Politico*, www.politico.com/story/2019/01/25/trump-shutdown-announcement-1125529.

[12] Damian Paletta, Mike DeBonis, and John Wagner (2019), "Trump Declares National Emergency on Southern Border in Bid to Build Wall," *Washington Post*, https://wapo.st/2SRQ6nx?tid=ss_mail.

[13] Jessica Taylor (2019), "Supreme Court Lets Trump Border Wall Move Forward, But Legal Fight Still Looms," NPR, www.npr.org/2019/07/26/745785115/supreme-court-lets-trump-border-wall-move-forward-but-legal-fight-still-looms.

[14] Emily Ekins (2019), "Americans Used to Support a Border Wall. What Changed Their Minds?" Cato Institute, www.cato.org/publications/commentary/americans-used-support-border-wall-what-changed-their-minds.

[15] See, for example, www.prri.org/spotlight/data-shows-how-passionate-and-partisan-americans-are-about-the-border-wall/ and https://abcnews.go.com/Politics/64-oppose-trumps-move-build-wall-asylum-30/story?id=62702683.

TABLE 8.1 *The relationship between group empathy and opinions about border policies*

	Opposition to the border wall		Opposition to family separation	
	β	S.E.	β	S.E.
Group empathy	.12**	.04	.17***	.04
Racial resentment	−.49***	.04	−.32***	.04
Party ID	−.41***	.04	−.24***	.04
Ideology	−.15**	.05	−.20***	.05
Political news exposure	−.03	.03	−.07*	.03
Black	.01	.03	−.04	.03
Latino	.03	.03	−.06*	.03
Female	.03†	.02	.09***	.02
Education	.05	.03	.04	.03
Age	−.06	.04	.09*	.04
Income	−.05	.05	−.06	.04
Married	.005	.02	−.02	.02
Employed	.03	.02	.03	.02
Catholic	−.02	.02	.02	.02
Church attendance	−.03	.03	−.05†	.03
Constant	1.00***	.04	.96***	.05
N	1,723		1,722	

Note: Coefficients estimated using OLS regression. Data are weighted. All variables are rescaled to run from 0 to 1. †$p \leq .10$, *$p \leq .05$, **$p \leq .01$, and ***$p \leq .001$, two-tailed.
Source: 2018 ANES Pilot Study (YouGov)

options ranging from "favor a great deal" to "oppose a great deal" on a 7-point scale. OLS regression results, presented in the first set of columns in Table 8.1, demonstrate that group empathy is significantly associated with opposition to the border wall, above and beyond powerful and substantively large effects of racial resentment, partisanship, and political ideology. Considering all the variables are rescaled from 0 to 1, moving from low to high scores on the GEI is associated with an increase of close to 1 point on the 7-point scale for opposition to the border wall. The association of racial resentment with opposition is much larger, accounting for a change of about half the entire policy opinion measure. The same is true for party identification: moving from strongly Democratic to strongly Republican affiliation reduces opposition to the wall by about 3 out of 7 points. These much stronger associations for racial resentment and partisanship are not surprising, given how highly politicized the policy had become by 2018 at the time of the survey. What is remarkable is that empathy for outgroups predicts opinions about the wall even after racism and partisanship are controlled for.

FAMILY SEPARATION

The Trump administration also engaged in separating undocumented immigrant families with children at the border, evidently in order to deter them from even attempting to enter the United States. Since the implementation of this "zero tolerance" immigration policy, officially launched in the spring of 2018, more than 2,700 children have been taken from their families – including those legally seeking asylum – as they arrived at the border. Children under thirteen, including many infants and toddlers, were sent to "tender age" shelters, while older children were held in detention centers and their parents were placed in criminal custody in separate facilities. As the government went public with this new strategy, images of children in chain-link cages dominated news cycles on several networks and around social media. Under increasing opposition and public outcry, Trump eventually signed an executive order on June 20, 2018, that seemed to end the family separation policy, albeit with no specific procedure or timeline for reunifying families. The administration then claimed the right to detain families and their children indefinitely, effectively replacing family separation with indefinite family detention. This would require modifying previous court orders that prohibited immigrant children from being held for more than twenty days. Several days after the executive order, a federal judge ordered the Trump administration to reunite all separated families with children under five within fourteen days and those with older children within thirty days, as well as barring the administration from any additional attempts to continue the practice of family separation. In July 2018, another federal judge denied the Trump administration's request to indefinitely detain immigrant families apprehended at the border.[16] Tragically, these court orders have gone largely unheeded.

The total number of children who remain separated from parents or guardians by immigration authorities is unknown. A 2019 report released by the US Department of Health and Human Services (HHS), Office of Inspector General, admitted that "thousands of children may have been separated during an influx that began in 2017, before the accounting required by the Court, and HHS has faced challenges in identifying separated children."[17] In other words, the Trump administration unofficially started its family separation policy almost a year prior to publicly announcing it, and hundreds or thousands of unidentified children likely remain separated from their families.

---

[16] Meagan Flynn (2018), "Federal Judge Denies Trump Administration's Request to Indefinitely Detain Families," *Washington Post*, https://wapo.st/2N33tLj?tid=ss_mail.

[17] See https://oig.hhs.gov/oei/reports/oei-BL-18-00511.pdf.

The safety conditions of the "unaccompanied" minors held at government-funded detention facilities has been widely criticized. According to HHS documents released in February 2019 during a House Judiciary Committee hearing, HHS's Office of Refugee Resettlement (ORR) received more than 4,500 allegations of sexual abuse or harassment of "unaccompanied" immigrant children held in US custody from October 2014 to July 2018.[18] The report shows that the number of complaints spiked during the enactment period of the administration's family separation policy. From March 2018 to July 2018, ORR received 859 complaints – the largest number of allegations during any five-month span in the previous four years.[19]

In addition to concerns about the immediate vulnerability of these children to abuse, medical professionals have also pointed out the potential for longer-term detrimental effects of family separation on a child's physical and psychological health. According to the American Academy of Pediatrics (AAP), "Highly stressful experiences, including family separation, can cause irreparable harm to lifelong development by disrupting a child's brain architecture."[20] The AAP further warns: "When children are separated from their parents, it removes the buffer of a supportive adult or caregiver to help mitigate stress and protect against substantial impacts on their health that can contribute to chronic conditions like depression, post-traumatic stress disorder and heart disease."[21]

These findings should lead policy makers to consider the long-term consequences of harsh immigration interventions on national security, particularly since increased border security was the administration's stated goal in the first place. Systematically undermining the physical and mental health of newcomers, many of whom will eventually end up in the country regardless of efforts to exclude them, is illogical if it boosts criminality. Even sending traumatized families back to their countries of origin may increase future insecurity, civil strife, and international conflict.[22]

Besides the physical and psychological trauma that family separation may inflict on children, there are also serious logistical problems the federal government faces in accommodating their basic needs. Many detention centers are inhospitably cold warehouses, with insufficient food, medical care, and sanitation, where people are housed in cage-like

---

[18] See www.axios.com/immigration-unaccompanied-minors-sexual-assault-3222e230-29e1-430f-a361-d959c88c5d8c.html.

[19] Matthew Haag (2019), "Thousands of Immigrant Children Said They Were Sexually Abused in US Detention Centers, Report Says," *New York Times*, www.nytimes.com/2019/02/27/us/immigrant-children-sexual-abuse.html.

[20] Devin Miller (2018), "AAP a Leading Voice Against Separating Children, Parents at Border," *AAP News*, www.aappublications.org/news/2018/06/14/washington061418.

[21] Ibid.

[22] Amanda Taub and Max Fisher (2019), "Trump's Refugee Cuts Threaten Deep Consequences at Home and Abroad," *New York Times*, www.nytimes.com/2019/09/11/world/middleeast/bahamas-refugees.html.

enclosures.[23] Many detainees refer to them as *las hieleras* (iceboxes) or *las perreras* (dog kennels). To deal the overflow of children as these centers hit their capacity, the Trump administration moved many to makeshift "tent cities." One of these was in the desert town of Tornillo, Texas, which at one point expanded to accommodate as many as 3,800 children.[24]

In the face of public outcry and negative coverage, administration officials insisted that the use of such facilities for children was temporary in lieu of other presumably longer-term, more appropriate arrangements. By January 2019, it was reported that the last children had been relocated from Tornillo, which marked the end of what journalist Robert Moore called "a detention camp that became the symbol of perhaps the largest mass incarceration of children not charged with a crime since the WWII internment of Japanese Americans."[25] Needless to say, we predict that empathy for outgroups will powerfully drive opposition to family separation policies.

To measure public opinion about the Trump administration's family separation policy, the 2018 ANES Pilot Study asked respondents: "Do you approve or disapprove of the practice of separating the children from those parents caught crossing the border illegally?" The response options again ranged on a 7-point scale from "approve extremely strongly" to "disapprove extremely strongly." The results of an OLS regression analysis are presented in the second set of columns in Table 8.1. As with opposition to the border wall, the GEI has a statistically and substantively significant effect on one's opposition to the government's policy of separating immigrant families. Moving from low to high scores on the GEI is associated with an increase in opposition to family separation of over 1 point on the 7-point scale, even after controlling for racial resentment, party identification, ideology, and political news exposure. This association is even larger than for the border wall, which is perhaps not surprising given how emotionally distressing the act of separating small children from their parents would be for most. Here group empathy is almost as strong a predictor as are ideology and partisanship, trailing only racial resentment.

DEFERRED ACTION ON CHILDHOOD ARRIVALS (DACA)

In June 2012, President Barack Obama initiated a government program called "Deferred Action on Childhood Arrivals" (DACA), which provided temporary protection from deportation and permission to work for certain immigrants

---

[23] Alan Shapiro (2017), "Children Should Be Cared for, Not Caged." AAP Voices, www.aap.org/en-us/aap-voices/Pages/Children-Should-Be-Cared-for-Not-Caged.aspx.

[24] Julio-Cesar Chavez, (2018), "Texas Desert Tent City for Immigrant Children Balloons in Size," Reuters, www.reuters.com/article/us-usa-immigration-tornillo/texas-desert-tent-city-for-immigrant-children-balloons-in-size-idUSKCN1MN004.

[25] Robert Moore (2019), "The Rise and Fall of the Tornillo Tent City for Migrant Children," *Texas Monthly*, www.texasmonthly.com/news/migrant-children-tornillo-tent-city-released.

known as "Dreamers" who were brought to the United States as children without documentation. The executive action was partly in response to Congress's continued failure to pass immigration reform – particularly, the Development, Relief, and Education for Alien Minors Act (aka the DREAM Act, first introduced in August 2001), which would provide legal status to this class of undocumented immigrants. The DACA program has benefited nearly 800,000 residents, allowing them to get driver's licenses, obtain renewable two-year work permits, qualify for in-state tuition, and attend college and graduate school.[26]

Declaring DACA an illegal and unconstitutional executive amnesty granted by President Obama, the Trump administration announced in September 2017 that it would shut down the program and lift its protections.[27] Reviewing the legality of the manner in which the administration moved to end DACA, several federal judges issued injunctions that required the program to continue accepting renewal applications while the case played out in court. The Justice Department then asked the Supreme Court to overturn those rulings. In the interim, the program was kept on life support for its existing beneficiaries, although new applications were no longer accepted. In June 2020, the Supreme Court blocked Trump's bid to end the program based on procedural grounds.[28] Writing the 5–4 majority opinion, Chief Justice John G. Roberts Jr. called the Trump administration's decision to rescind DACA "arbitrary and capricious." But Roberts also affirmed Trump's authority to cancel the program and left the door open for the president to try again if his administration could justify the policy change with adequate reasons and follow proper procedures. While the Supreme Court's decision has provided some immediate relief to the Dreamers, the ultimate fate of those affected by DACA remains in limbo and vulnerable to the whims of the executive, particularly in the absence of major legislative reform from Congress.

Despite the Trump administration's efforts to revoke DACA and the partisan polarization in Congress that has stymied legislative action on the legal protections and status of the Dreamers, the US public has generally been highly supportive of the DACA program. According to a CNN poll conducted in February 2018, 83 percent of respondents were in favor of continuing DACA, while only 12 percent were against it. Further, support cut across party lines:

---

[26] Maria Sacchetti (2017), "Their Lives Were Transformed by DACA. Here's What Will Happen If It Disappears," *Washington Post*, http://wapo.st/2wBES99?tid=ss_mail.

[27] Adam Edelman (2017), "Trump Ends DACA Program, No New Applications Accepted," NBC News, www.nbcnews.com/politics/immigration/trump-dreamers-daca-immigration-announcement-n798686.

[28] Adam Liptak and Michael D. Shear (2020), "Trump Can't Immediately End DACA, Supreme Court Rules," *New York Times*, www.nytimes.com/2020/06/18/us/trump-daca-supreme-court.html.

94 percent of Democrats, 83 percent of independents, and 67 percent of Republicans backed DACA.[29] Even as the issue became increasingly politicized amid legal challenges and renewed media attention, public support remained steady. A POLITICO/Morning Consult poll conducted with registered voters in June 2020 – right before the Supreme Court's decision on DACA – indicated that just 12 percent of respondents were in favor of deporting Dreamers; interestingly, even 69 percent of those who voted for Trump in 2016 said Dreamers should be protected.[30]

High levels of public support for DACA may very well be partly due to the common empathic framing of the policy as protecting blameless children who had no choice but to accompany their parents in crossing the border, who grew up knowing only the United States as home, and who in many cases thrived here (Gash et al. 2020; Haynes et al. 2016; see also Tafoya et al. 2019). That said, empathic triggers in the media and by pro-immigrant elites should resonate best among those high in group empathy to begin with. In an experiment, Haynes et al. (2016) found different reactions to episodic versus thematic frames about DACA, based on respondents' levels of individual trait empathy.[31] Individuals low in trait empathy were not affected by reading an article sympathetic to DACA recipients regardless of the framing style, whereas those high in trait empathy were significantly more supportive of DACA across all frames. As with opposition to family separation, group empathy is likely to be powerfully linked to support for DACA.

To measure the association between group empathy and opinions on DACA, we asked respondents: "As you may know, a program begun in 2012 called 'Deferred Action on Childhood Arrivals' (DACA) provided some protections for certain law-abiding US residents who were brought to the United States as children by parents who were undocumented. How strongly do you support or oppose DACA?" Response options ranged from "strongly oppose" to "strongly support" on a 7-point scale. Results in the first set of columns in Table 8.2 demonstrate that group empathy is indeed an important predictor of attitudes about DACA. Moving from low to high scores on the GEI is associated with more than a 2-point shift on the 7-point DACA support measure. This association is on par with that of SDO and much larger than ethnocentrism,

---

[29] Jennifer Agiesta (2018), "CNN Poll: 8 in 10 Back DACA, Supporters Hold Trump, GOP Responsible For Not Extending Program," CNN, www.cnn.com/2018/02/28/politics/cnn-poll-immigration-daca-trump/index.html.

[30] Anita Kumar (2020), "Poll: Trump Voters Want to Protect Dreamers," *Politico*, www.politico.com/news/2020/06/17/trump-supporters-dreamers-poll-323432.

[31] An "episodic frame" is a way of presenting an issue using "a specific example, case study, or event oriented report" whereas a "thematic frame" presents the issue via employing a "broader context, using generalities and abstractions instead of more concrete examples" (Haynes et al. 2016, 19).

TABLE 8.2 *The relationship between group empathy and opinions about DACA and the Muslim ban*

	Support for DACA		Opposition to the Muslim ban	
	β	S.E.	β	S.E.
Group empathy	.33***	.06	.15**	.05
SDO	−.31***	.06	−.38***	.06
Ethnocentrism	.005	.04	−.09**	.03
Immigration threat	−.14***	.04	−.23***	.04
Terrorism threat	−.08†	.04	−.10*	.04
Party ID	−.19***	.05	−.24***	.04
Ideology	−.17***	.05	−.26***	.05
Political news exposure	−.02	.04	−.01	.04
Black	−.06*	.03	.07*	.03
Latino	.04	.03	.07*	.02
Female	−.06**	.02	.01	.02
Education	.02	.04	.09*	.04
Age	−.03	.05	−.12**	.05
Income	−.01	.06	.01	.05
Married	−.04	.02	−.04†	.02
Employed	−.06**	.02	.02	.02
Metropolitan residence	.004	.04	.03	.04
Catholic	.07*	.03	.03	.03
Church attendance	.05	.03	−.02	.03
Constant	.88***	.07	.88***	.07
N	788		784	

Note: Coefficients estimated using OLS regression. Data are weighted. All variables are rescaled to run from 0 to 1. †$p \leq .10$, *$p \leq .05$, **$p \leq .01$, and ***$p \leq .001$, two-tailed.
Source: 2018 US Group Empathy Study (YouGov)

perceived threats from immigration and terrorism, ideology, partisanship, and a host of other controls.

THE MUSLIM BAN

In the previous chapter we examined public reactions to Trump's Muslim ban in its initial form as a campaign proposal, since that survey was conducted right before the 2016 presidential elections. We revisit this issue with a national survey conducted after several official versions of the Muslim ban had come into effect via Trump's executive orders – with each new one attempting to circumvent lower court challenges – until the Supreme Court handed down its own decision ultimately upholding the latest version of the ban.

The first version (often referred to as the "Muslim Ban 1.0") was issued on January 27, 2017, via an executive order entitled "Protecting the Nation from Foreign Terrorist Entry into the United States."[32] The executive order prohibited foreign nationals from seven predominantly Muslim countries – Iran, Iraq, Libya, Somalia, Sudan, Syria, and Yemen – from entering the United States for ninety days, suspended admissions of all Syrian refugees indefinitely, and prevented any other refugees from coming into the country for 120 days. Within a matter of days, federal judges blocked key provisions of the order, and the Ninth Circuit Court of Appeals rejected the Trump administration's request to resume the ban. Trump then issued a new version of the ban on March 6, 2017, which revised certain provisions (e.g., excluding Iraq from the banned countries list and providing exemption to those individuals who already held visas and green cards). However, this revised policy (dubbed "Muslim Ban 2.0") faced the same fate when a district court judge concluded that the order likely violated the Establishment Clause of the Constitution by targeting Muslims.[33]

The back-and-forth between federal courts and the Trump administration continued with a third version of the ban (aka "Muslim Ban 3.0," signed on September 24, 2017), which was yet again blocked. In December 2017, however, the Supreme Court granted the Trump administration's request to temporarily allow the latest ban to take full effect while the case was being litigated. Then on June 26, 2018, in a 5–4 ruling, the Supreme Court upheld President Trump's third version of the ban, reversing a series of lower court decisions that had ruled it unconstitutional and motivated by religious hostility. The ban that took effect barred or limited visitors and immigrants from five predominantly Muslim countries – Iran, Libya, Syria, Somalia, and Yemen (in addition to North Korean nationals and Venezuelan government officials along with their immediate family members). Although waivers were technically available, the waiver process was extremely stringent and burdensome even for parents, siblings, and grandparents who wished to visit their family members residing legally in the United States.

Given the explicit targeting of Muslims in the original ban, coupled with the administration's narrative criminalizing this group, we expect those with greater empathy for outgroups to be more likely to oppose this policy, even above and beyond the impact of partisanship, political ideology, and other predispositions. To empirically test this expectation, respondents were asked: "How strongly do you support or oppose the current policy that indefinitely

---

[32] See www.whitehouse.gov/presidential-actions/executive-order-protecting-nation-foreign-terrorist-entry-united-states/.

[33] For a comprehensive timeline of the events and actions concerning the Muslim ban, see www.cnn.com/2018/06/26/politics/timeline-travel-ban/index.html.

bars citizens of six Muslim-majority countries from entering the United States?" Response options ranged from "strongly support" to "strongly oppose" on a 7-point scale. The results are presented in the second set of columns in Table 8.2. Consistent with the results from 2016, group empathy once again has a significant and substantively large effect on opinions about this policy that Trump promptly executed after taking office. Moving from low to high scores on the GEI is associated with about a 1-point increase on the 7-point scale for opposition to the Muslim ban. This association is about the same magnitude and in the opposite direction of perceived threat of terrorism. For some at least, group empathy may counteract the negative effects of threat on security policies targeting marginalized groups. SDO seems to have a much larger effect on this policy, perhaps because it explicitly pits social groups against each other.

HURRICANE RELIEF FOR PUERTO RICO

On September 20, 2017, Hurricane Maria made landfall in Puerto Rico – the US territory whose residents are American citizens, albeit without federal voting rights or representation. Puerto Ricans were still recovering from Hurricane Irma that had pummeled the island a couple of weeks earlier when the island was struck again – this time with the strongest storm it had faced in eighty-five years. The entire island was left without electricity, which was not fully restored for months. The damage to the infrastructure combined with an already ailing economy crippled the island. For well over a year, survivors struggled without adequate access to shelter, food, clean water, sanitation facilities, healthcare, transportation, and many other basic human needs.

There was a heated debate about the total number of deaths that this devastating hurricane directly and indirectly inflicted on the people of Puerto Rico. According to a project report conducted by George Washington University's (GWU) Milken Institute School of Public Health, total *excess* mortality post-hurricane was estimated to be 2,975 (95% CI: 2,658–3,290) for the full study period from mid-September 2017 to mid-February 2018.[34] As part of the estimation methodology, GWU analyzed past mortality patterns to predict what the expected mortality rate would have been had Hurricane Maria not occurred (i.e., predicted mortality) and compared that rate to the actual deaths that occurred (i.e., observed mortality) while taking into account massive population displacement from the island in the aftermath of the hurricane.

---

[34] The project report can be accessed at https://publichealth.gwu.edu/sites/default/files/downloads/projects/PRstudy/Acertainment%20of%20the%20Estimated%20Excess%20Mortality%20from%20Hurricane%20Maria%20in%20Puerto%20Rico.pdf.

To put these numbers into perspective, the death toll of 2,975 estimated by the GWU report makes the devastation Hurricane Maria caused in Puerto Rico the worst natural disaster on American soil in the past 100 years and puts it on par with the number of people who died in the 9/11 terrorist attacks (a total of 2,996 people). However, Trump sought to refute the GWU study on Twitter: "3000 people did not die in the two hurricanes that hit Puerto Rico. When I left the Island, AFTER the storm had hit, they had anywhere from 6 to 18 deaths. As time went by it did not go up by much. Then, a long time later, they started to report really large numbers, like 3000"[35] and continued, "This was done by the Democrats in order to make me look as bad as possible when I was successfully raising Billions of Dollars to help rebuild Puerto Rico. If a person died for any reason, like old age, just add them onto the list. Bad politics. I love Puerto Rico!"[36] Shortly after contesting GWU's death toll estimate, Trump announced his intention to stop sending federal relief funds to Puerto Rico, claiming that the Puerto Rican government had been misusing the relief money.

Willison et al.'s (2019) comparative investigation of the federal response to hurricane disasters in Texas, Florida, and Puerto Rico indicate that, within the first nine days after the hurricanes hit, Harvey and Irma survivors had each received almost $100 million in FEMA dollars while Maria survivors had received just over $6 million in recovery aid. Within the first two months post-landfall, Harvey and Irma survivors each received nearly $1 billion. By comparison, it took twice the time (four months after landfall) for Hurricane Maria funds to reach that amount. Willison et al. (2019) found similar trends for total federal dollars received by survivors (including FEMA dollars), national flood-insurance payouts, and loans from the Small Business Association. Another key indicator of government response to natural disasters is federal staffing, which is critical to rescue, recovery, rebuilding, and long-term stabilization efforts. Willison et al.'s (2019) investigation finds that "federal staffing rates in Puerto Rico reached comparable levels in three times the amount of time as Texas and 30 times the amount of time for Irma."

The inequities in the US government response to the hurricane disasters in Texas and Florida versus Puerto Rico are aligned with similar gaps in US public approval of these relief efforts. A national poll conducted by Ipsos in early October 2017 indicated that the awareness of Hurricanes Harvey, Irma, and Maria and their resulting damage was nearly universal. However, public approval of the federal government's hurricane relief efforts in the mainland versus Puerto Rico was not uniform.[37] Over three-quarters of Americans approved a strong federal recovery response for both Hurricane Harvey in Texas and Hurricane Irma in Florida, while only 56 percent of Americans

---

[35] See https://twitter.com/realdonaldtrump/status/1040217897703026689?lang=en.

[36] See https://twitter.com/realdonaldtrump/status/1040220855400386560?lang=en.

[37] A summary report of the poll can be accessed at www.ipsos.com/en/perceptions-america-puerto-rico-disaster-relief-response.

approved of disaster aid for Puerto Rico following Hurricane Maria. Personal impact and self-interest surely had something to do with these reactions, but we suspect variation in group empathy likely also played an important role.[38] Given that Puerto Ricans are US citizens, group empathy may perhaps play a bigger role on the motivation to relieve their suffering than for policy issues like the border wall where the perceived threat is likely to be larger, the targeted outgroup is more distant, and the cause of suffering that triggers empathy is less direct.

Table 8.3 presents the results of an OLS regression analysis to examine the link between group empathy and hurricane relief for Puerto Rico. Respondents were asked: "As you may know, strong hurricanes have recently caused devastating loss of life and property damage in Puerto Rico. How strongly do you support or oppose additional government spending to assist Puerto Ricans in rebuilding their lives after these natural disasters?" Response options ranged from "strongly oppose" to "strongly support" on a 7-point scale, which were recoded to 0–1 as usual. The results show a substantively large and significant association between the GEI and support for hurricane relief for Puerto Rico. Moving from low to high scores on the GEI is associated with a shift of almost 1.5 points on the 7-point support scale. This association is second only to SDO, which has a massive effect on support. Group empathy has a much larger effect than ethnocentrism, party identification, and ideology.

SYMBOLS OFFENSIVE TO MINORITY GROUPS

We next examine how group empathy affects sensitivity to symbols historically associated with the oppression of minority groups. The focus is on two specific contexts: (1) discontinuing the use of Native American imagery, names, and mascots in sports and (2) removing Confederate monuments and memorials from public spaces. In both cases, we expect those high in group empathy to strongly support the removal of such symbols. These issues explicitly invoke sensitivity toward specific minority groups: Native Americans and African Americans. Our theory would therefore predict group empathy to be more strongly associated with these issues than those, such as the border wall, that invoke outgroup suffering only indirectly.

Native American Symbols

The appropriation of Native American names, mascots, and symbols in American sports has prompted increasing protest. While some sports teams

---

[38] Hurricane Harvey was responsible for 68 direct deaths and 35 indirect deaths in Texas, whereas Hurricane Irma caused 4 direct deaths and 80 indirect deaths in Florida (Willison et al. 2019), in contrast to the nearly 3,000 excess mortality cases in Puerto Rico (as estimated by the GWU study) caused by Hurricane Maria.

TABLE 8.3 *The relationship between group empathy and support for Puerto Rican hurricane relief*

	β	S.E.
Group empathy	.21***	.05
SDO	−.44***	.04
Ethnocentrism	.06†	.03
Party ID	−.10**	.03
Ideology	−.10*	.04
Political news exposure	.01	.03
Black	−.04	.02
Latino	−.001	.02
Female	.003	.02
Education	−.03	.03
Age	.08*	.04
Income	.02	.04
Married	−.02	.02
Employed	−.02	.02
Metropolitan residence	−.004	.03
Catholic	−.03	.02
Church attendance	.07*	.03
Constant	.81***	.06
N	795	

Note: Coefficients estimated using OLS regression. Data are weighted. All variables are rescaled to run from 0 to 1. †p ≤ .10, *p ≤ .05, **p ≤ .01, and ***p ≤ .001, two-tailed.
Source: 2018 US Group Empathy Study (YouGov)

still insist on keeping Native American references, many have decided to retire them. For instance, after a series of athletic sanctions, the University of North Dakota changed its nickname, the Fighting Sioux, to the Fighting Hawks.[39] The Cleveland Indians announced in 2018 that they would no longer use the cartoonish Chief Wahoo logo, though they retained the team name "Indians."[40]

---

[39] Pat Borzi (2016), "The Sioux Name Is Gone but North Dakota Fans Haven't Moved on," *New York Times*, www.nytimes.com/2016/03/03/sports/hockey/with-sioux-nickname-gone-north-dakota-hockey-fans-are-fighting-change.html.

[40] David Waldstein (2018), "Cleveland Indians Will Abandon Chief Wahoo Logo Next Year," *New York Times*, www.nytimes.com/2018/01/29/sports/baseball/cleveland-indians-chief-wahoo-logo.html.

While public awareness about the disparaging nature of stereotypical and/or misappropriated Native American symbols has increased, the Trump administration has been blatantly dismissive of the issue. Reacting to an Instagram post by Democratic Senator Elizabeth Warren of Massachusetts in January 2019, Trump tweeted: "If Elizabeth Warren, often referred to by me as Pocahontas, did this commercial from Bighorn or Wounded Knee instead of her kitchen, with her husband dressed in full Indian garb, it would have been a smash!"[41] A few weeks later, Trump tweeted: "Today Elizabeth Warren, sometimes referred to by me as Pocahontas, joined the race for President. Will she run as our first Native American presidential candidate, or has she decided that after 32 years, this is not playing so well anymore? See you on the campaign TRAIL, Liz!"[42] Some had already expressed concern about Trump's demeaning use of the name "Pocahontas" as a racial slur to mock Warren, who had once claimed Native American heritage. What many found even more appalling was the capitalization of the letters in the word "trail" in Trump's tweet as an explicit reference to the "Trail of Tears" – the forced relocation of Native Americans that killed thousands – as well as Trump's invocation of Wounded Knee – a massacre of Native Americans – as "punchlines" of sarcastic "jokes."[43]

In another incidence, Trump chose to honor a group of Navajo code talkers (who had helped the US Marine Corps send coded messages during World War II) in front of a White House portrait of Andrew Jackson. President Jackson was the architect of the "Trail of Tears," signing the "Indian Removal Act" in 1830 that banished more than 60,000 Native Americans from their ancestral homelands to clear those areas for white settlers. Jackson once talked about the Cherokee as an inferior race deserving extermination, exclaiming: "Established in the midst of a superior race, they must disappear."[44] Consequently, the Cherokees referred to him as the "Indian Killer." Despite this controversial legacy, Trump described himself as a big Andrew Jackson fan, objecting to replacing Jackson's visage with that of abolitionist icon Harriet Tubman on the front of the $20 bill, and moving Jackson's portrait to the Oval Office shortly after his inauguration.

The Trump administration's dismissiveness of Native American concerns has not been solely symbolic. Less than a week after taking office, Trump signed an executive order to revive the controversial Dakota Access Pipeline that transports oil through North Dakota. The order disregarded massive protest from Native Americans, who stated that the pipeline's crossing under Lake

---

[41] See https://twitter.com/realdonaldtrump/status/1084644517238714369?lang=en.

[42] See https://twitter.com/realdonaldtrump/status/1094368870415110145?lang=en.

[43] See https://www.npr.org/2019/02/12/694021594/why-trumps-attacks-on-sen-elizabeth-warren-are-dehumanizing-to-native-people.

[44] Eli Rosenberg (2017), "Andrew Jackson Was Called 'Indian Killer.' Trump Honored Navajos in front of His Portrait," *Washington Post*, http://wapo.st/2zJrIvH?tid=ss_mail.

Oahe threatened their water resources, environmental health, and the sacred sites of the nearby Standing Rock Sioux reservation.[45] In 2017, Trump also signed proclamations slashing the size of Grand Staircase-Escalante National Monument, which is sacred to many Native American tribes, by nearly 50 percent and Bears Ears National Monument by 85 percent. This amounted to "the largest combined rollback of federally protected land in the nation's history."[46] These actions opened thousands of acres of Native American land to the possibility of mining and development.

With all these considerations in mind, we expect that opinions about the use of Native American references and imagery are strongly driven by group empathy in the era of the Trump administration, independent of party identification and ideology as well as a host of other key predispositions. Given that these policy attacks are often explicitly and directly targeting a citizen minority group that poses no threat to the country and which has done nothing obvious to warrant such treatment, group empathy should be particularly powerful in driving opposition to them. Because this topic has not yet been highly politicized, partisanship might be expected to play a smaller role.

To measure views about removing these offensive symbols, we asked respondents: "How strongly would you support or oppose removing sports symbols, names, and imagery – such as Chief Wahoo of the Cleveland Indians or the Washington Redskins – that many Native American groups find offensive?" Response options ranged from "strongly oppose" to "strongly support" on a 7-point scale. The first set of columns in Table 8.4 presents OLS regression results. As predicted, group empathy is closely linked to support for removing such symbols. Moving from low to high scores on the GEI is associated with a nearly 2-point increase in support on the 7-point scale. This association rivals that of SDO and political ideology and is larger than that of partisanship and ethnocentrism. Perhaps not surprisingly, age also has a large and significant impact on views about these symbols, with younger respondents much more willing to see offensive Native American symbols removed.

Confederate Symbols

Over the past several years, an increasing number of Confederate flags, monuments, and memorials have been removed from public spaces across the country. These efforts gained momentum following the Charleston church massacre in June 2015, when a white supremacist killed nine African Americans

---

[45] Juliet Eilperin and Brady Dennis (2017), "Trump Administration to Approve Final Permit for Dakota Access Pipeline," *Washington Post*, http://wapo.st/2jZvvIm?tid=ss_mail.

[46] Kurtis Lee (2018), "'This Is Our Land … It's All We Have': Native Americans See President's Monument Proposal as an Assault on Their Culture," *Los Angeles Times*, https://enewspaper.latimes.com/infinity/article_share.aspx?guid=c6eba4b1-1bc1-448c-b40e-a111c30218f8.

TABLE 8.4 *The relationship between group empathy and support for the removal of symbols offensive to minority groups*

	Removal of symbols offensive to Native Americans		Removal of Confederate symbols	
	β	S.E.	β	S.E.
Group empathy	.24***	.06	.21***	.06
SDO	−.24***	.06	−.38***	.07
Ethnocentrism	−.05	.04	−.02	.04
Party ID	−.16***	.04	−.36***	.05
Ideology	−.24***	.05	−.16**	.06
Political news exposure	.03	.04	.09*	.04
Black	.07*	.03	.14***	.04
Latino	.07*	.03	.12***	.03
Female	−.04†	.02	−.05*	.02
Education	.09*	.04	.12**	.04
Age	−.30***	.05	−.16**	.05
Income	.01	.05	−.04	.06
Married	−.06*	.02	−.02	.03
Employed	−.07**	.02	−.05*	.02
Metropolitan residence	−.04	.04	.02	.04
Catholic	.03	.03	−.03	.04
Church attendance	−.01	.03	−.07*	.04
Constant	.78***	.07	.70***	.08
N	794		794	

Note: Coefficients estimated using OLS regression. Data are weighted. All variables are rescaled to run from 0 to 1. †p ≤ .10, *p ≤ .05, **p ≤ .01, and ***p ≤ .001, two-tailed.
Source: 2018 US Group Empathy Study (YouGov)

during a prayer service. The mass shooter's poses with Confederate emblems on social media accompanied by his racist posts intensified public debate about these symbols and contributed to the South Carolina legislature's decision to remove the Confederate flag from the State Capitol.[47]

While legislators have been taking action around the country to remove symbols of the Confederacy, public opinion has not yet reached consensus. Some believe the Confederacy defended slavery and white supremacy, and feel that memorializing this dark era of American history is inappropriate. Others

---

[47] Amanda Holpuch (2015), "Confederate Flag Removed from South Carolina Capitol in Victory for Activists," *The Guardian*, www.theguardian.com/us-news/2015/jul/10/confederate-flag-south-carolina-statehouse.

claim that these symbols are part of the South's cultural heritage, erected simply to honor fallen soldiers from the region.

Such public discord over Confederate symbols erupted into violence in August 2017 in Charlottesville, Virginia, during a "Unite the Right" rally. Hundreds of self-identified "alt-right" supporters, neo-Confederates, neo-fascists, neo-Nazis, Ku Klux Klan members, white supremacists, and various militias gathered to protest the planned removal of a statue of Confederate General Robert E. Lee. Armed with torches, adorned with swastikas, and offering the Nazi salute, these marchers were stark evidence of the resurgence of white supremacy in the United States. Marchers chanted racist and anti-semitic slogans such as "White Lives Matter," "You will not replace us," "Jews will not replace us," "Blood and soil," and "One people, one nation, end immigration."[48] The rally was confronted by a large group of counterprotestors, which included church clergy, racial justice and civil rights activists, and anti-fascist groups. Clashes between the white supremacists and counterprotestors turned deadly on August 12, 2017, when a self-proclaimed neo-Nazi sympathizer rammed his car into a crowd of counterprotestors, killing a young civil rights activist, Heather Heyer, and injuring several others.

In an exchange with reporters shortly after the incident, Trump reacted to the deadly attack in Charlottesville by suggesting that there were "very fine people on both sides" and "there is blame on both sides."[49] He continued his argument by stating:

I've condemned neo-Nazis. I've condemned many different groups. But not all of those people were neo-Nazis, believe me. Not all of those people were white supremacists, by any stretch. Those people were also there because they wanted to protest the taking down of a statue, Robert E. Lee. So – excuse me. And you take a look at some of the groups and you see – and you'd know it if you were honest reporters, which in many cases you're not, but many of those people were there to protest the taking down of the statue of Robert E. Lee. So this week it's Robert E. Lee. I noticed that Stonewall Jackson's coming down. I wonder, is it George Washington next week and is it Thomas Jefferson the week after?

Trump's comments triggered strong criticism from many, and we believe some of that energy springs from outgroup empathy in defiance of the hatred, racism, and bigotry on display. Even though the threat of harm was high, a diverse group of people stood up against white supremacy and political intolerance. In fact, one of the organizers of the counterprotests, a local minister named Brittany Caine-Conley, sent out a warning in advance of the rally: "There is an extremely high potential for physical violence and brutality directed at our

---

[48] For a review of white supremacist symbols and slogans spotted in Charlottesville, go to http://wapo.st/charlottesville-video?tid=ss_mail.

[49] Dana Farrington and Barbara Sprunt, (2017), "Transcript: Trump Shifts Tone Again on White Nationalist Rally in Charlottesville," NPR, www.npr.org/2017/08/15/543769884/transcript-trump-shifts-tone-again-on-white-nationalist-rally-in-charlottesville.

community. We need your help – we don't have the numbers to stand up to this on our own."[50] We suspect participating in high-risk protests – especially when the ingroup is not directly targeted – should be primarily driven by group empathy.

Even in the aftermath of the Charlottesville incident, many polls suggested that a majority of Americans opposed the removal of Confederate statues.[51] In an NPR/PBS Newshour/Marist poll conducted on August 14–15, 2017, when asked whether Confederate statues should remain as a historical symbol or be removed because they are offensive to some people, 62 percent said they should remain, while only 27 percent said they should go.[52] Nearly two-thirds of whites and Latinos supported keeping them. Even among African Americans, a plurality – 44 percent – said they should stay, with 40 percent supporting their removal and 16 percent unsure. Unsurprisingly, there was a sharp partisan divide over the issue. In an MSN poll (also conducted in August 2017 following the Charlottesville incident), 71 percent of Democrats supported removing Confederate monuments, while 87 percent of Republicans insisted they should stay.[53] Group empathy should be closely linked to support for removing Confederate symbols, because they are so closely tied to slavery and discrimination against African Americans. This particular effort, compared to the removal of Native American sports symbols, has been highly politicized over the last several years, with Republican elites often voicing displeasure about removing symbols of so-called Southern heritage. We would thus expect partisanship to be a much larger force here. Measures of racial animus such as SDO should also be powerful, since this is an explicitly racialized policy pitting mostly white and African American interests against each other. Moreover, witnessing violent events as in Charleston and Charlottesville related to Confederate symbols may shift public opinion over time by increasing issue awareness and empathy for the victims. Therefore, political news exposure is likely to be at least modestly associated with support for removing these symbols.

The second set of columns in Table 8.4 presents the results regarding attitudes about the use of Confederate symbols. Respondents were asked: "How strongly do you support or oppose removing Confederate flags,

---

[50] Farah Stockman (2017), "Who Were the Counterprotesters in Charlottesville?" *New York Times*, www.nytimes.com/2017/08/14/us/who-were-the-counterprotesters-in-charlottesville.html.

[51] Ariel Edwards-Levy (2017), "Polls Find Little Support for Confederate Statue Removal – But How You Ask Matters," *HuffPost*, www.huffpost.com/entry/confederate-statues-removal-polls_n_599de056e4b057 10aa59841c.

[52] See https://apps.npr.org/documents/document.html?id=3933461-NPR-PBS-NewsHour-Marist-Poll-Aug-17-2017.

[53] Jennifer Martinez (2017), "Poll Shows How Divided Americans Have Become in the Debate about Confederate Monuments and Flags," *Business Insider*, www.businessinsider.com/poll-confederate-monuments-flags-2017-8.

monuments, and memorials from public property?" Response options ranged from "strongly oppose" to "strongly support" on a 7-point scale. Once again, group empathy is a fairly large and significant predictor of support for removing symbols of the Confederacy, with movement from low to high scores on the GEI producing an almost 1.5-point shift in support. The size of the GEI coefficient in this model is similar to the previous one for Native American symbols, but, as expected, partisanship plays a much larger role. Also as predicted, exposure to political news is significantly associated with support for removing Confederate symbols.

BLACK LIVES MATTER

The "Black Lives Matter" movement arose to challenge what many view as unfair, violent, and often deadly treatment of African Americans by law enforcement and civilian vigilantes, coupled with the inability of the US criminal justice system to convict those responsible. It was launched in 2013 following the acquittal of George Zimmerman – a neighborhood watch volunteer in a gated community in Sanford, Florida – who stalked and killed an unarmed black teenager, Trayvon Martin, walking in that neighborhood where his father lived. The movement gained momentum with subsequent tragedies in 2014, including the fatal police shooting of another unarmed black teenager, Michael Brown, in Ferguson, Missouri, and the chokehold death of an unarmed black man, Eric Garner, during his arrest in Staten Island, New York. None of the officers involved in these cases were indicted.

Public sentiment regarding the movement has been mixed. Some view Black Lives Matter as an important effort to reduce systemic racism and violence against blacks in the United States, raising awareness about issues such as police brutality, racial profiling, and inequality in the criminal justice system. Others claim that the movement is extremist, provokes violence against law enforcement officials, and exaggerates the extent of racism in policing and criminal justice. As a result, countermovements like "All Lives Matter" and "Blue Lives Matter" have emerged, attempting to frame the movement's cause as a zero-sum competition, as if pronouncing that black lives matter somehow suggests other lives matter less.

As a presidential candidate, Trump openly rejected Black Lives Matter: "A lot of people feel that it is inherently racist. And it's a very divisive term. Because all lives matter. It's a very, very divisive term."[54] Referencing the July 2016 shooting of several police offers in Dallas, Texas, then-candidate Trump alleged

---

[54] David Weigel (2016), "Three Words That Republicans Wrestle with: 'Black Lives Matter,'" *Washington Post*, http://wapo.st/2a79a8t?tid=ss_mail.

without any evidence that Black Lives Matter might be responsible.[55] This argument mirrors the partisan gap between Republicans and Democrats regarding the issue. According to a Pew poll conducted in August 2017, the partisan divide was actually wider than the racial divide in support for Black Lives Matter, and the majority of the US public had a negative view of the movement.[56] Over the next few years, however, polling trends began to show a positive shift in majority sentiment.[57]

Despite its impact on US politics, systematic research about the opinion dynamics regarding Black Lives Matter is scarce. Applying the racial threat hypothesis to Black Lives Matter, Updegrove et al. (2020) suggest that whites may view law enforcement and its use of lethal force as a form of social control to maintain their dominance over the "threatening" African American population. However, they do not find empirical support for this hypothesis, and they call for a better theoretical alternative to explain attitudes about the movement. Group Empathy Theory can help provide such explanatory power. Let us illustrate with a harrowing incident of fatal police brutality in 2020 that shook the nation to its core.

Black Lives Matter came to the forefront of national agenda once again in late May of 2020 – taking the spotlight from the ongoing COVID-19 pandemic – when news cycles began running the appalling footage of an unarmed black man, George Floyd, being killed in police custody in Minneapolis, Minnesota. The police were responding to the 911 call of a deli employee who was accusing Floyd of using a counterfeit $20 bill to buy cigarettes. The footage showed Floyd in distress, repeatedly saying, "I can't breathe," while lying face down on the ground with his neck pressed under the knee of a white police officer, Derek Chauvin. According to the criminal complaint on file (substantiated by witness videos and security cameras), Chauvin did not remove his knee from Floyd's neck for nearly nine minutes even after Floyd had lost consciousness, including a whole minute after the paramedics arrived at the scene.[58] The footage also showed three other officers assisting Chauvin in keeping Floyd pinned to the ground at some point and otherwise standing guard over the scene, blocking witnesses.

We think group empathy is a primary driver of political attitudes and action in response to incidents like George Floyd's murder. For those who could empathize

---

[55] Jeremy Diamond (2016), "Trump: Black Lives Matter Has Helped Instigate Police Killings," CNN, www.cnn.com/2016/07/18/politics/donald-trump-black-lives-matter/index.html.

[56] Jonathan Easley (2017), "Poll: 57 Percent Have Negative View of Black Lives Matter Movement," The Hill, https://thehill.com/homenews/campaign/344985-poll-57-percent-have-negative-view-of-black-lives-matter-movement.

[57] Anagha Srikanth (2020), "Most Americans Support Protesters over Trump, Shifting Opinion from 2014 Black Lives Matter Protests: Poll," The Hill, https://thehill.com/changing-america/respect/equality/500883-most-americans-support-protesters-over-trump-shifting.

[58] "8 Minutes and 46 Seconds: How George Floyd Was Killed in Police Custody," *New York Times*, www.nytimes.com/2020/05/31/us/george-floyd-investigation.html?smid=em-share.

with Floyd, it must have been dreadful to listen to him imploring the police officer to take his knee off his neck so he could breathe, to no avail, and calling out to his mother as his life faded away. Nevertheless, not everyone who witnessed this atrocious incident had the same interpretation of it. Floyd was already handcuffed and lying subdued on the ground while Chauvin (with his hands nonchalantly in his pant pockets) kept digging his knee into Floyd's neck. So it would be a stretch to argue that the officer must have felt a "reasonable fear of an imminent threat to his life" – a defense the police often invoke. Nonetheless, some questioned whether Floyd's death was actually due to police misconduct, such as a Mississippi mayor who tweeted: "If you can say you can't breathe, you're breathing. Most likely that man died of overdose or heart attack."[59] Some chose to chalk it up to "a few bad apples" abusing their power in an otherwise fair law enforcement system. For example, in an interview with CNN's Jake Tapper, National Security Advisor Robert C. O'Brien said: "We have got great law enforcement officers, not – not the few bad apples, like the officer that killed George Floyd. But we got a few bad apples that have given – given law enforcement a bad name; 99.9 percent of these guys are heroes."[60] For others, this was more than just a few rogue police officers. It was a pattern of police brutality fueled by systemic racism targeting blacks and other people of color.

Emotional reactions to Floyd's killing were also varied. Whether or not they perceived Floyd's death as a product of systemic racism, many expressed sympathy for the victim. Yet many people felt more than just sympathy: they were enraged and disgusted, and some even felt compelled to go out on the streets in the midst of a pandemic to demand justice and an end to systemic racism. The protests were highly diverse. Americans from all races and ethnicities joined the protest movement despite the risk of contracting a highly infectious and deadly virus (which, at that point, had already claimed over 100,000 deaths). Protesters also risked physical harm at the hands of police and national guard units who at times resorted to excessive and violent force.[61]

The protests intensified and expanded across the United States and even spread to other nations – including the United Kingdom, Germany, New Zealand, and Canada – in a global display of solidarity.[62] While many of

[59] Associated Press (2020), "Crowd Protests White Mayor's Words about Black Man's Death," *Washington Post*, www.washingtonpost.com/national/mississippi-mayor-flouts-calls-to-resign-over-floyd-comments/2020/05/29/9e0944d2-a19a-11ea-be06-af5514ee0385_story.html.

[60] See http://transcripts.cnn.com/TRANSCRIPTS/2005/31/sotu.01.html.

[61] Tom McCarthy (2020), "Police Criticized over Heavy-Handed Response to Peaceful Protests across US," *The Guardian*, www.theguardian.com/us-news/2020/jun/02/police-criticized-heavy-handed-response-peaceful-protests-across-us.

[62] Zamira Rahim and Rob Picheta (2020), "Thousands around the World Protest George Floyd's Death in Global Display of Solidarity," CNN, www.cnn.com/2020/06/01/world/george-floyd-global-protests-intl/index.html.

these protests were entirely peaceful, incidents of looting and violence also erupted in some places. In response, Trump borrowed language dating back to a segregationist white police chief cracking down on protestors during the civil rights era. He tweeted on May 28, 2020: "These THUGS are dishonoring the memory of George Floyd, and I won't let that happen. Just spoke to Governor Tim Walz and told him that the Military is with him all the way. Any difficulty and we will assume control but, *when the looting starts, the shooting starts.* Thank you!" (emphasis added).[63] This was a very different tone than the one he displayed earlier the same month toward (mainly white) protestors who had stormed Michigan's capitol building, many of them heavily armed, demanding Governor Gretchen Whitmer lift strict coronavirus lockdown orders. His tweet in reaction to those armed protestors indicated quite the opposite approach: "The Governor of Michigan should give a little, and put out the fire. These are very good people, but they are angry. They want their lives back again, safely! See them, talk to them, make a deal."[64] Meanwhile, Trump's rival for the presidency in 2020, former vice president Joe Biden, delivered remarks that some referred to as being part of an "empathy offensive."[65] Calling for unity to confront systemic racism in light of Floyd's murder, Biden stated: "The country is crying out for leadership, leadership that can unite us, leadership that brings us together, that can recognize the pain and deep grief of communities that have had a knee on their neck for a long time."[66]

These varied reactions to the protests, we think, have a lot to do with group empathy. Some directed their focus and criticism on acts of vandalism, arson, and looting; others focused on peaceful acts of civil disobedience, why they were happening, and what they were demanding. One's rejection of Trump's framing of the protestors as merely "thugs" and "looters" should be partly influenced by group empathy. The very act of trying to understand – rather than dismiss or blatantly deny – the root causes of anger and rage behind outbursts of violent civil unrest can also be traced to group empathy. In his 1967 speech at Stanford University, Martin Luther King Jr. explicated

---

[63] See https://twitter.com/realDonaldTrump/status/1266231100780744704. Trump's tweet was later flagged by Twitter as a violation of their rules about "glorifying violence," which would instigate Trump's war on social media. See also Barbara Sprunt (2020), "The History Behind 'When The Looting Starts, The Shooting Starts,'" NPR, www.npr.org/2020/05/29/864818368/the-history-behind-when-the-looting-starts-the-shooting-starts.

[64] See https://twitter.com/realdonaldtrump/status/1256202305680158720?lang=en.

[65] Charlotte Alter (2020), "Joe Biden's Empathy Offensive," *Time*, https://time.com/5843586/joe-bidens-empathy-offensive. See also Kara Voght (2020), "As Trump Threatens Violence, Biden Offers Empathy and a Promise of 'Real Policy Reform,'" *Mother Jones*, www.motherjones.com/crime-justice/2020/05/biden-trump-george-floyd-minneapolis/.

[66] The full transcript of Biden's speech can be accessed at www.cnn.com/2020/06/02/politics/biden-philadelphia-transcript/index.html.

his thoughts on rioting – a tactic that was contrary to his own strategy of nonviolent resistance:

I think America must see that riots do not develop out of thin air. Certain conditions continue to exist in our society, which must be condemned as vigorously as we condemn riots. But in the final analysis, a riot is the language of the unheard. And what is it that America has failed to hear? It has failed to hear that the plight of the Negro poor has worsened over the last few years. It has failed to hear that the promises of freedom and justice have not been met. And it has failed to hear that large segments of white society are more concerned about tranquility and the status quo than about justice, equality, and humanity. And so in a real sense our nation's summers of riots are caused by our nation's winters of delay. And as long as America postpones justice, we stand in the position of having these recurrences of violence and riots over and over again. Social justice and progress are the absolute guarantors of riot prevention.[67]

To test the power of group empathy in explaining public reactions to Black Lives Matter, respondents were asked how strongly they support or oppose the movement on a 7-point scale ranging from "strongly oppose" to "strongly support." While the survey does not have a specific measure of perceived threat focusing on blacks, we did include measures of outgroup-oriented threat perceptions (mainly, perceived threat of immigration and terrorism), as well as SDO and ethnocentrism. The results, presented in the first set of columns in Table 8.5, show that group empathy indeed powerfully predicts opinions about this movement. Moving from low to high scores on the GEI produces more than a 2.5-point increase out of 7 in support for Black Lives Matter. This is similar to the power of party identification and larger than the impact of threat perceptions, SDO, ethnocentrism, and political ideology.

The evidence presented so far suggests group empathy is a key step toward increasing awareness and acknowledgement of systemic discrimination against blacks and other marginalized outgroups. As such, group empathy can help one develop a "motivated consciousness" to help boost the power of political disruption that social movements like Black Lives Matter employ in order to interrupt what Hayward (2020) refers to as privileged people's "motivated ignorance." This, in turn, may help rally a critical mass – even recruiting those who currently benefit from an unjust status quo – to mandate systemic change.

THE #METOO MOVEMENT

The issue of sexual harassment and assault has also drawn more attention during the Trump era. Statistics about the prevalence of sexual violence in the United States are shocking. According to the data assembled by RAINN (Rape, Abuse & Incest National Network) – the nation's largest anti–sexual violence organization –

---

[67] The full transcript of Martin Luther King Jr.'s "Other America" speech is available at www .crmvet.org/docs/otheram.htm.

TABLE 8.5 *The relationship between group empathy and support for contemporary social movements*

	Black Lives Matter		#MeToo	
	β	S.E.	β	S.E.
Group empathy	.36***	.05	.13*	.06
SDO	−.23***	.05	−.38***	.06
Ethnocentrism	.12***	.03	.03	.03
Immigration threat	−.11***	.03		
Terrorism threat	.09**	.03		
Party ID	−.36***	.04	−.40***	.05
Ideology	−.21***	.05	−.29***	.05
Political news exposure	−.01	.03	.03	.04
Black	.12***	.03	.03	.03
Latino	.06*	.02	.07**	.03
Female	−.04†	.02	−.0004	.02
Education	.05	.03	.04	.04
Age	−.07†	.04	−.08†	.05
Income	.03	.05	.07	.05
Married	−.05**	.02	−.05*	.02
Employed	−.03	.02	−.03	.02
Metropolitan residence	.02	.04	−.04	.04
Catholic	.02	.02	−.001	.02
Church attendance	−.01	.03	−.04	.03
Constant	.57***	.06	.89***	.06
N	788		792	

Note: Coefficients estimated using OLS regression. Data are weighted. All variables are rescaled to run from 0 to 1. $^†p \leq .10$, $^*p \leq .05$, $^{**}p \leq .01$, and $^{***}p \leq .001$, two-tailed.
Source: 2018 US Group Empathy Study (YouGov)

one out of six American women experience an attempted or completed rape at some point in their lives.[68] The numbers are even bleaker for women of color. More than 20 percent of African American women are raped at some point in their lifetimes, while one in three Latinas are subjected to some form of sexual violence.[69] Unfortunately, these statistics are almost certainly underestimates. As

[68] See www.rainn.org/statistics/criminal-justice-system.
[69] Sung Yeon Choimorrow, Marcela Howell, and Jessica González-Rojas (2018), "This Is a Defining Moment for Women of Color Who Survived Sexual Violence," Colorlines, www .colorlines.com/articles/defining-moment-women-color-who-survived-sexual-violence-op-ed.

per RAINN's statistics, three out of four sexual assaults go unreported; when survivors do report, 995 perpetrators will walk free out of every 1,000 sexual assaults.

What felt like a sea change in the discussion of sexual violence in the United States occurred in October 2017. Following news stories concerning sexual assault accusations against media mogul Harvey Weinstein, actress Alyssa Milano tweeted: "If you've been sexually harassed or assaulted, write 'me too' as a reply to this tweet."[70] In a matter of hours the tweet went viral, and thousands of women responded by showing support and sharing their own stories of sexual abuse. According to the Pew Research Center, the #MeToo hashtag was used roughly 19 million times on Twitter in the year following Milano's initial tweet.[71] Originally coined by Tarana Burke in 2006 as part of her local grassroots movement to help women of color who endured sexual violence, the phrase "Me Too" now represents a global call for action to empower survivors from all walks of life.

Many women have since decided to come forward with allegations of sexual violence, including against prominent figures in politics, business, and entertainment industries. One of the most high-profile "Me Too" cases was the sexual assault allegations against Trump's then-nominee for Supreme Court justice, Brett Kavanaugh, during his confirmation hearings. In her testimony in front of the Senate Judiciary Committee, Christine Blasey Ford, a professor of psychology, accused Kavanaugh of having sexually assaulted her when both were in high school. Not surprisingly, reactions to these accusations were sharply divided by party lines. In the end, Kavanaugh got his Senate confirmation in a 52–48 vote – the narrowest and most polarized Supreme Court confirmation vote since 1881.[72]

Responding to Ford's allegations against Kavanaugh and the #MeToo movement, Trump remarked: "It is a very scary time for young men in America, where you can be guilty of something you may not be guilty of. This is a very, very – this is a very difficult time. What's happening here has much more to do than even the appointment of a Supreme Court justice."[73] When asked if he had a message for young women, Trump's response was succinct: "Women are doing great." Later, at a political rally, President Trump mocked Ford's testimony and repeated his argument that the #MeToo movement was

[70] See https://twitter.com/alyssa_milano/status/919659438700670976?lang=en.

[71] Monica Anderson and Skye Toor (2018), "How Social Media Users Have Discussed Sexual Harassment Since #MeToo Went Viral," Pew Research Center, www.pewresearch.org/fact-tank/2018/10/11/how-social-media-users-have-discussed-sexual-harassment-since-metoo-went-viral.

[72] Jason Silverstein (2018). "Brett Kavanaugh Confirmed to Supreme Court by Smallest Margin Since 1881," CBS News, www.cbsnews.com/news/brett-kavanaugh-confirmed-to-supreme-court-by-smallest-margin-in-modern-history/.

[73] Jeremy Diamond (2018), "Trump Says It's 'A Very Scary Time for Young Men in America,'" CNN, www.cnn.com/2018/10/02/politics/trump-scary-time-for-young-men-metoo/index.html.

unfairly hurting men.[74] Trump's stance on this issue is not surprising, given the multitude of sexual harassment and assault accusations leveled against him personally.

There remains considerable public concern for the accused rather than the accuser in sexual assault cases, which has led to countermovements such as #ProtectOurBoys and #HimToo. A Pew survey fielded in February 2018 indicates that 31 percent of Americans think that "women claiming they have experienced sexual harassment or assault when it hasn't actually occurred" is a major problem.[75] In reality, false reporting of sexual assault is rare (Lisak et al. 2010). Further, public opinion about this issue is divided mostly along partisan lines. For example, an NPR/Ipsos poll finds 75 percent Republicans think the #MeToo movement has gone "too far," as compared to only 21 percent of Democrats.[76] Another poll, conducted by *The Economist*/YouGov in September 2018, asked: "If it were proven that Brett Kavanaugh sexually assaulted a woman when they were both high school students 36 years ago, do you think that does or does not disqualify Kavanaugh from being a Supreme Court Justice?"[77] Only 48 percent of the survey participants thought a *proven* sexual assault would be disqualifying. Also surprisingly, opinions were driven more by party identification than gender. While 46 percent of males and 50 percent of females considered a proven sexual assault as disqualifying, 71 percent of Democrats versus merely 27 percent of Republicans agreed that it would disqualify Kavanaugh. Interestingly, only 15 percent of blacks and 23 percent of Latinos thought a proven sexual assault would *not* disqualify Kavanaugh compared to 31 percent of whites. We suspect group empathy may explain such intergroup differences, even after controlling for partisanship, though perhaps not as much as for the race-targeted policies we discussed earlier since the wording of the GEI items focuses on racial/ethnic groups.

To empirically examine links between group empathy and the #MeToo movement, we focused on this high-profile example of the allegations against Brett Kavanaugh. Specifically, respondents were asked: "As a Supreme Court nominee, Brett Kavanaugh faced accusations of sexual misconduct by several women. In general, how strongly do you believe or disbelieve these claims?" Response options ranged from "I disbelieve them strongly" to "I believe them strongly" on a 5-point scale. The results, presented in the second set of columns in Table 8.5, show that the most powerful predictors of responses to this question are SDO, partisanship, and ideology. This is not surprising since

---

[74] Josh Dawsey and Felicia Sonmez (2018), "Trump Mocks Kavanaugh Accuser Christine Blasey Ford," *Washington Post*, https://wapo.st/2QpBUNE?tid=ss_mail.

[75] Nikki Graf (2018), "Sexual Harassment at Work in the Era of #MeToo," Pew Research Center, www.pewsocialtrends.org/2018/04/04/sexual-harassment-at-work-in-the-era-of-metoo.

[76] See www.ipsos.com/sites/default/files/2018-10/ipsos_npr_sexual_assault_topline_103118_final.pdf.

[77] The survey questionnaire and full results are available at https://d25d2506sfb94s.cloudfront.net/cumulus_uploads/document/m6ng12r04y/econTabReport.pdf.

a patriarchal, hierarchical view of the world associated with SDO and a conservative ideology likely leads one to side with an accused man in the absence of concrete evidence. And since Kavanaugh was the nominee of a Republican president, the effect of partisanship is also expectedly large. That said, group empathy also carries a significant if modest impact on opinions about this issue. Moving from low to high scores on the GEI is associated with close to a 1-point increase out of 5 in support for #MeToo. These results hint that, even though the GEI items focus on empathy for racial/ ethnic outgroups, the measure also captures support for other social groups experiencing discrimination.

LGBTQ RIGHTS AND PROTECTIONS

The LGBTQ community continues to face a great deal of stigmatization and discrimination in the United States and around the world. On the campaign trail, candidate Trump avoided anti-LGBTQ rhetoric and even promised to protect the rights of the LGBTQ community – a somewhat unprecedented strategy relative to previous GOP nominees. For instance, at a media interview in April 2016 during the primaries, Trump criticized North Carolina's controversial "bathroom bill" that required transgender people to use the restroom that matched the sex listed on their birth certificate. Trump said the state should allow people "to use the bathroom they feel is appropriate."[78] During his acceptance speech at the Republican National Convention in July 2016, Trump made reference to the mass shooting by an ISIS sympathizer at a gay nightclub in Orlando, Florida, a month before and proclaimed: "I will do everything in my power to protect our LGBTQ citizens from the violence and oppression of a hateful foreign ideology – believe me."[79]

After taking office, Trump moved significantly away from these commitments. With the encouragement of his religious and socially conservative vice president, Mike Pence, Trump began to roll back LGBTQ rights and protections in areas including healthcare, employment, education, and access to basic governmental and social services. For instance, in March 2017, Trump signed an executive order revoking key components of Obama's 2014 executive order to protect private LGBTQ employees from discrimination while working on government contracts. In May of that same year, Trump signed an executive order on "free speech and religious liberty," which paved the way for expansive religious exemptions that could potentially allow for discrimination based on sexual orientation and gender identity. A year later, Trump signed yet another executive order entitled

---

[78] Jose A. DelReal (2016), "Trump Criticizes Controversial NC Transgender Law," *Washington Post*, http://wapo.st/1Sdt82T?tid=ss_mail.

[79] Amanda Terkel (2016), "Donald Trump Promises to Protect the LGBTQ Community," *HuffPost*, www.huffpost.com/entry/donald-trump-lgbt_n_57918ba8e4b0fc06ec5c7fdd.

"Establishment of a White House Faith and Opportunity Initiative" that further protected those who refuse to comply with anti-discriminatory laws and regulations on religious grounds. The Justice Department filed a Supreme Court brief in September 2017 in support of the rights of a Colorado baker who refused to make a cake for a same-sex wedding.[80] In January 2018, the Office of Civil Rights (OCR) of the Department of Health and Human Services (HHS) announced the creation of a new office called the "Conscience and Religious Freedom Division," tasked with enforcing "conscience protections" for "health care providers who refuse to perform, accommodate, or assist with certain health care services on religious or moral grounds."[81] The Trump administration finalized its rollback of the Obama-era LGBTQ patient protections on June 12, 2020, coinciding with the fourth anniversary of the Orlando gay nightclub massacre, in the middle of Pride Month and despite the COVID-19 pandemic.[82]

The Trump administration also rescinded progressive policies intended to improve transgender rights in educational settings. Again contradicting his campaign stance, Trump ordered the Departments of Education and Justice to ignore Obama-era guidance in place since May 2016 that suggested the interpretation of Title IX (the law that prohibits sex discrimination in education) should also include transgender students. The Obama-era guidance had also directed public schools to allow transgender students to use the bathrooms and locker rooms that aligned with their gender identities. In February 2018, the Department of Education further announced that it would no longer investigate civil rights complaints from transgender students barred from using the bathroom of their choice.

The Trump administration also pursued a ban on transgender individuals serving in the military. In July 2017 Trump announced via Twitter: "After consultation with my generals and military experts, please be advised that the United States government will not accept or allow transgender individuals to serve in any capacity. Our military must be focused on decisive and overwhelming victory and cannot be burdened with the tremendous medical costs and disruption that transgender in the military would entail."[83] This was a sharp reversal of the Obama-era policy that allowed transgender people to openly serve. The policy stirred great controversy around the country, leading the administration to propose a revised policy that would allow transgender

---

[80] Masha Gessen (2017), "How Trump Uses 'Religious Liberty' to Attack LGBT Rights," *New Yorker*, www.newyorker.com/news/news-desk/how-trump-uses-religious-liberty-to-attack-lgbt-rights.

[81] US Department of Health and Human Services (HHS) (2018), "Conscience Protections for Health Care Providers," https://www.hhs.gov/conscience/conscience-protections/index.html.

[82] Dan Diamond (2020), "Trump Finalizes Rollback of LGBTQ Patient Protections," *Politico*, www.politico.com/news/2020/06/12/trump-lgbtq-patient-protections-315819.

[83] See https://twitter.com/realdonaldtrump/status/890193981585444864?lang=en; https://twitter.com/realDonaldTrump/status/890196164313833472.

individuals to stay in the military as long as they served in their biological sex and did not seek gender-transition surgery. Federal district court judges in several states blocked the policy from taking effect due to its discriminatory intent. However, in January 2019, the Supreme Court (in a 5–4 split decision with the two Trump-appointed conservative justices, Neil Gorsuch and Brett Kavanaugh, voting in favor) granted the Justice Department's request to allow the ban to take effect while challenges to the policy continue to play out in the lower courts.[84]

Interestingly, the following year, in June 2020, Justice Gorsuch along with Chief Justice Roberts would join with the four liberal-leaning justices in a landmark 6–3 decision, ruling that protections against workplace discrimination on the basis of "sex" under the Civil Rights Act of 1964 also cover "sexual orientation" or "gender identity" and should thus include LGBTQ employees. While this was a major blow to the Trump administration's anti-LGBTQ policy agenda and a milestone in the fight for LGBTQ rights and equality, the Supreme Court ruling did not apply to Trump's transgender ban in the military, and there remains critical areas where nondiscrimination protections are lacking, including healthcare, education, housing, and more.

Amid all these challenges and legal battles, the US public has been increasingly favorable toward LGBTQ rights. A CBS News Poll conducted in May–June 2020 indicated that 82 percent of respondents thought "gay, lesbian or bisexual people should be protected under civil rights laws."[85] This positive trend even extends to Republicans and conservatives. For instance, according to the 2020 SCOTUSPoll, 74 percent of Republicans agreed it should be illegal for employees to be fired based on their sexual orientation, and 69 percent of Republicans thought the same for transgender people.[86] As Robert Jones, CEO of the Public Religion Research Institute (PRRI), puts it: "Whether you're talking about marriage equality, nondiscrimination protection – everybody has moved. Seniors have moved, white evangelicals have moved, base Republicans have moved."[87] It thus appears that neither party identification, ideology, nor religion can be the sole driver of these opinions. We suspect group empathy is at play.

Those high in group empathy should display solidarity with the LGBTQ community. To measure attitudes toward LGBTQ people, two questions were

---

[84] Ariane de Vogue and Zachary Cohen (2019), "Supreme Court Allows Transgender Military Ban to Go into Effect," CNN, www.cnn.com/2019/01/22/politics/scotus-transgender-ban/index .html.

[85] See www.pollingreport.com/lgbt.htm.

[86] A report of the results from this poll can be accessed at https://projects.iq.harvard.edu/files/ scotus-poll/files/scotuspoll-summary.pdf.

[87] Lisa Lerer, Giovanni Russonello, and Isabella Grullón Paz (2020), "On LGBTQ Rights, a Gulf between Trump and Many Republican Voters," *New York Times*, www.nytimes.com/2020/06/ 17/us/politics/lgbtq-supreme-court-trump-republicans.html.

TABLE 8.6 *The relationship between group empathy and support for LGBTQ rights*

	Extending governmental protections for LGBTQ		Allowing LGBTQ to openly serve in the US military	
	β	S.E.	β	S.E.
Group Empathy	.17**	.06	.20***	.06
SDO	-.47***	.06	-.40***	.06
Ethnocentrism	.03	.03	.002	.04
Party ID	-.14***	.04	-.19***	.04
Ideology	-.10†	.05	-.14*	.06
Political news exposure	.07†	.04	.04	.04
Black	-.04	.03	-.08*	.03
Latino	.001	.03	.02	.03
Female	.005	.02	-.02	.02
Education	.03	.04	.03	.04
Age	-.03	.05	-.14**	.05
Income	.12**	.05	.04	.06
Married	-.04†	.02	-.02	.02
Employed	.01	.02	-.02	.02
Metropolitan residence	.001	.04	.03	.05
Catholic	.04	.03	.06*	.03
Church attendance	-.14***	.03	-.16***	.04
Constant	.78***	.07	.84***	.08
N	794		794	

Note: Coefficients estimated using OLS regression. Data are weighted. All variables are rescaled to run from 0 to 1. †$p \leq .10$, *$p \leq .05$, **$p \leq .01$, and ***$p \leq .001$, two-tailed.
Source: 2018 US Group Empathy Study (YouGov)

asked: (1) "How strongly do you support or oppose government protections against discrimination in housing and employment for people of different sexual orientations (such as gay, lesbian, and transgender individuals)?" and (2) "How strongly do you support or oppose allowing gays, lesbians, and transgender individuals from serving openly in the US military?" Response options ranged from "strongly oppose" to "strongly support" on a 7-point scale. The results of OLS regression analyses are presented in Table 8.6. For both outcome variables, the effect of group empathy is statistically significant and substantively important. Moving from low to high scores on the GEI is associated with more than a 1-point increase on the 7-point scale in support for both protecting LGBTQ rights in general and allowing them to serve openly in the US military. SDO again produces the largest effect, but the GEI is about as influential as party identification and ideology – an impressive result.

All in all, these results strongly corroborate our theoretical expectation that group empathy is a significant, and often primary, determinant of attitudes and reactions to Trump-era policies and issues concerning minorities. Moreover, group empathy may not only influence domains closely related to race/ethnicity but also opinions regarding other groups who experience discrimination and stigmatization such as women and the LGBTQ community.

RACIAL/ETHNIC GAPS IN REACTIONS TO TRUMP-ERA POLICIES AND ISSUES

We have shown in previous chapters many instances where blacks and Latinos have taken very different positions on a variety of policy issues, and group empathy helped explain those differences. We next explore whether racial/ethnic gaps persist across this wide array of policies pursued by the Trump administration and, if so, how group empathy fares in explaining such gaps. Figure 8.1 presents average intergroup differences for all of the outcomes examined. These results indicate large gaps between black and white respondents, with somewhat smaller but still often significant differences between whites and Latinos. In almost every case except for LGBTQ rights, blacks and Latinos took significantly more progressive positions than whites, and the differences are often substantively large.[88] As other studies have shown, African Americans are far more opposed to the border wall than are whites, in this case by 25 percentage points. They are even more opposed than Latinos, by almost 10 percentage points. Blacks in this sample are also over 10 percentage points more opposed to family separation than are whites and 5 percentage points more supportive of DACA. Latinos almost always fall between blacks and whites on these issues, even when they involve what might be considered ingroup interests related to immigration. We apply the same approach as in previous chapters to explore whether such racial/ethnic differences of opinion about Trump-era policies and issues are accounted for, at least in part, by differences in group empathy.

The first step in determining whether group empathy explains racial/ethnic gaps in policy opinion is to see if the groups continue to differ on the GEI as we previously observed. In addition to the GEI, we also measured empathy for a variety of specific groups: whites, African Americans, Arabs, Latinos, undocumented immigrants, Native Americans, and the LGBTQ community. As in previous surveys, two questions were designed to tap the affective and cognitive components of group-specific empathy. The first, measuring empathic concern, read: "For each of the following specific groups, how concerned do you feel about

---

[88] Some of these differences persisted even after including the GEI, along with other political predispositions and socio-demographic influences in the models, as seen in Tables 8.1 through 8.6, so it is expected that some differences of opinion across these groups are not fully driven by group empathy and that other forces are likely also at play.

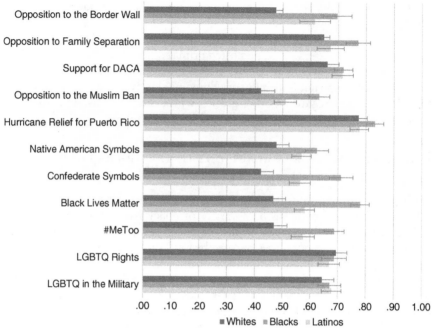

FIGURE 8.1   Racial/ethnic gaps in group-salient policy opinions
Note: The bars represent predictive margins calculated after OLS regression. The lines represent 95 percent confidence intervals. Data are weighted. All variables are rescaled to run from 0 to 1. Estimates from full model available in the online appendix.
Source: 2018 ANES Pilot Study (YouGov) and 2018 US Group Empathy Study (YouGov)

the challenges they face in our society these days?" Response options ranged from "not at all concerned" to "very concerned" on a 5-point scale. The second question, measuring perspective taking, read: "Regardless of the challenges another group faces, sometimes it is easier and other times more difficult to understand what members of a given group are going through. How easy is it for you to 'put yourself in the shoes' of individuals from each of the following groups in our society?" Response options ranged from "not easy at all" to "very easy" on a 5-point scale. We then generated an index by combining the two.

As Figure 8.2 displays, African Americans and Latinos score significantly higher on the GEI as well as group-specific empathy for all racial/ethnic minority groups as well as undocumented immigrants. This pattern is similar to previous studies. While African Americans report higher levels of empathy for the LGBTQ community than whites do, the levels of empathy whites and Latinos exhibit for this group do not significantly differ. One interesting difference we observe in the Trump era, which we did not observe in our previous surveys, is that African Americans and Latinos express significantly

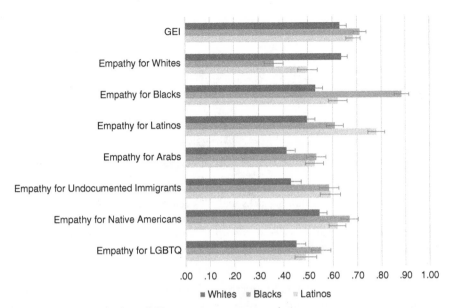

FIGURE 8.2 Racial/ethnic differences in group empathy
Note: The bars represent predictive margins calculated after OLS regression. The lines represent 95 percent confidence intervals. Models also control for gender, education, age, income, marital status, household size, employment status, metropolitan residence, religion (Catholic), and political news exposure. Data are weighted. All variables are rescaled to run from 0 to 1. Estimates from full model available in the online appendix.
Source: 2018 US Group Empathy Study (YouGov)

less group empathy toward whites than the white respondents do for their ingroup. In earlier intergroup comparisons of empathy toward whites, minority respondents did not differ from the majority. The reason for this change is open to speculation, but one potential explanation might be a backlash against Trump and his mostly white supporters.

Can these minority–majority differences in group empathy explain the policy opinion gaps between whites and nonwhites in the Trump era? To find out, we conducted generalized structural equation modeling (GSEM) analyses. Bootstrapping with bias-corrected confidence intervals were employed to test the significance of indirect effects. The following figures present the results of individual path analyses for each dependent variable.

We first return to ANES data to analyze the mediational role of group empathy in explaining intergroup differences in opinions about the border wall and family separation. Figure 8.3 presents the path coefficients obtained via GSEM. As previously shown in Figure 8.1, both African Americans and Latinos displayed significantly higher opposition to the border wall than whites.

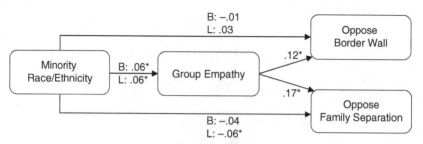

FIGURE 8.3 The role of group empathy in explaining racial/ethnic gaps in opinions about border policies

Note: Path coefficients estimated using generalized structural equation modeling based on the full models. "B" denotes blacks and "L" denotes Latinos. White respondents constitute the baseline category. All indirect paths are statistically significant. Data are weighted. All variables are rescaled to run from 0 to 1. *p ≤ .05, one-tailed.

Source: 2018 ANES Pilot Study (YouGov)

In the fully specified model including the GEI along with a host of other political factors, such intergroup differences disappeared (see Table 8.1). As for the family separation policy, blacks on average showed higher opposition than both whites and Latinos (also shown in Figure 8.1). The differences between whites and Latinos, on the other hand, were not significant given the overlapping 95 percent confidence intervals. In the fully specified model presented in Table 8.1, white–black differences disappeared and, most surprisingly, Latinos were significantly less opposed to family separation than whites after controlling for the GEI and all of the other explanatory variables. The GSEM technique tests whether group empathy can at least partially explain these findings. The bootstrap results suggest that the indirect effects are statistically significant for both blacks and Latinos across both policy issues. Because minorities score significantly higher on the GEI and, in turn, the GEI significantly increases opposition to the border wall and family separation policies, we observe a positive and significant indirect path between race/ethnicity and these two policy outcomes.

We extended these analyses to all of the policy outcomes tapped in our national survey. Figure 8.4 presents path coefficients for policies that target undocumented immigrants, Muslims, and other minority groups in the Trump era. As seen in Figure 8.1, opinion differences between Latinos and whites for many of these policies are smaller than the black–white comparisons, though still very often significant. There are also certain issues such as LGBTQ rights where all three groups display similar positions. This sometimes leaves less variation for group empathy to explain. Still, in many cases there are large racial/ethnic opinion differences, and group empathy is likely responsible.

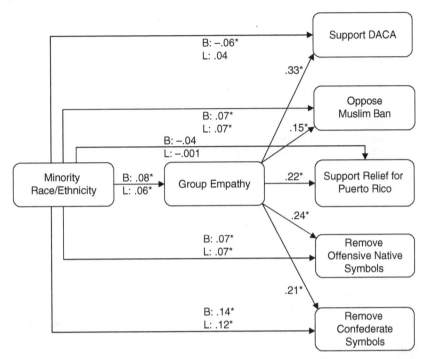

FIGURE 8.4 The role of group empathy in explaining racial/ethnic gaps in opinions about Trump-era policies and issues
Note: Path coefficients estimated using generalized structural equation modeling based on the full models. "B" denotes blacks and "L" denotes Latinos. White respondents constitute the baseline category. All indirect paths are statistically significant. Data are weighted. All variables are rescaled to run from 0 to 1. *p ≤ .05, one-tailed.
Source: 2018 US Group Empathy Study (YouGov)

Interestingly, African Americans display significantly less support for DACA than whites do when group empathy along with SDO, ethnocentrism, party identification, ideology, political news exposure, and socio-demographic factors are controlled (refer back to Table 8.2). However, the positive and significant indirect effect of group empathy partially suppresses this negative direct effect. Since African Americans are significantly higher in group empathy than whites, and group empathy in turn has a large, statistically significant positive effect on support for DACA, blacks end up supporting DACA somewhat more on average as a group.

As for opposition to Trump's Muslim ban, group empathy at least partially explains the differences between African Americans and Latinos on the one hand and whites on the other. Both minorities remain significantly less supportive of the ban even after the GEI and a host of other key factors are controlled for. A similar pattern can be seen for removing symbols offensive to

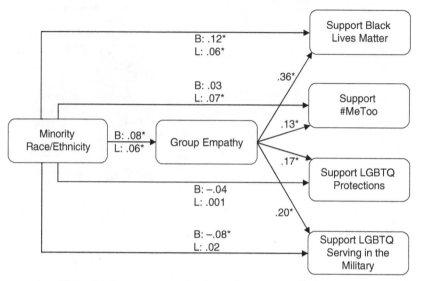

FIGURE 8.5 The role of group empathy in explaining racial/ethnic gaps in opinions about contemporary social movements
Note: Path coefficients estimated using generalized structural equation modeling based on the full models. "B" denotes blacks and "L" denotes Latinos. White respondents constitute the baseline category. All indirect paths are statistically significant. Data are weighted. All variables are rescaled to run from o to 1. *p ≤ .05, one-tailed.
Source: 2018 US Group Empathy Study (YouGov)

Native Americans and Confederate symbols. The coefficients for both blacks and Latinos remain statistically significant in the fully specified regression models. While the bootstrap procedure suggests significant indirect effects via group empathy, further mediating influences seem to be also at play in order to fully explain these intergroup differences. By comparison, group empathy substantively explains white–black differences in support for hurricane relief to Puerto Rico. Referring back to Figure 8.1, blacks were much more supportive of aid to Puerto Rico, while whites and Latinos did not significantly differ from one another. As Figure 8.4 shows, the direct effect of race/ethnicity on this outcome variable is no longer significant for blacks in the fully specified model, while the indirect effect through group empathy is large and significant.

We also conducted GSEM analyses to explain intergroup differences in support for contemporary social movements defending the rights of blacks, women, and the LGBTQ community (presented in Figure 8.5). We find that a significant proportion, though not all, of the differences between whites and nonwhites in support of Black Lives Matter is explained by group empathy. The same is true for group differences in support of Kavanaugh's accusers.

Differences between Latino and white support for government protections of the LGBTQ community and the LGBTQ openly serving in the military are not large to begin with (as Figure 8.1 shows) but there is still some significant effect via the indirect path. Group empathy also mediates some of the difference between African Americans and whites when it comes to LGBTQ rights, but the pattern of results is quite different. Prior works find that African Americans – especially those who identify as religious conservatives – do not show interest in combating intolerance leveled at gays and lesbians (McKenzie and Rouse 2013). Looking at the direct paths illustrated in Figure 8.5, African Americans are significantly *less* supportive of LGBTQ serving in the military, but group empathy has the potential to counterbalance those differences. African American respondents high in group empathy are much more supportive of the LGBTQ community, and they are higher not only in general group empathy but also group-specific empathy toward LGBTQ people than whites to begin with (as shown in Figure 8.2). In other words, group empathy significantly reduces the overall difference between whites and blacks on these issues.

Overall, these results largely corroborate our theoretical expectation that group empathy helps explain the racial and ethnic gaps in reactions to the policies and issues salient in the era of the Trump administration. Support for the removal of Confederate symbols and the Black Lives Matter movement are mainly ingroup concerns for African Americans, but the fact that group empathy also mediates Latino reactions to those issues is particularly supportive of Group Empathy Theory. By the same token, the border wall, family separation, and DACA may all be considered Latino concerns. The fact that differences between blacks and whites on these issues are at least partially explained by group empathy is quite remarkable. Of course, other predispositions such as ideology, partisanship, or ethnocentrism can also help explain these differences in policy views across racial/ethnic groups. In fact, in additional analyses not reported here, these other predispositions have just such an effect. What we can say, however, is that group empathy matters as much or more than those alternative explanations.[89]

CONCLUSION

The Trump era has been characterized by extreme partisan polarization, incendiary and divisive discourse, and policy proposals that seem to target stigmatized groups in American society. The role of empathy, particularly for marginalized outgroups, has thus become ever more critical as the public is frequently exposed to rhetoric and policies that otherize, criminalize, and even dehumanize vulnerable communities.

---

[89] These additional results are available in the online appendix.

Even children are not spared from this inflammatory discourse. At a roundtable held at the Morrelly Homeland Security Center, Trump alleged that some undocumented immigrant children crossing the US border are actually members of the MS-13 gang, who "exploited the loopholes in our laws to enter the country as unaccompanied alien minors," adding, "They look so innocent. They're not innocent."[90] The Trump administration's discourse to justify stricter immigration policies is often devoid of empathy even in the face of tragedy.[91] Following the deaths of two Guatemalan immigrant children in US custody, Trump tweeted: "Any deaths of children or others at the Border are strictly the fault of the Democrats and their pathetic immigration policies that allow people to make the long trek thinking they can enter our country illegally. They can't. If we had a Wall, they wouldn't even try!"[92] Trump appointees and allies often amplify this rhetoric. For instance, in defense of Trump's family separation policy, Brian Kilmeade – a host of the Fox News show *Fox & Friends* – said: "Like it or not, these are not our kids. Show them compassion, but it's not like he is doing this to the people of Idaho or Texas. These are people from another country."[93]

Amid this exclusionary rhetoric, hate crimes have increased substantially during the Trump era. Using data from the Anti-Defamation League's Hate, Extremism, Anti-Semitism, Terrorism (HEAT) map, Feinberg, Branton, and Martinez-Ebers (2019) examine the correlation between counties that hosted one of Trump's 275 presidential campaign rallies in 2016 and incidents of hate crimes in subsequent months.[94] They find that counties that had hosted a 2016 Trump campaign rally experienced, on average, a 226 percent increase in reported hate crimes over comparable counties that did not host such a rally. In another study, employing time-series and panel regression techniques, Edwards and Rushin (2018) find a statistically significant surge in reported hate crimes across the United States following Trump's election, which indicates strong empirical support for what they refer to as the "Trump Effect"

---

[90] Seung Min Kim (2018), "Trump Warns against Admitting Unaccompanied Migrant Children: 'They're Not Innocent,'" *Washington Post*, https://wapo.st/2IERsoJ?tid=ss_mail.

[91] Karen Tumulty (2019), "Trump's Tweets on Children Dying in US Custody Are a New Low," *Washington Post*, www.washingtonpost.com/opinions/2018/12/29/with-trump-there-is-no-bottom/?tid=ss_mail.

[92] See https://twitter.com/realdonaldtrump/status/1079082188665171971?lang=en.

[93] Eugene Scott (2018), "Fox News Host's 'Not Our Kids' Statement, and the Limits of Compassion," *Washington Post*, https://wapo.st/2KbxCdj?tid=ss_mail.

[94] To estimate a rally's impact on subsequent hate crime rates, Feinberg et al. (2019) aggregate hate-crime incident data and Trump rally data to the county level, while controlling for factors like previous crime rates, the presence of active hate groups, the size of the minority population, and so on. See Ayal Feinberg, Regina Branton, and Valerie Martinez-Ebers (2019), "Counties That Hosted a 2016 Trump Rally Saw a 226 Percent Increase in Hate Crimes," *Washington Post*, www.washingtonpost.com/politics/2019/03/22/trumps-rhetoric-does-inspire-more-hate-crimes/?utm_term=.17deb591529e.

hypothesis. Their results further demonstrate that counties that voted for Trump by the widest margins in the 2016 presidential election also saw the largest subsequent spikes in reported hate crimes.

Several studies have tied this surge in hate crimes to the rising nationalism, populism, and far-right politics occurring not just in the United States but around the globe. As Bieber (2018, 535) puts it: "The increase of hate crimes around the Brexit and Trump elections suggests both an increased polarization during the campaign, but also the (perceived) change in social norms that nationalist and xenophobic attitudes have become more acceptable and thus radical individuals and groups feel more empowered to act upon them." One of the latest examples of how perpetrators of hate crimes may feel validated by the Trump administration's inflammatory discourse and policies is the March 2019 attack on two mosques in Christchurch, New Zealand, that resulted in the death of forty-nine people. In a manifesto entitled "The Great Replacement" posted online, the shooter referred to Donald Trump as "a symbol of renewed white identity and common purpose."[95] Although Trump promptly condemned the massacre via Twitter, when asked by reporters whether he perceived white nationalism as a rising threat around the world, he responded: "I don't really. I think it's a small group of people that have very, very serious problems."[96] However, according to official records, domestic terrorism has claimed more American lives than international terrorism since 9/11, and it is increasingly driven by white supremacist ideology.[97]

The Charlottesville "alt-right" rally in 2017 is only one example of violent white nationalist extremism in the United States in recent years. Another occurred on August 3, 2019, in the border town of El Paso, Texas, when a mass shooter killed twenty-three people and injured dozens. The shooter had driven almost ten hours from Allen, Texas, to the southern border to specifically target the Latinx community in El Paso, which constitutes the majority of the city's population.[98] Before the massacre, the shooter released a white supremacist screed to explain his reasoning for the attack. He bemoaned an immigrant "invasion," echoing Trump's own language at recent rallies.[99] For instance, in Florida in May 2019, Trump had bemoaned thousands of

---

[95] Alexander Smith, Caroline Radnofsky, Linda Givetash, and Vladimir Banic (2019), "New Zealand Mosque Shooting: Attacker's Apparent Manifesto Probed," NBC News, www.nbcnews.com/news/world/new-zealand-mosque-terrorist-may-have-targeted-country-because-it-n983601.

[96] Colby Itkowitz and John Wagner (2019), "Trump Says White Nationalism Is Not a Rising Threat after New Zealand Attacks: 'It's a Small Group of People,'" *Washington Post*, https://wapo.st/2JfRInJ?tid=ss_mail.

[97] Tim Arango, Nicholas Bogel-Burroughs, and Katie Benner (2019), "Minutes before El Paso Killing, Hate-Filled Manifesto Appears Online," *New York Times*, www.nytimes.com/2019/08/03/us/patrick-crusius-el-paso-shooter-manifesto.html.

[98] Ibid.

[99] Peter Baker and Michael D. Shear (2019), "El Paso Shooting Suspect's Manifesto Echoes Trump's Language," *New York Times*, https://www.nytimes.com/2019/08/04/us/politics/trump-mass-shootings.html.

immigrants "marching up" to the border and asked the cheerful crowd: "How do you stop these people?" An audience member yelled: "Shoot them!" Laughing along with his followers at the comment, he chose to respond jokingly: "That's only in the Panhandle you can get away with that stuff. Only in the Panhandle."[100]

It is thus important to consider how elite rhetorical strategies like Trump's may affect the climate of empathy across groups in American society. The present moment allows us to examine very different presidential discourses that could promote or undermine empathy for marginalized groups as they attempt to protect the nation from real threats both economic and military in nature. The stigmatizing rhetoric of contemporary populist leaders like Trump ("They're bringing crime. They're rapists"[101]) stands in stark contrast to the inclusive rhetoric of politicians like Obama ("Learning to stand in somebody else's shoes, to see through their eyes, that's how peace begins"[102]). That said, empathic rhetoric is not exclusive to one party or another over time. For example, the iconic conservative Ronald Reagan offered a very different tone than Trump's border wall narrative ("Rather than talking about putting up a fence, why don't we work out some recognition of our mutual problems?"[103]), as did George W. Bush by tempering his policies with the rhetoric of "compassionate conservatism."[104] The more moderate approaches of Reagan and Bush were grounded in an effort to expand their base of support among minority groups, including Latino immigrants.[105]

We suspect Trump's divisive approach has fundamentally limited his ability to expand beyond his base. Meanwhile, opponents of the president have increasingly found ways to connect, organize, and unify diverse constituencies – wherein group empathy functions as one of the key common denominators – in active opposition against Trump's divisive policies. The reaction to divisiveness might be a more explicit place for group empathy in our politics.

Trump's rhetorical strategy highlights threats to specific ingroups, an approach that inherently assumes empathy for outgroups will be too scarce to

---

[100] A video recording of this exchange at the Florida rally can be accessed at https://www.pbs.org/newshour/politics/watch-trump-asks-what-to-do-about-migrants-crossing-border-rallygoer-suggests-shoot-them.

[101] The full text of this quote can be accessed at http://wapo.st/1HPABjR?tid=ss_mail.

[102] See https://obamawhitehouse.archives.gov/realitycheck/the-press-office/remarks-president-barack-obama-student-roundtable-istanbul.

[103] See www.vox.com/2017/1/29/14429368/reagan-bush-immigration-attitude.

[104] For an interview with President Bush on his take on compassionate conservatism, see www.bushcenter.org/catalyst/opportunity-road/george-w-bush-on-compassionate-conservatism.html.

[105] We continue discussing the role leadership plays in promoting group empathy at the macro level in the final chapter.

outweigh protective reactions. The evidence does not corroborate this assumption. While outgroup empathy is much less common than ingroup empathy, it can nevertheless powerfully temper the impulse to support policies that increase the suffering of other groups to benefit one's own. We think this finding represents one of our key scholarly contributions, one that also provides a normative benefit. Powerful empathic reactions occur among minority outgroups facing the highest threats as well as among whites high in reactive empathy. These results suggest that elite rhetorical strategies relying on threats meant to trigger public fear and anger underestimate the possibility of an empathic backlash.

As the election results in 2018 in the United States suggest, many people respond to divisive politics by building coalitions, organizing, and mobilizing across lines of difference. While the Trump administration has encouraged nationalism, exclusionary politics, and even hate crimes, we are also bearing witness to a rising activism, resistance, and political participation in opposition. By creating cross-cutting cleavages within communities over a common denominator of compassion and perspective taking, group empathy may play a pivotal role for mobilizing citizens against policies that increase human suffering. Group empathy can powerfully counteract the effects of perceived threats, racial animus, and social dominance tendencies that lead one to view other groups as inferior and undeserving. In short, empathy for outgroups can trump hatred.

9

Group Empathy, Brexit, and Public Opinion in the United Kingdom

> Oh, I have suffered / With those that I saw suffer!
>
> William Shakespeare, *The Tempest* (circa 1611)

Following the Brexit vote to leave the European Union, racially and religiously motivated hate crimes soared in the United Kingdom.[1] Emboldened by the victory of the Leave campaign that largely ran on an anti-immigrant, anti-refugee platform, those who may once have been somewhat reluctant to share negative views about immigrants publicly, let alone act on them, began to do so more openly. While attacks on minority-owned small businesses, racist graffiti on the neighborhoods and homes of immigrant families, and incidents of verbal and physical harassment in public and private spaces increased, so did acts driven by outgroup empathy.

Empathy toward those being targeted after Brexit was manifest in various ways – through social media, public institutions, nongovernmental organizations, and on the streets. Thousands of people stood up against racism via protests and demonstrations around the United Kingdom. Empathy for stigmatized outgroups was also manifested in smaller but creative acts. For instance, a local artist transformed a racist graffiti incident into a positive message. Disturbed by the words "Speak English" sprayed on a wall in Walthamstow, north London, Chris Walker photoshopped a version that exclaimed "[We] Speak English [Bengali, Bulgarian, Cockney, French, Lithuanian, Panjabi (sic), Polish, Tamil, Turkish, Urdu]," listing several languages spoken in the area by residents who originated from other parts of the world.[2]

---

[1] Tara John (2017), "Hate Crimes Soared in Parts of the UK after Brexit," *Time*, https://time.com /4985332/hate-crime-uk-2017/.

[2] Greg Evans (2018), "Artist Turns a Piece of Racist Graffiti into Something a Lot More Positive," *Independent*, www.indy100.com/article/racist-graffiti-english-language-walthamstow-london-artist-chris-walker-8658966.

More racist graffiti – "No Blacks, No Blacks" – was spray-painted on the front door of an immigrant from the Congo in Greater Manchester only five days after he and his ten-year-old son moved in.[3] Jackson Yamba posted a photo of his vandalized door on Twitter, noting: "My front door in Salford was painted over a week ago with this abhorrent racist graffiti – after reporting it to @gmpolice they still haven't been here to investigate. How do I assure my traumatised 10 year old that he is safe in his home?"[4] Massive public support in reaction to Yamba's tweet compelled the police to launch a hate crime investigation, which subsequently led to the apprehension of the perpetrator. Meanwhile, a crowdfunding campaign raised over £2,000 for the father and son in a matter of hours. The organizer of the fundraiser, Mark Donne, noted: "Let's replace the door with a beautiful one. Or, frankly, let's raise as much as we can to show love, solidarity & friendship with the Yamba family – they can spend on whatever they choose. A new door cannot remove the trauma they've suffered, but the gesture can offer reassurance, support & put a smile back on that little boy's face."[5]

Some British citizens began wearing safety pins as a sign of solidarity with marginalized communities who found themselves all the more vulnerable in the post-Brexit surge of racism and xenophobia. The idea was developed by a Twitter user with the intent to signal that the wearer of the safety pin would be an ally or would provide a safe place for anyone feeling targeted in everyday activities, such as deciding whom to sit next to on a public transport. Originally from the United States, the campaign's founder referred to herself as an "undercover immigrant" given the fact that she is white and a native English speaker, adding: "I am not a British citizen, I cannot vote but I am a part of this society. I am married to an Englishman and have lived here for six years. It is important for me to stand with others who can't go undercover."[6] The safety pin idea was criticized by some circles as a superficial gimmick aimed at making white Britons feel good about themselves without taking any real action. Supporters of the idea, on the other hand, emphasized that the pins were more than just a symbolic gesture, instead signifying the pledge to document, report, and intervene whenever they witnessed abusive or discriminatory behavior. Only a few months after the Brexit referendum, the safety pin idea would be exported to the United States in response to the rise of hate speech and crimes targeting Muslims, Latinos, blacks, and other minorities in the wake of Trump's presidential election victory in November 2016.

---

[3] Josh Halliday (2019), "Salford Man Targeted with Racist Graffiti 'Overwhelmed' By Support," *The Guardian*, www.theguardian.com/uk-news/2019/feb/18/salford-dad-jackson-yamba-targeted-with-racist-graffiti-overwhelmed-by-support.

[4] See https://twitter.com/jacksonyamba/status/1096865024444981249?lang=en.

[5] See www.gofundme.com/f/lets-buy-jackson-yamba-amp-his-son-a-brand-new-door.

[6] Zak Brophy (2016), "The Humble Safety Pin Makes an Anti-Racism Point," BBC News, www.bbc.com/news/uk-36661097.

Group Empathy Theory was conceived as a general approach that can explain political attitudes and behavior across a variety of social divisions and political contexts. Its basic tenets and assumptions are not limited to any particular group, country, setting, or period. It should be applicable to any heterogeneous societal structure replete with ingroup–outgroup dynamics both hostile and hospitable. This chapter explores the power of group empathy to explain public opinion dynamics in the contemporary British context surrounding Brexit.

DEBATES ABOUT PUBLIC OPINION DYNAMICS SURROUNDING BREXIT

On June 23, 2016, in what was dubbed the Brexit referendum, a slim majority (51.9 percent) of UK voters opted to leave the European Union. The result came as a huge shock to many, including the majority of Members of Parliament, who stated they would have preferred to stay (Goodwin & Milazzo 2017). Indeed, most UK political experts saw the referendum itself as a failed gambit by the sitting prime minister at the time, David Cameron, to publicly rebuff the far-right wing of his Conservative Party who had been clamoring for some time about EU restrictions on British trade and, especially, open immigration policies. Cameron abruptly resigned the day after the referendum, after months of campaigning against leaving the EU and repeatedly branding it an act of "economic self-harm."[7]

As of this writing, the political and economic processes triggered by that fateful ballot referendum are still unfolding. Cameron's prediction of the impact of Brexit – shared by most of the world's economists – seems to be playing out as he cautioned. The outcome roiled world stock markets and immediately undermined the value of the British currency. However, support for Brexit also appears to be growing since the referendum. Boris Johnson, the leading political figure in the Vote Leave campaign, was selected in July 2019 by his party to assume the prime minister position vacated by Theresa May following her failed attempts to pass a Brexit deal. Johnson loudly claimed that leaving the EU without a clear settlement of many issues surrounding trade and immigration – the so-called hard Brexit option that nearly every economist in print predicted to be disastrous for the nation – would be far preferable to holding a second referendum or requesting further delay so that the negotiations with the EU could continue.[8] He then secured what he called "a huge, great stonking mandate" from the British people to "Get Brexit Done" (his campaign

---

[7] Heather Stewart, Rowena Mason, and Rajeev Syal (2016), "David Cameron Resigns after UK Votes to Leave European Union," *The Guardian*, www.theguardian.com/politics/2016/jun/24/david-cameron-resigns-after-uk-votes-to-leave-european-union.

[8] Common elite messages on these dimensions did seem to have a clear impact on vote choice (Goodwin et al. 2020).

slogan and main focus) by pulling off the biggest Conservative Party victory since 1987 in the December 2019 snap general election.[9] Johnson delivered his promise of getting the United Kingdom officially out of the European Union on January 31, 2020.[10]

In the immediate aftermath of the referendum, some evidence seemed to flatly contradict the argument that Brexit support was driven mostly by economic anxiety among working-class UK citizens who were losing jobs and wages in competition with new immigrants from the broader EU. The evidence showed that support for Brexit was actually highest in places where migrants were most scarce.[11] Others pointed out, however, that it was *changes* in the local percentage of migrants from the EU that significantly drove the vote. For instance, Goodwin and Heath (2016, 329) found that "even though areas with relatively high levels of EU migration tended to be more pro-Remain, those places which had experienced a sudden influx of EU migrants over the last ten years tended to be more pro-Leave." This could then be due to either economic or attitudinal factors. Still, most empirical analyses of the individual-level causal antecedents of Brexit support have found that negative views of immigrants, and especially their cultural impact on the United Kingdom, were among the best predictors (Goodwin & Milazzo 2017; Gormley-Heenan & Aughey 2017; Patel & Connelly 2019; Swales 2016). But work continues to be done on exactly how immigration and the anxieties it provokes drive up support for risky and potentially economically devastating policies like Brexit.

While we suspect that anti-immigrant affect might have a lot to do with Brexit and similar electoral results both in the UK and throughout Europe, we think the political psychology underlying that affect may be tied to whether an individual can readily put themselves into the shoes of those coming to the United Kingdom for work or to pursue a better life. Just as with the power of group empathy in the US context, so do we predict it should matter in Britain. To be sure, standard explanations having little to do with group empathy might continue to drive support as well, but Group Empathy Theory predicts that interpersonal and intergroup differences in this particular predisposition matter at least as much as commitments to party or ideological leanings.

---

[9] Sam Knight (2019), "Boris Johnson Wins, and Britain Chooses the Devil It Knows," *New Yorker*, www.newyorker.com/news/letter-from-the-uk/boris-johnson-wins-and-britain-chooses-the-devil-it-knows.

[10] The United Kingdom's official exit was followed by a transition period to allow UK–EU negotiations to continue as per their future relationship, particularly in the areas of trade and security. See Tom Edgington (2020), "Brexit: What Is the Transition Period," BBC News, www.bbc.com/news/uk-politics-50838994.

[11] Chris Lawton and Robert Ackrill (2016), "Hard Evidence: How Areas with Low Immigration Voted Mainly for Brexit," *The Conversation*, http://theconversation.com/hard-evidence-how-areas-with-low-immigration-voted-mainly-for-brexit-62138.

We suspect that group empathy significantly undergirds British attitudes about Brexit, because the referendum was consistently framed in large part as a move to "protect" the United Kingdom from "outsiders" posing economic, cultural, and/or existential threats to national interests. These outsiders included European immigrants who were free to move as a result of EU laws. The elite propaganda of the Leave campaign also relied heavily on the narrative of a river of non-European immigrants ostensibly streaming into the United Kingdom, from South Asia, Africa, and the Middle East. The Syrian refugee crisis, which had placed a huge strain on Germany and other northern European nations, was also often invoked in the run-up to the referendum.

It is no coincidence that the Syrian refugee crisis, prompted by massive human suffering in a predominantly Muslim country that descended into civil war in 2011, has served as a rhetorical touchstone for many of the ethnonationalist, far-right parties in Western Europe. Opening one's doors to the poor and dispossessed hailing from countries shattered by brutality and oppression is surely challenging and risky for any developed nation. Using Brexit as a case, we explore whether outgroup empathy can help explain why some citizens in those receiving countries are more willing to take such a risk.

To be clear, we do not propose outgroup empathy as a substitute for racial/ ethnic animosities or other commonly employed factors to explain policy preferences. However, group empathy should explain additional variance because some UK citizens will find it more difficult than others to take the perspective of those coming to the shores of Britain as a result of political and economic crises in their homelands. This should be true even among many citizens who harbor no strong negative affect toward outgroups per se but simply lack the motivation to care about their well-being.

HYPOTHESES AND DATA

We hypothesize that those high in group empathy will hold little support for Brexit, even above and beyond other relevant predispositions such as party attachments, ideology, and authoritarianism (H1a). Group empathy should also significantly affect British attitudes about immigration, welfare preferences, and foreign aid, as well as perceptions of group-based discrimination and support for equal opportunities for marginalized groups (H1b). Moreover, as in the US context, nonwhite minorities in the United Kingdom should display higher levels of group empathy than the majority (H2a) and that such differences should significantly explain intergroup variation in British political opinions (H2b). Our theory suggests that nonwhite British citizens, even those who do not hail from the countries currently sending the largest number of migrants, should be better able to take the newcomers' perspective. On average, their support for Brexit is likely to be lower, even if they may stand to suffer the most in downward wage pressure and competition for jobs due to the EU's freedom of movement for workers policy.[12]

We have the opportunity to revisit a critical claim the theory makes about the distinction between intergroup empathy and interpersonal empathy. Empathy for outgroups should operate much differently than individual empathy often expressed toward close intimates and friends (H3). In fact, there are situations where they might even work in directly opposite directions. Empathy toward one's closest friends and family might push some to want to close borders against outsiders in order to protect their kin from perceived threats they attribute to immigrants. Alternatively, others high in individual empathy might actually feel close to newcomers, especially if they themselves hail from groups that were once considered foreign. In other words, individual-level empathy can cut both ways, as other research has suggested (Feldman et al. 2020). However, group empathy should motivate one to push strongly against Brexit and support immigrants and other vulnerable groups in the United Kingdom. While minorities should display higher levels of group empathy than do whites, we do not expect to find intergroup differences in individual empathy since it is a universal human trait that occurs more naturally without the social prerequisites or life experiences that group empathy requires.

To test these hypotheses, we use data from the British Election Study (BES) – the longest-running social science survey in the United Kingdom since its launch in 1964. A four-item version of the Group Empathy Index (GEI) was included in Wave 14 fielded by YouGov in May 2018. A total of 7,691 respondents were administered the GEI. As discussed in Chapter 3, we chose four items out of the original fourteen-item scale: two perspective taking and two empathic concern items with the highest factor loadings using data from the 2013/14 US Group Empathy Two-Wave Study (see Table 9.1). For the BES, the short version of the GEI maintained the Likert-type wording of the items in statement format with response options on a 5-point scale ranging from "does not describe me well at all" to "describes me extremely well."[13] A Cronbach's alpha test yields high reliability ($\alpha = .90$). A confirmatory factor analysis (CFA) with oblique rotation further

---

[12] According to Clarke et al. (2017, 12): "At the end of 2015, the argument that immigration was having negative effects on domestic workers, a view being pushed by UKIP and Nigel Farage, appeared to be legitimized in a widely circulated report by the Bank of England. The analysis suggested that rising immigration could drive down wages for low-skilled British workers, estimating that a 10-percentage-point increase in the proportion of immigrants was associated with a nearly 2 per cent reduction in pay for semi- and unskilled workers in service industries such as care homes, shops and bars."

[13] As discussed in Chapter 3, for the ANES, we transformed the Likert-type statement format of the GEI items into a construct-specific question format to address concerns about acquiescence bias. The predictive power of the GEI remains robust to the changes in the number of items used and these formatting decisions.

TABLE 9.1 *Four-item Group Empathy Index (GEI) in Likert statement format*

Perspective taking items

- I sometimes try to better understand people of other racial or ethnic groups by imagining how things look from their perspective.
- Before criticizing somebody from another racial or ethnic group, I try to imagine how I would feel if I were in their place.

Empathic concern items

- I often have tender, concerned feelings for people from another racial or ethnic group who are less fortunate than me.
- When I see someone being taken advantage of due to their race or ethnicity, I feel protective toward them.

Note: Response options are: (1) Does not describe me well at all; (2) Describes me slightly well; (3) Describes me moderately well; (4) Describes me very well; (5) Describes me extremely well.

affirms a unidimensional model, given that only one factor has an eigenvalue of over 1 (3.08) and all four items load very highly (.86 and over). For comparative purposes, both a simple summative index of the four items as well as a CFA-based factor score were created. The results are identical across these two measurement types. As noted earlier in Chapter 3, just like the full fourteen-item GEI, the short version of the GEI employs its CFA-based factor score form in the analyses of the BES data.

The 2018 BES Wave 14 included a ten-item individual empathy measure in addition to the GEI. This allowed us to compare the predictive power of each type of empathy.[14] The items of the individual empathy scale were geared toward measuring respondents' empathic abilities primarily reserved for their inner circle. For instance, one item stated: "After being with a friend who is sad about something, I usually feel sad." Response options ranged from "strongly disagree" to "strongly agree" on a 4-point scale. Similar to the GEI, the measure of individual empathy was generated using the factor scores of the ten items.

As in the other chapters of this book, the analyses that follow control for key socio-demographic factors, including minority race/ethnicity, gender, education, age, income, marital status, employment status, household size, and religion.[15] For political controls, we generated a 9-point party identification variable by grouping center-left and left-wing parties on one side and center-right and right-wing parties

---

[14] The items of this individual empathy scale are provided in the Appendix at the end.
[15] To be consistent with the US models, we continue using the "Catholic" dummy variable in the British models.

on the other.[16] This grouping is parsimonious and largely coincides with the Brexit positions of the British parties at the time of the referendum, so it makes the tests of group empathy's effects on Brexit and related attitudes highly stringent.[17] Other controls include ideology, measured with a 10-point left–right scale, and authoritarianism, also measured on a 10-point scale where "0" is libertarian and "10" denotes authoritarian.[18]

All measures are set on equal footing via linear transformation and range from 0 to 1. The analyses use sampling weights to draw inferences about the general British population. YouGov constructs the weights for the BES samples at the regional level in which Scotland, England, Wales, and London are weighted separately to match population values. The weights are then adjusted to account for the oversampling of Scottish and Welsh respondents.

RESULTS

We theorize that group empathy is strongly linked to policy opinions, especially about issues concerning group rights and resources. Perhaps the most salient political issue in this current political moment in the United Kingdom is Brexit. Group empathy should be significantly associated with opposition to Brexit, since the Leave campaign's rhetorical strategy in the EU referendum appealed to exclusionary, nationalist, and anti-immigrant sentiments (Clarke et al. 2017). The BES Wave 14 survey asked respondents: "In the EU referendum debate, do you think of yourself as closer to either the 'Leave' or 'Remain' side?" As Table 9.2 shows, while authoritarianism, left/right ideology, and party identification are the top three determinants of Brexit support, group empathy also has a very large and highly significant effect ($p \leq .01$). Support for Britain to remain in the EU was 22 percentage points more likely as the GEI moved from its minimum to maximum score. Younger and more educated respondents were also more likely to oppose Brexit.

As predicted, individual empathy does not have a statistically significant effect on Brexit support ($p > .10$). This is no doubt in part because empathy

---

[16] Specifically, we grouped Labour, Liberal Democrats, Scottish National Party (SNP), Plaid Cymru, and Green Party versus the Conservative Party and the United Kingdom Independence Party (UKIP). As a robustness check, we also ran analyses replacing this ordinal and aggregated party identification measure with separate party variables (using "other/no party" as the reference category) in the models. The results, available in the online appendix, are fully consistent.

[17] While the Conservative Party's official position in the referendum campaign was neutral, "intra-party divisions contributed to the Leave vote as Conservative supporters received mixed messages from their party" (Lynch & Whitaker 2018, 32).

[18] The child-rearing scale to measure authoritarianism was not administered in the sample of respondents who received the GEI. So the models include this alternative authoritarianism scale. The items used to generate this scale are provided in the Appendix at the end.

TABLE 9.2 *The relationship between group empathy and opposition to Brexit*

	β	S.E.	Change in Probability
Group empathy	.55**	.20	.22
Individual empathy	.29	.36	.12
Party ID	−.89***	.17	−.34
Ideology	−1.15***	.28	−.43
Authoritarianism	−1.80***	.24	−.62
Minority	.18	.21	.07
Female	.11	.09	.04
Education	.56**	.19	.22
Age	−1.00***	.31	−.33
Income	.13	.20	.05
Married	.01	.09	.01
Employed	.16	.10	.07
Household size	−.23	.32	−.09
Catholic	−.07	.15	−.03
Constant	1.61***	.36	
N	1,518		

Note: Coefficients estimated using binary probit. Data are weighted. All variables are rescaled to run from 0 to 1. †p ≤ .10, *p ≤ .05, **p ≤ .01, and ***p ≤ .001, two-tailed.
Source: 2018 British Election Study (YouGov)

at the individual level can cut both ways. While it might lead some to want to extend a hand to those in need, it could also lead others to want to protect intimates from perceived external threats such as increased job competition or personal security concerns attributed to strangers in one's community. This is the sort of pattern found in other studies that focus on individual empathy (Feldman et al. 2020), rather than the group-based form we explore.

The BES Wave 14 survey also had several questions to tap immigration-related opinions. One such question asked respondents on a 10-point scale if they think the United Kingdom should allow many fewer or many more immigrants into the country (*support for increased immigration*). The survey also asked whether they think immigration undermines or enriches Britain's cultural life (*perceived cultural impact of immigration*) and whether they think it is bad or good for the economy (*perceived economic impact of immigration*), both on a 7-point scale. In line with the US findings, the results of OLS regression analyses, presented in Table 9.3, show that the GEI is a top predictor of British immigration attitudes (p ≤ .001), performing even better than party identification and ideology and only surpassed by authoritarianism.

TABLE 9.3 *The relationship between group empathy and opinions about immigration in the United Kingdom*

	Support for increased immigration		Perceived cultural benefits of immigration		Perceived economic benefits of immigration	
	β	S.E.	β	S.E.	β	S.E.
Group empathy	.22***	.03	.37***	.04	.30***	.03
Individual empathy	−.08	.05	−.05	.07	−.06	.06
Party ID	−.14***	.03	−.20***	.03	−.14***	.03
Ideology	−.05	.04	−.02	.05	−.03	.05
Authoritarianism	−.43***	.03	−.47***	.04	−.36***	.04
Minority	.02	.03	.11**	.04	.10**	.03
Female	−.0001	.01	.01	.02	−.03†	.01
Education	.09**	.03	.11**	.03	.13***	.04
Age	−.09*	.04	−.03	.05	−.01	.05
Income	−.02	.03	.04	.04	.06†	.03
Married	.02†	.01	.02	.02	.01	.02
Employed	.01	.01	.002	.02	.0002	.02
Household size	−.09†	.05	−.10†	.06	−.15**	.06
Catholic	.004	.02	.003	.03	−.002	.03
Constant	.66***	.06	.69***	.07	.71***	.07
N	1,555		1,577		1,576	

Note: Coefficients estimated using OLS regression. Data are weighted. All variables are rescaled to run from 0 to 1. †p ≤ .10, *p ≤ .05, **p ≤ .01, and ***p ≤ .001, two-tailed.
Source: 2018 British Election Study (YouGov)

As in the Brexit results, individual empathy has no significant impact on immigration support.

Group empathy should also affect British people's support for prosocial policies that redistribute wealth between groups in society. The BES Wave 14 survey asked respondents on a 5-point scale: "Do you think that the amount of money families on welfare receive is too high or too low?" We coded the variable so that increased values would indicate higher support for welfare by assigning the lowest score for the "much too high" option and the highest score for "much too low." Ordered probit results, presented in the first set of columns in Table 9.4, indicate that group empathy has a highly significant effect on welfare preferences (p ≤ .001). Regarding marginal effects, the probability of considering the amount of welfare money much too high drops from 14 to 5 percent as the GEI moves from its minimum to maximum score. By comparison, individual empathy has no statistically significant effect on welfare attitudes.

TABLE 9.4 *The relationship between group empathy and opinions about welfare and foreign aid in the United Kingdom*

	Support for welfare		Support for foreign aid	
	β	S.E.	β	S.E.
Group empathy	.58***	.16	1.22***	.16
Individual empathy	.44	.29	.69**	.28
Party ID	−.56***	.14	−.14	.13
Ideology	−.91***	.24	−.42*	.21
Authoritarianism	−1.57***	.21	−2.80***	.25
Minority	.20	.19	.26	.20
Female	−.03	.07	.09	.07
Education	−.21	.16	.69***	.15
Age	.22	.24	.08	.25
Income	−.53***	.16	.42**	.16
Married	−.14†	.07	−.08	.07
Employed	−.14†	.08	.22**	.08
Household size	−.02	.29	−.37	.30
Catholic	.28*	.14	.23	.16
N	1,430		1,583	

Note: Coefficients estimated using ordered probit. Data are weighted. All variables are rescaled to run from 0 to 1. †$p \leq .10$, *$p \leq .05$, **$p \leq .01$, and ***$p \leq .001$, two-tailed.
Source: 2018 British Election Study (YouGov)

Chapter 7 demonstrated that group empathy significantly increases Americans' support for US foreign aid. The BES Wave 14 survey also included a measure of opinions about foreign aid, which allowed us to retest this relationship in the British context. Specifically, respondents reported how much they agreed/disagreed with the statement "Britain should stop all government spending on overseas aid" on a 5-point scale. We recoded the variable so the increasing values would indicate increase in support to continue British foreign aid. The results of an ordered probit analysis, displayed in the second set of columns in Table 9.4, demonstrate that group empathy has the second-largest effect on one's policy position on foreign aid ($p \leq .001$), behind only authoritarianism. As the GEI moves from the lowest to highest score, the probability of opposing foreign aid decreases from 36 percent to less than 9 percent – a highly substantive impact. While statistically significant, individual empathy's impact is smaller, leading to about an 11 percentage point change in the probability of supporting foreign aid ($p \leq .05$). Overall, the British results on the group empathy–foreign aid link successfully replicate the US findings.

Another group-based issue we analyzed is perceptions of discrimination in British society at large. Group Empathy Theory predicts that those high on the GEI will be more cognizant of and sensitive to the discrimination of marginalized groups. There was strong empirical support for this assertion in the US context and, thanks to the BES, we were able to test it in the United Kingdom. The BES Wave 14 survey asked how much discrimination respondents think there is for or against various groups, including black and other ethnic minorities, whites, Muslims, Christians, women, and men. Response options ranged from "0" for "a lot of discrimination in favour" to "10" for "a lot of discrimination against." Based on the theory, the GEI should have a significant effect on perceptions of discrimination targeting blacks and other ethnic minorities, Muslims, and women as disadvantaged groups. We would not expect the GEI to be positively associated with perceptions of discrimination against whites, Christians, or men, given their dominant status in society. The results of OLS regression analyses, presented in Table 9.5, show that the GEI and left/right ideology are the top two predictors of perceived discrimination against black and other ethnic minority groups, as well as Muslims. The power of the GEI is on par with that of authoritarianism when predicting perceived discrimination against women. In contrast, individual empathy does not significantly affect perceived discrimination concerning any of these minority groups. The impact of the GEI is negative and significant vis-à-vis perceptions of discrimination against whites in the United Kingdom, meaning that those higher in group empathy are less likely to perceive reverse discrimination targeting whites. As expected, the GEI is not significantly associated with perceptions of discrimination against Christians and males. Individual empathy, once again, has no significant impact on any of these outcome variables.

While people may be aware of group-based discrimination, only some – particularly those who score higher in group empathy – will be motivated to remedy this by providing equal opportunities to marginalized groups. To test this expectation, we analyzed the impact of group empathy on support for equal opportunity policies directed toward (1) ethnic minorities, (2) women, and (3) the LGBTQ community. Specifically, survey respondents evaluated whether they think attempts to give equal opportunities to each of these groups in Britain have gone too far or have not gone far enough on a 5-point ordinal scale. Ordered probit analyses, displayed in Table 9.6, demonstrate that group empathy is the strongest predictor of support for equal opportunity policies to benefit ethnic minorities above and beyond all other political and socio-demographic factors.[19] The probability of strongly supporting

---

[19] Covariates of income, marital status, and household size were dropped from these models because there were no observations for these variables in predicting group empathy's effect on equal opportunity views.

TABLE 9.5 *The relationship between group empathy and awareness of group-based discrimination in the United Kingdom*

	Minorities		Muslims		Women		Whites		Christians		Men	
	β	S.E.	β	S.E.	β	S.E.	β	S.E.	β	S.E.	β	S.E.
Group empathy	.13***	.03	.17***	.04	.06*	.03	-.13***	.03	.004	.03	.003	.03
Individual empathy	-.02	.06	-.01	.08	.04	.05	.08	.07	.08	.06	.01	.06
Party ID	-.04	.03	-.06†	.03	-.08**	.03	.04	.03	.04	.03	.03	.03
Ideology	-.17***	.05	-.15**	.06	-.05	.05	.18***	.05	.11**	.04	.16***	.05
Authoritarianism	-.09**	.04	-.10**	.04	-.06*	.03	.25***	.04	.21***	.03	.09**	.03
Minority	.08**	.03	.004	.04	.06**	.02	-.06	.04	-.01	.03	-.08***	.03
Female	.06***	.01	.06***	.02	.10***	.01	-.05***	.01	-.01	.01	-.14***	.01
Education	.05†	.03	-.01	.03	-.03	.02	-.04	.03	.02	.02	-.02	.02
Age	.03	.05	-.09†	.06	.01	.04	.03	.05	.0003	.05	.02	.05
Income	.002	.03	-.03	.04	.0005	.03	-.03	.03	-.02	.03	.02	.03
Married	-.02†	.01	-.02	.02	-.01	.01	-.005	.02	.01	.01	.02	.01
Employed	-.04*	.02	-.04*	.02	-.02†	.01	.01	.02	-.01	.01	.01	.02
Household	-.05	.05	-.09	.06	-.08†	.05	.05	.05	.08	.06	.10***	.05
Catholic	-.02	.02	-.06*	.03	-.04†	.02	-.01	.03	.07***	.02	.02	.02
Constant	.66***	.06	.76***	.07	.60***	.05	.26***	.06	.26***	.06	.30***	.05
N	1,523		1,521		1,526		1,521		1,438		1,512	

Note: Coefficients estimated using OLS regression. Data are weighted. All variables are rescaled to run from 0 to 1. †p ≤ .10, *p ≤ .05, **p ≤ .01, and ***p ≤ .001, two-tailed.

Source: 2018 British Election Study (YouGov)

TABLE 9.6 *The relationship between group empathy and support for equal opportunity policies in the United Kingdom*

	Equal opportunity for ethnic minorities		Equal opportunity for women		Equal opportunity for LGBTQ	
	β	S.E.	β	S.E.	β	S.E.
Group empathy	1.22***	.32	.56*	.27	.91***	.28
Individual empathy	−.40	.53	.89†	.52	.30	.54
Party ID	−.35	.31	−.45*	.23	−.52**	.21
Ideology	−1.03*	.50	−.95**	.34	−.72*	.32
Authoritarianism	−1.04**	.36	−.34	.35	−.99**	.35
Minority	.69**	.27	.11	.24	.15	.17
Female	.22†	.12	.48***	.12	.21†	.13
Education	.51†	.27	.11	.26	−.38	.26
Age	−.26	.33	.21	.32	−.99***	.30
Employed	−.05	.12	−.04	.11	−.02	.11
Catholic	.09	.19	−.02	.20	.19	.16
N	493		499		488	

Note: Coefficients estimated using ordered probit. Data are weighted. All variables are rescaled to run from 0 to 1. $^{†}p \leq .10$, $^{*}p \leq .05$, $^{**}p \leq .01$, and $^{***}p \leq .001$, two-tailed.

Source: 2018 British Election Study (YouGov)

equal opportunity actions for minorities increases from 4 to 23 percent as one moves from the minimum to maximum level of group empathy.

The second set of columns in Table 9.6 shows that group empathy also affects support for equal opportunity policies designed to benefit women ($p \leq .05$). Moving from the minimum to maximum score on the GEI, the probability of responding that such attempts for women have not gone nearly far enough increases from 7 to 17 percent. Surprisingly, individual empathy has actually a larger effect than group empathy on support for equal opportunity for women, albeit with marginal statistical significance ($p \leq .10$). This is not an effect we expected a priori, but it does make a lot of sense. As mothers, wives, daughters, and friends, women represent close intimates in nearly every person's life, so individual empathy might easily and naturally apply to attitudes and behaviors concerning women's rights.

The third set of columns in Table 9.6 demonstrates that, group empathy is among the top three determinants, along with age and authoritarianism, of supporting equal opportunity acts for the LGBTQ community ($p \leq .001$). The predicted probability of selecting the option that such attempts have not gone far enough increases from 21 percent to nearly 40 percent as the GEI goes from its minimum to maximum value.

Individual empathy, on the other hand, is not significant. The fact that group empathy not only influences one's attitudes toward racial/ethnic groups but also nonracial/nonethnic ones – in this case, women and the LGBTQ community – is in line with the US findings discussed in the previous chapter on group empathy in the Trump era.

THE ROLE OF OUTGROUP EMPATHY IN EXPLAINING INTERGROUP DIFFERENCES

Group Empathy Theory asserts that because minorities are likely to suffer discrimination in society as they grow up, they should display higher group empathy. The US data supports this prediction handsomely, finding that racial/ethnic minority groups score consistently higher than whites on group empathy, and group empathy explains intergroup differences in a host of political attitudes and behavior. We now test this key tenet of the theory in the British context. The US data included stratified oversamples of African Americans and Latinos, thus allowing us enough degrees of freedom to calculate indirect effects separately per each minority group. Because the BES Wave 14 data does not have oversamples of racial/ethnic minority groups, we generated a dichotomous variable for minority race/ethnicity by coding any nonwhite ethnicity or mixed background as "1" versus "0" if the respondent was white British and from any other white background.

We first check whether there are policy differences between whites and nonwhites that group empathy can explain. As Figure 9.1 demonstrates, nonwhites on average are indeed more strongly opposed to Brexit, more supportive of immigration, welfare, and foreign aid. They are also on average more cognizant of discrimination and supportive of equal opportunity policies concerning marginalized outgroups (with the exception of the LGBTQ community). We next test the prediction that British nonwhites should display higher levels of group empathy, on average, than white citizens. Consistent with the US findings, nonwhite minorities score significantly higher on the GEI than whites do ($M_{Nonwhite}$ = .53; M_{White} = .43). This difference holds in a regression analysis, as Table 9.7 presents, with all of the socio-demographic controls included in the model that predicts group empathy in Chapter 4 ($p \leq .05$). By contrast, British whites and nonwhites do not differ in individual empathy as demonstrated by a comparison of means (M_{White} = .69 and $M_{Nonwhite}$ = .68) and regression results (also presented in Table 9.7).

Generalized structural equation modeling (GSEM) analyses, followed by a bootstrap procedure with bias-corrected confidence intervals, test the significance of the indirect effects. The results corroborate the hypothesis that group empathy significantly explains minority–majority differences in policy

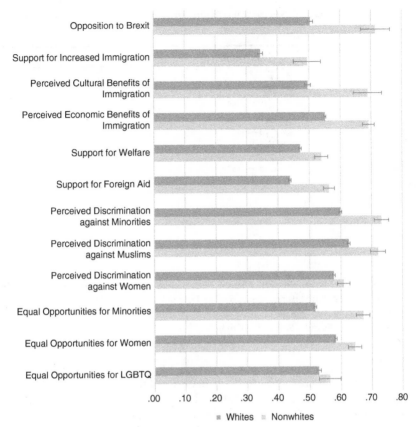

FIGURE 9.1 Policy opinion gaps between whites and nonwhites in the United Kingdom
Note: The bars represent the means for each outcome of interest among whites and nonwhite minorities. The lines represent 95 percent confidence intervals. Data are weighted. All variables are rescaled to run from 0 to 1.
Source: 2018 British Election Study (YouGov)

preferences across all outcomes of interest that initially indicate intergroup differences, even after controlling for political and socio-demographic factors.[20]

CONCLUSION

The results in this chapter show that the political relevance of group empathy is not exclusive to the United States. Group Empathy Theory seems to travel well to the British context. Group empathy powerfully predicts opposition to Brexit.

---

[20] Full results for all these GSEM analyses are located in the online appendix.

TABLE 9.7 *Differences in socio-demographic predictors of group empathy versus individual empathy*

	Group empathy		Individual empathy	
	β	S.E.	β	S.E.
Minority	.06*	.03	−.03	.02
Female	.06***	.01	.07***	.01
Education	.14***	.02	.04**	.01
Age	−.15***	.04	−.04	.03
Income	−.02	.03	−.01	.02
Married	−.003	.01	−.002	.01
Employed	−.04***	.01	−.03**	.01
Household size	−.02	.04	−.01	.03
Catholic	.07***	.02	.02*	.01
Constant	.40***	.03	.66***	.02
N	3,029		2,026	

Note: Coefficients estimated using OLS regression. Data are weighted. All variables are rescaled to run from 0 to 1. $^{\dagger}p \leq .10$, $^{*}p \leq .05$, $^{**}p \leq .01$, and $^{***}p \leq .001$, two-tailed.
Source: 2018 British Election Study (YouGov)

It also displays a systematic effect on British political views and attitudes in a host of other important policy domains including immigration, social welfare redistribution, foreign aid, perceived discrimination, and equal opportunity policies. And, as in the United States, racial/ethnic differences in group empathy seem to account for many of the intergroup differences in policy views. The statistical effect of the GEI rivals and at times surpasses that of party identification, ideology, and authoritarianism. This is in contrast to the mostly insignificant effects of individual empathy. In other words, these results corroborate our hypotheses and support the claim that the GEI is an original measure of outgroup empathy that can help us better understand and explain British public opinion.

Obviously, the political contexts in the United States and the United Kingdom are distinct in many respects, but they are also moving in several parallel ways. Both countries made pivotal decisions around the same time – the EU referendum in June 2016 and the US presidential election in November 2016 – that pit two contrasting messages against one another in deciding their trajectories. The Brexit and Trump victories highlight rising group conflict in both nations. According to Norris and Inglehart (2019, 391), "Growing acceptance of multiculturalism in British society seems to have triggered an authoritarian backlash among the minority of racist and xenophobic sectors of society who endorse these values as a form of collective security to protect 'Us' from 'Them.'" They point to a similar "cultural backlash" in the United States that led to Trump's victory. The United Kingdom's Leave campaign to "Take *Back* Control" and Trump's appeals to "Make America Great *Again*" [emphases ours] both attempted to invoke a reconstructed, romanticized past when the white majority was dominant and ethnic diversity was low. The glorified nations of the past that these two campaigns alluded to were not pluralistic or multicultural. In contrast, the Remain campaign's "Britain Stronger in Europe" and Hillary Clinton campaign's "Stronger Together" slogans both represented progressive appeals for integration, multiculturalism, and civic nationalism. Ironically, the Vote Remain and Clinton campaigns were just as *nostalgic* as the Vote Leave and Trump campaigns, in the sense that they wanted to go "*back* to the future" that was also a romanticized version of reality. The naive liberal assumption that political progress moves in a linear fashion once more proved to be false as the timeline of history yet again skewed into a tangent of far-right ethnic nationalism in these countries amid the Brexit and Trump victories.

It should not be lost on the reader that neither the Brexit campaign nor Trump won in a landslide. In the case of Brexit, Vote Leave won by a margin of less than 4 percent, with 17,410,742 votes to leave versus 16,141,241 to remain. In the United States, Trump lost the popular vote by nearly 2.9 million votes but won the Electoral College by taking swing states like Michigan and Wisconsin with razor-thin margins. While some pundits call the campaign strategies of Vote Leave and Trump innovative, others see it as reverting back to the old playbook of ethnic entrepreneurship. The innovative side of the Vote Leave campaign was using new technology that allowed for tailoring its messages and reaching out to "untapped" demographics based on various algorithms. Yet both the Vote Leave and Trump campaigns were able to move some voters by renormalizing age-old discourses of protectionism and xenophobia.

The history of colonialism in Britain, and that of slavery in the United States, continue to nourish the idea of social dominance and white racial resentment among some societal circles, which may be just enough to tilt the pendulum in favor of ethnic entrepreneurs. In an effort to exculpate Britain from the troubles Africa has been experiencing in the postcolonial era, Boris Johnson once argued: "The continent may be a blot, but it is not a blot upon our conscience. The problem is not that we were once in charge, but that we are not in charge any more."[21] He concluded his neocolonialist argument by exclaiming: "The best fate for Africa would be if the old colonial powers, or their citizens, scrambled once again in her direction; on the understanding that this time they will not be asked to feel guilty." This is not the only time Johnson made such controversial

---

[21] Boris Johnson (2002), "Africa Is a Mess, but We Can't Blame Colonialism," *The Spectator*, https://blogs.spectator.co.uk/2016/07/boris-archive-africa-mess-cant-blame-colonialism/.

remarks. Having served also as mayor of London (2008–16) and foreign secretary (2016–18), Johnson has a long record of "jokes" that mock marginalized groups, such as calling gay men "tank-topped bumboys," black people "piccaninnies" with "watermelon smiles," and Muslim women in burkas "letterboxes" and "bank robbers."[22]

In Chapter 3 we found that group empathy overwhelmingly increases people's proclivity to intervene to stop racially charged jokes and to support stigmatized groups. Only time will tell if a critical mass of citizens, perhaps drawing on a wellspring of group empathy, might alter the trajectory of political discourse to condemn – not condone – social dominance, bigotry, and xenophobia. Of course, we do not think that all those who voted to leave the EU were driven by xenophobia or racial resentment while those who voted to remain in the EU were moved solely by group empathy. The same goes for those who voted for Boris Johnson in the United Kingdom or Donald Trump in the United States. The reality is far more complex, and our own data show this repeatedly. Party identities, ideology, authoritarianism, and some other factors such as pocketbook considerations all play a role. However, group empathy (or lack thereof) may tip the scale on one side or the other and, thus, can be a game changer.[23]

---

[22] Adam Bienkov (2019), "Boris Johnson Called Gay Men 'Tank-Topped Bumboys' and Black People 'Piccaninnies' with 'Watermelon Smiles,'" *Business Insider*, www.businessinsider.com/boris-johnson-record-sexist-homophobic-and-racist-comments-bumboys-piccaninnies-2019-6.

[23] Group empathy deficit and the revival of ethnonationalist politics are discussed in greater detail in the next, final chapter.

10

Cultivating Group Empathy and Challenging Ethnonationalist Politics

> I am loath to close. We are not enemies, but friends. We must not be enemies. Though passion may have strained, it must not break our bonds of affection. The mystic chords of memory, stretching from every battlefield and patriot grave to every living heart and hearthstone all over this broad land, will yet swell the chorus of the Union, when again touched, as surely they will be, by the better angels of our nature.
>
> Abraham Lincoln's first inaugural address (March 4, 1861)

We have presented a great deal of evidence in this book about a politically consequential phenomenon that has received little attention to date: the tendency for some citizens to empathize with members of other groups, even when those groups compete directly for rights, resources, and security. The ability to take another person's perspective and to experience their emotions is quite common in humans, and social psychologists have studied empathy for many years. Most often, however, this process occurs among close intimates: parents and children, siblings, friends, and extended family.

Experiencing empathy for cherished members of one's ingroup is understandable from an evolutionary perspective. Such deep and reflexive attachments to the emotional lives of our nearest and dearest can serve as a powerful mechanism for reciprocity and protection. Not surprisingly, perhaps, these intimate bonds can actually fuel animosity toward outgroup members who might cause us and our loved ones harm. By the previous logic, empathizing with outgroups – including those who have experienced oppression, discrimination, or misfortune – should be relatively less common than empathizing with close intimates and ingroup members, for the simple reason that such outgroups will compete with ours. And indeed that is what we found whenever we tested both constructs in the same model. Among British citizens, scores on individual empathy (primarily directed at one's family and circle of friends) are substantially higher (M = .69) than empathy for outgroup members (M = .47), a difference that is highly statistically significant as well (p ≤ .001). We find similar differences in the 2015 US Group Empathy Study. More politically consequential, however, is the variation across individuals on each of these dimensions and their distinct effects on political attitudes and behavior.

We showed in Chapters 4 and 9 that empathy for one's intimates is quite equally distributed across groups in society since it is a universal innate trait. By contrast, there are substantive differences between majority and minority citizens in both the United States and the United Kingdom when it comes to outgroup empathy, with minorities displaying much higher levels. This is as predicted, since group empathy is a socially acquired trait cultivated through various life experiences that enable one to emotionally and cognitively react to the suffering of another group. Such life experiences are more direct and more prevalent in minority communities. As for its political consequences, individual empathy – the kind we feel toward close family and friends – is a very poor predictor of policy views concerning group rights and issues. Empathy for outgroups, on the other hand, significantly increases support for egalitarian policies that redistribute rights and resources more fairly across groups regardless of their origin, race/ethnicity, religion, and so on.

All this goes to show that empathy for outgroups is a unique and previously understudied force in politics. Our primary measure of it, the Group Empathy Index (GEI), is not simply a stand-in for racial resentment, social dominance orientation (SDO), ethnocentrism, authoritarianism, linked fate, partisanship, or political ideology, which have been at the heart of models predicting support for policies related to redistribution and intergroup competition. Moreover, analyses across different policy issues and domains consistently demonstrate that group empathy drives political attitudes and behaviors above and beyond many of these commonly employed predictors of public opinion.

The GEI is a valid and reliable tool for explaining policy views in a cross-national context. The scale performs almost identically in the United Kingdom and in the United States. Unlike racial resentment, for example, the items used to build the GEI do not mention specific racial or ethnic groups. This is critical because it allows us to more easily take the theory on the road and test it in other places. From a practical standpoint, our questions are less likely to run afoul of social norms about the discussion of sensitive topics like race and ethnicity in many countries. Finally, the ability to use very similar questions in comparative settings means we can better investigate the universal role the construct plays in politics around the world without being concerned about measurement bias. We are excited for scholars to extend the use of the GEI into other multicultural societies, where different groups struggle to cooperate and compromise as they live side by side.

WHY GROUP EMPATHY MATTERS

The skeptics might ask whether empathy for outgroups really matters above and beyond threats and interests that seem to be at the core of all our political disputes. Is it politically consequential, or is it just another concept thought up by academics who are safely ensconced in their offices, never needing to venture out into the real world? To the contrary, we think the evidence presented throughout this book convincingly demonstrates the political consequences of group empathy in democratic societies, at times superseding perceptions of threat, personal and/or ingroup interests, and even partisan identities.

Chapter 5 detailed how strongly group empathy was associated with opposition to profiling Arabs in the context of homeland security, particularly among minorities. In two separate nationally representative samples, African Americans in particular, and Latinos to a somewhat lesser extent, were much more likely than whites to take the side of an Arab passenger who was searched and questioned after making an ambiguous comment on the phone before boarding an airplane. These reactions occurred despite the fact that African Americans and Latinos both perceive themselves to be at higher risk than whites do from terrorist attacks. And across all three racial/ethnic groups, group empathy is strongly associated with opposition to discriminatory practices and trading civil liberties for security. Importantly, these associations are often stronger than ones driven by predispositions such as ideology, racial resentment, SDO, authoritarianism, and the like.

We also found strong associations between group empathy and support for pro-immigration policies in several chapters (most notably Chapters 6 and 8). This might be where our work has one of its largest impacts given the contemporary policy debate. Current immigration policy trends in the United States strike many as distinctly lacking in empathy for those who arrive on America's borders seeking a better life. Above and beyond commitments to party and racial animus, group empathy powerfully drives opposition to exclusionary policies such as building a wall on the US southern border, family separation, strict travel and immigration bans against citizens of several predominantly Muslim countries, ending political asylum protections, and so on.

In June 2019, US news outlets carried a heartbreaking photograph of a young father and daughter, refugees from El Salvador seeking asylum, drowned on the banks of the Rio Grande after they attempted to cross into the United States.[1] The haunting picture of a father and daughter face-down in the water – the toddler tucked inside her dad's shirt with her arm around his neck – went viral,

---

[1] Azam Ahmed and Kirk Semple (2019), "Photo of Drowned Migrants Captures Pathos of Those Who Risk It All," *New York Times*, www.nytimes.com/2019/06/25/us/father-daughter-border-drowning-picture-mexico.html.

triggering cries from around the world for more compassionate treatment of immigrants and asylum seekers. For instance, one commenter, "Michael C," reacting in the response section of the *New York Times* report, wrote: "I can only say that the plight of the immigrant father and mother to be freed from the endless hardship of their home country and offer their children and themselves a better life in a different country is EXACTLY what each and every one of us on the other side would do if we were in their shoes. No matter the obstacles, we would do no different than these people, make it our life's priority to get to a better place."[2] Reactions like this one are obvious appeals to empathy for those who come to our shores with nothing but their shirts, and their children, on their backs.

Not everyone reacted empathically to the tragedy at Rio Grande. In response to many reactions triggered by the picture, the acting director of US Citizenship and Immigration Services, Ken Cuccinelli, blamed the father, claiming in an interview that he was unconcerned that the photo would be associated unfavorably with the administration's immigration policies. He argued:

The reason we have tragedies like that on the border is because those folks, that father didn't want to wait to go through the asylum process in the legal fashion, so decided to cross the river. ... Until we fix the attractions in our asylum system, people like that father and that child are going to continue to come through a dangerous trip.[3]

This response attempts to separate the audience from the victims and ignores the forces – such as the risk of violence, death, and economic despair – that have pushed people toward the US borders for centuries. It makes pretense that the asylum process under Trump is a viable option for all who might seek it when in reality the administration has drastically narrowed opportunities while essentially working to dismantle the US asylum system.[4] The United States, even as unwelcoming as it may be, is still perceived by many immigrants as a better place than where they come from. Making the United States less attractive than other places is self-defeating. Fewer immigrants came to the US shores during the Great Recession between 2008 and 2011, but an economic recession is obviously no solution to the problems associated with immigration.

Group empathy is also powerfully linked to support for foreign policy actions, including humanitarian aid and military intervention, as the evidence in Chapter 7 demonstrates. The ability and motivation to take the perspective of and care about someone in another country experiencing great hardship dramatically increases support for foreign aid. Group

[2] Ibid.
[3] Caroline Kelly, Catherine E. Shoichet, and Priscilla Alvarez (2019), "Ken Cuccinelli Blames Drowned Man in Border Photograph for Own, Daughter's Deaths," CNN, www.cnn.com /2019/06/27/politics/ken-cuccinelli-drowned-father-daughter-fault/index.html.
[4] See   www.amnesty.org/en/latest/research/2018/10/usa-treatment-of-asylum-seekers-southern-border/.

empathy was not just independently powerful: it was more powerful than many of the other key factors (including partisanship, ideology, political trust, and perceived threats) as a predictor of humanitarian aid. Interestingly, the race/ethnicity of the citizens in the target country featured in the experimental vignettes did not moderate the impact of group empathy: those high in the GEI were more likely to support policies and actions to end the suffering of either European or Arab conflict victims, and they did so to an almost identical degree. Group empathy was also a far larger predictor of humanitarian aid and military support for the victims of the Syrian civil war than party identification or ideology, a quite surprising result given how influential those dimensions are in standard models of public opinion across a host of domains.

In Chapter 9 we found that, among British citizens, group empathy is a better predictor of support for immigration than any other predisposition or socio-demographic factor, save authoritarianism. It is also one of the top determinants of opposition to Brexit. In both US and British samples, group empathy predicts not only race/ethnicity-related policy attitudes but also public support for issues related to other marginalized minority groups, including women's and LGBTQ rights. And, just as in the United States, nonwhite British citizens score significantly higher in group empathy than their white compatriots, and group empathy helps explain intergroup differences in almost all of the political outcomes we examined. The British results thus suggest Group Empathy Theory is applicable across national borders.

In sum, we have strong evidence, accumulated over many studies spanning several years and two countries, that group empathy structures public opinion across a broad spectrum of policy domains. The skeptic might still wonder whether this predisposition is really distinct from other constructs that political psychologists have been exploring for decades, such as racial animus, authoritarian personality, SDO, party identification, or political ideology. We explored this possibility in Chapter 3 across multiple predictive validity tests as well as in our other empirical chapters by testing the effects of group empathy while controlling for these factors. The consistent finding was that group empathy impacts public opinion quite independently from, and often much more powerfully than, many of these other more familiar dimensions. We do not argue that group empathy is completely distinct from traits like authoritarianism, racial animus, political ideology, or party identification. However, group empathy may be a quite basic predisposition learned very early in youth, somewhat independent of these other forces. As a set of skills learned from lived experience, outgroup empathy might in fact help structure other group predispositions, tempering hostility toward outgroups and even moderating political predispositions like partisanship and ideology.

Some may claim that group empathy is simply a luxury for "liberal elites" – those with wealth who need not worry about falling out of the middle class or becoming victims of crime at the hands of undocumented immigrants or others who do not belong in their communities. Perhaps a trusting and generous view of the world – believing it to be filled with people who are kind and not out to do us harm – is only well and good until one's regular route to school or work is riddled with criminal activity or when your bus line is targeted by terrorists. To this critique, we would respond that real existential concerns cannot explain why some score so low on the GEI while others score highly. In our studies, whites who do not perceive themselves to be at high risk of terrorism still score lower on group empathy than blacks and Latinos who do. Income rarely has anything to do with group empathy in our data, and when it does it is generally associated with declines in the GEI rather than increases.

And finally, it is important to remember that many of the so-called problems that have been linked to immigrants and minorities – that they commit more crime, reduce natives' wages and income, and increase drug trafficking – find little support in systematic empirical studies. The best guess of scholars who study both legal and illegal immigration is that newcomers provide a net benefit economically and actually *reduce* crime rates in the communities where they are concentrated (Adelman et al. 2018; Blau & Mackie 2017). It is therefore simply unfounded to insist that empathizing with the struggles of immigrants is born of naiveté about the costs of welcoming those newcomers.

The ability to take the perspective of another, especially someone quite different than oneself, and the motivation to act upon the emotions that others are feeling is a package of skills that might be acquired as a result of some basic experiences with others, via discussions with family, and in interactions with diverse friends, neighbors, and groups. Our hunch, in other words, is that empathy comes from contact with the world over time but beginning at a very young age. This hint gives us some ideas about normative advice we would offer those who wish to increase group empathy across social divisions in their own communities and nations.

SOCIALIZING EMPATHY FOR OUTGROUPS

After reviewing the evidence presented in this book, one might decide that group empathy is a normative good for society and that we should therefore increase it whenever possible. Cooperation and compromise across national borders and between racial/ethnic groups not only produces peace and security: it also produces freer markets and greater worldwide economic growth. Despite the angry and outraged protestations of populist leaders of late, there is little evidence that ethnic segregation, immigration shutdowns, travel bans, trade barriers, or physical walls between countries help make the world more prosperous or secure. Moreover, many of these interventions are expensive and impractical. We have to learn to solve our problems together with compromise and mutual respect.

Perhaps individual empathy, focused inward toward one's close family and friends, was a critical resource for our early ancestors. They needed to protect themselves in small groups from outsiders who posed regular threats to their territory, food sources, fresh water, and so on. We suspect that the popularity of many contemporary leaders who peddle ethnonationalist sentiments are capitalizing on such deeply ingrained predispositions to protect "us" without thinking of the costs to larger national and global collectives. However, in large multicultural societies stretching over vast geographic areas, ingroup solidarity is less adaptive, if for no other reason than it is very hard to identify the "us" and the "them" reliably. In our most optimistic vision, empathy for outgroups might be a key tool for reducing conflicts and forging compromises within such complex human societies around the world. But how can this set of skills and motivations be cultivated in individuals, so that they might see the world through the eyes of strangers very different than themselves?

Given what we have learned in writing this book, we know the road to increasing group empathy on a large scale will be long and difficult. The tendency to prioritize family and cherished ingroups in need when extending trust, compassion, rights, and resources has deep evolutionary roots. Outgroup empathy should thus be less common and probably represents a rather recent development in the history of our species, as distinct human groups have come into regular contact in long-term settlements. That said, we find over and over that empathizing with outgroups in the contemporary world does actually occur through various socializing processes and that, when activated, it is highly politically consequential.

As discussed in Chapter 4, we suspect group empathy develops at an early age as a result of experiences and interactions with family, friends, community members, and perhaps broader forces like politics and the media. Personal exposure to discrimination (or witnessing discrimination against others), the quality and quantity of contact with other groups, and perceiving less intergroup economic competition are all positively associated with outgroup empathy. Some are more likely than others to have these life experiences, all else equal. To investigate the origins of group empathy, we looked into various demographic differences in the GEI, beginning with factors like race/ethnicity, gender, education, and age. We found large differences in group empathy between whites and nonwhites in almost every sample, with whites scoring somewhat lower than African Americans and Latinos. We postulated that a primary reason for this consistent gap was intergroup differences in experiences with discrimination and prejudice. Young people who are raised hearing about the unfair treatment their ancestors faced, and that they might continue to face, likely develop some of the skills and motivations that fall into the package we call group empathy.

Chapter 4 also demonstrated that the dynamics of the ingroup identification–outgroup empathy link operate differently across different groups in society. We found that whites who identify more strongly with their ingroup display lower levels of outgroup empathy, as Social Identity Theory (SIT) would predict – in line with its tenets of ingroup favoritism/outgroup discrimination. But for minorities, the relationship is instead positive and thus contrary to SIT. Our results showed that higher ingroup identification is indeed associated with higher levels of outgroup empathy among both blacks and Latinos. This is exactly how we theorized in Chapter 2. Minorities who identify strongly with their ingroup – and thus embrace their collective histories, memories, and experiences – are much more likely than low ingroup identifiers to develop empathy for other marginalized groups. Therefore, Group Empathy Theory presents an important modification to SIT by empirically showing that, among minorities, ingroup identification *facilitates* – rather than hinders – outgroup empathy.

Recall our reference in Chapter 4 to "The Talk," in which black parents instruct their children in detail how to stay safe in encounters with police officers. This type of experience, we suspect, leads kids to grow up with a different lens for interpreting police interactions with members from other groups. They might be wary about the treatment of others at the hands of law enforcement and more hesitant to assume those being detained have actually done anything wrong. Even more benign experiences – like being tailed in a clothing store by a member of the staff applying a racial stereotype about shoplifters – might lead an individual to have greater sensitivity toward others who are being racially profiled in similar circumstances. Hearing these stories of discrimination from one's family and friends, or witnessing these types of events at a distance through the mass media, might further motivate individuals to practice empathy for members of other groups. Over time, this practice could lead to exactly the types of reactions that produce higher scores on the GEI and the attitudinal and behavioral political consequences we have documented in this book.

If exposure to discrimination shapes group empathy, we would expect group empathy itself might ironically be more difficult to come by as ethnic conflict declines. Of course, we would not recommend exposing people to group conflict or discrimination so that they might better empathize with the difficulties other groups face. Direct exposure to discrimination cannot be the only way to learn empathy for groups other than one's own. After all, some whites in our samples, in both the United States and Britain, score very highly on the group empathy dimension without reporting high levels of personal experience with being a target of prejudice or mistreatment. Just as interpersonal empathy for close family and friends is ubiquitous across groups, intergroup empathy also has the potential to be fostered among members of every race and ethnicity. Members of dominant racial/ethnic groups can be socialized to take the perspective of even those very unlike themselves and to become motivated to care about the suffering of others. These are skills and motivations that any person can learn, and many do.

Empathizing with those quite different than us might come from other sources. Reflecting on the similarities between our cherished ingroups and others requires some exposure to history – and possibly direct conversations with people who come from different backgrounds. We suspect that many of the social benefits of what some call "cosmopolitanism" stem from exactly this sort of contact between groups. Positive interactions while traveling to other places and meeting other people who have different traditions and cultures but share many of the same basic commitments and life experiences can improve one's ability to take another group's perspective. For those who travel with a purpose beyond leisure, joining programs such as the Peace Corps to help and engage with overseas communities may further enhance and maximize one's empathic abilities.

Our findings demonstrate that education is a stronger predictor of outgroup empathy than any other socio-demographic dimension we examined. We suspect that education has its effect on empathy through encouraging benign and constructive contact between groups and also by reducing the likelihood of zero-sum economic competition between groups. More years of education provide more opportunities for people, not only to be in diverse environments but to listen to the stories of other groups, to become friends with people from different backgrounds, and to benefit from the various problem-solving skills that others have developed. Educational environments are thus among the places most likely to foster shared experiences that help us practice empathy. That said, educational experiences are most effective in cultivating group empathy if they go beyond simply acquiring cold historical facts about the issues and problems that concern other groups, which may be important for increasing one's knowledge but not enough for motivating that person to genuinely care.

PROMOTING GROUP EMPATHY AT THE SOCIETAL LEVEL: THE ROLE OF LEADERSHIP?

It seems the United States has become a battleground for a litany of social divisions – race/ethnicity, gender, immigration status, class, sexual orientation, and so on. The media's ratings-driven incentives lead them to focus on the most dramatic news and hostile voices in hot-button issues. The political arena has become even more contentious over the last several decades with the widening of ideological divisions among elites inside the Washington beltway. All the while, Americans find themselves drawn to sensationalist media coverage, partisan bickering, and one-sided stories circulating within their social networks. This negative climate has made it all the more difficult to address long-standing historical inequalities, health disparities, and features of the justice system that produce unfair outcomes for some groups.

This battleground atmosphere has led us to focus on exploring the ways outgroup empathy conditions responses to discrimination and intolerance leveled against racial/ethnic minorities and other disadvantaged groups. Yet we still need to know more about where outgroup empathy comes from. We have investigated individual-level correlates that provide some hints: education, contact across lines of difference, and exposure to discrimination all seem to boost outgroup empathy. But what about broader societal-level forces? Can group empathy develop and change at the macro level as a result of public appeals and policy actions of leaders? We suspect outgroup empathy is not *solely* a product of family socialization in early life that waits around to be triggered by riveting examples of discrimination and mistreatment of outgroups. Since we are focusing on a prosocial disposition, it makes sense to acknowledge how prosocial political developments may likewise encourage the development of group empathy.[5]

Shogan's (2009) study on the political utility of empathy provides an interesting analysis of the ways several US presidents fared in attempting to cultivate empathy among the public via the bully pulpit. She posits that Abraham Lincoln developed a high capacity for empathy in his early life, which he retained and took advantage of throughout his political career (see also Goodwin 2005). In his early twenties, Lincoln traveled down the Mississippi River as a hired hand, during which time he was exposed to "the savage cruelties of slavery for the first time," and later he often retold how "his heart bled" (Shogan 2009, 862). Another deeply impactful experience for Lincoln occurred in 1841 on a riverboat trip. Lincoln recounted the horrors he observed to his traveling companion, Joshua Speed, in a letter:

> You may remember, as I well do, that from Louisville to the mouth of the Ohio there were, on board, ten or a dozen slaves, shackled together with irons. That sight was a continual torment to me; and I see something like it every time I touch the Ohio, or any other slave-border. It is hardly fair for you to assume, that I have no interest in a thing which has, and continually exercises, the power of making me miserable. . . . I do oppose the extension of slavery because my judgment and feeling so prompt me; and I am under no obligations to the contrary.[6]

Shogan (2009) argues that the manner in which Lincoln recounted his experiences and the emotional reaction to them exemplifies a strong sense of empathy. Lincoln would utilize his empathic skills in a tactical manner to put

---

[5] We thank the anonymous reviewer for bringing this important point to our attention.

[6] Abraham Lincoln (1855), "Letter to Joshua F. Speed," August 24, https://quod.lib.umich.edu/l/lincoln/lincoln2/1:339?rgn=div1;view=fulltext.

himself in the shoes of his opponents – and the broader public – to forecast their strategy and then elicit support from them for political purposes. So Lincoln's ability to empathize on a personal level helped him to persuade others and to lead (Shogan 2009; see also Goodwin 2005). Shogan essentially sets Lincoln's example as a foundational model, though it is difficult to determine where Lincoln's personal empathy ended and his political pragmatism began.

Bill Clinton serves as another empathic model for Shogan (2009). She posits that, like Lincoln, Clinton understood and internalized the political value of empathy. He successfully employed it as his "I feel your pain" mantra, which first garnered national acclaim in responding to a concerned voter during his 1992 presidential debate against the incumbent president George H. W. Bush who, in contrast, appeared out of touch and disinterested (infamously, even checking his watch at one point). Once in office, Clinton enlarged the White House's casework operation to get insights from citizens reaching out for his help and would employ stories of hardship and misfortune to push policies such as Family and Medical Leave. However, Shogan (2009) also suggests it is debatable whether or not Clinton's empathic gestures were genuine, particularly given other acts of dishonesty exhibited in key aspects of his political career. A formidable challenge therefore lies in discriminating between what some view as Clinton's keen ability to understand constituents as an "empathizer-in-chief" versus what others would describe as a "mastery of spectacle" or political crutch that Clinton relied on perhaps too often to "compensate for his own personal and political failures" (Shogan 2009, 868).

Still another formidable case of empathic leadership up for debate is that of Barack Obama. From his early community-organizing experiences to the height of his presidency, Obama has claimed to rely heavily on empathy as a compass for his approach to governance. In his 2006 book *The Audacity of Hope: Thoughts on Reclaiming the American Dream*, Obama stresses that empathy should rest at the center of one's moral code and be employed by elected officials and appointed judges to make more equitable decisions to positively impact society and people's lives. Once in the Oval Office, President Obama often invoked the concept in his speeches, imploring the public to consider the perspectives of those less fortunate. The Obama administration also made explicit overtures to various minority communities and engaged in efforts to build intergroup coalitions.[7] During the 2020 presidential election cycle, former vice president Joe Biden adopted Obama's rhetorical empathic approach to present himself as the antithesis of Donald Trump, who routinely eschewed

---

[7] At the same time, critics note that Obama had some shortfalls in converting such empathic overtures into substantive policy outcomes. Furthermore, his policies of immigrant deportations and overseas drone strikes (which often resulted in civilian casualties) seemed to lack the empathy he otherwise touted and exemplified (see Orelus 2016).

empathy in his words and actions, resulting in an "empathy gap" between the two political rivals.[8]

It is possible that empathic calls to action might elevate levels of outgroup empathy among constituents. However, it is also plausible that such political appeals can deepen intergroup and within-group gaps in empathy, due to what Tesler (2016) coins "the spillover of racialization" that made public opinion more polarized by racial attitudes and race during Obama's presidency. If that is the case, at the intergroup level, minorities might have become more receptive to Obama's empathic appeals than whites on average. Among whites, Tesler's (2016) "two sides of racialization" – i.e., white racial liberals becoming increasingly Democratic versus white racial conservatives turning into more right-wing Republicans during the Obama era – might have also exacerbated within-group gaps in empathy. As Biden renewed the Obama-era empathy rhetoric to challenge Trump in 2020 (particularly with his aforementioned "empathy offensive"[9] in solidarity with the protests for George Floyd and Black Lives Matter), the trends once again appear intent on repeating themselves into the foreseeable future.

It is an arduous endeavor to estimate how much any president's calls to empathy might change policy making, let alone the prevalence of this trait in society. As Edwards (2003, 2012) has long demonstrated, presidents are rarely able to move public sentiment in their preferred directions. So we suspect the president's use of the bully pulpit is likewise limited when it comes to promoting empathy in the general public. Johnson (2010) explores the role of leadership in shaping "affective citizenship," which involves how people feel about others and themselves in public domains. She analyzes several emotions – empathy, love, fear, anxiety, and hope – in relation to the leadership styles and practices of Tony Blair, David Cameron, Kevin Rudd, and Barack Obama. With regard to Obama, Johnson (2010, 505) draws key insights into the difficulty of actually navigating the promise and subsequent policy impact of a leader's empathic overtures, noting: "There is a problem that Obama's rhetoric cannot address (partly for strategic electoral reasons). Even if it is successfully mobilized, empathy itself cannot ensure desirable outcomes (not least because views of what constitutes desirable or good outcomes differ)." Notwithstanding these challenges, we encourage scholars to continue exploring how governing styles might affect outgroup empathy in

---

[8] A May 2020 Quinnipiac poll reported on the "empathy gap" between Biden and Trump. When asked whether each candidate "cares about average Americans," 61 percent of respondents agreed that Biden cared compared to 42 percent for Trump. See Aaron Blake (2020), "Trump's Biggest Deficit against Biden: Empathy," *Washington Post*, www.washingtonpost.com/politics/2020/05/22/trumps-biggest-deficit-against-biden-empathy/.

[9] Charlotte Alter (2020), "Joe Biden's Empathy Offensive," *Time*, https://time.com/5843586/joe-bidens-empathy-offensive. See also Kara Voght (2020), "As Trump Threatens Violence, Biden Offers Empathy and a Promise of 'Real Policy Reform,'" *Mother Jones*, www.motherjones.com/crime-justice/2020/05/biden-trump-george-floyd-minneapolis/.

the mass public. We suspect group empathy is hard to move and learned fairly early in life. If so, presidents may be more likely to promote empathy among younger generations. This would be important for future studies to consider.

TRACING CAUSALITY

Our survey results repeatedly show that members of minority groups in both the United States and Britain hold higher levels of group empathy than whites – and that they are also more likely to have life experiences that might cause these differences. The evidence we have presented on the origins of group empathy is mostly circumstantial, however, so some may worry that these are but correlations between self-reported perceptions and attitudes in adulthood when what we really need are objective, longitudinal measures of the circumstances in which people are raised.

The strongest evidence in favor of our theory on the development of group empathy would come from a close examination of the socializing experiences of young people. The ideal design would be one in which experiences across lines of difference were randomly, or as close to randomly as possible, assigned to some young people but withheld from others. Then we could compare those who had group empathy-building experiences to those without. As long as everyone had an equal chance of getting into a group that engaged in the type of contact that fostered group empathy, we could be sure that this was an important cause of the dimension we have spent this book exploring.

Such data are very hard to come by, especially in representative samples large enough to compare the experiences of youths as they mature in a given society. One tantalizing clue, however, comes from an ingenious study by Mo and Conn (2018) that investigates the impact of participating in the Teach for America program on levels of prejudice. They employ a regression discontinuity design to compare students who just exceeded the entrance exam score required for admission to Teach for America with those who fell just below a qualifying score. These two groups were similar in many ways, having scored nearly identically on the exam, but different in that one participated in the program and the other did not. What Mo and Conn discovered was that teaching for two years in an underprivileged school led to significant changes in the belief systems of these mostly middle-class white participants. These teachers came to base their views about poverty more on the structural and institutional sources, rather than stereotypical and individualistic explanations that placed the blame on the work ethic, moral values, or poor decision making of those living in poverty. While the authors did not measure changes in group empathy, we would suspect that this is most likely what underlies the shift in beliefs about the sources of poverty.

The obvious advantage of evidence like the one in Mo and Conn's study is that it helps rule out the concerns about spurious relationships that potentially confound some observational studies. As discussed in Chapter 4, we must take seriously the possibility that the correlations we found between factors like group empathy and educational attainment, for example, are driven by a third force. Perhaps those who are high in empathy are also drawn to settings where they will interact with diverse others in the hopes of further expanding their horizons and having new experiences. The most readily accessible of such environs for young people is school. Of course, the cost of higher education – where some of the most diverse and empathy-enriching interactions may occur – remains prohibitive for many. If so, income should be positively associated with group empathy, although we rarely find it is. All these forces create a very difficult interplay to disentangle when attempting to find the real causal levers one might pull in order to grow empathic skills and motivation to care for others much different than themselves.

We continue to look for additional evidence in social and educational settings that facilitate causal inferences. For instance, two of us regularly teach a variety of undergraduate courses in political science at the University of Texas at El Paso (UTEP), for which we incorporate into our curriculum a substantial service learning component.[10] Students volunteer at local organizations and interact with members of the El Paso community throughout the semester. These service learning experiences are documented and reported on at the end of the course, and they reveal hints suggesting students' empathy for others has improved. Students who spent time, especially for the first time, with others from very different backgrounds than their own have often come away with stories that indicate a better understanding and heightened concern about the struggles of the communities they engaged with. In the next section, we contemplate the impact of such educational experiences on group empathy and discuss our plans for systematic research in applied settings.

ACTIVATING GROUP EMPATHY VIA EDUCATIONAL EXPERIENCES

As we have repeated many times throughout this book, it seems unlikely that group empathy is innate. Instead, it is built incrementally through socialization processes where experience *nurtures* one's affective and cognitive empathic abilities. So what happens when life experiences that can help develop empathy for outgroups are not readily available during childhood and adolescence? Are there ways educators can help fill such gaps in early life

[10] The incorporation of service learning and, more broadly, a wide range of community engagement and leadership opportunities into the curriculum has earned recognition as a best practice at UTEP and continues to blossom among a growing cohort of community-engaged scholars, both in the Paso Del Norte Region and at other universities around the country (see Núñez & Gonzalez 2018).

development by incorporating simulated experiences in and outside the classroom?

Following the assassination of Martin Luther King Jr. in 1968, third-grade teacher Jane Elliott in Riceville, Iowa (an all-white, all-Christian town) decided to go beyond merely lecturing to her students about discrimination, racism, and prejudice. In a two-day exercise, she divided her class into two groups: on the first day, those with blue eyes would be treated as superior while the ones with brown eyes would be the inferior group, and on the second day, the roles would be reversed. The "superior" group received preferential treatment and positive reinforcement by the teacher while the "inferior" students were forced to wear collars (to be easily identified as members of the discriminated outgroup) and were subjected to unfair treatment such as negative commentaries, less recess time, and not being able to use the drinking fountain or playground equipment. In a matter of hours, those put in the superior position and favored by their teacher were extremely buoyant and performing better in class activities, whereas the ones designated as inferior began showing signs of distress and performing poorly on tests. At the end of the two-day exercise, Elliott carefully explained to her students the purpose of this activity and reported that she was able to deliver a much more concrete lesson about discrimination and racism now that her third-graders were able to personally experience – albeit briefly – how it feels to be treated unfairly for no other reason than a difference in eye color.[11]

We believe such pioneering exercises of group empathy, if taught effectively, might make life-changing impressions – especially among those who may have had little prior opportunity to walk in the shoes of those less fortunate. In a high-school reunion fourteen years later, Elliott was able to observe her long-lasting impact on those now-grown students as they talked about the exercise and shared personal anecdotes, as documented in a PBS film *A Class Divided*. Recalling the collar they were forced to wear as a badge of inferiority, one said: "You know you hear these people talking about, you know, different people and how they're, you know, different and they'd like to have them out of the country: 'I wish they'd go back to Africa.' ... And sometimes I just wish I had that collar in my pocket. I could whip it out and put it on and say, 'Wear this, and put yourself in their place.'"

Of course, we cannot treat the task of group-empathy building as if it is a simple classroom activity to be completed. One brief exposure to the injustice of discrimination is unlikely to alter one's entire outlook on others. Still, with powerful instructional strategies like the one Elliott designed, experiences that trigger group empathy can be simulated in an educational setting and may activate one's awareness of and sensitivity to other groups' struggles. Such "simulated and coached" socialization is highly desirable at a young age,

---

[11] The footage of this class exercise would become a documentary film called *The Eye of the Storm*, which originally aired on ABC in 1970.

ideally during kindergarten and primary school. But during secondary school and beyond, effective instructional activities may still establish a positive trajectory on the road to greater outgroup empathy.

Community Engagement and Service Learning

One key educational strategy is community engagement that provides experiential service learning. A number of studies show a significant connection between service learning and interpersonal empathy (e.g., Lundy 2007; Scott & Graham 2015). These opportunities can also increase intergroup empathy. To check this, we collected preliminary data by embedding service-learning into our introductory, undergraduate-level government courses. These courses are mandatory for all majors and are conducted in a large-class setting with approximately 300 students, so we were able to obtain a large number of observations with good variation in students' backgrounds and educational interests. Specifically, we required students to complete community service work up to a certain number of hours in various organizations and events designated by UTEP's Center for Community Engagement. At the end of their service learning experiences, students submitted personal reflections in the form of journal entries.

A content analysis of these journal entries suggest that community service work in organizations related to assisting disadvantaged groups did indeed trigger group-empathic responses, especially among those who expressed relatable background experiences. For instance, some of our students volunteered for Project SHINE, which helps elderly immigrants and refugees improve their English proficiency, civics knowledge, and health literacy, and also prepares them for the US citizenship test. One student who served as a tutor for the citizenship test wrote: "I enjoyed teaching reading and writing skills to my students that they need in order to do the reading and writing portions of the citizenship test. With my bilingual abilities, I enjoyed spreading my knowledge to my students since I once in the past only spoke Spanish but as the years went by, I began speaking English. . . . This experience has taught me to reflect on the struggles people undergo in this nation in order to succeed."

Some journal entries indicated service learning may also help students – especially those with no similar life experiences or no prior interaction with certain marginalized outgroups – to combat prejudices that may stand in the way of group empathy. To illustrate, after volunteering at a local shelter that serves the homeless, as well as recently arrived immigrants and refugees, one student wrote: "I was able to interact with a lot of Spanish-speaking people, handing out bags of food. There were fifty bags of basic food necessities inside each bag, but I also noticed a lot of people taking advantage of the free food. They wanted two or three bags instead of appreciating the one bag they received. If I do this again, I would not be as judgmental as I was the first time around. Everyone has a different story and a different background, not that I did not love helping them but I should worry more on that than accusing them of being ungrateful." Remarks like this encourage us to design field experiments to systematically investigate the causal relationships between intergroup contact, prejudice reduction, and group empathy that arise from service learning (see Paluck & Green 2009).

Service learning can also help facilitate empathy for nonracial/nonethnic disadvantaged groups. Some of our students, for instance, signed up for organizations and events that help people with disabilities. One student who served as a volunteer for the Ability Awareness Week activities wrote: "I learned how to help people around the university with disabilities and what it is like to be in their shoes. We set up an obstacle course where people had to go around cones while in a wheelchair for ten minutes. People realized that it wasn't easy at all." Service learning may thus propel students to go beyond pity or sympathy and help them learn how to take the perspective of such underserved groups. This is important because simply feeling sad about the struggles of a certain outgroup (in this case, the disabled community) may not be sufficient to drive people into action; learning to take such outgroup's perspective may change that.

At the end of the semester, we conducted exit surveys (which included the GEI) with our students as well as students in other sections of the introductory government courses that did not require service learning. Compared to those who did not engage in community service as part of their coursework, students who participated in service learning exhibited higher levels of group empathy.[12] These preliminary findings are encouraging and merit further inquiry to obtain more systematic evidence regarding the effects of experiential learning on group empathy. In future iterations of our courses that embed service learning, we plan to follow a panel design with a pretest to record students' preexisting levels of group empathy and compare them to the posttest levels upon completion of their community engagement experiences. We also plan to conduct field experiments by randomly assigning students to different sorts of volunteer roles with variation in contact with disadvantaged community members. Such applied, randomized field interventions would provide a rigorous test of the socialization hypothesis underlying Group Empathy Theory.

Simulation and Gamification

In addition to service learning and community engagement activities, we also employ simulation and gamification techniques in some of our courses to help activate and boost group empathy. Games with an educational purpose rather than for pure entertainment, also dubbed as "serious games," are increasingly

---

[12] The results of these analyses are available in the online appendix.

used by instructors, civil rights activists, practitioners, and researchers (Ritterfeld et al. 2009). Some of these games are specifically designed to trigger empathy and help instigate social change. However, "serious games" require careful design and tactful execution to achieve their purpose. As Huang and Tettegah (2015, 399) put it: "There must be a connection to prior experiences, or the long-term memory, for the player to feel connected to the character's plight. Otherwise, the experience becomes a game, not a serious game."

We teach a course on Latinx politics, which requires students to research and discuss the issue of undocumented immigration. To facilitate a discussion that considers not only the economic, cultural, and security-based aspects but also the humanitarian face of this issue, we assign our students *The Migrant Trail*. This web-based game allows one to assume the role of an undocumented immigrant as well as that of a border patrol agent. The immigrant's goal is to cross the harsh Sonoran desert on the USA–Mexico border without getting caught by the border patrol or getting left behind by the "coyote" they paid for safe passage. The player chooses an avatar from a selection of several immigrants with different backgrounds and motives. On their harrowing journey, immigrants need to make tough choices to survive such as whether to leave behind a member of the crossing party who was bitten by a scorpion or give their last tube of antibiotic ointment to save the person. If players decide to play the role of the border patrol, they are informed that their job is not just apprehending undocumented immigrants but also providing first aid to the injured and locating the remains of the immigrants who died during the perilous journey.

Living in the border town of El Paso right next to its "sister city" Ciudad Juárez, many of our students at UTEP are familiar with the struggles of immigrants like the ones featured in the game. Some of them are Dreamers themselves, some have family members and friends who are undocumented, others have loved ones on the other side of the border striving for an opportunity to start a new life in the United States, and still others have border patrol agents among their close circles.

The reactions to the game were quite empathic even among students for whom undocumented Latino immigrants constitute an outgroup. For instance, a white female student stated: "I was not familiar at all with the actual realities of the journey. I do have a vivid imagination but was shocked when my migrant character died with only 15 miles to go to pickup. My migrant character was Diego, a young man in his twenties. If he couldn't make it, what hope does anyone else have?" She then expressed willingness to help inspired by what she observed in the game: "I loved the times when the group would come across friendly hikers or a hydration station left by a goodwill group. I would like to be part of an effort to help like that." Such responses indicate that group empathy triggered or bolstered by games like *The Migrant Trail* may not only elicit positive attitudes toward stigmatized groups in distress but also encourage prosocial behavior to help them.

We also teach an upper-division undergraduate course on ethnic conflict and civil wars, which is another ideal venue for increasing group empathy via gamification. One of the instructional games we assign in this course is *Darfur Is Dying* – a game designed by University of Southern California students in cooperation with humanitarian aid workers who have had extensive experience in Darfur. The first phase of the game involves the player selecting an avatar to forage for water. Most avatars are young children aged 10–14, with an adult female and an adult male option as well. The player tries to get water to the refugee camp while trying to avoid the Janjaweed militias on the way to a well. If the player's avatar is captured, the game provides brief information on what type of abuse and violence the avatars would have to endure in real life depending on their gender and age. If players pass this stage, they then go back to the refugee camp to continue their efforts to survive under the constant threat of militia attacks. Throughout the game, vital information is provided about the humanitarian crisis in Darfur. At the end of the game, players have the option to engage in real-world political activism, such as sending a message to the president and/or signing a petition for Congress to pass legislation to help refugees.

In an experimental study, Peng et al. (2010) find that playing *Darfur Is Dying* elicited significantly greater role-taking ability and increased one's willingness to help the Darfurian people compared to reading a text conveying the same information. In line with such research, we believe the power of this type of simulation is that it not only triggers *reactive* empathy (in the form of compassion and sympathy) but also creates a virtual platform to experience *parallel* empathy that mimics to some extent the emotional state of Darfurian refugees. In students' reflection essays, we frequently came across words like fear, anger, frustration, and anxiety, suggesting parallel empathy was experienced. To illustrate, one student wrote:

The game *Darfur Is Dying* took me on a bit of an emotional roller coaster in that, in my first attempt, I treated it as a video game without even thinking about the reality behind it. However, after my avatar was caught and I read the consequences, I remembered that this was the reality for a lot of people in Darfur and instantly felt uneasy and sad. My avatar in the first attempt was Abok and the consequences of her being caught are as follows: "Girls in Darfur face abuse, rape and kidnapping by the Janjaweed." Young girls would risk all of this just so that they could have water to sustain themselves and their families. I instantly felt terrible because while playing the game, I was carelessly drinking a bottle of filtered water without even thinking about it. My second attempt was unsuccessful as well. This time I chose the mother, but because she carried more water, she was not quick enough to hide before the Janjaweed spotted her. In this attempt, I felt extremely stressed out and anxious the entire time. All I wanted to do was get the water to the camp and every time the Janjaweed would come into sight, I could feel my heart begin pounding. It is terrible that these people had to go through so much and risk their lives just to have water. This is just a game, but it is alarming and should not be taken lightly.

Another web-based game that puts players through the experience of being a refugee is *Against All Odds*, which was developed for the UN Refugee Agency (UNHCR). In the first stage, players have to survive interrogation and persecution by their own government and need to make hard choices in order to flee their country for safety. The subsequent stages of the game virtually put players through the process of claiming asylum, going through integration challenges, and experiencing discrimination that refugees often face in a foreign land. As Group Empathy Theory would predict, those with relatable experiences reacted most empathically to the game, with one student writing: "Situating myself in a new country felt almost like a déjà vu. I came here not knowing any English in late middle school, and many difficulties in terms of culture shock and language barriers felt personal." For some, such relatable experiences were more indirect (through their friends and family) yet still instigated highly empathic responses: "This makes me think about how my parents must have felt when they immigrated from Mexico not knowing the language or how to get around in the US. Although we have never gotten into much detail, I have heard stories on how difficult it was for them in the beginning." While relatable backgrounds help facilitate group empathy, even those who did not have prior similar experiences expressed empathic concern (perhaps more in a reactive rather than parallel form) and perspective taking. One student said: "All of these experiences made me have more sympathy and be more understanding of refugees. I have honestly learned a lot from the other side of the whole immigration/refugee issue. As someone who is focused on a homeland security career, this type of knowledge helps me understand the reasons behind desperate attempts by foreign individuals trying to reach and stay in the US."

Our ethnic conflict and civil wars course also employs *PeaceMaker* – a game that simulates the Israeli-Palestinian conflict. In this game, the player can take the role of the Israeli prime minister or the Palestinian president. The goal is to bring peace to the region using various decisional strategies in dealing with events presented via real-world photos and video footage. Students played only one side of the conflict in the first week and then they were instructed to switch roles and play the other side the following week. As in the *Darfur Is Dying* game, *PeaceMaker* seemed to have triggered reactive empathy as students displayed high levels of sympathy for the victims of this intractable conflict. Expressions of parallel empathy, such as stress and frustration with the peace process, were also abundant in students' reflection essays.

Playing only one side increased empathy for one's "virtual ingroup" while decreasing feelings of concern and perspective taking for the other. Many were cognizant of this effect. For instance, one student said: "It was strange, however, that in such a short time I did feel pride in my own 'people.' So, I can understand how nationalism can cause this conflict to go on as much as it has." Similarly, another student commented:

Throughout the game I was trying to make the right decisions in order to protect my people. I considered them my people since I was their leader and my decisions could affect them greatly. I would constantly worry or be nervous in some way about the outcome of a decision or action taken. I think that playing as the leader of a specific side will lead to a change in perspective over a conflict. ... You will be looking out for the best interest of yourself, your people, and your country, and your actions will be based on this. I definitely do think that it affected my own personal attitudes because at the moment I was not thinking about doing what was best for the other side but doing what was best for my side.

Such ingroup-focused, one-sided empathic reactions were largely replaced by mutual empathy for both sides when students changed their leadership role from one nation to the other. A student wrote: "This game made me feel responsible and very much stressed. I wanted both communities not only to have a voice but to come together. Fixing a Palestinian problem while leaving an Israeli one on hold made me feel accountable." Another student noted: "This game made me realize how difficult it is to reach conciliation in the area. Before, I would arrogantly make statements such as 'why don't they just resolve everything already?' without taking into consideration the various aspects to the process. You try to do the right thing for one side and it quickly backfires from the other." This is consistent with the results of a previous experimental study, which found that American and Turkish students displayed heightened perspective taking abilities for both the Israeli and Palestinian sides in the 2014 Gaza operation after playing the *PeaceMaker* game (Cuhadar & Kampf 2014).

In addition to qualitative analyses of the reflection essays, the results of an exit survey conducted at the end of the ethnic conflict and civil wars course further corroborate that incorporating instructional games into the curriculum has a highly positive impact on students' group-based empathic concern and perspective taking abilities.[13] The more students played *Darfur Is Dying*, the more empathy they displayed toward refugees. As for the *PeaceMaker* game, the quantitative results indicate that playing both the Israeli and Palestinian leader roles simultaneously increased empathy for both Muslims and Jews.

Gamification offers significant potential for enhancing group empathy, particularly in areas where students may feel detached due to issue unfamiliarity and complexity such as ethnic conflict and civil wars abroad. In the future, we plan to conduct a field experiment by randomly assigning students a gamification-based curriculum versus a traditional, text-based

---

[13] These results are provided in the online appendix.

curriculum to systematically observe whether such an intervention affects group empathy and, in turn, political attitudes and behavior.

GROUP EMPATHY AND THE CURRENT POLITICAL MOMENT

The reader might wonder if the authors have some partisan motivation for writing this book, given that some may interpret the findings as a strong indictment of the Trump administration and its policies. It cannot be denied that the 2016 US presidential election seemed like an explicit clash of worldviews, between those who wished to pursue the benefits of a diverse society and cooperation and those seeking a more protectionist stance against threats and competition at home and abroad. Hillary Clinton chose a bridging campaign slogan – "Stronger Together" – rooted in empathy and cooperation across lines of difference. Donald Trump's slogans – "America First" and "Make America Great Again" – were much more inwardly focused.

Despite noting the obvious in our observations of the current political context, we nonetheless insist that this book is not a partisan treatise. Our underlying goal is not to persuade readers how to vote. The role of empathy for outgroups in driving politics has been mostly overlooked to date, and this book is about filling that gap in our understanding. Further, we do not believe Trump or any other individual is the root cause either for the levels of group empathy currently displayed by Americans or any other citizenry or for its substantive effects on public opinion.

Why would we argue that Trump is not primarily responsible for the significance of group empathy as a driver of public opinion in all these domains? Could not the current political moment – with news story after news story written about policies such as the construction of the border wall, family separation, and closing the border to refugees fleeing for their lives – somehow make group empathy more salient and consequential in public opinion about these issues? We do think that the revival of white nationalism and attacks on racial/ethnic minorities in the Trump era are becoming part of Americans' collective memory, contributing to the life experiences that may boost group empathy even for those who are not personally affected but nevertheless witness these moments. Indeed, the ANES pilot study and our national survey – both conducted in 2018, coinciding with Trump's presidential term – demonstrate that exposure to political news has a highly significant impact on group empathy. An OLS regression analysis of the ANES data (with key political and socio-demographic controls) indicates a major shift in predictive margins from .48 to .63 in the GEI (measured on a 0–1 scale) as political news exposure moves from the lowest to highest level ($p \leq .001$). In other words, those who follow what is going on in government and public affairs, at least in this particular political moment, display substantively higher levels of outgroup empathy. This would also explain why we have observed an upward trend in group empathy among whites in our latest surveys. But it is also worth noting that we began collecting data in 2012, long before Trump's campaign for president. The predictive power of our group empathy measure, the GEI, is therefore clearly not confined to the period after Trump emerged as a political force. Empathy for outgroups was a politically important dimension before, and it remains so now.

We would suggest, however, that the relative scarcity of group empathy in society was something Trump capitalized upon during his campaign. His strongest supporters, and those who continue to support many of the most divisive policies, score significantly lower on this dimension. Does this mean they lack empathy of all kinds? Of course not. In terms of individual and ingroup empathy, there are small to nonexistent differences on average between all voting groups, just as we found with regard to racial/ethnic groups. Trump supporters, however, are simply not as likely to put themselves in the shoes of marginalized groups or to show concern for their suffering. In a CNN interview in June 2019, as the Trump administration ramped up its policy for separating children from their parents at the border, a CNN reporter asked one Trump supporter how he felt about those families. He replied: "These people that we have coming across the border illegally are breaking the rules. I have no feelings for them at all."[14] As with thousands of public interviews in America along with our own evidence across several years, this sentiment is common among Trump's followers. It is also common in Britain among those who succumb to ethnonationalist, protectionist appeals. We suspect it is common elsewhere as well.

The current political moment is therefore not a historical high point or a transitory period in the relevance of group empathy. Back in 2006, then-senator Barack Obama urged Northwestern University graduates at their commencement ceremony to cultivate more empathy for marginalized others: "There's a lot of talk in this country about the federal deficit. But I think we should talk more about our empathy deficit – the ability to put ourselves in someone else's shoes; to see the world through those who are different from us – the child who's hungry, the laid-off steelworker, the immigrant woman cleaning your dorm room."[15] He then added: "As you go on in life, cultivating this quality of empathy will become harder, not easier. There's no community service requirement in the real world, no one forcing you to care. You'll be free to live in neighborhoods with people who are exactly like yourself, and send

---

[14] Martin Savidge, Tristan Smith, and Emanuella Grinberg (2018), "What Trump Supporters Think of Family Separations at the Border," CNN, www.cnn.com/2018/06/19/us/trump-voters-family-separation/index.html.

[15] A transcript and video of Obama's 2006 commencement speech is available at www.northwestern.edu/newscenter/stories/2006/06/barack.html.

your kids to the same schools, and narrow your concerns to what's going in your own little circle." The United States has indeed long suffered an "empathy deficit" that can be traced back to the very beginnings of the country, including the treatment of Native Americans and the practice of slavery. It is not a provisional phase. So we do not think the Trump administration single-handedly created this political momentum of what many citizens around the world, from all backgrounds and races, identify as cruel, heartless, and inhumane. Trump has, however, deftly taken advantage of this widespread deficit of empathy across social, religious, and national divisions. Others are doing so as well, as our evidence on the link between group empathy and public support for Brexit shows.

Trump, Brexit, and the rise of populist candidates and parties across Europe, South America, and many other parts of the world all share a virulent, anti-immigrant policy platform. These leaders have not created a wave – they have only caught it. But why did this brand of politics, built on a coalition of voters who lack empathy for those less fortunate than they, become so dominant in contemporary politics? It is very difficult to say. Many have pointed to economic anxieties, driven by the perception that others in the global community seem to be benefiting more from free markets and open international trade. The middle and working classes in the more advanced democracies have seen their wages stagnate, their standard of living decline, and quality housing near their place of work gradually disappear, and some started to blame immigrants as the scapegoats for the shrinking pie. Some have argued that perhaps relative deprivation is the catalyst, a trigger that turns people inward toward the well-being of their ingroups, families, and close friends. But the evidence here does not provide strong support for such explanation.

Whenever the economic anxiety of the working and lower middle classes is invoked to explain the rise of Trump in the United States, Brexit in Britain, Le Pen in France, and so on, one must consider that nonwhite citizens voted overwhelmingly for the alternatives in these elections. Racial/ethnic minorities control far less wealth, on average, and have lower incomes than whites in advanced industrialized countries. Their wages have also stagnated, especially since the Great Recession. Yet these real economic threats do not seem to trigger anti-immigrant sentiment or strict immigration policy support among minority citizens, at least not in the two countries we have explored so far. And, not coincidentally, these same minority groups express significantly higher levels of outgroup empathy despite their own precarious economic status compared to the majority's more advantageous positioning in the socio-economic strata.

So, we ask again, what are the roots of these growing ethnic antagonisms in such advanced multicultural societies? The evidence, ours and others', rules out strictly material and existential threats. Economic threats cannot be responsible, because people both low and high in group empathy are being squeezed by income stagnation in many modern democracies. Security concerns cannot explain these changes either since terrorism is not on the rise, and those most vulnerable are not the lowest in outgroup empathy.

What if economic forces have their effect more indirectly on these processes? Income polarization causes segregation, and segregation makes it harder for people to witness the lives and struggles of people much different than they, especially on terms that foster empathy. The next generation of children therefore do not share schools, churches, neighborhoods, and even entire towns with those who cannot afford to be there. If socio-economic position is correlated with race, ethnicity, and immigration status as strongly as it is in many nations, the seeds of empathy across lines of difference will be unlikely to sprout and thrive. The economic forces that have reduced human poverty – at least in certain parts of the world and for certain segments of society – over the last several decades are also the same ones that have bred income polarization. By separating the haves from the have-nots not only economically but ethnically and spatially, free-market multicultural societies may be naturally politically destabilizing.

This macroeconomic explanation for the rise of ethnonationalist, anti-immigrant politics is difficult to test against many alternatives. We would predict, however, that, were racial/ethnic groups segregated as if randomly and left for a generation, the young people in these groups might register lower levels of group empathy. Enos's 2017 book *The Space between Us* provides a good model. He finds that, when people are close enough to see the problems in other communities but still live in segregated spaces within those mostly urban areas, prejudice and hostility actually increase. Enos did not measure outgroup empathy in his surveys, but we would expect to find differences in that dimension based on the ratio of intergroup contact and residential segregation that he found so potent. While proximity may lead to outgroup empathy via increased intergroup contact, it can also be a drag on its formation over time. True and permanent integration, where people experience similar costs and benefits and share the same daily struggles, creates a more conducive environment for intergroup empathy to grow. Income polarization works against this possibility. While people may not want to sacrifice the economic benefits of free market opportunities, we should be cognizant of what is lost when people do not share experiences across lines of difference.

So what could further explain the trend of rising populist, ethnonationalist parties and candidates, with policy platforms that seem to lack empathy for the plight of others both without and within their own borders? Our suspicion is that all multicultural societies are vulnerable to strategic elites who attempt to mobilize a fairly large segment of the population that is neither able nor motivated to empathize with those from other groups. Taking the flipside from Lincoln's first inaugural address that we reference at the outset of this chapter, there are votes to be captured by appealing to the *worst* angels of our nature. Even cataclysmic events accompanied by horrendous bloodshed and loss of life – including the American Civil War, the Holocaust and many other genocides, and the ongoing Israeli-Palestinian conflict – have not guaranteed the power of group empathy in our governments, parties, and policies.

Many have argued that anti-immigration sentiment is driven by racial animus or ethnocentrism. Perhaps. We suspect, however, that the inability to put oneself in the shoes of someone very different on many dimensions is not simply a consequence of racism. Group empathy encompasses a package of skills and motivations that come from life experiences many people share, from all walks of life. For those people, the impact of racism on policy views is blunted and sometimes neutralized entirely. Yet we suspect that others who lack group empathy are more vulnerable to falling prey to the demagoguery of political opportunists who play the race, religion, or nativist card to gain votes.

Ingroup interest is generally the default setting for societies. The success of these populist movements – not just in this current political moment but also repeatedly throughout history – has been that they present themselves as a protector of ingroup interests at all costs while declaring that all punitive actions pledged against outgroups can be justified as self-defense. Pursuing such Machiavellian-like discourse, Trump openly frames immigration as an *invasion* to legitimatize many of his anti-immigrant and inhumane policies (including family separation and the Muslim ban) as part of a *just war* to defend American interests.[16] Similarly, to convince British voters to support Brexit in the run-up to the EU referendum, Nigel Farage – then-leader of the far-right UK Independence Party (UKIP) – launched his infamous poster showing a long line of refugees and immigrants (who were crossing the Croatia–Slovenia border in 2015) with the slogan "Breaking Point" in capital letters followed by "The EU has failed us all. We must break free of the EU and take back control."[17] While many have condemned such incendiary rhetoric, nationalist propaganda stemming from populist leaders resonates strongly with certain segments of the society in its appeals to ingroup interests that come natural to the human psyche.

Empathy for outgroups, on the other hand, is learned. It does not come as naturally as empathy toward loved ones; it is nurtured through socialization. So it may be overpowered if it does not build up a critical mass. We should also emphasize that group empathy does not force us to naively surrender our ingroup interests for the sake of others. Those who are highly empathic

---

[16] Thomas Kaplan (2019), "How the Trump Campaign Used Facebook Ads to Amplify His 'Invasion' Claim," *New York Times*, www.nytimes.com/2019/08/05/us/politics/trump-campaign-facebook-ads-invasion.html.

[17] Ishaan Tharoor (2016), "New Pro-Brexit Ad Gets Linked to Nazi-Era Propaganda," *Washington Post*, http://wapo.st/1tyxDwk?tid=ss_mail.

toward the suffering of outgroups still want to protect their families and kin and still care about their own interests. Having high group empathy does not require one to support policies such as open borders or unconditional acceptance of refugees. A person who is highly empathic toward undocumented immigrants and refugees may still support robust legal proceedings and background checks that may require detention of asylum seekers while their case is under review. Still, we expect such a person would be strongly opposed to overcrowded and inhumane detention conditions, indeterminate detention without due process, and elite and public discourses that stigmatize and demonize immigrants.

Even though it does not have to be a zero-sum competition, outgroup empathy may nevertheless clash with ingroup interests if people feel overwhelmed. As we mentioned in Chapter 7 on foreign policy, Turkey has taken in millions of Syrian refugees who could not make it to other, wealthier European countries. As a developing nation itself, this created a serious strain on its economy, healthcare system, and social services. While most Turkish citizens initially supported opening their country's doors to their neighbors in distress, many have since changed their position and started demanding a limit on the number of refugees the country should accept – especially after seeing other European countries not pulling their weight and after feeling its impact on Turkey's already frail infrastructure. Over the past years, Mexico has also accommodated a recurrent stream of refugees and immigrants from Latin American countries and within its own population, traversing the country on their way to the US border. Many Mexicans, especially those we believe to be high in group empathy, tried to help them on their long, strenuous journey by offering them food, medical assistance, and even shelter. Yet many have since become weary of the persistent stream of immigrants and refugees, particularly as US immigration and asylum policies have tightened. According to Roberto Sarabia, who works at a small grocery store in a southern Mexican border town: "People previously opened their doors to these migrants, but they do not have much extra money here. What little they could give, they've already given."[18] In both the Turkish and Mexican examples, even the most empathic and generous of good Samaritans may thus eventually perceive their efforts to be futile once all resources are exhausted to the point that it threatens the basic well-being of their own families. This is not to say that their group empathy suddenly expires but rather follows the old idiom that *the spirit is willing but the flesh is weak*.

The revival of far-right, xenophobic, and racist political movements that take advantage of the empathy deficit is also partly facilitated by the ill-conceived campaign strategies of some left-wing politicians and liberal parties against the strong appeal of ingroup interests that populist leaders profit from. Even highly

---

[18] Maya Averbuch and Mary Beth Sheridan (2019), "Threatened by Trump, Exhausted by Caravans, Mexico Struggles with Migrant Surge," *Washington Post*, https://wapo.st /2Ukhyfm?tid=ss_mail.

empathic members of society may feel unmotivated by appeals for altruistic political action on behalf of outgroups if they feel that their own interests are ignored or their support is taken for granted. By contrast, populist politicians and parties effectively mobilize their constituents by pitting their ingroup interests against the interests of outsiders via scaremongering tactics and rhetorical cues, such as warning of an "invasion" of immigrants who are coming to "replace" them. Under such circumstances, opposition parties and candidates with pro-immigrant, pro-minority agendas have to find a way to demonstrate to their constituencies that outgroup empathy and ingroup interests are not mutually exclusive. Instead of employing a narrow discourse of outgroup empathy embellished by emotional stories of struggling individuals with the hopes to appeal to the "the better angels of our nature," a stronger case would be to explain how outgroup empathy is not purely altruistic and selfless but can very well be rational and self-serving. Strategically crafted elite discourse based on factual information should focus on effectively relaying the message that empathy-driven action to help other groups is not only morally right but may also simultaneously advance ingroup interests if executed sensibly and effectively. For instance, foreign aid can help poor nations achieve sustainable development and subsequently reduce undocumented immigration as people find new opportunities becoming available to them in their homelands, rich in family histories and culture that many would much prefer not to abandon for economic reasons. Well-planned humanitarian military interventions and peacebuilding efforts in troubled areas can likewise help resolve violent conflict and in turn curb refugee flows of communities who otherwise would flee in tears only as a last resort to survive. And instead of allowing opportunists to promote hateful, exclusionary politics and an unjust system, a peaceful, egalitarian movement could better help prevent the kind of mass unrest and radicalization that would threaten national security.

As governments and economies become more integrated around the world, the rewards for peaceful coexistence, cooperation, and compromise will continue to grow. Citizens and elected officials of many nations now stand at a crossroads both new and yet hauntingly familiar. Empathy for those very different than ourselves is not so common and was surely risky in the distant past. It may have been most feasible and safest in the days before technology brought all humans into such close contact to look inward and empathize only with our closest neighbors. The trust we build now between ourselves and our more distant neighbors, however, is vital for humans to thrive in the centuries to come. We now face problems on a global scale – such as the COVID-19 pandemic as we discuss in the Epilogue that follows – requiring the immediate attention, collaboration, and compromise of the international community. We must begin the difficult work of cultivating empathy and trust across what many will feel are great lines of human difference and division. That challenge – the cultivation of group empathy – pales in comparison to the costs of inaction.

Politicians will always have an incentive to frame group rights and interests in zero-sum terms, to appeal to homogenous ingroups, to shun outsiders, and to create boundaries that they feel duty-bound to defend at all costs. There are some, however, who innately and automatically resist such strategies and who see through thinly veiled attempts to capitalize on the politics of human conflict and suffering.

The discoveries in this book give us some hope that diverse human societies can thrive. There will always be a force that can be mobilized, springing from the recognition that most of those so different than ourselves are seeking only precisely what we would want at minimum for ourselves, our families, and our friends: health, safety, and happiness. Our closest neighbors are now not so removed from communities on the other side of the world, with whom we can visit and talk so easily, at least in digital form. To survive, we must embrace the work of extending our empathy to those members of our human family just over the horizon – by seeing us in them.

Group Empathy in Response to the COVID-19 Pandemic

From now on, it can be said that plague was the concern of all of us. Hitherto, surprised as he may have been by the strange things happening around him, each individual citizen had gone about his business as usual, so far as this was possible. And no doubt he would have continued doing so. But once the town gates were shut, every one of us realized that all, the narrator included, were, so to speak, in the same boat, and each would have to adapt himself to the new conditions of life. Thus, for example, a feeling normally as individual as the ache of separation from those one loves suddenly became a feeling in which all shared alike and – together with fear – the greatest affliction of the long period of exile that lay ahead.

Albert Camus, *The Plague* (1947)[1]

As we were putting the finishing touches on our book, the COVID-19 pandemic suddenly turned the world upside down. Nations were placed under quarantine and economies came to a halt as billions of people followed medical guidelines to help prevent healthcare systems from becoming overwhelmed. The most vulnerable populations were older adults and those with underlying medical conditions. While people from all racial/ethnic groups were affected, the virus hit minority communities hardest, with African Americans and Latinos accounting for a disproportionate number of infections and deaths.[2] Many people abided by the stay-at-home orders and wore masks when they had to go out, in order to protect others even if they did not consider themselves to be at high risk. However, others took to the streets, often unmasked and armed, to demand the immediate reopening of businesses of all kinds.

---

[1] Excerpt from *The Plague* by Albert Camus, translated by Stuart Gilbert, translation copyright © 1948, copyright renewed 1975 by Stuart Gilbert. Used by permission of Alfred A. Knopf, an imprint of the Knopf Doubleday Publishing Group, a division of Penguin Random House LLC. *La Peste*. copyright © Editions Gallimard, Paris, 1947. All rights reserved.

[2] Centers for Disease Control and Prevention (CDC) (2020), "COVID-19 in Racial and Ethnic Minority Groups," www.cdc.gov/coronavirus/2019-ncov/need-extra-precautions/racial-ethnic-minorities.html.

Meanwhile, the Trump administration immediately tried to focus the public's attention on where the virus originated from, labeling it the "Wuhan virus" or the "Chinese virus," thereby framing the public health crisis as an external threat with racial undertones.[3] Trump also began chiding certain states for not opening their economies earlier, stirring partisan discord, and even encouraging protesters to "liberate" their states via a series of tweets.[4] Amid the scapegoating and incitement, coupled with the devastating health toll and socio-economic consequences of the pandemic, hate crimes against people of Asian descent markedly increased in the United States and around the world.[5]

Trump also used the pandemic as a pretext for his political agenda to restrict immigration. On April 20, 2020, he tweeted: "In light of the attack from the Invisible Enemy, as well as the need to protect the jobs of our GREAT American Citizens, I will be signing an Executive Order to temporarily suspend immigration into the United States!"[6] The executive order he ended up signing later that week issued a sixty-day pause to certain categories of immigration, with exemptions.[7] While more limited than the sweeping immigration ban he previously boasted of, the executive order still affected a large number of immigrants, including the spouses and children of legal permanent residents as well as family members of US citizens (a category Trump often derided as "chain immigration" even though his own wife, Melania Trump, benefited from it for her parents' immigration to the United States). In another political maneuver, Trump halted funding to the World Health Organization (WHO), undermining its ability to fight the pandemic and help nations in need.[8] He would later unilaterally declare (without the consent of Congress) the severance of all US ties with the WHO over allegations about the organization's

---

[3] Katie Rogers, Lara Jakes, and Ana Swanson (2020), "Trump Defends Using 'Chinese Virus' Label, Ignoring Growing Criticism," *New York Times*, www.nytimes.com/2020/03/18/us/politics/china-virus.html.

[4] Kevin Liptak (2020), "Trump Tweets Support for Michigan Protesters, Some of Whom Were Armed, as 2020 Stress Mounts," CNN, www.cnn.com/2020/05/01/politics/donald-trump-michigan-gretchen-whitmer-protests/index.html.

[5] Human Rights Watch, "Covid-19 Fueling Anti-Asian Racism and Xenophobia Worldwide: National Action Plans Needed to Counter Intolerance," www.hrw.org/news/2020/05/12/covid-19-fueling-anti-asian-racism-and-xenophobia-worldwide.

[6] https://twitter.com/realDonaldTrump/status/1252418369170501639.

[7] Nick Miroff, Maria Sacchetti, and Arelis R. Hernández (2020), "Trump Signs Order Pausing Immigration for 60 Days, with Exceptions," *Washington Post*, www.washingtonpost.com/immigration/coronavirus-trump-immigration-suspension/2020/04/22/4f0efdb8-84c1-11ea-ae26-989cfce1c7c7_story.html.

[8] John Hudson, Josh Dawsey, and Souad Mekhennet (2020), "Trump Expands Battle with WHO Far Beyond Aid Suspension," *Washington Post*, www.washingtonpost.com/national-security/trump-expands-battle-with-world-health-organization-far-beyond-aid-suspension/2020/04/25/72c754e6-856e-11ea-9728-c74380d9d410_story.html.

preferential treatment of China and incompetence in handling the pandemic.[9]

All of these developments surrounding the pandemic led us to once again consider the power of group empathy as a determinant of public opinion and political action. We were able to explore the public's reactions to COVID-19 in March 2020 via a nationally representative survey fielded by YouGov with 850 participants (585 whites and 265 nonwhites). The survey included the short, four-item version of the Group Empathy Index (GEI) in construct-specific question format (Cronbach's alpha = .89). We asked respondents how strongly, on a 5-point scale, they supported sending aid to foreign countries to help those suffering from COVID-19. Group empathy is the leading predictor of support for coronavirus-related foreign aid, above and beyond partisanship, ideology, feelings about whites versus blacks, political news exposure, and socio-demographic factors in the model, as shown in Table E.1 ($p \leq .001$).

As a discriminant validity check, we also analyzed the effect of group empathy on a different dependent variable: concern about oneself or a family member getting ill with the coronavirus disease. As predicted, the effect of the GEI is significant but much smaller, only about half as strong as in the first model (also reported in Table E.1). This makes sense since the target of concern in this question is not other groups but the well-being of the respondents and their close intimates. This also shows that the effect of group empathy we observe on coronavirus-related foreign aid is not a product of concern about the COVID-19 pandemic getting worse elsewhere and eventually coming back to infect the respondents themselves. It is about concern for others.

Further consistent with Group Empathy Theory, the effect of the GEI on support for coronavirus relief to foreign countries is much higher – almost two times greater in magnitude – among nonwhites as compared to whites (see Table E.2).[10] In fact, analyses with white and nonwhite subsamples show that group empathy has the largest coefficient size (.61) and statistical significance ($p \leq .001$) among minority respondents, by far exceeding any other factor in the model. In comparison, while highly significant ($p \leq .001$), the effect size of the GEI (.35) is slightly surpassed by that of the white–black feeling thermometer (.37) among whites. The number of political factors that are statistically significant and thus qualified to explain white support for coronavirus-related foreign aid is also much more varied compared to the nonwhite model. Although not as strong as group empathy or the feeling thermometer, the effects of ideology, partisanship, and political news exposure are all statistically significant among whites, whereas none of these political variables

[9] Berkeley Lovelace Jr. (2020), "Trump Says the US Will Cut Ties with World Health Organization," CNBC, www.cnbc.com/2020/05/29/trump-says-the-us-will-cut-ties-with-world-health-organization.html.

[10] Because the survey does not include stratified oversamples of minority groups, we pooled all of the minority respondents and created a dichotomous white/nonwhite variable for these subanalyses.

TABLE E.I *The relationship between group empathy and coronavirus-related opinions*

	COVID-19 foreign aid		COVID-19 health concern	
	β	S.E.	β	S.E.
Group empathy	.46***	.06	.26***	.06
White–black feeling thermometer	−.28*	.13	.04	.13
Party ID	−.06	.05	−.16**	.06
Ideology	−.07	.06	−.15*	.08
Political news exposure	.13**	.05	−.01	.05
Black	−.03	.04	−.04	.05
Latino	.02	.04	.01	.06
Other minorities	.03	.05	−.04	.05
Female	−.03	.02	−.02	.03
Education	−.01	.04	−.09†	.06
Age	−.04	.06	−.12*	.06
Income	−.11†	.07	.01	.08
Married	−.01	.03	.01	.03
Employed	.01	.03	−.06**	.03
Urban residence	.05	.04	.05	.04
Catholic	.03	.03	.03	.04
Church attendance	−.01	.04	.06	.05
Constant	.42***	.10	.47***	.10
N	630		630	

Note: Coefficients estimated using OLS regression. Data are weighted. All variables are rescaled to run from 0 to 1. $^†p \le .10$, $^*p \le .05$, $^{**}p \le .01$, and $^{***}p \le .001$, two-tailed.
Source: 2020 US Group Empathy Study (YouGov)

(including the feeling thermometer measure) are significant in predicting nonwhite support other than group empathy.

We will continue this line of investigation by exploring the link between group empathy and other coronavirus-related attitudes as the crisis further unfolds. We are particularly interested in how group empathy may condition one's support for government assistance directed at vulnerable outgroups who are most severely affected by the pandemic, attitudes about Asian Americans, and the trade-offs associated with staying at home versus reopening the economy.

This tragedy has revealed the fragility of our way of life. A virus has no nationality. It fails to heed immigration laws, and no wall is tall enough to prevent its global spread. In an instant, the world can seem so much smaller. But the very interconnectedness that makes us vulnerable to the spread of a virus also makes us stronger, as nations pool their resources and ingenuity in the search for

TABLE E.2 *Racial/ethnic differences in the relationship between group empathy and support for coronavirus relief to other nations*

	Whites		Nonwhites	
	β	S.E.	β	S.E.
Group empathy	.35***	.07	.61***	.12
White–black feeling thermometer	−.37**	.13	−.20	.21
Party ID	−.12†	.06	.12	.09
Ideology	−.13*	.07	.04	.12
Political news exposure	.18***	.05	.02	.08
Female	−.04	.03	.001	.04
Education	−.02	.05	−.05	.09
Age	−.08	.06	−.02	.11
Income	−.06	.08	−.21*	.10
Married	−.01	.03	.02	.05
Employed	−.01	.03	.08	.05
Urban residence	.03	.04	.14	.09
Catholic	.02	.03	−.02	.06
Church attendance	.11**	.04	−.20**	.07
Constant	.55***	.10	.27†	.15
N	452		181	

Note: Coefficients estimated using OLS regression. Data are weighted. All variables are rescaled to run from 0 to 1. †$p \le .10$, *$p \le .05$, **$p \le .01$, and ***$p \le .001$, two-tailed.
Source: 2020 US Group Empathy Study (YouGov)

a cure. We hope that the hardships people have endured will help pierce social divisions and bring all groups a bit closer. Unfortunately, the best evidence we have at the moment suggests the pandemic is polarizing by race/ethnicity and class, given that nonwhites and blue-collar workers in cities are suffering so much more than rural whites who live in less densely populated areas and white-collar workers who have more flexibility to work remotely. Competition for scarce resources got even tougher as unemployment hit its highest levels since the Great Depression.[11] The pandemic also proved to be further deepening the partisan fault lines (that are especially brittle in an election year), rather than uniting Democrats and Republicans against a common threat.[12]

[11] Greg Iacurci (2020), "Unemployment Is Nearing Great Depression Levels. Here's How the Eras Are Similar – and Different," CNBC, www.cnbc.com/2020/05/19/unemployment-today-vs-the-great-depression-how-do-the-eras-compare.html.

[12] Dominic Tierney (2020), "Not Even the Coronavirus Will Unite America," *The Atlantic*, www.theatlantic.com/ideas/archive/2020/03/not-even-coronavirus-will-unite-america/608698/.

The post–COVID-19 world will, we suspect, be a harsh testing ground for the power of empathy to improve intergroup relations. On the one hand, shared experiences of loss and suffering around the world might help cultivate group empathy among and between the nations of Earth and lead to long-standing cooperation for mutual recovery. On the other hand, groups may turn inward, becoming more protectionist and conflict-prone. Yet, even in this bleak scenario, the role of group empathy is still (if not more) vital. Considering all the systematic evidence provided in this book, if our theory is correct, those who suffer the most end up being the most empathic. And those who carry empathy for others carry the antibody to fight the infection of hatred, bigotry, and injustice.

******

Right before this manuscript went into final production, Joe Biden was elected President of the United States over incumbent Donald Trump. The 2020 election was particularly historic given that the winning ticket included Kamala Harris – the first female and first minority Vice President of Black and Asian descent. While racial resentment had been tightly linked to Trump's rise to power, we suspect group empathy was a primary driver of his demise. After a tumultuous first term marked by the rollout of inhumane policies such as family separation, the fueling of racial tensions, and a mismanaged COVID-19 pandemic response leaving hundreds of thousands dead, over 80 million Americans had seen enough. Biden, for his part, deployed an "empathy offensive" as a core component of his campaign to combat Trumpism and the politics of division. Consequently, "Amtrak Joe" achieved the rare feat of ousting a first-term president from office with record voter turnout despite a raging pandemic.

Biden was explicit and intentional in using empathy as a foundational principle and rhetorical tool: indeed, the giant video screens flanking the stage where he gave his victory speech read "The People Have Chosen Empathy." However, the 2020 election was far from an ultimate or unequivocal repudiation of Trumpism. While Biden now holds the record for most votes accumulated by a presidential candidate in any American election, Trump received the second highest number of votes to date and refused to concede. Instead, he constantly attempted to undermine the legitimacy of the outcome and the electoral system as a whole, leaving the country as divided as ever. Trump actually managed to garner more than 10 million additional votes than in the 2016 election and even attracted some additional minority votes in states such as Florida and Texas. And in some states that flipped Democratic, like Georgia, the margin was less than .5 percentage points. So the appeal of ethnonationalism and populism remains alive and well. Still, it may have been empathy that helped tilt the balance just enough to deny Trump a second term. Moving forward, scholars and other political observers should continue unearthing the role empathy plays among the citizenry and leaders as the country faces the daunting challenge of putting itself back together.

Appendix

STUDY 1: 2012 US GROUP EMPATHY PILOT STUDY (GFK)

This study was fielded by GfK in August/September 2012. GfK employs an online respondent pool, called KnowledgePanel, that is representative of the US population. Panel members are randomly recruited through probability-based sampling, and households are provided with access to the Internet and hardware if needed. The overall completion rate among those who had already agreed to be in the GfK pool was 56 percent. The completion rate by respondents' race/ethnicity was 67 percent for whites, 50 percent for African Americans, and 52 percent for Latinos. The cumulative response rate (CUMRR1, which is similar to the AAPOR RR1 metric) – based on the formulas developed by Callegaro and DiSogra (2008) for online panels – was around 5 percent, which is usual for GfK samples of this type. The average respondent was forty-seven years old, with some college experience, and earning around $40,000–$49,999 in annual household income. Approximately 50 percent of respondents were women; 31 percent identified as liberal, and 29 percent identified as conservative.

STUDY 2: 2013/14 US GROUP EMPATHY TWO-WAVE STUDY (GFK)

This study was fielded by GfK in December 2013/January 2014 in two waves. There was a seven- to ten-day lag between each wave. The completion rate in the first wave among those who had already agreed to participate in KnowledgePanel was 67 percent for whites, 51 percent for African Americans, and 46 percent for Latinos. In the second wave, the completion rate was 77 percent for whites, 71 percent for African Americans, and 77 percent for Latinos. The cumulative response rate (CUMRR1) was 4.9 percent in Wave 1 and 6.8 percent in Wave 2. The average respondent was forty-eight years old, with some college experience, and earning around $40,000–$49,999 in annual household income. Approximately 49 percent of respondents were women; 31 percent identified as liberal, and 31 percent identified as conservative.

Ethnocentrism (adopted from Bizumic et al. 2009)

Instructions

Below are a series of statements with which you may either agree or disagree. For each statement, please indicate the degree of your agreement/disagreement.

[Exploitativeness – Intergroup Ethnocentrism] In dealing with other ethnic and cultural groups, our first priority should be that we make sure that we are the ones who end up gaining and not the ones who end up losing.

[Purity – Intergroup Ethnocentrism] I would be very happy for a member of my family marrying a person from a different cultural or ethnic group. (R)

[Group Cohesion – Intragroup Ethnocentrism] For the sake of our future, all the people of my cultural or ethnic group need to pull together, bury our disagreements, and unite in a common group identity.

[Superiority – Intergroup Ethnocentrism] Our cultural or ethnic group is NOT more deserving and valuable than others. (R)

[Devotion – Intragroup Ethnocentrism] No matter what happens, I will ALWAYS support my cultural or ethnic group and never let it down.

[Preference – Intergroup Ethnocentrism] I do NOT prefer members of my own cultural or ethnic group to others. (R)

Answer Scale
- Strongly agree
- Somewhat agree
- Neither agree nor disagree
- Somewhat disagree
- Strongly disagree

STUDY 3: 2015 US GROUP EMPATHY STUDY (MTURK)

This study was fielded in September 2015 via Mechanical Turk (MTurk) – a Web-based interface to recruit individuals for a wide array of tasks requiring human intelligence. Participants were compensated for their time. MTurk offers a convenience sample, but social science studies using this platform are common and the data generated are generally of high quality. Berinsky et al. (2012) compare their MTurk sample to: (1) a number of samples used in experiments published in leading political science journals; (2) a high-quality Internet panel sample; and (3) probability samples used in the Current Population Survey (CPS) and the American National Election Studies (ANES). They find that the effects of experimental manipulations observed in the MTurk population comport well with those conducted in other samples.

The study involved two surveys with separate samples. The first was designed to compare the effects of the Group Empathy Index (GEI) and the Interpersonal Reactivity Index (IRI) on political attitudes and behavior. A total of 300 respondents took part in that survey. The average respondent was thirty-eight years old, with some college experience, and earning around $40,000–$49,999 in annual household income. Approximately 48 percent of respondents were women; 47 percent identified as liberal, and 24 percent identified as conservative. The second MTurk survey was designed as a manipulation check for the racial/ethnic nonverbal cues used in the experimental vignettes of the 2013/14 US Group Empathy Study. A total of 125 respondents participated in the manipulation check. The average respondent was thirty-nine years old, with some college experience, and earning around $30,000–$39,999 in annual household income. Approximately 50 percent of respondents were women; 53 percent identified as liberal, and 23 percent identified as conservative.

Interpersonal Reactivity Index (IRI) (adopted from Davis 1980)

Instructions

For each item below, please indicate how well it describes you. Please read each item carefully and answer as honestly as you can.

Perspective-Taking Scale

Before criticizing somebody, I try to imagine how I would feel if I were in their place.

If I'm sure I'm right about something, I don't waste much time listening to other people's arguments. (R)

I sometimes try to understand my friends better by imagining how things look from their perspective.

I believe that there are two sides to every question and try to look at them both.

I sometimes find it difficult to see things from the "other guy's" point of view. (R)

I try to look at everybody's side of a disagreement before I make a decision.
When I'm upset at someone, I usually try to "put myself in his shoes" for a while.

Empathic Concern Scale

When I see someone being taken advantage of, I feel kind of protective toward them.
When I see someone being treated unfairly, I sometimes don't feel very much pity for them. (R)
I often have tender, concerned feelings for people less fortunate than me.
I would describe myself as a pretty soft-hearted person.
Sometimes I don't feel sorry for other people when they are having problems. (R)
Other people's misfortunes do not usually disturb me a great deal. (R)
I am often quite touched by things that I see happen.

Answer Scale

- Describes me extremely well
- Describes me very well
- Describes me moderately well
- Describes me slightly well
- Does not describe me well at all

STUDY 4: 2016 US GROUP EMPATHY TESS STUDY (GFK)

This survey experiment was sponsored by Time-sharing Experiments for the Social Sciences (TESS) and fielded by GfK in September/October 2016. Of 885 panel members that GfK invited to participate, a total of 508 respondents completed the study. The overall completion rate was 57.4 percent. The average respondent was forty-eight years old, with some college experience, and earning around $40,000–$49,999 in annual household income. Approximately 49 percent of respondents were women; 34 percent identified as liberal, and 27 percent identified as conservative.

STUDY 5: 2018 BRITISH ELECTION STUDY (YOUGOV)

The British Election Study (BES) Wave 14 was fielded by YouGov in May 2018. Of 31,063 respondents who participated in Wave 14, 20,393 of them had also taken part in Wave 13. This corresponds to an overall wave-on-wave retention rate of 66 percent. A total of 4,191 respondents took all of the fourteen BES waves up to that point, which equals to about 13 percent of respondents who were originally surveyed in the first wave. The average respondent was fifty-two years old, with some college experience, and earning around £30,000–£39,999 in annual household income. Approximately 56 percent of respondents were women;

38 percent placed themselves on the left, and 40 percent on the right of the left–right scale.

Individual Empathy

[basicEmpathy] How much do you agree or disagree with the following statement?

[empathy1] I can usually figure out when my friends are scared.

[empathy2] I can usually realize quickly when a friend is angry.

[empathy3] I can usually figure out when people are cheerful.

[empathy4] I am not usually aware of my friends' feelings. (R)

[empathy5] When someone is feeling "down" I can usually understand how they feel.

[empathy6] After being with a friend who is sad about something, I usually feel sad.

[empathy7] My friends' unhappiness doesn't make me feel anything. (R)

[empathy8] Other people's feelings don't bother me at all. (R)

[empathy9] I don't become sad when I see other people crying. (R)

[empathy10] My friends' emotions don't affect me much. (R)

Answer Scale
- Strongly disagree
- Disagree
- Agree
- Strongly agree

Authoritarianism

[al_scale] 0–10 scale derived from adding and scaling variables al1, al2, al3, al4, and al5. 0 is libertarian, 10 is authoritarian.

How much do you agree or disagree with the following statements?

[al1] Young people today don't have enough respect for traditional British values.

[al2] For some crimes, the death penalty is the most appropriate sentence.

[al3] Schools should teach children to obey authority.

[al4] Censorship of films and magazines is necessary to uphold moral standards.

[al5] People who break the law should be given stiffer sentences.

Answer Scale
- Strongly disagree
- Disagree
- Neither agree nor disagree
- Agree
- Strongly agree

STUDY 6: 2018 US GROUP EMPATHY STUDY (YOUGOV)

The survey was fielded by YouGov in October 2018. YouGov interviewed 1,402 respondents who were then matched down to a sample of 1,050 to produce the final dataset. Respondents were matched to a sampling frame on gender, age, race, and education. The frame was constructed by stratified sampling from the 2016 American Community Survey (ACS) one-year sample with selection within strata by weighted sampling with replacements (using the person weights on the public use file). The matched cases were weighted to the sampling frame using propensity scores. The matched cases and the frame were combined and a logistic regression was estimated for inclusion in the frame. The propensity score function included gender, age, race/ethnicity, years of education, and region. The propensity scores were grouped into deciles of the estimated propensity score in the frame and post-stratified according to these deciles. The weights were then post-stratified on 2016 presidential vote choice, and a four-way stratification of gender, age, race, and education, to produce the final weight. The RR3 response rates for this study were 78.1 percent for whites, 28.8 percent for blacks, and 31.4 percent for Latinos. The average respondent was approximately forty-six years old, with some college experience, and earning around $40,000–$49,999 in annual household income. Approximately 57 percent of respondents were women; 32 percent identified as liberal, and 26 percent identified as conservative.

STUDY 7: 2018 ANES PILOT STUDY (YOUGOV)

The survey was fielded by YouGov in December 2018. Of 6,500 panelists YouGov invited to complete the survey, 3,322 started the questionnaire while 3,178 did not respond. Of those who started, 101 were ineligible due to citizenship status and 311 did not answer the entire questionnaire. Of the remaining 2,910 who completed the questionnaire, 131 were rejected after quality-control checks (e.g., completion time and item nonresponse). The final dataset consists of 2,500 cases selected by a sample matching procedure. The matching procedure involved respondents being matched to US citizens in the 2016 American Community Survey (ACS) sample by gender, age, race, and education. Matched cases were weighted to the ACS frame using a propensity score model based on the prior variables as well as geographic region. After data collection, the sample was weighted by YouGov to match population characteristics for 2016 presidential candidate choice, gender, age, race, and education. The average respondent was approximately fifty years old, with some college experience, and earning around $50,000–$59,999 in annual household income. About 56 percent of respondents were women; 30 percent identified as liberal, and 30 percent identified as conservative.

STUDY 8: 2020 US GROUP EMPATHY STUDY (YOUGOV)

The survey was fielded by YouGov in March 2020. YouGov interviewed 949 respondents who were then matched down to a sample of 850 to produce the final dataset. Respondents were matched to a sampling frame on gender, age, race, and education, similar to the sampling procedure employed in the 2018 US Group Empathy Study described earlier, and based on stratified sampling from the 2017 American Community Survey (ACS) sample. The RR3 response rate for this study was 47.1 percent. The average respondent was approximately forty-nine years old, with some college experience, and earning around $50,000–$59,999 in annual household income. About 55 percent of respondents were women; 26 percent identified as liberal, and 38 percent identified as conservative.

References

Adelman, Robert M., Charis E. Kubrin, Graham C. Ousey, and Lesley W. Reid. 2018. "New Directions in Research on Immigration, Crime, Law, and Justice." *Migration Letters* 15(2): 139–46.

Albertson, Bethany, and Shana Kushner Gadarian. 2013. "Who's Afraid of Immigration? The Effects of Pro- and Anti-immigrant Threatening Ads among Latinos, African Americans, and Whites." In *Immigration and Public Opinion in Liberal Democracies*, eds. Gary Freeman, Randall Hansen, and David Leal, pp. 286–304. New York: Routledge.

Allport, Gordon W. 1954. *The Nature of Prejudice*. Oxford: Addison-Wesley.

Alsultany, Evelyn A. 2006. "From Ambiguity to Abjection: Iraqi-Americans Negotiating Race in the United States." In *The Arab Diaspora: Voices of an Anguished Scream*, eds. Zahia Smail Salhi and Ian Richard Netton, pp. 127–42. New York: Routledge.

Altemeyer, Bob. 1981. *Right-Wing Authoritarianism*. Winnipeg: University of Manitoba Press.

Altemeyer, Bob. 1996. *The Authoritarian Specter*. Cambridge, MA: Harvard University Press.

Alterman, Arthur I., Paul A. McDermott, John S. Cacciola, and Megan J. Rutherford. 2003. "Latent Structure of the Davis Interpersonal Reactivity Index in Methadone Maintenance Patients." *Journal of Psychopathology and Behavioral Assessment* 25 (4): 257–65.

Alvarez, R. Michael, and Tara L. Butterfield. 2000. "The Resurgence of Nativism in California? The Case of Proposition 187 and Illegal Immigration." *Social Science Quarterly* 81(1): 167–79.

Aristotle. 1991. *The Art of Rhetoric*, trans. Hugh Lawson-Tancred. London: Penguin.

Baron, Reuben M., and David A. Kenny. 1986. "The Moderator–Mediator Variable Distinction in Social Psychological Research: Conceptual, Strategic, and Statistical Considerations." *Journal of Personality and Social Psychology* 51(6): 1173–82.

Baron-Cohen, Simon, Therese Jolliffe, Catherine Mortimore, and Mary Robertson. 1997. "Another Advanced Test of Theory of Mind: Evidence from Very High Functioning Adults with Autism or Asperger Syndrome." *Journal of Child Psychology and Psychiatry* 38(7): 813–22.

Baron-Cohen, Simon, Sally Wheelwright, Jacqueline Hill, Yogini Raste, and Ian Plumb. 2001. "The 'Reading the Mind in the Eyes' Test Revised Version: A Study with Normal Adults, and Adults with Asperger Syndrome or High-Functioning Autism." *Journal of Child Psychology and Psychiatry and Allied Disciplines* 42(2): 241–51.

Barreto, Matt A., Benjamin F. Gonzalez, and Gabriel R. Sanchez. 2013. "Rainbow Coalition in the Golden State? Exposing Myths, Uncovering New Realities in Latino Attitudes toward Blacks." In *Black and Brown in Los Angeles: Beyond Conflict and Coalition*, eds. Josh Kun and Laura Pulido, pp. 203–32. Los Angeles: University of California Press.

Ben-Ami Bartal, Inbal, Jean Decety, and Peggy Mason. 2011. "Empathy and Pro-Social Behavior in Rats." *Science* 334(6061): 1427–30.

Ben-Ami Bartal, Inbal, David A. Rodgers, Maria Sol Bernardez Sarria, Jean Decety, and Peggy Mason. 2014. "Pro-Social Behavior in Rats Is Modulated by Social Experience." *eLife* 3: e01385.

Bass, Gary. 2008. *Freedom's Battle: The Origins of Humanitarian Intervention.* New York: Knopf.

Batson, C. Daniel, and Nadia Y. Ahmad. 2009a. "Empathy-Induced Altruism: A Threat to the Collective Good." In *Altruism and Prosocial Behavior in Groups*, eds. Shane R. Thye and Edward J. Lawler, pp. 1–23. Bingley: Emerald Group Publishing Limited.

Batson, C. Daniel, and Nadia Y. Ahmad. 2009b. "Using Empathy to Improve Intergroup Attitudes and Relations." *Social Issues and Policy Review* 3(1): 141–77.

Batson, C. Daniel, Johee Chang, Ryan Orr, and Jennifer Rowland. 2002. "Empathy, Attitudes, and Action: Can Feeling for a Member of a Stigmatized Group Motivate One to Help the Group?" *Personality and Social Psychology Bulletin* 28(12): 1656–66.

Batson, C. Daniel, and Jay S. Coke. 1981. "Empathy: A Source of Altruistic Motivation for Helping." In *Altruism and Helping Behavior*, eds. J. Philippe Rushton and Richard M. Sorrentino, pp. 167–87. Hillsdale, NJ: Lawrence Erlbaum.

Batson, C. Daniel, Tricia R. Klein, Lori Highberger, and Laura L. Shaw. 1995. "Immorality from Empathy-Induced Altruism: When Compassion and Justice Conflict." *Journal of Personality and Social Psychology* 68(6): 1042–54.

Batson, C. Daniel, Marina P. Polycarpou, Eddie Harmon-Jones, Heidi J. Imhoff, Erin C. Mitchener, Lori L. Bednar, Tricia R. Klein, and Lori Highberger. 1997. "Empathy and Attitudes: Can Feeling for a Member of a Stigmatized Group Improve Feelings toward the Group?" *Journal of Personality and Social Psychology* 72(1): 105–18.

Berger, Martin A. 2011. *Seeing through Race: A Reinterpretation of Civil Rights Photography.* Berkeley: University of California Press.

Berinsky, Adam J. 2007. "Assuming the Costs of War: Events, Elites, and American Public Support for Military Conflict." *Journal of Politics* 69(4): 975–97.

Berinsky, Adam J., Gregory A. Huber, and Gabriel S. Lenz. 2012. "Evaluating Online Labor Markets for Experimental Research: Amazon.com's Mechanical Turk." *Political Analysis* 20(3): 351–68.

Bieber, Florian. 2018. "Is Nationalism on the Rise? Assessing Global Trends." *Ethnopolitics* 17(5): 519–40.

Binder, Norman E., J. L. Polinard, and Robert D. Wrinkle. 1997. "Mexican American and Anglo Attitudes toward Immigration Reform: A View from the Border." *Social Science Quarterly* 78(2): 324–37.

Bizumic, Boris, John Duckitt, Dragan Popadic, Vincent Dru, and Stephen Krauss. 2009. "A Cross-Cultural Investigation into a Reconceptualization of Ethnocentrism." *European Journal of Social Psychology* 39(6): 871–99.

Blalock, Hubert M. 1967. *Toward a Theory of Minority-Group Relations*. New York: John Wiley & Sons.

Blau, Francine D., and Christopher Mackie, eds. 2017. *The Economic and Fiscal Consequences of Immigration*. Washington, DC: The National Academies Press.

Bloom, Paul. 2017. *Against Empathy: The Case for Rational Compassion*. New York: HarperCollins.

Bobo, Lawrence, and Vincent L. Hutchings. 1996. "Perceptions of Racial Group Competition: Extending Blumer's Theory of Group Position to a Multiracial Social Context." *American Sociological Review* 61(6): 951–72.

Book, Angela S., Vernon L. Quinsey, and Dale Langford. 2007. "Psychopathy and the Perception of Affect and Vulnerability." *Criminal Justice and Behavior* 34(4): 531–44.

Borjas, George J. 2001. *Heaven's Door: Immigration Policy and American Economy*. Princeton, NJ: Princeton University Press.

Borjas, George J., Jeffrey Grogger, and Gordon H. Hanson. 2010. "Immigration and the Economic Status of African-American Men." *Economica* 77(306): 255–82.

Bowers, Jake. 2011. "Making Effects Manifest in Randomized Experiments." In *Cambridge Handbook of Experimental Political Science*, eds. James N. Druckman, Donald P. Green, James H. Kuklinski, and Arthur Lupia, pp. 459–80. New York: Cambridge University Press.

Brader, Ted, Nicholas A. Valentino, Timothy J. Ryan, and Ashley E. Jardina. 2010. "The Racial Divide on Immigration Opinion: Why Blacks Are Less Threatened by Immigrants." APSA 2010 Annual Meeting Paper. Available at SSRN: https://ssrn.com/abstract=1642984.

Brader, Ted, Nicholas A. Valentino, and Elizabeth Suhay. 2008. "What Triggers Public Opposition to Immigration? Anxiety, Group Cues, and Immigration Threat." *American Journal of Political Science* 52(4): 959–78.

Brady, Henry E., and Paul M. Sniderman. 1985. "Attitude Attribution: A Group Basis for Political Reasoning." *American Political Science Review* 79(4): 1061–78.

Branton, Regina. 2007. "Latino Attitudes toward Various Areas of Public Policy: The Importance of Acculturation." *Political Research Quarterly* 60(2): 293–303.

Branton, Regina, Erin C. Cassese, Bradford S. Jones, and Chad Westerland. 2011. "All along the Watchtower: Acculturation Fear, Anti-Latino Affect, and Immigration." *Journal of Politics* 73(3): 664–79.

Brewer, Marilynn B. 1979. "In-Group Bias in the Minimal Intergroup Situation: A Cognitive-Motivational Analysis." *Psychological Bulletin* 86(2): 307–24.

Brewer, Marilynn B. 1999. "The Psychology of Prejudice: Ingroup Love or Outgroup Hate?" *Journal of Social Issues* 55(3): 429–44.

Breyer, Thiemo. 2020. "Empathy, Sympathy, and Compassion." In *The Routledge Handbook of Phenomenology of Emotion*, eds. Thomas Szanto and Hilge Landweer, pp. 429–40. New York: Routledge.

Brown, Lisa M., Margaret M. Bradley, and Peter J. Lang. 2006. "Affective Reactions to Pictures of Ingroup and Outgroup Members." *Biological Psychology* 71(3): 303–11.

Bueno de Mesquita, Bruce, and David Lalman. 1992. *War and Reason: Domestic and International Imperatives*. New Haven, CT: Yale University Press.

Buie, Dan H. 1981. "Empathy: Its Nature and Limitations." *Journal of the American Psychoanalytic Association* 29(2): 281–307.

Burk, James. 1999. "Public Support for Peacekeeping in Lebanon and Somalia: Assessing the Casualties Hypothesis." *Political Science Quarterly* 114(1): 53–78.

Burris, Val. 2008. "From Vietnam to Iraq: Continuity and Change in Between-Group Differences in Support for Military Action." *Social Problems* 55(4): 443–79.

Cainkar, Louise. 2002. "No Longer Invisible: Arab and Muslim Exclusion after September 11." *Middle East Report* 224: 22–9.

Cainkar, Louise. 2009. *Homeland Insecurity: The Arab American and Muslim American Experience after 9/11*. New York: Russell Sage Foundation.

Callegaro, Mario, and Charles DiSogra. 2008. "Computing Response Metrics for Online Panels." *Public Opinion Quarterly* 72(5): 1008–32.

Cao, Xiaoxia. 2010. *Pathways to Eliciting Aid: The Effects of Visual Representations of Human Suffering on Empathy and Help for People in Need*. PhD Dissertation, University of Pennsylvania.

Chavez, Leo. 2008. *The Latino Threat: Constructing Immigrants, Citizens, and the Nation*. Palo Alto, CA: Stanford University Press.

Cheon, Bobby K., Dong-mi Im, Tokiko Harada, Ji-Sook Kim, Vani A. Mathur, Jason M. Scimeca, Todd B. Parrish, Hyun Wook Park, and Joan Y. Chiao. 2011. "Cultural Influences on Neural Basis of Intergroup Empathy." *NeuroImage* 57(2): 642–50.

Chong, Alberto, and Mark Gradstein. 2008. "What Determines Foreign Aid? The Donors' Perspective." *Journal of Development Economics* 87(1): 1–13.

Chong, Dennis, Jack Citrin, and Patricia Conley. 2001. "When Self-Interest Matters." *Political Psychology* 22(3): 541–70.

Chong, Dennis, and Dukhong Kim. 2006. "The Experiences and Effects of Economic Status among Racial and Ethnic Minorities." *American Political Science Review* 100 (3): 335–51.

Christov-Moore, Leonardo, Elizabeth A. Simpson, Gino Coudé, Kristina Grigaityte, Marco Iacoboni, and Pier Francesco Ferrari. 2014. "Empathy: Gender Effects in Brain and Behavior." *Neuroscience & Biobehavioral Reviews* 46(4): 604–27.

Cialdini, Robert B., Stephanie L. Brown, Brian P. Lewis, Carol Luce, and Steven L. Neuberg. 1997. "Reinterpreting the Empathy-Altruism Relationship: When One into One Equals Oneness." *Journal of Personality and Social Psychology* 73(3): 481–94.

Cikara, Mina, Emile G. Bruneau, and Rebecca R. Saxe. 2011. "Us and Them: Intergroup Failures of Empathy." *Current Directions in Psychological Science* 20(3): 149–53.

Clarke, Harold D., Matthew J. Goodwin, and Paul Whiteley. 2017. *Brexit: Why Britain Voted to Leave the European Union*. New York: Cambridge University Press.

Cliffordson, Christina. 2001. "Parents' Judgments and Students' Self-Judgments of Empathy: The Structure of Empathy and Agreement of Judgements Based on the Interpersonal Reactivity Index (IRI)." *European Journal of Psychological Assessment* 17(1): 36–47.

Collins, W. Andrew. 2003. "More than Myth: The Developmental Significance of Romantic Relationships during Adolescence." *Journal of Research on Adolescence* 13(1): 1–24.

Conrad, Courtenay R., Sarah E. Croco, Brad T. Gomez, and Will H. Moore. 2018. "Threat Perception and American Support for Torture." *Political Behavior* 40(4): 989–1009.

Cooper, Bridget. 2011. *Empathy in Education: Engagement, Values and Achievement.* New York: Continuum.

Coplan, Amy. 2011. "Understanding Empathy." In *Empathy: Philosophical and Psychological Perspectives*, eds. Amy Coplan and Peter Goldie, pp. 3–18. New York: Oxford University Press.

Council on American-Islamic Relations (CAIR). 2002. *The Status of Muslim Civil Rights in the United States: Stereotypes and Civil Liberties.* Washington, DC: CAIR.

Craig, Maureen A., and Jennifer A. Richeson. 2012. "Coalition or Derogation? How Perceived Discrimination Influences Intraminority Intergroup Relations." *Journal of Personality and Social Psychology* 102(4): 759–77.

Cuhadar, Esra, and Ronit Kampf. 2014. "Learning about Conflict and Negotiations through Computer Simulations: The Case of PeaceMaker." *International Studies Perspectives* 15(4): 509–24.

Cummings, Scott, and Thomas Lambert. 1997. "Anti-Hispanic and Anti-Asian Sentiments among African Americans." *Social Science Quarterly* 78(2): 338–53.

Dancygier, Rafaela M. 2010. *Immigration and Conflict in Europe.* New York: Cambridge University Press.

Davis, Darren W. 2006. *Negative Liberty: Public Opinion and the Terrorist Attacks on America.* New York: Russell Sage Foundation.

Davis, Darren W., and Brian D. Silver. 2004. "Civil Liberties vs. Security: Public Opinion in the Context of the Terrorist Attacks on America." *American Journal of Political Science* 48(1): 28–46.

Davis, Mark H. 1980. "A Multidimensional Approach to Individual Differences in Empathy." *JSAS Catalog of Selected Documents in Psychology* 10(4): 85–102.

Davis, Mark H. 1983. "Measuring Individual Differences in Empathy: Evidence for a Multidimensional Approach." *Journal of Personality and Social Psychology* 44(1): 113–26.

Davis, Mark H. 1994. *Empathy: A Social Psychological Approach.* Boulder, CO: Westview Press.

Dawson, Michael C. 1994. *Behind the Mule: Race and Class in African-American Politics.* Princeton, NJ: Princeton University Press.

De Corte, Kim, Ann Buysse, Lesley L. Verhofstadt, Herbert Roeyers, Koen Ponnet, and Mark H. Davis. 2007. "Measuring Empathic Tendencies: Reliability and Validity of the Dutch Version of the Interpersonal Reactivity Index." *Psychologica Belgica* 47(4): 235–60.

de la Garza, Rodolfo O., Angelo Falcón, and F. Chris Garcia. 1996. "Will the Real Americans Please Stand Up: Anglo and Mexican-American Support of Core American Political Values." *American Journal of Political Science* 40(2): 335–51.

de la Garza, Rodolfo O., Angelo Falcón, F. Chris Garcia, and John A. Garcia. 1993. "Attitudes toward U.S. Immigration Policy: The Case of Mexicans, Puerto Ricans and Cubans." *Migration World Magazine* 21(2–3): 13–6.

Decety, Jean, and Philip L. Jackson. 2004. "The Functional Architecture of Human Empathy." *Behavioral and Cognitive Neuroscience Reviews* 3(2): 71–100.

Decety, Jean, Greg J. Norman, Gary G. Berntson, and John T. Cacioppo. 2012. "A Neurobehavioral Evolutionary Perspective on the Mechanisms Underlying Empathy." *Progress in Neurobiology* 98(1): 38–48.

Doyle, Michael W. 1986. "Liberalism and World Politics." *American Political Science Review* 80(4): 1151–69.

Duan, Changming, and Clara E. Hill. 1996. "The Current State of Empathy Research." *Journal of Counseling Psychology* 43(3): 261–74.

Dymond, Rosalind F. 1949. "A Scale for the Measurement of Empathic Ability." *Journal of Consulting Psychology* 13(2): 127–33.

Eagly, Alice H. 1987. *Sex Differences in Social Behavior: A Social-Role Interpretation.* Hillsdale, NJ: Lawrence Erlbaum Associates.

Eagly, Alice H., Paul W. Eastwick, and Mary Johannesen-Schmidt. 2009. "Possible Selves in Marital Roles: The Impact of the Anticipated Division of Labor on the Mate Preferences of Women and Men." *Personality and Social Psychology Bulletin* 35(4): 403–14.

Edwards, George C. III. 2003. *On Deaf Ears: The Limits of the Bully Pulpit.* New Haven, CT: Yale University Press.

Edwards, George C. III. 2012. *Overreach: Leadership in the Obama Presidency.* Princeton, NJ: Princeton University Press.

Edwards, Griffin, and Stephen Rushin. 2018. "The Effect of President Trump's Election on Hate Crimes." Available at SSRN: https://papers.ssrn.com/sol3/papers.cfm?abstract_id=3102652.

Eisenberg, Nancy, Richard A. Fabes, and Tracy L. Spinrad. 2006. "Prosocial Development." In *Handbook of Child Psychology, Vol. 3: Social, Emotional, and Personality Development*, ed. Nancy Eisenberg, pp. 646–718. New York: Wiley.

Eisenman, David P., Deborah Glik, Michael Ong, Qiong Zhou, Chi-Hong Tseng, Anna Long, Jonathan Fielding, and Steven Asch. 2009. "Terrorism-Related Fear and Avoidance Behavior in a Multiethnic Urban Population." *American Journal of Public Health* 99(1): 168–74.

Eklund, Jakob, Teresia Andersson-Stråberg, and Eric M. Hansen. 2009. "'I've Also Experienced Loss and Fear': Effects of Prior Similar Experience on Empathy." *Scandinavian Journal of Psychology* 50(1): 65–9.

Enos, Ryan D. 2017. *The Space between Us: Social Geography and Politics.* New York: Cambridge University Press.

Erikson, Erik H., Joan M. Erikson, and Helen Q. Kivnick. 1989. *Vital Involvement in Old Age: The Experience of Old Age in Our Time.* New York: Norton.

Este-McDonald, James. 2011. "Expanding the Hurwitz/Peffley Model: How Race Shapes Public Opinion on Foreign Aid." APSA 2011 Annual Meeting Paper. Available at SSRN: https://ssrn.com/abstract=1902748.

Ethier, Kathleen A., and Kay Deaux. 1994. "Negotiating Social Identity When Contexts Change: Maintaining Identification and Responding to Threat." *Journal of Personality and Social Psychology* 67(2): 243–51.

Evans, Gareth. 2008. *The Responsibility to Protect: Ending Mass Atrocity Crimes Once and for All.* Washington, DC: Brookings Institution Press.

Eyerman, Ron. 2001. *Cultural Trauma: Slavery and the Formation of African American Identity.* New York: Cambridge University Press.

Falcón, Angelo. 1988. "Black and Latino Politics in New York City: Race and Ethnicity in a Changing Urban Context." In *Latinos and the Political System*, ed. F. Chris Garcia, pp. 171–94. Notre Dame, IN: University of Notre Dame Press.

Fearon, James D. 1994. "Domestic Political Audiences and the Escalation of International Disputes." *American Political Science Review* 88(3): 577–92.

Feldman, Stanley. 2003. "Enforcing Social Conformity: A Theory of Authoritarianism." *Political Psychology* 24(1): 41–74.

Feldman, Stanley, and Leonie Huddy. 2005. "Racial Resentment and White Opposition to Race-Conscious Programs: Principles or Prejudice?" *American Journal of Political Science* 49(1): 168–83.

Feldman, Stanley, Leonie Huddy, Julie Wronski, and Patrick Lown. 2020. "The Interplay of Empathy and Individualism in Support for Social Welfare Policies." *Political Psychology* 41(2): 343–62.

Feldman, Stanley, and Karen Stenner. 1997. "Perceived Threat and Authoritarianism." *Political Psychology* 18(4): 741–70.

Filson, Darren, and Suzanne Werner. 2002. "A Bargaining Model of War and Peace: Anticipating the Onset, Duration, and Outcome of War." *American Journal of Political Science* 46(4): 819–38.

Finlay, Krystina A., and Walter G. Stephan. 2000. "Reducing Prejudice: The Effects of Empathy on Intergroup Attitudes." *Journal of Applied Social Psychology* 30(8): 1720–37.

Forgiarini, Matteo, Marcello Gallucci, and Angelo Maravita. 2011. "Racism and the Empathy for Pain on Our Skin." *Frontiers in Psychology* 2(Article 108): 1–7.

Foyle, Douglas C. 1999. *Counting the Public in: Presidents, Public Opinion and Foreign Policy.* New York: Columbia University Press.

Gaddis, S. Michael, and Raj Ghoshal. 2015. "Arab American Housing Discrimination, Ethnic Competition, and the Contact Hypothesis." *The ANNALS of the American Academy of Political and Social Science* 660(1): 282–99.

Gaertner, Samuel L., and John F. Dovidio. 2000. *Reducing Intergroup Bias: The Common Ingroup Identity Model.* Philadelphia, PA: Psychology Press.

Galinsky, Adam D., and Gordon B. Moskowitz. 2000. "Perspective-Taking: Decreasing Stereotype Expression, Stereotype Accessibility, and In-Group Favoritism." *Journal of Personality and Social Psychology* 78(4): 708–24.

Gartner, Scott Sigmund, and Gary M. Segura. 2000. "Race, Casualties, and Opinion in the Vietnam War." *Journal of Politics* 62(1): 115–46.

Gash, Alison, Daniel Tichenor, Angelita Chavez, and Malori Musselman. 2020. "Framing Kids: Children, Immigration Reform, and Same-Sex Marriage." *Politics, Groups, and Identities* 8(1): 44–70.

Gay, Claudine. 2006. "Seeing Difference: The Effect of Economic Disparity on Black Attitudes toward Latinos." *American Journal of Political Science* 50(4): 982–97.

Ghareeb, Edmund, ed. 1983. *Split Vision: The Portrayal of Arabs in the American Media.* Washington, DC: American-Arab Affairs Council.

Gimpel, James G., and James R. Edwards, Jr. 1999. *The Congressional Politics of Immigration Reform.* Boston, MA: Allyn & Bacon.

Gleichgerrcht, Ezequiel, and Jean Decety. 2014. "The Relationship between Different Facets of Empathy, Pain Perception and Compassion Fatigue among Physicians." *Frontiers in Behavioral Neuroscience* 8(Article 243): 243–51.

Goemans, Hein Erich. 2000. *War and Punishment: The Causes of War Termination and the First World War.* Princeton, NJ: Princeton University Press.

Goff, Phillip Atiba, Matthew Christian Jackson, Brooke Allison Lewis Di Leone, Carmen Marie Culotta, and Natalie Ann DiTomasso. 2014. "The Essence of Innocence: Consequences of Dehumanizing Black Children." *Journal of Personality and Social Psychology* 106(4): 526–45.

Goodwin, Doris Kearns. 2005. *Team of Rivals: The Political Genius of Abraham Lincoln.* New York: Simon & Schuster.

Goodwin, Matthew J., and Oliver Heath. 2016. "The 2016 Referendum, Brexit and the Left Behind: An Aggregate-Level Analysis of the Result." *Political Quarterly* 87(3): 323–32.

Goodwin, Matthew J., Simon Hix, and Mark Pickup. 2020. "For and Against Brexit: A Survey Experiment of the Impact of Campaign Effects on Public Attitudes toward EU Membership." *British Journal of Political Science* 50(2): 481–95.

Goodwin, Matthew J., and Caitlin Milazzo. 2017. "Taking Back Control? Investigating the Role of Immigration in the 2016 Vote for Brexit." *British Journal of Politics and International Relations* 19(3): 450–64.

Gormley-Heenan, Cathy, and Arthur Aughey. 2017. "Northern Ireland and Brexit: Three Effects on 'The Border in the Mind.'" *British Journal of Politics and International Relations* 19(3): 497–511.

Gowa, Joanne. 2011. *Ballots and Bullets: The Elusive Democratic Peace*. Princeton, NJ: Princeton University Press.

Gramby-Sobukwe, Sharon. 2005. "Africa and US Foreign Policy: Contributions of the Diaspora to Democratic African Leadership." *Journal of Black Studies* 35(6): 799–801.

Gratz, Alan. 2017. *Refugee*. New York: Scholastic Press.

Greenwald, Anthony G., and Thomas F. Pettigrew. 2014. "With Malice toward None and Charity for Some: Ingroup Favoritism Enables Discrimination." *American Psychologist* 69(7): 669–84.

Hainmueller, Jens, and Michael J. Hiscox. 2010. "Attitudes toward Highly Skilled and Low-Skilled Immigration: Evidence from a Survey Experiment." *American Political Science Review* 104(1): 61–84.

Hall, Stuart. 1997. "The Spectacle of the 'Other.'" In *Representation: Cultural Representations and Signifying Practices*, ed. Stuart Hall, pp. 223–79. London: Sage.

Hamada, Basyouni I. 2001. "The Arab Image in the Minds of Western Image-Makers." *Journal of International Communication* 7(1): 7–35.

Hamm, Mark S. 1997. *Apocalypse in Oklahoma*. Boston, MA: Northeastern University Press.

Hanmer, Michael J., and Kerem Ozan Kalkan. 2013. "Behind the Curve: Clarifying the Best Approach to Calculating Predicted Probabilities and Marginal Effects from Limited Dependent Variable Models." *American Journal of Political Science* 57(1): 263–77.

Hanson, Gordon H. 2007. *The Economic Logic of Illegal Immigration*. New York: Council on Foreign Relations.

Harrell, Erika. 2007. "Black Victims of Violent Crime." US Department of Justice, Bureau of Justice Statistics Special Report. Available at: www.bjs.gov/content/pub/pdf/bvvc.pdf.

Hayes, Andrew F., and Kristopher J. Preacher. 2010. "Quantifying and Testing Indirect Effects in Simple Mediation Models When the Constituent Paths Are Nonlinear." *Multivariate Behavioral Research* 45(4): 627–60.

Haynes, Chris, Jennifer Merolla, and S. Karthick Ramakrishnan. 2016. *Framing Immigrants: News Coverage, Public Opinion, and Policy*. New York: Russell Sage Foundation.

Hayward, Clarissa Rile. 2020. "Disruption: What Is It Good For?" *Journal of Politics* 82 (2): 448–59.

Henry, Charles P. 2010. "The Rise and Fall of Black Influence on U.S. Foreign Policy." In *African Americans in Global Affairs: Contemporary Perspectives*, ed. Michael L. Clemons, pp. 192–221. Lebanon, NH: Northeastern University Press.

Henry, Patrick J., and David O. Sears. 2002. "The Symbolic Racism 2000 Scale." *Political Psychology* 23(2): 253–83.

Henry, Patrick J., and David O. Sears. 2009. "The Crystallization of Contemporary Racial Prejudice across the Lifespan." *Political Psychology* 30(4): 569–90.

Hersch, Eitan. 2013. "Long-Term Effect of September 11 on the Political Behavior of Victims' Families and Neighbors." *Proceedings of the National Academy of Sciences of the United States of America* 110(52): 20,959–63.

Hetherington, Marc J., and Jonathan D. Weiler. 2009. *Authoritarianism and Polarization in American Politics*. New York: Cambridge University Press.

Hetherington, Marc J., and Jonathan D. Weiler. 2018. *Prius or Pickup? How the Answers to Four Simple Questions Explain America's Great Divide*. New York: Houghton Mifflin Harcourt.

Hoeffler, Anke. 2014. "Can International Interventions Secure the Peace?" *International Area Studies Review* 17(1): 75–94.

Hoffman, Martin L. 1984. "Interaction of Affect and Cognition in Empathy." In *Emotions, Cognition, and Behavior*, eds. Carroll E. Izard, Jerome Kagan, and Robert B. Zajonc, pp. 103–31. New York: Cambridge University Press.

Hoffman, Martin L. 1990. "Empathy and Justice Motivation." *Motivation and Emotion* 14(2): 151–72.

Hoffman, Martin L. 2000. *Empathy and Moral Development: Implications for Caring and Justice*. New York: Cambridge University Press.

Hopkins, Dan. 2014. "The Enduring Political Impact of 9/11 for Those Who Were Closest." FiveThirtyEight. https://fivethirtyeight.com/features/the-enduring-political-impact-of-911-for-those-who-were-closest/.

Huang, Wen-Hao David, and Sharon Y. Tettegah. 2015. "Cognitive Load and Empathy in Serious Games: A Conceptual Framework." In *Gamification: Concepts, Methodologies, Tools, and Applications*, pp. 390–403. Hershey, PA: IGI Global.

Huddy, Leonie, Stanley Feldman, and Erin Cassese. 2009. "Terrorism, Anxiety, and War." In *Terrorism and Torture: An Interdisciplinary Perspective*, eds. Werner G. K. Stritzke, Stephan Lewandowsky, David Denemark, Joseph Clare, and Frank Morgan, pp. 290–312. New York: Cambridge University Press.

Huddy, Leonie, Stanley Feldman, Charles Taber, and Gallya Lahav. 2005. "Threat, Anxiety, and Support for Antiterrorism Policies." *American Journal of Political Science* 49(3): 593–608.

Huddy, Leonie, Stanley Feldman, and Christopher Weber. 2007. "The Political Consequences of Perceived Threat and Felt Insecurity." *The ANNALS of the American Academy of Political and Social Science* 614(1): 131–53.

Huddy, Leonie, Lilliana Mason, and Lene Aarøe. 2015. "Expressive Partisanship: Campaign Involvement, Political Emotion, and Partisan Identity." *American Political Science Review* 109(1): 1–17.

Hughes, Michael, and Melvin E. Thomas. 1998. "The Continuing Significance of Race Revisited: A Study of Race, Class, and Quality of Life in America, 1972 to 1996." *American Sociological Review* 63(6): 785–95.

Hurwitz, Jon, Mark Peffley, and Jeffery Mondak. 2015. "Linked Fate and Outgroup Perceptions: Blacks, Latinos, and the U.S. Criminal Justice System." *Political Research Quarterly* 68(3): 505–20.

Islam, Mir Rabiul, and Miles Hewstone. 1993. "Dimensions of Contact as Predictors of Intergroup Anxiety, Perceived Out-Group Variability, and Out-Group Attitude: An Integrative Model." *Personality and Social Psychology Bulletin* 19(6): 700–10.

Jackson, Nancy B. 1996. "Arab Americans: Middle East Conflicts Hit Home." In *Images That Injure: Pictorial Stereotypes in the Media*, ed. Paul Lester, pp. 63–6. Westport, CT: Praeger.

Jamal, Amaney. 2008. "Civil Liberties and the Otherization of Arab and Muslim Americans." In *Race and Arab Americans Before and After 9/11: From Invisible Citizens to Visible Subjects*, eds. Amaney Jamal and Nadine Naber, pp. 114–30. New York: Syracuse University Press.

Jardina, Ashley. 2019. *White Identity Politics*. New York: Cambridge University Press.

Jentleson, Bruce W., and Rebecca L. Britton. 1998. "Still Pretty Prudent: Post-Cold War American Public Opinion on the Use of Military Force." *Journal of Conflict Resolution* 42(4): 395–417.

Johnson, Carol. 2010. "The Politics of Affective Citizenship: From Blair to Obama." *Citizenship Studies* 14(5): 495–509.

Johnson, James D., Nelgy Olivo, Nathan Gibson, William Reed, and Leslie Ashburn-Nardo. 2009. "Priming Media Stereotypes Reduces Support for Social Welfare Policies: The Mediating Role of Empathy." *Personality and Social Psychology Bulletin* 35(4): 463–76.

Jones-Correa, Michael, ed. 2005. *Governing American Cities: Interethnic Coalitions, Competition, and Conflict*. New York: Russell Sage Foundation.

Kalkan, Kerem Ozan, Geoffrey C. Layman, and Eric M. Uslaner. 2009. "'Bands of Others'? Attitudes toward Muslims in Contemporary American Society." *Journal of Politics* 71(3): 847–62.

Kaufmann, Karen. 2003. "Cracks in the Rainbow: Group Commonality as a Basis for Latino and African-American Political Coalitions." *Political Research Quarterly* 56 (2): 199–210.

Keely, Charles B. 1971. "Effects of the Immigration Act of 1965 on Selected Population Characteristics of Immigrants to the United States." *Demography* 8(2): 157–69.

Kerr, Willard A., and Boris J. Speroff. 1954. "Validation and Evaluation of the Empathy Test." *Journal of General Psychology* 50(2): 369–76.

Kinder, Donald R., and Cindy D. Kam. 2010. *Us against Them: Ethnocentric Foundations of American Opinion*. Chicago, IL: University of Chicago Press.

Kinder, Donald R., and Tali Mendelberg. 2000. "Individualism Reconsidered." In *Racialized Politics: The Debate about Racism in America*, eds. David O. Sears, Jim Sidanius, and Lawrence Bobo, pp. 44–74. Chicago, IL: University of Chicago Press.

Kinder, Donald R., and Lynn Sanders. 1996. *Divided by Color: Racial Politics and Democratic Ideals*. Chicago, IL: University of Chicago Press.

Kinder, Donald R., and David O. Sears. 1981. "Prejudice and Politics: Symbolic Racism versus Racial Threats to the Good Life." *Journal of Personality and Social Psychology* 40(3): 414–31.

Kinder, Donald R., and Nicholas Winter. 2001. "Exploring the National Divide: Blacks, Whites, and Opinion on National Policy." *American Journal of Political Science* 45 (2): 439–56.

King, Martin Luther. 2012. *A Gift of Love: Sermons from Strength to Love and Other Preachings*. Boston, MA: Beacon Press.

Kriner, Douglas, and Francis Shen. 2010. *The Casualty Gap: The Causes and Consequences of American Wartime Inequalities.* New York: Oxford University Press.

Krupnikov, Yanna, and Spencer Piston. 2016. "The Political Consequences of Latino Prejudice against Blacks." *Public Opinion Quarterly* 80(2): 480–509.

Kteily, Nour S., Jim Sidanius, and Shana Levin. 2011. "Social Dominance Orientation: Cause or 'Mere Effect'? Evidence for SDO as a Causal Predictor of Prejudice and Discrimination against Ethnic and Racial Outgroups." *Journal of Experimental Social Psychology* 47(1): 208–14.

Kulczycki, Andrzej, and Arun P. Lobo. 2001. "Deepening the Melting Pot: Arab-Americans at the Turn of the Century." *Middle East Journal* 55(3): 459–73.

Kull, Steven. 2011. "Preserving American Public Support for Foreign Aid." In *The 2011 Brookings Blum Roundtable Policy Briefs*, pp. 53–60. Washington, DC: Brookings.

Lahav, Gallya, and Marie Courtemanche. 2012. "The Ideological Effects of Framing Threat on Immigration and Civil Liberties." *Political Behavior* 34(3): 477–505.

Lai, Eric Yo Ping, and Dennis Arguelles. 2003. *The New Face of Asian Pacific American: Numbers, Diversity and Change in the 21st Century.* San Francisco, CA: UCLA Asian American Studies Center Press.

Lamm, Claus, C. Daniel Batson, and Jean Decety. 2007. "The Neural Substrate of Human Empathy: Effects of Perspective-Taking and Cognitive Appraisal." *Journal of Cognitive Neuroscience* 19(1): 42–58.

Leach, Colin Wayne, Russell Spears, Nyla R. Branscombe, and Bertjan Doosje. 2003. "Malicious Pleasure: Schadenfreude at the Suffering of Another Group." *Journal of Personality and Social Psychology* 84(5): 932–43.

Lelkes, Yphtach, and Rebecca Weiss. 2015. "Much Ado about Acquiescence: The Relative Validity and Reliability of Construct-Specific and Agree-Disagree Questions." *Research & Politics* 2(3): 1–8.

Light, Michael T., and Ty Miller. 2018. "Does Undocumented Immigration Increase Violent Crime?" *Criminology* 56(2): 370–401.

Lind, Rebecca Ann, and James A. Danowski. 1998. "The Representation of Arabs in U.S. Electronic Media." In *Cultural Diversity and the U.S. Media*, eds. Yahya R. Kamalipour and Theresa Carilli, pp. 156–67. New York: State University of New York Press.

Lisak, David, Lori Gardinier, Sarah C. Nicksa, and Ashley M. Cote. 2010. "False Allegations of Sexual Assault: An Analysis of Ten Years of Reported Cases." *Violence against Women* 16(12): 1318–34.

Litvack-Miller, Willa, Daniel McDougall, and David M. Romney. 1997. "The Structure of Empathy during Middle Childhood and Its Relationship to Prosocial Behavior." *Genetic, Social and General Psychology Monographs* 123(3): 303–24.

Lopez, Linda, and Adrian D. Pantoja. 2004. "Beyond Black and White: General Support for Race-Conscious Policies among African Americans, Latinos, Asian Americans and Whites." *Political Research Quarterly* 57(4): 633–42.

Lundy, Brenda L. 2007. "Service Learning in Life-Span Developmental Psychology: Higher Exam Scores and Increased Empathy." *Teaching of Psychology* 34(1): 23–7.

Lynch, Philip, and Richard Whitaker. 2018. "All Brexiteers Now? Brexit, the Conservatives and Party Change." *British Politics* 13(1): 31–47.

Maoz, Zeev, and Bruce Russett. 1993. "Normative and Structural Causes of the Democratic Peace, 1946–1986." *American Political Science Review* 87(3): 624–38.

Masuoka, Natalie. 2008. "Defining the Group: Latino Identity and Political Participation." *American Politics Research* 36(1): 33–61.

Masuoka, Natalie, and Jane Junn. 2013. *The Politics of Belonging: Race, Public Opinion, and Immigration.* Chicago, IL: University of Chicago Press.

Mathur, Vani A., Tokiko Harada, Trixie Lipke, and Joan Y. Chiao. 2010. "Neural Basis of Extraordinary Empathy and Altruistic Motivation." *NeuroImage* 51(4): 1468–75.

Matthews, Miriam, Shana Levin, and Jim Sidanius. 2009. "A Longitudinal Test of the Model of Political Conservatism as Motivated Social Cognition." *Political Psychology* 30(6): 921–36.

McClain, Paula D., and Albert K. Karnig. 1990. "Black and Hispanic Socioeconomic and Political Competition." *American Political Science Review* 84(2): 535–45.

McClain, Paula D., and Joseph Stewart Jr. 2002. *"Can We All Get Along?" Racial and Ethnic Minorities in American Politics.* Boulder, CO: Westview Press.

McFarland, Sam. 2010. "Authoritarianism, Social Dominance, and Other Roots of Generalized Prejudice." *Political Psychology* 31(3): 453–77.

McKenzie, Brian D., and Stella M. Rouse. 2013. "Shades of Faith: Religious Foundations of Political Attitudes among African Americans, Latinos, and Whites." *American Journal of Political Science* 57(1): 218–35.

Mehrabian, Albert, and Norman Epstein. 1972. "A Measure of Emotional Empathy." *Journal of Personality* 40(4): 525–43.

Merolla, Jennifer L., and Elizabeth J. Zechmeister. 2009. *Democracy at Risk: How Terrorist Threats Affect the Public.* Chicago, IL: University of Chicago Press.

Merskin, Debra. 2004. "The Construction of Arabs as Enemies: Post-September 11 Discourse of George W. Bush." *Mass Communication and Society* 7(2): 157–75.

Miklikowska, Marta. 2018. "Empathy Trumps Prejudice: The Longitudinal Relation between Empathy and Anti-Immigrant Attitudes in Adolescence." *Developmental Psychology* 54(4): 703–17.

Milner, Helen V., and Dustin H. Tingley. 2010. "The Political Economy of U.S. Foreign Aid: American Legislators and the Domestic Politics of Aid." *Economics & Politics* 22 (2): 200–32.

Mo, Cecilia Hyunjung, and Katharine M. Conn. 2018. "When Do the Advantaged See the Disadvantages of Others? A Quasi-Experimental Study of National Service." *American Political Science Review* 112(4): 721–41.

Monroe, Kristen R. 1996. *The Heart of Altruism: Perceptions of a Common Humanity.* Princeton, NJ: Princeton University Press.

Morris, Irwin L. 2000. "African American Voting on Proposition 187: Rethinking the Prevalence of Interminority Conflict." *Political Research Quarterly* 53(1): 77–98.

Mueller, John E. 1973. *War, President, and Public Opinion.* New York: Wiley.

Mueller, John E. 1994. *Policy and Opinion in the Gulf War.* Chicago, IL: University of Chicago Press.

Nelson, Thomas E., and Donald R. Kinder. 1996. "Issue Frames and Group-Centrism in American Public Opinion." *Journal of Politics* 58(4): 1055–78.

Nincic, Miroslav, and Donna J. Nincic. 2002. "Race, Gender, and War." *Journal of Peace Research* 39(5): 547–68.

Norris, Pippa, and Ronald Inglehart. 2019. *Cultural Backlash: Trump, Brexit, and Authoritarian Populism.* New York: Cambridge University Press.

Núñez M., Gina, and Azuri L. Gonzalez, eds. 2018. *Community Engagement and High Impact Practices in Higher Education.* Dubuque, IA: Kendall Hunt.

Nunnally, Shayla C. 2012. *Trust in Black America: Race, Discrimination, and Politics.* New York: New York University Press.

Obama, Barack. 2006. *The Audacity of Hope: Thoughts on Reclaiming the American Dream.* New York: Crown Publishers.

O'Brien, Ed, Sara H. Konrath, Daniel Grühn, and Anna Linda Hagen. 2012. "Empathic Concern and Perspective Taking: Linear and Quadratic Effects of Age across the Adult Life Span." *Journals of Gerontology, Series B: Psychological Sciences and Social Sciences* 68(2): 168–75.

Oliver, Eric J., and Janelle Wong. 2003. "Intergroup Prejudice in Multiethnic Settings." *American Journal of Political Science* 47(4): 567–82.

Orelus, Pierre Wilbert. 2016. *Race, Power, and the Obama Legacy.* New York: Routledge.

Otfinoski, Steven. 2018. *The Selma Marches for Civil Rights: We Shall Overcome.* North Mankato, MN: Capstone Press.

Padilla, Amado M., and William Perez. 2003. "Acculturation, Social Identity, and Social Cognition: A New Perspective." *Hispanic Journal of Behavioral Sciences* 25(1): 35–55.

Page, Scott E. 2007. *The Difference: How the Power of Diversity Creates Better Groups, Firms, Schools, and Societies.* Princeton, NJ: Princeton University Press.

Paluck, Elizabeth Levy, and Donald P. Green. 2009. "Prejudice Reduction: What Works? A Review and Assessment of Research and Practice." *Annual Review of Psychology* 60: 339–67.

Panagopoulos, Costas. 2006. "Arab and Muslim Americans and Islam in the Aftermath of 9/11." *Public Opinion Quarterly* 70(4): 608–24.

Patel, Tina G., and Laura Connelly. 2019. "'Post-Race' Racisms in the Narratives of 'Brexit' Voters." *The Sociological Review* 67(5): 968–84.

Paxton, Pamela Marie, and Stephen F. Knack. 2012. "Individual and Country-Level Factors Affecting Support for Foreign Aid." *International Political Science Review* 33 (2): 171–92.

Peffley, Mark, and Jon Hurwitz. 2010. *Justice in America: The Separate Realities of Blacks and Whites.* New York: Cambridge University Press.

Peng, Wei, Mira Lee, and Carrie Heeter. 2010. "The Effects of a Serious Game on Role-Taking and Willingness to Help." *Journal of Communication* 60(4): 723–42.

Perea, Juan F., ed. 1997. *Immigrants Out! The New Nativism and the Anti-Immigrant Impulse in the United States.* New York: New York University Press.

Pérez, Efrén O., and Marc J. Hetherington. 2014. "Authoritarianism in Black and White: Testing the Cross-Racial Validity of the Child Rearing Scale." *Political Analysis* 22(3): 398–412.

Perreault, Stephane, and Richard Y. Bourhis. 1999. "Ethnocentrism, Social Identification, and Discrimination." *Personality and Social Psychology Bulletin* 25 (1): 92–103.

Pettigrew, Thomas F. 1998. "Intergroup Contact Theory." *Annual Review of Psychology* 49(1): 65–85.

Pratt, Robert A. 2017. *Selma's Bloody Sunday: Protest, Voting Rights, and the Struggle for Racial Equality.* Baltimore, MD: Johns Hopkins University Press.

Preston, Stephanie D., and Frans De Waal. 2002. "Empathy: Its Ultimate and Proximate Bases." *Behavioral and Brain Sciences* 25(1): 1–20.

Pulos, Steven, Jeff Elison, and Randy Lennon. 2004. "Hierarchical Structure of the Interpersonal Reactivity Index." *Social Behavior and Personality* 32(4): 355–60.

Ramakrishnan, S. Karthick. 2014. "Asian Americans and the Rainbow: The Prospects and Limits of Coalitional Politics." *Politics, Groups, and Identities* 2(3): 522–29.

Richardson, Deborah R., Georgina S. Hammock, Stephen M. Smith, Wendi Gardner, and Manuel Signo. 1994. "Empathy as a Cognitive Inhibitor of Interpersonal Aggression." *Aggressive Behavior* 20(4): 275–89.

Ritterfeld, Ute, Michael Cody, and Peter Vorderer, eds. 2009. *Serious Games: Mechanisms and Effects*. New York: Routledge.

Rogers, Carl R. 1959. "A Theory of Therapy, Personality, and Interpersonal Relationships, as Developed in the Client-Centered Framework." In *Psychology: A Study of a Science*, ed. Sigmund Koch, pp. 184–256. New York: McGraw-Hill.

Rohall, David E., and Morten G. Ender. 2007. "Race, Gender, and Class: Attitudes toward the War in Iraq and President Bush among Military Personnel." *Race, Gender & Class* 14(3/4): 99–116.

Rumble, Ann C., Paul A.M. Van Lange, and Craig D. Parks. 2010. "The Benefits of Empathy: When Empathy May Sustain Cooperation in Social Dilemmas." *European Journal of Social Psychology* 40(5): 856–66.

Russett, Bruce. 1993. *Grasping the Democratic Peace: Principles for a Post-Cold War World*. Princeton, NJ: Princeton University Press.

Russett, Bruce, and Miroslav Nincic. 1976. "American Opinion on the Use of Military Force Abroad." *Political Science Quarterly* 91(3): 411–31.

Said, Edward S. 1997. *Covering Islam: How the Media and the Experts Determine How We See the Rest of the World*. New York: Vintage.

Sanchez, Gabriel R. 2006. "The Role of Group Consciousness in Latino Public Opinion." *Political Research Quarterly* 59(3): 435–46.

Sanchez, Gabriel R. 2008. "Latino Group Consciousness and Perceptions of Commonality with African Americans." *Social Science Quarterly* 89(2): 428–44.

Sassenrath, Claudia, Sara D. Hodges, and Stefan Pfattheicher. 2016. "It's All about the Self: When Perspective Taking Backfires." *Current Directions in Psychological Science* 25(6): 405–10.

Sawyier, Fay Horton. 1975. "A Conceptual Analysis of Empathy." *Annual of Psychoanalysis* 3: 37–47.

Schildkraut, Deborah J. 2002. "The More Things Change ... American Identity and Mass and Elite Responses to 9/11." *Political Psychology* 23(3): 511–35.

Schildkraut, Deborah J. 2009. "The Dynamics of Public Opinion on Ethnic Profiling After 9/11: Results from a Survey Experiment." *American Behavioral Scientist* 53(1): 61–79.

Schulte-Rüther, Martin, Hans J. Markowitsch, N. Jon Shah, Gereon R. Fink, and Martina Piefke. 2008. "Gender Differences in Brain Networks Supporting Empathy." *NeuroImage* 42(1): 393–403.

Schuman, Howard. 2000. "The Perils of Correlation, the Lure of Labels, and the Beauty of Negative Results." In *Racialized Politics: The Debate about Racism in America*, eds. David O. Sears, Jim Sidanius, and Lawrence Bobo, pp. 302–23. Chicago, IL: University of Chicago Press.

Schuman, Howard, Charlotte Steeh, Lawrence Bobo, and Maria Krysan. 1997. *Racial Attitudes in America: Trends and Interpretations*. Cambridge, MA: Harvard University Press.

Scott, Katharine E., and James A. Graham. 2015. "Service-Learning: Implications for Empathy and Community Engagement in Elementary School Children." *Journal of Experiential Education* 38(4): 354–72.

Scuzzarello, Sarah, Catarina Kinnvall, and Kristen R. Monroe, eds. 2009. *On Behalf of Others: The Psychology of Care in a Global World.* Oxford: Oxford University Press.

Sears, David O. 1988. "Symbolic Racism." In *Eliminating Racism: Profiles in Controversy*, eds. Phyllis A. Katz and Dalmas A. Taylor, pp. 53–84. New York: Plenum Press.

Sears, David O. 1993. "Symbolic Politics: A Socio-Psychological Theory." In *Explorations in Political Psychology*, eds. Shanto Iyengar and William J. McGuire, pp. 113–49. Durham, NC: Duke University Press.

Sears, David O., and Jack S. Levy. 2003. "Childhood and Adult Political Development." In *Oxford Handbook of Political Psychology*, eds. David O. Sears, Leonie Huddy, and Robert Jervis, pp. 60–109. New York: Oxford University Press.

Sears, David O., and Nicholas A. Valentino. 1997. "Politics Matters: Political Events as Catalysts for Preadult Socialization." *American Political Science Review* 91(1): 45–65.

Segal, Elizabeth A., Karen E. Gerdes, Jennifer Mullins, M. Alex Wagaman, and David Androff. 2011. "Social Empathy Attitudes: Do Latino Students Have More?" *Journal of Human Behavior in the Social Environment* 21(4): 438–54.

Semmerling, Tim Jon. 2006. *"Evil" Arabs in American Popular Film: Orientalist Fear.* Austin, TX: University of Texas Press.

Shaheen, Jack G. 2003. "Reel Bad Arabs: How Hollywood Vilifies a People." *The ANNALS of the American Academy of Political and Social Science* 588(1): 171–93.

Shaw, Laura L., C. Daniel Batson, and R. Matthew Todd. 1994. "Empathy Avoidance: Forestalling Feeling for Another in Order to Escape the Motivational Consequences." *Journal of Personality and Social Psychology* 67(5): 879–87.

Shogan, Colleen J. 2009. "The Contemporary Presidency: The Political Utility of Empathy in Presidential Leadership." *Presidential Studies Quarterly* 39(4): 859–77.

Sidanius, Jim, and Felicia Pratto. 2001. *Social Dominance: An Intergroup Theory of Social Hierarchy and Oppression.* New York: Cambridge University Press.

Sides, John, and Kimberly Gross. 2013. "Stereotypes of Muslims and Support for the War on Terror." *Journal of Politics* 75(3): 583–98.

Sirin, Cigdem V., Nicholas A. Valentino, and José D. Villalobos. 2016a. "Group Empathy in Response to Nonverbal Racial/Ethnic Cues: A National Experiment on Immigration Policy Attitudes." *American Behavioral Scientist* 60(14): 1676–97.

Sirin, Cigdem V., Nicholas A. Valentino, and José D. Villalobos. 2016b. "Group Empathy Theory: The Effect of Group Empathy on US Intergroup Attitudes and Behavior in the Context of Immigration Threats." *Journal of Politics* 78(3): 893–908.

Sirin, Cigdem V., Nicholas A. Valentino, and José D. Villalobos. 2017. "The Social Causes and Political Consequences of Group Empathy." *Political Psychology* 38(3): 427–48.

Sirin, Cigdem V., and José D. Villalobos. 2019. "The Study of Discrete Emotions in Politics." In *The Oxford Encyclopedia of Political Decision Making*, ed. David P. Redlawsk. Oxford: Oxford University Press (Online Edition).

Skitka, Linda J., Christopher W. Bauman, Nicholas P. Aramovich, and G. Scott Morgan. 2006. "Confrontational and Preventative Policy Responses to Terrorism: Anger

Wants a Fight and Fear Wants 'Them' to Go Away." *Basic and Applied Social Psychology* 28(4): 375–84.

Skitka, Linda J., Christopher W. Bauman, and Elizabeth Mullen. 2004. "Political Tolerance and Coming to Psychological Closure Following the September 11, 2001, Terrorist Attacks: An Integrative Approach." *Personality and Social Psychology Bulletin* 30(6): 743–56.

Slade, Shelley. 1981. "The Image of the Arab in America: Analysis of a Poll on American Attitudes." *Middle East Journal* 35(2): 143–62.

Slantchev, Branislav L. 2004. "How Initiators End Their Wars: The Duration of Warfare and the Terms of Peace." *American Journal of Political Science* 48(4): 813–29.

Slovic, Paul. 2007. "'If I Look at the Mass I Will Never Act': Psychic Numbing and Genocide." *Judgment and Decision Making* 2(2): 79–95.

Slovic, Paul, Daniel Västfjäll, Arvid Erlandsson, and Robin Gregory. 2017. "Iconic Photographs and the Ebb and Flow of Empathic Response to Humanitarian Disasters." *Proceedings of the National Academy of Sciences* 114(4): 640–44.

Sniderman, Paul M., Gretchen C. Crosby, and William G. Howell. 2000. "The Politics of Race." In *Racialized Politics: The Debate about Racism in America*, eds. David O. Sears, Jim Sidanius, and Lawrence Bobo, pp. 236–79. Chicago, IL: University of Chicago Press.

Sniderman, Paul M., and Thomas Piazza. 1993. *The Scar of Race*. Cambridge, MA: Harvard University Press.

Sniderman, Paul M., and Philip E. Tetlock. 1986. "Symbolic Racism: Problems of Motive Attribution in Political Analysis." *Journal of Social Issues* 42(2): 129–50.

Sobel, Richard. 2001. *The Impact of Public Opinion on U.S. Foreign Policy since Vietnam: Constraining the Colossus*. New York: Oxford University Press.

South Asian American Leaders of Tomorrow (SAALT). 2001. *American Backlash: Terrorists Bring War Home in More Ways Than One*. Washington, DC.

Stam, Allan. 1996. *Win, Lose, or Draw*. Ann Arbor, MI: University of Michigan Press.

Staub, Ervin. 1989. *The Roots of Evil: The Origins of Genocide and Other Group Violence*. New York: Cambridge University Press.

Stenner, Karen. 2005. *The Authoritarian Dynamic*. New York: Cambridge University Press.

Stephan, Walter G., and Krystina Finlay. 1999. "The Role of Empathy in Improving Intergroup Relations." *Journal of Social Issues* 55(4): 729–43.

Stotland, Ezra. 1969. "Exploratory Investigations of Empathy." *Advances in Experimental Social Psychology* 4(1): 271–314.

Stürmer, Stefan, Mark Snyder, Alexandra Kropp, and Birte Siem. 2006. "Empathy-Motivated Helping: The Moderating Role of Group Membership." *Personality and Social Psychology Bulletin* 32(7): 943–56.

Suleiman, Michael W. 1988. *The Arabs in the Mind of America*. Brattleboro, VT: Amana.

Suleiman, Michael W. 1999. "Islam, Muslims, and Arabs in America: The Other of the Other of the Other … " *Journal of Muslim Minority Affairs* 19(1): 33–48.

Suleiman, Ramzi, Reem Yahya, Jean Decety, and Simone Shamay-Tsoory. 2018. "The Impact of Implicitly and Explicitly Primed Ingroup–Outgroup Categorization on the Evaluation of Others' Pain: The Case of the Jewish–Arab Conflict." *Motivation and Emotion* 42(3): 438–45.

Sullivan, Patricia L. 2008. "Sustaining the Fight: A Cross-Sectional Time-Series Analysis of Public Support for Ongoing Military Interventions." *Conflict Management and Peace Science* 25(2): 112–35.

Swales, Kirby. 2016. *Understanding the Leave Vote*. London: NatCen Social Research.

Swigonski, Mary E. 1994. "The Logic of Feminist Standpoint Theory for Social Work Research." *Social Work* 39(4): 387–93.

Sze, Jocelyn A., Anett Gyurak, Madeleine S. Goodkind, and Robert W. Levenson. 2012. "Greater Emotional Empathy and Prosocial Behavior in Late Life." *Emotion* 12(5): 1129–40.

Tafoya, Joe R., Melissa R. Michelson, Maria Chávez, and Jessica L. Lavariega Monforti. 2019. "I *Feel* Like I Was Born Here: Social Identity, Political Socialization, and DeAmericanization." *Latino Studies* 17(1): 48–66.

Tafoya, Sonya. 2007. "Shades of Belonging: Latinos and Racial Identity." In *Race, Class, and Gender in the United States: An Integrated Study*, ed. Paula S. Rothenberg, pp. 218–21. New York: Worth Publishers.

Tajfel, Henri. 1981. *Human Groups and Social Categories: Studies in Social Psychology*. New York: Cambridge University Press.

Tajfel, Henri, and John C. Turner. 1979. "An Integrative Theory of Intergroup Conflict." In *The Social Psychology of Intergroup Relations*, eds. William G. Austin and Stephen Worchel, pp. 33–48. Monterey, CA: Brooks/Cole.

Tedin, Kent L., and Richard W. Murray. 1994. "Support for Biracial Political Coalitions among Blacks and Hispanics." *Social Science Quarterly* 75(4): 772–89.

Terry, Janice J. 1985. "Mistaken Identity: Arab Stereotypes in Popular Writing." Washington, DC: American-Arab Affairs Council.

Tesler, Michael. 2016. *Post-Racial or Most-Racial? Race and Politics in the Obama Era*. Chicago, IL: University of Chicago Press.

Tesler, Michael, and David O. Sears. 2010. *Obama's Race: The 2008 Election and the Dream of a Post-Racial America*. Chicago, IL: University of Chicago Press.

Tomz, Michael R., and Jessica L. P. Weeks. 2013. "Public Opinion and the Democratic Peace." *American Political Science Review* 107(4): 849–65.

Torabi, Mohammad R., and Dong-Chul Seo. 2004. "National Study of Behavioral and Life Changes since September 11." *Health Education & Behavior* 31(2): 179–92.

Transue, John E. 2007. "Identity Salience, Identity Acceptance, and Racial Policy Attitudes: American National Identity as a Uniting Force." *American Journal of Political Science* 51(1): 78–91.

Truax, Charles B., and Robert Carkhuff. 1967. *Toward Effective Counseling and Psychotherapy: Training and Practice*. New Brunswick, NJ: Aldine Transaction.

Turner, John C., Michael A. Hogg, Penelope J. Oakes, Stephen D. Reicher, and Margaret S. Wetherell. 1987. *Rediscovering the Social Group: A Self-Categorization Theory*. Cambridge, MA: Blackwell Publishing.

Uhlaner, Carole J. 1991. "Perceived Discrimination and Prejudice and the Coalition Prospects of Blacks, Latinos, and Asian Americans." In *Racial and Ethnic Politics in California*, eds. Byran O. Jackson and Michael B. Preston, pp. 339–71. Berkeley, CA: IGS Press.

Unger, Lynette S., and Lakshmi Thumuluri. 1997. "Trait Empathy and Continuous Helping: The Case of Voluntarism." *Journal of Social Behavior and Personality* 12(3): 785–800.

Updegrove, Alexander H., Maisha N. Cooper, Erin A. Orrick, and Alex R. Piquero. 2020. "Red States and Black Lives: Applying the Racial Threat Hypothesis to the Black Lives Matter Movement." *Justice Quarterly* 37(1): 85–108.

Valentino, Nicholas A., Ted Brader, and Ashley E. Jardina. 2013. "Immigration Opposition among U.S. Whites: General Ethnocentrism or Media Priming of Attitudes about Latinos?" *Political Psychology* 34(2): 149–66.

Valentino, Nicholas A., Vincent L. Hutchings, and Ismail K. White. 2002. "Cues That Matter: How Political Ads Prime Racial Attitudes during Campaigns." *American Political Science Review* 96(1): 75–90.

Valentino, Nicholas A., and David O. Sears. 1998. "Event-Driven Political Communication and the Preadult Socialization of Partisanship." *Political Behavior* 20(2): 129–54.

Valentino, Nicholas A., and David O. Sears. 2005. "Old Times There Are Not Forgotten: Race and Partisan Realignment in the Contemporary South." *American Journal of Political Science* 49(3): 672–88.

Valentino, Nicholas A., Stuart N. Soroka, Shanto Iyengar, Toril Aalberg, Raymond Duch, Marta Fraile, Kyu S. Hahn, Kasper M. Hansen, Allison Harell, Marc Helbling, Simon D. Jackman, and Tetsuro Kobayashi. 2019. "Economic and Cultural Drivers of Immigrant Support Worldwide." *British Journal of Political Science* 49(4): 1201–26.

Västfjäll, Daniel, Paul Slovic, Marcus Mayorga, and Ellen Peters. 2014. "Compassion Fade: Affect and Charity Are Greatest for a Single Child in Need." *PLOS ONE* 9(6): e100115.

Villalobos, José D. 2011. "Promises and Human Rights: The Obama Administration on Immigrant Detention Policy Reform." *Race, Gender & Class* 18(1–2): 151–70.

Wagner, R. Harrison. 2000. "Bargaining and War." *American Journal of Political Science* 44(3): 469–84.

Wang, Yu-Wei, M. Meghan Davidson, Oksana F. Yakushko, Holly Bielstein Savoy, Jeffrey A. Tan, and Joseph K. Bleier. 2003. "The Scale of Ethnocultural Empathy: Development, Validation, and Reliability." *Journal of Counseling Psychology* 50(2): 221–34.

Ward, Brian, and Tony Badger, eds. 1996. *The Making of Martin Luther King and the Civil Rights Movement*. New York: New York University Press.

Weisz, Erika, and Jamil Zaki. 2018. "Motivated Empathy: A Social Neuroscience Perspective." *Current Opinion in Psychology* 24: 67–71.

Westheider, James E. 1997. *Fighting on Two Fronts: African Americans and the Vietnam War*. New York: New York University Press.

Wilcox, Clyde, Joseph Ferrera, and Dee Allsop. 1993. "Group Differences in Early Support for Military Action in the Gulf: The Effects of Gender, Generation, and Ethnicity." *American Politics Research* 21(3): 343–59.

Willison, Charley E., Phillip M. Singer, Melissa S. Creary, and Scott L. Greer. 2019. "Quantifying Inequities in US Federal Response to Hurricane Disaster in Texas and Florida Compared with Puerto Rico." *BMJ Global Health* 4(1): e001191.

Yancey, George A. 2003. *Who Is White? Latinos, Asians, and the New Black/Nonblack Divide*. Boulder, CO: Lynne Rienner Publishers.

Zahn-Waxler, Carolyn, Marian Radke-Yarrow, Elizabeth Wagner, and Michael Chapman. 1992. "Development of Concern for Others." *Developmental Psychology* 28(1): 126–36.

Zainiddinov, Hakim. 2016. "Racial and Ethnic Differences in Perceptions of Discrimination among Muslim Americans." *Ethnic and Racial Studies* 39(15): 2701–21.

Zillmann, Dolf. 2006. "Empathy: Affective Reactivity to Other's Emotional Experiences." In *Psychology of Entertainment*, eds. Jennings Bryant and Peter Vorderer, pp. 151–82. New York: Lawrence Erlbaum.

Zogby, John. 1990. *Arab America Today: A Demographic Profile of Arab Americans.* Washington, DC: Arab American Institute.

Index

A page in bold followed by an n indicates a footnote. A page in bold italics indicates a figure or table.

Books in the series

Susan Welch, Lee Sigelman, Timothy Bledsoe, and Michael Combs, *Race and Place: Race Relations in an American City*

Cara J. Wong, *Boundaries of Obligation in American Politics: Geographic, National, and Racial Communities*

John R. Zaller, *The Nature and Origins of Mass Opinion*

Alan S. Zuckerman, Josip Dasović, and Jennifer Fitzgerald, *Partisan Families: The Social Logic of Bounded Partisanship in Germany and Britain*

CPSIA information can be obtained
at www.ICGtesting.com
Printed in the USA
LVHW091652110421
684169LV00001B/27